THE PRICE OF FEAR

AL-QAEDA AND THE TRUTH BEHIND THE FINANCIAL WAR ON TERROR

IBRAHIM WARDE

I.B. TAURIS
LONDON · NEW YORK

Published in 2007 by I.B.Tauris & Co. Ltd
6 Salem Road, London W2 4BU
175 Fifth Avenue, New York, NY 10010
www.ibtauris.com

In the United States of America and Canada distributed by Palgrave Macmillan, a division
of St Martin's Press, 175 Fifth Avenue, New York, NY 10010

ISBN: 978 1 85043 424 5

A full CIP record for this book is available from the British Library
A full CIP record for this book is available from the Library of Congress

Library of Congress catalog card: available

Typeset in Goudy Old Style by A. & D. Worthington, Newmarket, Suffolk
Printed and bound in Great Britain by CPI Bath

Contents

Acknowledgements v

Introduction: The Fog of Financial War vii

PART I. THE MYTHOLOGY OF TERRORIST FINANCING

1. Fantasy, Fiction, and Terrorist Financing 3

PART II. RULES OF FINANCIAL ENGAGEMENT

2. Framing the Guilty: The Financial Terrain 23

3. The Flawed Money Laundering Template 35

PART III. NARRATIVE AND DYNAMICS

4. Money and the War on Terror Narrative 53

5. The Usual Suspects 63

6. Dynamics of the Financial War 77

PART IV. WAR AND CONSEQUENCES

7. Targets and Collateral Damage 93

8. "Gated Finance" and Other Contradictions of the Financial War 107

9. The Question of Islamic Charities 127

PART V. ASSESSMENTS AND RECOMMENDATIONS

10. "Catastrophic Successes": Assessing the Financial War   153

11. Rethinking Money and Terror   163

Epilogue: The Last Happy Warriors   183

Notes   197

Index   253

Acknowledgements

This book builds on a number of academic and professional projects I have been involved in over the years. My work on financial regulation and money laundering goes back to the monographs, *Foreign Banking in the United States* and *The Regulation of Foreign Banking in the United States*, I wrote and updated for IBPC throughout the 1990s. A later project, which dealt with issues of Middle Eastern politics and global finance, was my book *Islamic Finance in the Global Economy*, published in 2000 by Edinburgh University Press.

In conducting research for this book, I was affiliated with a number of academic institutions. I would like to thank Roger Owen and Thomas Mullins at Harvard University's Center for Middle Eastern Studies, Philip Khoury and Richard Samuels at the Massachusetts Institute of Technology, and Leila Fawaz and Laurent Jacque at the Fletcher School of Law and Diplomacy, Tufts University.

My work as a consultant has taken me to a number of countries: Bahrain, France, Germany, Ireland, Italy, Jordan, Lebanon, Malaysia, Qatar, Saudi Arabia, Singapore, Switzerland, the United Arab Emirates, and the United Kingdom. In those countries, conversations with bankers, government and law enforcement officials, academics, and experts were invaluable. A number of ideas in this book were first developed in articles for *Le Monde diplomatique*. I would like to thank the editors, in particular Alain Gresh and Serge Halimi, for their help and guidance. Most of all, I would like to thank my family, my wife Christiane and my son Antoine, for their unwavering support.

The Fog of Financial War

The first casualty when war comes is truth.
Hiram Johnson

Most of the material that you were dealing with had no connection to anything in the real world, not even the kind of connection that is contained in a direct lie. Statistics were just as much a fantasy in their original version as in the rectified version.
George Orwell

The message is that there are known "knowns"–there are things that we know that we know. There are known "unknowns"–that is to say, there are things that we now know we don't know. But there are also unknown "unknowns," things we do not know we do not know. And each year we discover a few more of those unknown unknowns.
Donald Rumsfeld

The "war on terror" began on the financial front. On September 24, 2001, President George W. Bush, standing in the Rose Garden outside the White House, and flanked by Treasury Secretary Paul O'Neill and Secretary of State Colin Powell, announced: "This morning, a major thrust of our war on terrorism began with a stroke of a pen. Today, we have launched a strike on the financial foundation of the global terror network." [1] A presidential order that had taken effect that day "one minute after midnight" blacklisted 27 individuals and groups–"terrorist organizations, individuals, terrorist leaders, a corporation that serves as a front for terrorism and several nonprofit organizations." The presidential statement made it clear that this was just a beginning: in the open-ended war on terror, many more financial attacks would be forthcoming. [2]

The first strike was also meant to be a shot heard around the world. Since most of the assets linked to terrorism were outside the United States, the financial war was from the start a global one. The President gave notice to the international financial community: "If you do business with terrorists, if you support or sponsor them, you will not do business with the United States of America."[3] A fact sheet issued by the White House that day expanded the class of targeted groups to all those who are "associated with" designated terrorist groups, and established the US ability to "block the U.S. assets of, and deny access to U.S. markets, those foreign banks that refuse to freeze terrorist assets."[4] Within days, under American leadership, the campaign was taken up by international bodies. Members of the G-7 pledged to pursue "a comprehensive strategy to disrupt terrorist funding around the world."[5] On September 28 the United Nations Security Council passed Resolution 1373, which required all nations to keep their financial systems free of terrorist funds. The Financial Action Task Force (FATF), the Paris-based organization in charge of policing money laundering, which had until then been spurned by the Bush administration,[6] was formally appointed as global policeman on matters of terrorist financing. The World Bank and the International Monetary Fund added terrorist financing and money laundering controls to their monitoring of countries' economic activities.[7] Countless international, regional, and national bodies pledged to deprive all suspected terrorist networks of financial and logistical support.

The hastily passed and symbolically charged USA PATRIOT legislation (the acronym stood for "Uniting and Strengthening America by Providing Appropriate Tools Required to Intercept and Obstruct Terrorism"), signed by President Bush on October 26, 2001, provided additional tools aimed at terror financiers. It considerably beefed up financial controls, by expanding the anti-money laundering arsenal, broadening definitions of terrorism and financial institutions, widening prosecutorial powers, and prohibiting American banks and other financial institutions from accepting funds from shell banks domiciled in offshore financial centers. In addition many of the controversial sections of the law, including permission given to the Federal Bureau of Investigation (FBI) and other law enforcement agencies to expand wiretapping, detention, or eavesdropping on lawyers, were justified by the need to "disrupt" the financing of terror.

A massive surveillance of domestic and international financial flows was also under way soon after the attacks. First Data Corporation, one of the world's largest processors of credit card transactions, and whose subsidiaries include Western Union, offered as early as September 13 to open its books to US investigators.[8] And under a series of broad US subpoenas, the massive database of Brussels-based Swift (the Society for Worldwide Interbank Financial Telecommunications), which links 7,800 banks and financial institutions worldwide and processes some 11 million sets of transfer instructions and confirmations daily, was tapped for information on activity by suspected terrorists. The secret Terrorist Finance Tracking Program was managed by the Central Intelligence Agency under the supervision of the Treasury Department.[9]

A week after the first strike, President Bush trumpeted "progress on the financial front" as he announced more blacklisted accounts.[10] The financial assault has since broadened and deepened. Initially limited to terror groups with "global reach," it soon expanded far beyond the perpetrators of the attacks on the World Trade Center and those who posed a direct threat to the United States. It extended to movements such as Hamas and Hezbollah, and the dragnet engulfed informal remittance networks (hawalas) and mainstream Islamic charities. In the weeks following the 9/11 attacks, the pace of financial strikes was frantic. The financial front—though briefly upstaged by the swift military offensive in Afghanistan—dominated the headlines. In its 100-day progress report, the White House announced that "the United States and its allies have been winning the war on the financial front" and assured that "denying terrorists access to funds is a very real success in the war on terrorism." [11]

The most spectacular strike occurred on the morning of November 7, 2001, when special agents from the US Customs Service, the Internal Revenue Service (IRS), the Office of Foreign Assets Control (OFAC), and the FBI descended on offices of Al-Barakaat, a remittance and telecommunications company based in Somalia and Dubai. It was the first time the administration had targeted US-based companies and individuals suspected of aiding and financing terrorists. There were simultaneous and equally dramatic operations against the company in foreign countries, highlighting unprecedented strides in international cooperation. The announcement was made with great fanfare by President Bush, with the most prominent members of the cabinet at his side. The company was described as the "quartermaster of terror," and stood accused of sending $15–25 million annually to Al-Qaeda. There were even suggestions that Usama Bin Laden was a founder and co-owner of the company.

It later appeared that those accusations were baseless and that Al-Barakaat was innocent of terrorist charges. The episode, discussed in detail in Chapter 7, shone a new light on the financial war. Countries ranging from Canada to Sweden, judging the "evidence" furnished by the US unconvincing, refused to comply with requests for further crackdowns against the company and its executives. In the US, after a long battle, the company was discreetly exonerated of being linked to terrorists—so discreetly in fact that many top Treasury officials still mention the closure of Al-Barakaat as a spectacular victory in the war on terror. A top government official later confessed, "This is not normally the way we would have done things. We needed to make a splash. We needed to designate now and sort it out later." [12] The Al-Barakaat episode, though illustrative of every dysfunction of the financial war, is still perceived in the literature of law enforcement as a shining trophy.[13]

Following the invasion of Iraq, that country became the new center of gravity for the financial war. On March 20, 2003, hours before bombs started falling on Iraq, President Bush signed an executive order to confiscate $1.4 billion that had been held in US banks. Many of those assets had been frozen by executive order following the 1990 invasion of Kuwait.[14] Now they were to be seized and disposed of. The action marked only the second time since World War II that the US government had taken ownership of a substantial amount of frozen foreign assets.[15] The executive order also required the government to identify, freeze, and seize Iraqi assets worldwide.

In many respects, however, the financial strike against Iraq was different from the strikes that followed the 9/11 attacks. For one thing, it was largely eclipsed by military and diplomatic developments, and as a result was mostly ignored by the mainstream media.[16] At the same time, the elements of surprise and improvisation that existed after the World Trade Center attacks were now absent. A substantial bureaucratic apparatus armed with an unprecedented legal and regulatory arsenal and intent on muscle flexing was firmly in place. Most significantly the money question was an integral part of the "regime change" strategy. Despite intensive preparations for war with Iraq, no budgetary provisions had been made for it. This was in part because war critics would seize on the economic argument, but also because the war was supposed to "pay for itself." [17] For one thing, much of the "authorized discourse" insisted that an Iraqi invasion would be a "cakewalk" and that the Iraqis—indeed the entire Islamic world—would erupt in joy.[18] Equally important, Iraq was potentially a rich country. On March 27, a week after the war started, when the question of war costs was first officially mentioned, Defense Undersecretary Paul Wolfowitz, a leading architect of the war, told the House Committee on Appropriations: "There's a lot of money to pay for this that doesn't have to be U.S. taxpayer money, and it starts with the assets of the Iraqi people. ... On a rough recollection, the oil revenues of that country could bring between $50 and $100 billion over the course of the next two or three years. ... We're dealing with a country that can really finance its own reconstruction, and relatively soon." [19]

The personal wealth of Saddam Hussein was to be included in those financial calculations, and the quest for "Saddam's billions" was thus part of the build-up to the war. Months before the start of the war, large financial investigative teams were placed in Iraq by the Treasury Department "on a long-term basis to obtain access to individuals who it says have knowledge of the flow and location of Iraqi funds." [20] Those teams worked closely with the FBI, the intelligence community, and the Department of Defense. In the words of Juan Zarate, then Deputy Assistant Secretary for Terrorist Financing and Financial Crimes at the Treasury Department, "The hunt for Iraqi assets will be a long-term effort. It requires dogged investigation, including interrogations, witness interviews and document exploitation, as well as intensive diplomatic efforts worldwide and vigorous intelligence work." [21] Finding those assets became "the top priority" of the Treasury Department. According to Secretary John Snow, "The order authorizes the Treasury to marshal the assets and to use the funds for the benefit and welfare of the Iraqi people." [22] On August 28, 2003, executive order 13315 placed Iraq's state assets under US control. It required US banks to search for and freeze assets they found belonging to the former Iraqi regime, its senior officials, and their family members. As the insurgency grew, hopes for a swift and profitable reconstruction faded, but an added rationale, the need to deprive insurgents of funds, lent further urgency to the financial war.

The financial front

In addition to being where the war on terror started, the financial terrain may also well be the widest and most durable front of that war, as well as the least controversial and most prone to spin and political manipulation. The financial front was the one front to which every single country was expected to contribute. Long after the removal of the Taliban regime in Afghanistan and the official ending of the "military phase" of the Iraqi war, respectively on December 12, 2001 and May 1, 2003, the financial front was still steadily expanding. In that respect, the contrast between the military front and the financial one was striking. Militarily, the steady broadening of the war on terror, which culminated with the war in Iraq, was deeply unpopular internationally, and generated a great deal of defections. The "coalition of the willing" was, to use the expression of Senator John Kerry during the 2004 presidential campaign, more like a "coalition of the coerced and the bribed." [23] As chaos spread in Iraq, the coalition kept shrinking, from 38 nations and 50,000 troops in mid-2003, to 27 countries and about 22,000 troops at the end of 2005, with most of the remaining countries announcing that they would end their participation in 2006. [24] The exact opposite happened on the financial front. All members of the United Nations officially signed on to the financial war, doing their part in freezing accounts, signing treaties, creating new bureaucracies, overhauling legislation, and otherwise committing to starving terrorists of funds. [25] Even now, hardly a day goes by without news of a new country enacting or tightening "money laundering/terrorist financing" laws or signing a related bilateral or multilateral agreement.

The breadth and softness of the financial front makes it especially vulnerable to political manipulation. The goal of separating the terrorists from their money is unexceptionable and the financial argument itself is highly plausible. The sheer magnitude of the destruction caused by the 9/11 attacks left little doubt that huge resources had been involved. Even after it was revealed that the actual cost of the 9/11 operations was modest—in the $300,000 to $500,000 range[26]—the broader paradigm was never seriously challenged: money is the sinew of war, and attempts at apocalyptic terror involving nuclear, chemical, and biological weapons justified extreme measures. The involvement of Usama Bin Laden, the scion of an immensely wealthy Saudi family, who first appeared on the radar screen as the "financier" of the Mujahideen, and the fact that 15 out of the 19 hijackers were Saudis, suggested that money had been central to the conspiracy. Yet there is a central paradox about money. Although money matters can, at the basic level, be understood by anyone, more involved financial arguments are likely to bore and confuse. Claims and accusations on money matters are not easily verifiable. Indeed, they are often, literally, irrefutable. To quote former Citicorp Chairman John Reed, "money is information on the move."[27] As such, unlike, say, weapons of mass destruction, the non-existence of which was eventually established, allegations about money are routinely exempted from the physical verification test. The most fanciful claims can be made, and it is nearly impossible to prove or disprove them. The financial front is also highly conducive to "pseudo-events"[28]—freezing accounts, issuing new regulations, creating new agencies and committees, convening conferences and meetings, announcing new policy measures, and other forms of bureaucratic "busyness"—which, to paraphrase former Treasury Secretary Paul O'Neill, make it easy to confuse "activity" with "progress."[29] By the same token, the "vigorous" prosecution of the financial war is assumed to be effective.[30] Although considered the province of "financial warriors"—technocrats belonging to a vast specialized bureaucracy were assumed to know what they were doing and not to be second-guessed—financial decisions are seldom politically innocent. A Treasury Department official confessed to the Los Angeles Times that the Department's early decisions and announcements were "premature and politically driven."[31] Equally significant, the financial front is irresistible to politicians whenever they need to show they are "doing something," or whenever they want to grandstand or change the subject.

The first strike of the war on terror was a case in point. The general public was in a state of shock, and the administration, which had been fixated on Iraq and had not taken the Al-Qaeda threat seriously despite repeated warnings of an impending attack involving hijacked airplanes on US soil,[32] wanted to do something bold and dramatic. Inexplicably there were no contingency plans at the time for an immediate military attack on Afghanistan, and no forces in the immediate area. At the National Security Council meeting held in the White House bunker on the evening of September 11, Donald Rumsfeld said that it could take up to 60 days before the military could put together major military strikes in the country that sheltered the Taliban.[33] The idea of a financial attack came up as early as September 17 as a fitting substitute.[34] It was, in the words of President Bush, "something that could be done immediately,"[35] with the added advantage that it would provide a much needed "scorecard," since concrete, albeit spurious, results could be announced.[36] The President ordered to "seize some assets, and quickly."[37] Treasury General Counsel David Aufhauser later described a frantic weekend search: "It was almost comical. We just listed out as many of the usual suspects as we could and said, Let's go freeze some of their assets."[38] And President Bush insisted that he ought to make the announcement himself— one filled with hoopla and military metaphors—to drive home the point that this would be a "completely different kind of war."[39]

A barely noticed aspect of the first strike was that it could not have made much of a dent on the alleged treasure of Al-Qaeda, since most of the accounts listed had either already been frozen by Bill Clinton three years earlier following the 1998 African embassy bombings, or affected accounts of organizations that were either extinct, or operating in a much reduced capacity.[40] In both cases, the presidents had invoked the International Emergency Economic Powers Act (IIEPA) to freeze the assets of Usama Bin Laden, Al-Qaeda, and related entities. As noted by former National Security Council officials Daniel Benjamin and Steven Simon, in both cases, "the move made news, but had little effect."[41] In 1998 and even more so in 2001, the political logic was compelling: the financial strikes conveyed a message of forceful action; they elicited strong popular support and generated no criticism or second guessing. In the words of Benjamin and Simon, "Cutting off the terrorists' finances sounded appealing and played to the public's sense that the world of international finance was one great machine in which every moving piece could be found."[42]

That the strikes failed to have an impact on terrorist funding was almost beside the point. After all, who could disagree with the idea of drying up terrorist funding, or that of punishing terror's paymasters, especially if such actions would prevent future attacks? Financial measures designed to stem terror financing were thus just as uncontroversial as the thorough searching of passengers at the airport—perhaps inconvenient, but a negligible price to pay for everyone's safety. Few voices were raised in criticism. Nearly five years after the September 11 attacks, at a time when most Americans were critical of the administration, support for intrusive financial controls was strong. Following the disclosure of the Terrorist Finance Tracking Program, which provided for the monitoring of virtually all international financial transfers, seven out of ten Americans supported the program, including majorities of Republicans (83 percent), independents (67 percent), and Democrats (58 percent).[43] From the early days of the war on terror, analysts and commentators of every political stripe were generally supportive of such policies. Many who expressed misgivings about military strikes had no qualms about financial ones. Mark Weisbrot, co-director of the liberal Center for Economic and Policy Research, wrote, "These financial measures are going to be far more important and effective in fighting terrorism than anything that falls out of a B-1 bomber. According to US intelligence sources, Bin Laden has supplied the Taliban with more than $100 million a year since 1996. This is a major source of income for the government, and probably buys him a lot of protection, too."[44] The empirical evidence did not support the claim that Bin Laden supplied the Taliban with an annual stipend of this magnitude, but commentators such as Weisbrot, who vigorously questioned the rationale behind military strikes, continued to take the financial one at face value.

Over time, many aspects of the escalating war on terror (the extension of the war to Iraq, the treatment of war prisoners, the torture, the assaults on liberty, privacy, and civil rights, etc) became deeply contentious, yet the financial front was largely immune to such criticisms. As summarized by the *Economist*, the argument was that "choking off the money that funds terrorism sounded, after September 11th, like a neat and peaceable way to help prevent future attacks."[45]

The financial war has consumed vast swaths of the US government's budget and bureaucracy. It has affected the lives and activities of people and organizations around the world. It has generated acres of column inches and headlines. But it has been subjected to virtually no critical scrutiny. The discourse of finance, of transfer-monitoring, and asset control seems so technocratic, so divorced from the slippery world of politics that no one has yet thought to ask the question: is this an effective way to defeat terror? And if not, why is it being pursued? These questions need to be addressed as a matter of urgency because, as this book will demonstrate, the financial war has political, social, and economic consequences that have nothing to do with terrorism, but which may endanger America's national interests and the security of the world in the long term.

The parallel universe of the financial war

Richard Perle, the influential Chairman of the Defense Policy Board, the Pentagon advisory group, said in the wake of the September 11 attacks that "terrorism must be decontextualised."[46] The discussion of terrorism, especially in the period immediately following the attacks, was largely detached from context, history, and politics. On the subject of terrorist financing, a veritable "parallel universe" has taken shape, built around dubious axioms, assumptions, and founding myths.

The central axiom is that money is the "lifeblood" or the "oxygen" of terror. As he asked "the world to stop payment" on September 24, 2001, President Bush asserted that "money is the lifeblood of terrorist operations." Secretary of State Colin Powell went on to explain: "Terrorists require a financial infrastructure. They require safe-havens. They require places that will get them succor and comfort. We're going after all of them in every way that we can." [47] The same theme was used by British Chancellor of the Exchequer Gordon Brown as he announced a series of post-September 11 financial controls to take effect throughout the European Union: "If fanaticism is the heart of modern terrorism, finance is its lifeblood." [48] The much abused lifeblood and oxygen metaphors[49] have been ritually invoked whenever action was taken on the financial front. In pressing to include anti-money laundering legislation in the USA PATRIOT legislation, Representative John J. LaFalce of New York argued that terrorism would end only when "our law enforcement becomes armed with the appropriate arsenal of tools to either cut off or trace the lifeblood of terrorism: money." Otherwise the country would be fighting "terrorism with one hand tied behind our back." [50] Influential think tanks all concurred. A Heritage Foundation study stated: "Cut off these flows, and the terrorist's activities will be stunted no matter how fanatical the devotion of their followers." [51] Whenever the subject of terrorist financing comes up, whether in the media, in Congress, or in courtrooms, the metaphor is inevitably dredged up. On certain occasions, a second, related axiom was articulated. It stated, in the words of David Aufhauser, former General Counsel at the Treasury Department, that "money is the mother of intent." [52]

Those axioms were forcefully stated, yet they rested on a number of assumptions, most of which were so self-evident that they were seldom if ever expressed. The master assumption of the financial war is that there is a more or less finite stash of cash "out there," which is periodically tapped for terrorist operations. The roots of this assumption, and related ones (terrorists are motivated by money, acts of terror require substantial financing, financiers and paymasters are a necessary part of any terrorist attack, etc), are to be found in the entrenched belief that Al-Qaeda's treasure consists essentially of Usama Bin Laden's "300 million inheritance," and in the prevailing law enforcement mindset (discussed in the next chapter). Once that stash is seized in its entirety, terrorism will be deprived of its lifeblood and will stop. Indeed, the finite stash of cash assumption is the financial counterpart to the "head count" approach common to counter-insurgency strategies—"the yardstick by which success is measured." [53] One can find countless statements to the effect that the way of ending terrorism is to kill all the terrorists. Drawing lists of "bad guys" and checking them off as they are arrested is a staple of law enforcement. On various occasions, President Bush would for example assert that "75% of Al-Qaeda leadership has been killed or captured." By the same token, as he left office, David Aufhauser boasted that thanks to his efforts, "Al Qaeda's cash flow had been reduced by two-thirds." [54] Oblivious to the possibility that money could be replenished, another Treasury official told the *Washington Post*, "There are limitless quantities of drugs. What is not so easily replaceable is the money." [55] For that reason, seizing terrorist assets, rather than seizing contraband or imprisoning top thugs, had become the top priority of the agency.

Finance as a residual explanation

Another reason why the idea that money causes terror was able to get such currency was the resolute foreclosing of any political or social explanations of terrorism in the aftermath of 9/11. The Bush administration, with its emphasis on the simplicities of good and evil, was not in the business of "understanding terrorism." Nonetheless, the law enforcement and intelligence agencies needed at least to explain why terror occurred in certain places and at certain times. Insofar as certain subjects, such as American foreign policy, could not be brought up, finance subtly stepped into the breach as the residual explanation of choice.

The World Trade Center attacks had been made possible by money, the "oxygen" of terror. In the months immediately following 9/11, the absence of terrorist acts was interpreted as proof positive that "financial networks were strangled" and that the financial offensive was working.[56] The reappearance of terrorism in various parts of the world—a development that could not be squared either with the overall logic of the war on terror, or with the justifications of the war in Iraq—was frequently interpreted as a sign that some terrorist money was still "out there." The money warriors, while taking stock of their successes, would on occasion recognize that terror financiers had not been dealt with harshly enough, or that terrorists had found new ways of hiding their money—in sum, that more needed to be done on the financial terrain. After every terrorist attack—and in every instance of post-September 11 terrorism, the cost of the attacks was proved to be negligible—there would be calls for "doing more" on the financial front.[57]

In other words, whenever events contradicted the official storyline, the financial argument was bound to resurface. In the months preceding the war in Iraq, the dominant discourse claimed not only that a war was necessary, but also that it would be a "cakewalk"—that American troops would, in the words of Vice-President Dick Cheney, "be greeted with flowers and sweets," that reconstruction would be smooth, and democracy would take root in Iraq and flourish in the Middle East. Most significantly, "regime change" in Iraq was to deal a fatal blow to terrorism.[58] And on May 1, 2003, there was an official proclamation of "mission accomplished." The notion that there would be a substantial Iraqi resistance was thus a logical impossibility, which is why the war planners simply failed to plan for the postwar.[59]

Later, a number of milestones—the killing of Saddam Hussein's sons, the arrest of Saddam Hussein himself,[60] the return to "sovereignty," the elections and referendum, the killing of Abu Musab al-Zarqawi, etc—were to spell the end of the insurgency. Every one of these milestones was actually followed by a recrudescence of terrorism. With the insurgency repeatedly said to be in its "last throes," money provided the much needed post-hoc hypothesis: the insurgents were really foreigners, and dead-enders, and anti-American attacks could be attributed to undiscovered cash.[61] In the words of one writer: "US officials think another $3 billion (belonging to Saddam Hussein), give or take a million or two, is sloshing around in banks in Syria, Lebanon, Jordan and Turkey. That translates into a lot of body bags in Iraq." [62]

Conversely, any pause in the insurrection would be attributed to the drying up of financial resources. A lull in December 2003 in the city of Tikrit, the birthplace of Saddam Hussein and a stronghold of anti-American resistance, was reflexively attributed to the seizure of $2 million in cash. Tikrit Commander Major General Raymond T. Odierno, in accounting for the drop in the number of attacks to six per day, from 22 per day a month earlier, explained: "For the first time in the last 30 days, I truly feel we've gotten into their cycle of financing. We have indications they're having trouble financing attacks." [63]

Even as many American officials came to terms with the fact that they were facing an insurrection, the financial argument would periodically reappear, occasionally broadening the list of "usual suspects." The New York Times reported in October 2004 that "the core of the Iraqi insurgency now consisted of as many as 50 militant cells that draw on 'unlimited money' from an underground financial network run by former Baath Party leaders and Saddam Hussein's relatives. Their financing is supplemented in great part by wealthy Saudi donors and Islamic charities that funnel large sums of cash through Syria, according to these officials, who have access to detailed intelligence reports." [64] Some "evidence" was adduced: "Only half the estimated $1 billion the Hussein government put in Syrian banks before the war has been recovered, Pentagon officials said. There is no tally of money flowing through Syria to Iraq from wealthy Saudis or Islamic charities, but a Pentagon official said the figure is 'significant.'" [65]

A mainstay of the discourse on terrorism, and a corollary of the finan-cial argument for terror, was that there is a "market" for terror attacks—a mechanical relationship between the money available and the occurrence of terrorist acts. "Terrorism experts" took to opining on the fluctuations of the terror market with the same confidence displayed by stock market analysts. At any given time, one could learn about how much an attacker, a suicide bomber, or a suicide bomber's family would receive as a reward for carrying out a terrorist attack. In early 2004, Israeli officials quoted in the *New York Times* claimed that each attack brought its Palestinian planners an amount ranging from $673 to $1,122.[66] Around the same time, it was estimated that the reward for conducting a strike in Iraq was $500, as opposed to $3,000 for the killing of an American soldier.[67] Almost a year later, the going rate in parts of Baghdad for planting roadside bombs was said to be $100–300 for each explosive.[68]

Of course, one troublesome aspect of the terrorism-for-profit argument was that most terrorists were suicide bombers—which led many analysts to broaden the economic rationality argument. Some asserted the afterlife benefits of martyrdom.[69] Others emphasized the financial benefits for survi-vors. *U.S. News and World Report* quoted the explanation of Yehudit Barsky, identified as yet another "Islamic charities expert:" "Without the money that terrorists know will go to their families when they die, it would be harder for organizations to recruit. Cut off that support system of money funneled to families, and you'll be left with very few young men willing to die for terror and destroy their family as well." [70] In the same vein, Israeli counter-terrorism expert Boaz Ganor, arguing that the families of suicide bombers during the intifada could receive as much as $25,000, wrote: "From this perspective, perpetrating suicide attacks could be considered by a youngster from a large family as an altruistic act for his family's benefit." [71] The financial argument is dubious on many levels. Even if the amounts mentioned were correct (a very big if), it would be hard to believe that the financial compensation would be the only, or even the main, motivation of suicide bombers. Indeed, none of the serious empirical works on suicide bombing places much empha-sis on money as a causal factor.[72]

An alternative approach to terrorist financing

In a 2003 testimony before the Senate Banking Committee, former counter-terrorist czar Richard Clarke expressed his frustration:

> The questions we asked then [in 1995] of the CIA were never answered—and we asked them for six years: how much money does it cost to be al Qaeda? What's their annual operating budget? Where do they get their money? Where do they stash their money? Where do they move their money? How? Those

questions we asked from the White House at high levels for five or six years
were never answered because, according to the intelligence community, it was
too hard.[73]

Clearly, it never occurred to him, or to other top officials, that these were
perhaps not the proper questions to ask. The same questions are still insis-
tently asked today. Unlike other aspects of the war on terror, which at least
since the beginning of the second term of the Bush administration have
been seriously questioned, the terrorist financing paradigm has remained
unchanged. As a result, in the financial war there would be neither learning
curve nor corrective actions.[74]

Contrary to what is commonly said, money is not the oxygen or lifeblood of terror. Such slogans suggest that once money is "taken away" from
terrorists, terrorism will stop. "Money warriors" have the causality wrong:
terror does not exist because there is money; rather, money appears where
there is support for terror. The principal question ought to be, "why is there
support for terror?" Only after such a question is adequately answered, and
once the nature of the support network (its characteristics, its grievances,
the incentive systems of its members, etc) is understood, can the question
which dominates the financial war—"where does the money come from?"—be
properly addressed.

Another entrenched belief is that acts of terror, because of their destruc-
tiveness, cost a lot of money. The empirical evidence suggests otherwise.
More than half of the American casualties in Iraq have been caused by
crude, often home-made improvised explosive devices (IEDs), "sometimes
made with multiple artillery shells and Iranian TNT, sometimes disguised
as bricks, boosted with rocket propellant, and detonated by a cell phone or
a garage door opener."[75] The September 11 attacks cost somewhere between
$300,000 and $500,000.[76] Over a period of less than two years, 19 people
lived modest lives while planning a massive attack. What they lacked in
money, they more than made up for in wile, imagination, and motivation.
The principal weapons of the attacks were of course hijacked planes that
were turned into missiles, with box cutters used to subdue the crews and the
passengers. No subsequent terrorist attack has cost more than $50,000. Most
in fact cost much less, yet reactions to the July 7, 2005 London bombing
attacks—when four simultaneous bombs during the rush hour in London's
public transport system (in three Underground subway trains and a double-
decker bus) killed 56 people (52 civilians plus the four suicide bombers)
and injured over 700—suggest that, almost four years after the September
11 attacks, the financial lessons had yet to sink in. Indeed, as had been the
case after every single terrorist attack, before any evidence surfaced about the
perpetrators and their methods, the focus was on terrorist financing.

On the day of the London attacks, Colonel David Hunt, Fox News's military analyst and author of a book on terrorism,[77] appeared on Bill O'Reilly's top-rated US talk show for instant commentary. Predictably, it didn't take long before the "expert" addressed the money question:

> There's too much money in the Muslim world that's unaccounted for that's going to terrorist funding. This operation in London took six months to a year, thousands of dollars, passports, logistic cells and you have to get at that money. What I mean by that is—the Bank of Saudi Arabia [sic], the Bank of Yemen [sic]. If you've got money, we're taking it and redistributing it. I'm talking about Biblical Justice to stop this. We've got to get people's attention.[78]

The host, Bill O'Reilly, agreed that the solution was "to take their money" but he deplored the fact that "you can't force banks in the Arab world to tell you where their money is." To which Colonel Hunt had a ready answer:

> No, but I can get inside their bank—and people listening in the business know this. You can get inside a bank's computer—hit "send" and take it. I'm telling you—you asked what to do. You get at this money. There's $500 billion of unaccounted for money that travels around the Muslim world and forms a "zakat", which is a tithing in the Muslim community and "hawala" which is given—borrowed money [sic].[79]

Just as predictable was the announcement of sweeping measures against terrorist financing. It took only five days for Chancellor of the Exchequer Gordon Brown to say: "Blocking terrorists' access to financial systems is a critical preventive measure."[80] The Chancellor's language was almost identical to that used after the September 11 attacks. In his words, "Just as there will be no safe haven for those who perpetrate terrorism, there will be no hiding place for those who finance terrorism."[81] He urged European Union finance ministers to step up the fight against financing for groups accused of terrorism. He said that the crackdown on terrorist financing would be placed at the center of the United Kingdom's presidency of the European Union, and that the issue would be put "at the top of the agenda" of the upcoming annual meetings of the International Monetary Fund and the World Bank.[82] Among the measures he announced on July 12, 2005 were the seizure of suspects' assets, the exchange of data between financial authorities, the introduction of a code of conduct to prevent the abuse of charities, and new controls on cross-border financial transfers. Incidentally, most of these measures had been drawn up following the Madrid bombings 16 months earlier, but the follow-through was deemed insufficient. Gordon Brown also announced the establishment of a new group working across government to identify targets for asset-freezing, and demanded a report by March 2006 from the chairman of the Serious and Organized Crime Agency, former

MI5 chief Sir Stephen Lander, on how to crack down on suspicious transactions.[83]

Those measures were to apply far beyond the United Kingdom and the European Union. According to the Chancellor, "Some states outside the EU have taken very little action, in spite of what happened on September 11," singling out Burma, Nauru, and Nigeria, countries that had been designated a month earlier "as non-co-operative" by the Financial Action Task Force (FATF).[84] The rationale was that "you're only as strong as your weakest link. Where there are countries that are not taking action to cut off the sources of terrorist finance, we will clearly have continuing problems."[85] The Chancellor said that the European Union was "prepared to offer help" to other countries that had not yet put in place sophisticated technical systems to stop money laundering.[86]

Stuart Levey, Treasury Undersecretary for Terrorism and Financial Crimes, wrote in the *Financial Times* that such attacks occurred because Europe was "exploited by terrorists as a haven for raising, moving and storing money,"[87] and called for a "stepping up" of "the war on terrorist financing."[88]

Some six months after the attacks, a little-noticed news item reported that, according to Scotland Yard, the four coordinated suicide bombings had cost all of £500 (less than $1,000).[89] To be sure, as in the past, the financial warriors had an instant retort: what cost a lot of money were not the acts of terror themselves, but the organization and infrastructure that sustained such attacks. To quote legendary New York District Attorney Robert Morgenthau:

> Large enterprises with thousands of employees cannot exist without cash. That is as true for Osama bin Laden's operation as any other. A private army with associates around the world cannot be maintained on a shoestring budget. Mr. bin Laden needs money for weapons, food, clothing, travel and training, and to pay off local leaders who allow him to remain in power.[90]

But none of the recent attacks would be recognizable in such descriptions. In London, the "paymaster" was also one of the suicide bombers. Mohammad Sidique Khan, a teacher's assistant by profession, and "a respected figure in his local community of Dewsbury, West Yorkshire," had provided the money needed to purchase the inexpensive and widely available materials needed to produce home-made peroxide-based bombs.[91] There was nothing to attract the attention either of the banks or of law enforcement: none of the banking transactions of the bombers were out of the ordinary, no "dirty money" or cross-border transfers were involved, three of the suicide bombers were born and raised in the United Kingdom, and the fourth was born in Jamaica and was a convert to Islam.

What are we to make of the steady decrease in the cost of terrorist attacks? One explanation is related to technological developments, which resulted in the democratization of violence, the privatization of war, and the advent of virtual networks. There is also the process of learning, adaptation, and socialization that has taken place since September 11. The "deadly expertise" of Al-Qaeda has quickly spread to potential terrorists worldwide,[92] not least thanks to the Internet. Jean-Louis Bruguière, the veteran French anti-terrorism judge, likes to compare permutations of Islamic radicalism to the mutations of a virus—an aspect of the problem that is often overlooked.[93] Since being "degraded" as a result of the Afghan war, Al-Qaeda "has been reduced to an ideological label, a state of mind, and a mobilizational outreach program to incite attacks worldwide."[94] All those developments give the lie to the persistent assertion that "no organization runs for long without money."[95] In reality, greater levels of militancy and motivation, fueled in no small measure by the war in Iraq, and growing perceptions that the war on terror is really a war against Islam,[96] have functioned as a substitute for the lack of financial resources.

The mistake of financial warriors is to look at terrorist financing as a subfield of criminology—a self-contained, free-standing field insulated from politics. They like to consider the financial war as a technical matter, best left to experts, where official proclamations are taken at face value: frozen amounts are to be subtracted from the terrorists' stash of money, and the terrorist threat is assumed to be reduced accordingly. In their parallel universe, the principal building block is the money laundering template, which grew out of the law enforcement agencies' battles against organized crime and drug trafficking. Although money laundering is fundamentally different from terrorist financing, the two have become virtually indistinguishable following the September 11 attacks. Money laundering is about "hiding and legitimizing proceeds derived from illegal activities."[97] Terrorist financing, in contrast, is not driven by a crime-for-profit logic and has seldom anything to do with cleaning dirty money.

Arguably the "softest front" of the war on terror (i.e. one where attacks can be waged easily without fear of retaliation or short-term political repercussions, and where prosecutors often choose to wage unrelated battles), the financial terrain is in reality permeated by politics. Financial attacks, as we saw, are often simply a way of "changing the subject" or of showing decisive action. The financial terrain is particularly inviting to punitive warfare. It is impenetrable to most observers and in particular to the media, casualties are largely invisible, and political consequences only manifest themselves in the long term. Like all economic sanctions, financial attacks are often the consequence of frustration or pique. In other words, overkill comes easily;

it brings satisfaction, and its collateral damage is not immediately visible. In the long run, however, such actions can create a boomerang effect: policies which are good and sensible when used reasonably and sparingly become counter-productive when used indiscriminately or with excessive vigor. For example, many of the initial reporting requirements imposed on Islamic charities were necessary, and in fact long overdue. Yet over time, a systematic ratcheting up of these measures, along with countless fishing expeditions and gratuitous attacks, had the opposite effect. By creating perceptions that the charities were being unfairly singled out, and that the war on terror had morphed into a war on Islam, support, including financial support, to radicalism has increased—yet by virtue of the "catastrophic success" of the financial war,[98] it has gone further underground, and largely out of the reach of the financial warriors.

Politics is also central to explaining how the war on terror came to be launched and how it evolved, and how as a result terrorism has mutated. This book discusses how the narrative of terrorism financing came to be shaped, and analyzes the tools and weapons of that war. In an interesting illustration of Joseph Nye's "paradox of American power," it shows that political and economic muscle can impose policies but not desired outcomes.[99] Those policies did not make a dent in terrorist financing, though they did reshape the global financial system, and brought about significant, though mostly unintended, political and economic consequences.

This brings us to the question of policy effectiveness. Surprisingly it is Donald Rumsfeld who, in a confidential memo sent on October 16, 2003 to four of his top military and civilian advisers, raised the issue most lucidly. The document, which was mysteriously leaked a few days later to USA Today,[100] asked two sets of questions. One dealt with the effectiveness of the war on terror:

> Today we lack metrics to know if we are winning or losing the global war on terror. Are we capturing, killing or deterring and dissuading more terrorists every day than the madrassas and the radical clerics are recruiting, training and deploying against us? ... Is our current situation such that "the harder we work, the behinder we get?"

The other addressed the need for an integrated, long-term strategy:

> Does the US need to fashion a broad integrated plan to stop the next generation of terrorists? The US is putting relatively little effort into a long-range plan, but we are putting a great deal of effort into trying to stop terrorists. The cost-benefit ratio is against us! Our cost is billions against the terrorists' costs of millions.[101]

What came to be called the "long hard slog" memo was a remarkable document, sharply different in style and content from any official declaration. It was sober, reflective, and free of the bluster usually associated with the Defense Secretary. It asked probing questions about what constituted victory. It also clearly suggested that the long-term solution to the problem of terror was primarily a political one, even addressing those "soft power" issues that are usually summarily dismissed by hawks. Much of the discussion of the effectiveness of the financial war will address questions raised in the memo (which it should be said did not seem, at least until 2005, to have much of an impact on Pentagon policy).

All this is certainly not meant to downplay the importance of money. Although most recent acts of terror have been conducted on a shoestring, money—though not a causal factor, and not, as is commonly repeated, the lifeblood of terror—is a significant facilitator and enabler. More money undoubtedly results in deadlier attacks. In the future, as terrorists attempt to gain access to weapons of mass destruction, money is bound to assume an even greater role, which is all the more reason to address the issue in an intelligent and effective manner. Policies based on an inappropriate understanding are bound to be counter-productive, since their actual impact will be to cause collateral damage, which is likely to increase recruitment and support—including financial support.

This book is divided into five parts. Part I explains how prevalent beliefs about terrorist financing came to be formed and why they proved impervious to contrary empirical evidence. Part II explains the "rules of financial engagement." It describes the origin of mindsets, assumptions, and policy templates underlying the financial war. Chapter 2 maps the financial terrain. It discusses the impact of prosecutorial tools largely designed to "frame the guilty," the implications of globalized finance on regulation and law enforcement, and the emergence of economic sanctions as "weapons of first resort." Chapter 3 deals specifically with the money laundering template, which was developed during the war on drugs, and was uncritically transposed to the fight against terrorist financing, despite fundamental differences between the two logics.

Part III focuses on the narrative and dynamics of the financial war. Chapter 4 explains how the money question came to fit the broader war on terror narrative. The financial argument served in part to obscure political grievances and was central to both the first and the second Bush doctrines. The first doctrine, articulated following the September 11 attacks, drew no distinction between those who financed acts of terror and those who committed them. The second doctrine, which came to define the Bush administration, was that of preemption: if money is indeed the "oxygen" of terror, then it makes sense to seize it preemptively. Chapter 5 reassesses the role of many of the "usual suspects" of financial war narrative: the Saudis, rich Arabs, drugs and crime, gold and diamonds, hawalas and Islamic banks. Chapter 6 discusses the multiple dynamics—political, bureaucratic, and legal—of the financial war and the overarching logic of "martial finance."

Part IV deals with the impact and consequences of the financial war. Chapter 7 addresses the disconnect between guilt and retribution, and the collateral damage caused by the financial war, with a special focus on Al-Barakaat, the Somali remittance company wrongly accused of being a secret financier of Al-Qaeda. The case vividly illustrates a common asymmetry: the high-profile closure of the company was presented as a policy triumph, yet it brought further devastation to one of the world's poorest countries. Chapter 8 explores the many contradictions of the financial war: between liberalization and criminalization (and the resulting logic of "gated finance"), between "following the money" and systematic interdiction, between escalation and diminishing returns, between soft power and unilateralism, and between courting Islamic moderates and targeting their money. The question of Islamic charities, discussed in some detail in Chapter 9, may be at once the least understood and the most consequential aspect of the financial war. Reforming Islamic charities was long overdue, but heavy-handed policies and indiscriminate attacks have lent credence to the view that the war on terror was a war against Islam.

Part V is about assessments and recommendations. Chapter 10 focuses on a paradox: the financial warriors are constantly touting their achievements, yet acts of terror keep increasing. The concluding chapter revisits the question of money and terror. It suggests an alternative paradigm based on a logic of insurrection. Terrorist financing appears wherever there is support for terror, and the question of support is essentially about politics. Such a paradigm casts doubt on the usefulness of tools which assume a crime-for-profit logic. In addition to reviewing the existing empirical evidence, the chapter makes a number of policy recommendations.

PART I
THE MYTHOLOGY OF
TERRORIST FINANCING

1

Fantasy, Fiction, and Terrorist Financing

The great enemy of the truth is very often not the lie—deliberate, contrived and dishonest—but the myth—persistent, persuasive and unrealistic.
John F. Kennedy

He who captures the symbols by which the public feeling is for the moment contained, controls by that much the approaches to public policy.
Walter Lippmann

Ideology is a lot easier, because you don't have to know anything or search for anything. You already know the answer to everything. It's not penetrable by facts. It's absolutism.
Paul O'Neill

In *Liar's Poker*, his classic portrait of Wall Street in the go-go 1980s, Michael Lewis described how, as a brash investment banker, he went about "inventing logical lies" in order to explain otherwise unexplainable events to nervous clients. Asked why the dollar fell, he would confidently say: "Several Arabs had sold massive holdings of gold, for which they received dollars. They were selling those dollars for marks and thereby driving the dollar lower." In the words of the investment banker turned author:

> Most of the time when markets move, no one has any idea why. A man who can tell a good story can make a good living as a broker. It was the job of people like me to make up reasons, to spin a plausible yarn. And it's amazing what people will believe. Having selling out of the Middle East was an old standby. Since no one ever had any clue what the Arabs were doing with their money or why, no story involving Arabs could ever be refuted. So if you didn't know why the dollar was falling, you shouted out something about Arabs.[1]

Shouting something about Arabs and their money would be unavoidable in the wake of the September 11 attacks. For one thing, no one knew anything specific about the attacks. The magnitude of the destruction suggested that a huge financial and logistical infrastructure had been at work. With the involvement of Usama Bin Laden, a man usually described as a Saudi "billionaire" and "terrorist financier," and the participation of 15 Saudi hijackers, the plausibility of the financial argument happened to coincide with a common stereotype. Indeed, as Jack Shaheen's comprehensive study of their portrayal by Hollywood suggests, Arabs had long been associated with "vile oil sheikhs with an eye for Western blondes and arms deals and intent on world domination, or with crazed terrorists." [2] By joining two of the three most common stereotypes—the billionaire and the bomber—the events of September 11 gave such crude stereotypes the ring of truth (the third stereotype was the belly dancer). [3]

Since facts were scarce, speculation ran rampant. Plausible yarns and logical lies filled the blanks. All the observations made by Michael Lewis about the world of finance in the 1980s—that nothing said about the Arabs and their money could be refuted, that stories about Middle Eastern investors were the residual explanation of choice for any unexplainable event, that people would believe anything—need to be placed in the context of the immediate period following September 11. The shock had been severe, and a paranoid atmosphere prevailed. It was widely assumed that numerous terrorists were in the United States and that other deadly attacks on US soil were imminent; Vice-President Dick Cheney was for weeks in an "undisclosed location," anthrax-laced letters were found around Washington, killing five people and resulting in a temporary closing of Congress. It was in that atmosphere that the "parallel universe" of terrorist financing took shape.

Essayist Joan Didion wrote insightfully about the process by which certain hypotheses about terror gelled over time into "fixed ideas." [4] Insofar as finance was the first front of the global war on terror, an instant canon on terrorist financing appeared in the days after the September 11 attacks. The "laundry list" became so familiar that it came to be mindlessly repeated: the Bin Laden $300 million fortune, business fronts legal and illegal, Islamic charities, the Saudis, rich Arabs, hawalas, drugs, gold and diamonds, petty crime. [5] From the popular press to weighty studies of prestigious think tanks, lists of usual suspects were almost identical. Repetition looked like corroboration. The lackadaisical way in which the terrorist financing discourse was constructed stood in sharp contrast with the authoritative way in which dubious "facts" were cited and recited.

Starting in 2004, considerable new information came out about the financial war on terror, but such evidence had little impact on perceptions or policies. Key players such as former Treasury Secretary Paul O'Neill, former counter-terrorism "czar" Richard Clarke, or Michael Scheuer, who headed the "virtual Bin Laden station" at the Central Intelligence Agency, published memoirs or contributed to books debunking much of what was commonly believed about the financial war. The publication of the 9/11 Commission Report in August 2004 helped gain a clearer understanding of the reality of terrorist financing, and contradicted, as will be discussed later, much of the canon.[6] The Commission's report, complemented by a terrorist financing monograph,[7] was based on "a comprehensive review of government materials on terrorist financing from essentially every law enforcement, intelligence and policy agency involved in the effort," and "included interviews of current and former government personnel, from intelligence analysts and street agents, up to and including members of the cabinet."[8]

Much of the 9/11 Commission Report could be criticized—the overly cautious conclusions of a group composed of an equal number of Democrats and Republicans, the failure to provide context or see the "big picture"[9]—but the sheer accumulation of fact and detail was invaluable. On matters of finance, the report and the attached monograph made a number of important points: they showed how little money is needed for terror attacks; they debunked the "urban legend" of the $300 million Bin Laden personal fortune; they established, contrary to the belief in some finite stash of cash, that money provided to terror groups fluctuated wildly and correlated with political developments; they hinted at the politicization of terrorist financing inquiries, and at how shadowy financial and logistical support networks had a way of appearing as needed. The 9/11 Commission Report did generate considerable media coverage, but such coverage was dominated by the political implications of the reports (the apportioning of blame between the Clinton and the Bush administrations, matters of intelligence reform and bureaucratic reorganization, etc). The financial aspects were barely mentioned in the mainstream media, and as a result, the implications for the financial war were left unaddressed.

Unlike other aspects of the war on terror, early beliefs about terrorist finance proved remarkably resilient. One possible explanation is the general plausibility of any argument about "the Arabs and their money." Another is the steady drumbeat of financial allegations that followed the attacks. In the 100 days following September 11, the financial war was a primary focus of media attention. Only the brief war in Afghanistan, which by the standards of other armed conflicts received scant media coverage, occasionally upstaged it. Above all, the financial war was politically convenient: it obscured the political and ideological dimension of political Islam. So it is no surprise that over time, "fixed ideas" about terrorist financing were well entrenched, and axioms and assumptions were thoroughly internalized. Facts and factoids were made to fit within this worldview. Neither policy-makers nor the media gave much play to later stories that debunked the dominant terrorist financing narrative.[10]

The elusive $300 million: The life and times of a factoid

Since Usama Bin Laden was singled out in 1998 as "public enemy number 1," the financial war was driven by the belief that his $300 million fortune formed the core of the Al-Qaeda funding network. In the 9/11 Commission Report, the figure was shown to be fictive—and was, or should have been, known to be so at least since 1999.[11] Yet the story lives on to this day. A Google search of keywords "Bin Laden" and "$300 million" conducted in April 2006 yielded no fewer than 154,000 hits.

Usama Bin Laden was a scion of one of the wealthiest Saudi families. He had come to prominence during the Afghan jihad, primarily because of his role in finance and logistics. Since the early 1990s, he resurfaced as the financier behind just about every high-profile attack attributed to Islamic extremists. So entrenched was the financier image that it took a while for intelligence agencies to realize that his role went far beyond that of mere financier—that he was in fact a terrorist leader and mastermind who was as much a recipient as a provider of financial support.

The $300 million factoid seems to have originated in 1996, when a State Department analyst inserted it in a "fact sheet" on Usama Bin Laden.[12] The figure was apparently arrived at by a rough calculation based on approximate figures. The analyst divided assets of the Bin Laden Group, which he esti-mated to be $5 billion, by the number of sons, which he estimated to be 20.[13] He arrived at a $250 million figure, which he rounded up to $300 million. The calculation rested on vague estimates and many dubious assumptions about the Bin Laden family, inheritance laws and practices, the actual worth of the privately held company, and its ownership structure.[14] Though it did not even rise to the level of a "back-of-the-envelope" calculation, the figure soon gained canonic status. More tabloid-like sources took further license with the figure, freely adding a zero, and certain books have claimed that Bin Laden's personal fortune was in the $3 billion range.[15]

The intelligence and law enforcement communities had initially bought the $300 million story hook, line, and sinker. Indeed, "intelligence reporting" dating from November 1998 bizarrely saw in that figure the convergence of diverse estimates—it "probably originated from rumors in the Saudi business community" but was also a "reasonable estimate" of Bin Laden's inheritance "as of a few years earlier"—which were also independently verified by the intelligence community.[16] In the words of the September 11 Commission:

The intelligence community thought it had adequately verified this number by valuing Bin Ladin's investments in Sudan as well as what he could have inherited from his father's construction empire in Saudi Arabia. Finished intelligence supported the notion that Bin Ladin's "fortune" was still intact by concluding that Bin Ladin could only have established al Qaeda so quickly in Afghanistan if he had ready access to significant funds.[17]

An early *Time* magazine account called any attempt to figure out the question of Bin Laden's family and personal wealth "a fact checker's migraine." [18] One reason for the confusion about Usama Bin Laden's wealth could be attributed to the casual conflation of three very distinct periods in his life and business fortunes. First were the years preceding 1991. He was then still formally part of the family business, the giant Saudi Binladin Group (SBG),[19] on good terms with the Saudi establishment, and a hero of the Afghan jihad. In 1991, however, he fell out with the Saudi royal family, and left for the Sudan.[20] During the Sudan years (1991–96), Bin Laden was coopted by the Sudanese Islamist regime and started a string of "legitimate" businesses. He played a dual role, that of a wealthy businessman and increasingly that of a global jihadist. In 1994, he was stripped of the Saudi citizenship. He was also disowned by his family, his shares of the family business were sold, and the proceeds of the sale were confiscated by the Saudi government. In 1996, under international pressure, he was expelled from the Sudan, and again stripped of his holdings in that country.[21] According to the September 11 Commission monograph on terrorist financing:

> When Bin Ladin was pressured to leave Sudan in 1996, the Sudanese government apparently expropriated his assets and seized his accounts, so that he left Sudan with practically nothing. When Bin Ladin moved to Afghanistan in 1996, his financial situation was dire; it took months for him to get back on his feet. While relying on the good graces of the Taliban, Bin Ladin reinvigorated his fund-raising efforts and drew on the ties to wealthy Saudi nationals that he developed during his days fighting the Soviets in Afghanistan.[22]

So between 1996 and 2001, Bin Laden was a "guest" and sometime patron of the Taliban regime. Whatever financial resources he accumulated over time came from a broad support network of jihadists. In 1998, his proclamation of jihad, followed by his indictment in the United States and the attacks against US embassies in Kenya and Tanzania, turned him into the "public enemy number 1" of the United States. Since that time, he was mostly on the run, though still protected by the Taliban rulers (until their fall in December 2001). He is now said to be hiding among tribes and supporters probably in lawless areas of Afghanistan and Pakistan.

Most accounts of Bin Laden after September 11 would mix and match elements of the three periods. Hence the familiar portrait of a cave-dwelling heir and tycoon with close ties to the Saudi establishment who ran his business empire and made shrewd moves in the stock market, all the while plotting terrorist acts.[23] The enduring legend became that "of the world's richest terrorist, a business-savvy nomad who has used a vast inheritance and a constellation of companies to finance a global network of violence."[24]

Yet as early as 1999, US government officials discovered that the $300 million figure was bogus. The National Security Council (NSC) organized inter-agency trips to Saudi Arabia in 1999 and 2000. For the first time, information was based on sources from the Saudi government as well as the Bin Laden family. It revealed that although Bin Laden was indeed once a wealthy man—who from 1970 to 1994 received a family income in the neighborhood of $1 million a year—he was also divested in 1994 of his share of the family business, as he lost his Saudi citizenship and was disowned by his family.[25] At the time, he still had business interests in the Sudan. Two years later, however, when he left the Sudan for Afghanistan, the Sudanese government expropriated all his assets.[26]

But the myth of Bin Laden as a rich financier persisted.[27] With almost no exception, every post-September 11 news article, every think tank report, every book of "revelations" on terrorist financing has repeated the assertion that Usama Bin Laden has a $300 million personal fortune which "formed the basis of the financing for al Qaeda."[28] Some did not resist the urge to embellish. Indeed, with every telling, the tale of Bin Laden's wealth seemed to grow taller. When describing Bin Laden's "global cash machine," even respectable publications went tabloid. One could read, for example:

> Every time a soft drink is sold in the world, there is a chilling possibility that Osama bin Laden's wealth increases—and with it the power of his terrorist network to wage war on the West. Most drinks contain gum arabic, a substance that prevents particles settling in the bottom of a can or bottle. Much of it is produced in Sudan by the Gum Arabic Company, in which bin Laden has owned a large slice.[29]

The other strange thing about that factoid was that the $300 million figure has been unchanged since 1996: despite a life of danger, Bin Laden's wealth has been remarkably stable—no gains or losses, no expenses payments or subsidies to the Taliban hosts, no confiscations, and no accretions of any sort were factored in. Although the mention of the figure became a fixture of the literature on terrorist financing, creative license was never absent: for some, the $300 million was the amount of Bin Laden's original inheritance or the result of the sale of his Sudanese businesses; for others it was the "current value" of his share in the family business; others still considered the $300 million figure to be the total budget of Al-Qaeda; one publication kept the number, but changed the currency from dollars to pounds sterling.[30]

To be sure, mentions of the figure were occasionally followed by caveats, which should logically have amounted to discrediting it, but did not. A typical account went as follows: "Taking into account his many brothers, Bin Laden's share of his father's estate has been estimated at $300 million. Some officials believe his current net worth is about one-tenth of that, as a result of his lavish support for the Afghan war against the Soviet Union and for terrorist causes. Other analysts suspect he is all but tapped out."[31] Other sources, citing a United Nations panel report issued in August 2002, deduct amounts frozen and factor in "secretly-managed investments" to place the $300 million as a high-end estimate: "despite 144 U.N. member states having frozen some $112 million in suspected al-Qaeda assets since September 11, the terror network continues to enjoy access to tens of millions of dollars in secretly managed investments—estimated to be worth somewhere between $30 million and $300 million."[32] Peter L. Bergen's oral history, perhaps the most rigorous study of the terrorist, put his inheritance at $20 million.[33] Such caveats were nonetheless of little consequence, since they were typically buried deep inside articles and reports. Thus the "hard," albeit fictitious, number remained in a public mind ready to believe only the most extreme assertions. The 9/11 Commission monograph on terrorist financing called the story of the $300 million inheritance "an urban legend [that] was nevertheless hard to shake."[34] Indeed, long after it was discredited, the factoid was still being cited by government officials and can still be found in just about every piece of writing on terrorist financing.[35]

Faith-based finance

Journalist Ron Suskind, who has written extensively on the Bush White House and on a number of Bush appointees and advisers,[36] has called the Bush administration the "faith-based presidency."[37] Everybody knows about the President's deep Christian faith, which formed the basis for the political biography—that of an aimless if not dissolute youth set straight by God—he successfully presented to the voters in 2000 and 2004, and about the role played by the Christian right in both elections. In a 2000 presidential debate, he called Jesus Christ his favorite political philosopher. When asked by Bob Woodward whether prior to attacking Iraq he had sought the counsel of his father (who had waged the First Gulf War), George W. Bush replied: "There is a higher father that I appeal to."[38] But more fundamentally, according to Suskind, "faith has also shaped his presidency in profound, nonreligious ways:" "The president has demanded unquestioning faith from his followers, his staff, his senior aides and his kindred in the Republican Party. Once he makes a decision—often swiftly, based on a creed or moral position—he expects complete faith in its rightness."[39]

Whatever predisposition the Bush administration had against the empirical approach was greatly reinforced by the climate of fear created by the September 11 attacks. As President Bush famously put it, "facing clear evidence of peril, we cannot wait for the final proof, the smoking gun that could come in the form of a mushroom cloud."[40] Resolve, decisiveness, steadfastness became virtues—indeed ends in themselves—regardless of whether the underlying decisions were right or wrong. The black-or-white, with-us-or-against-us style is not conducive to the rigorous exploration of a complex and messy reality. President Bush once told Senator Joseph Biden, "I don't do nuance."[41]

Such intolerance of doubt and doubters led to the departure of key appointees who held a different policymaking philosophy. When she resigned her position as administrator of the Environmental Protection Agency, Christie Whitman told Suskind: "In meetings, I'd ask if there were any facts to support our case. And for that, I was accused of disloyalty!"[42] By the same token, Treasury Secretary Paul O'Neill, who was asked to resign after only two years in the job, discovered early on that "hard-eyed analysis would be painted as disloyalty."[43] One day, as he was trying to explain to George W. Bush the complex budgetary implications of tax cuts, the president looked at him "with a flat, inexpressive stare" and finally said: "I won't negotiate with myself. It's that simple." O'Neill later remarked that he "wanted to say to the President that all sound analysis is about negotiating with yourself."[44] The loyal economic adviser Lawrence Lindsey was fired for suggesting that a war in Iraq war could cost $200 billion. At the time, though the war was imminent, it was not included in the budget and any reference to costs was taboo.[45] Following the departure of these officials, true believers had free rein, and recent budgets were mostly remarkable for "numbers that didn't quite compute."[46] A number of moderate Republicans have expressed worries about the President's "faith-based" posture. Bruce Bartlett, a domestic policy adviser to Ronald Reagan and a Treasury official in the George H.W. Bush administration, put it bluntly: "[H]e dispenses with people who confront him with inconvenient facts. He truly believes he's on a mission from God. Absolute faith like that overwhelms a need for analysis. The whole thing about faith is to believe things for which there is no empirical evidence."[47] To keep facts from intruding, tight discipline was expected, so that public officials would always stay "on message."

Even more revealing of the administration's attitude was an encounter between Ron Suskind and a senior aide to George W. Bush in the summer of 2002. The aide was displeased with one of the journalist's articles, and criticized him for being part of "the reality-based community" which included people who "believe that solutions emerge from your judicious study of discernible reality." The aide added: "That's not the way the world really works anymore. We're an empire now, and when we act, we create our own reality. And while you're studying that reality—judiciously, as you will—we'll act again, creating other new realities, which you can study too, and that's how things will sort out. We're history's actors ... and you, all of you, will be left to just study what we do." [48]

Claims about weapons of mass destruction and the subsequent war in Iraq have shown that the White House aide was deadly serious. The non-existence of weapons of mass destruction was in the final analysis irrelevant. What mattered more were "the new realities" created by the war. Indeed the rationales for the war kept shifting,[49] and as Paul Wolfowitz, the leader of the pro-war faction, explained bluntly, weapons of mass destruction were more convenient pretext than cause. In his words, "The truth is that for reasons that have a lot to do with the U.S. government bureaucracy we settled on the one issue that everyone could agree on, which was weapons of mass destruction as the core reason." [50]

For all the reasons discussed in this chapter, the parallel reality of terror-ist financing was especially resistant to empirical verification. So even more so than in other aspects of the war on terror, as the "reality-based" approach clashed with the "faith-based" one, the latter was bound to win. Safely insulated from empirical challenge, the financial war could thus be discussed in binary, Manichean, black-and-white terms (good versus evil, with us or against us) which favored non sequiturs, circular reasoning, and tautologies.

"Funding evil:" Terrorist financing between theology and arithmetic

The theme of evil was a fixture of the Bush administration's post-September 11 rhetoric. Evil had great resonance with religious fundamentalists and presented many rhetorical advantages. Calling someone evil closes off debate, since anyone saying otherwise must be either equally evil, or perhaps lacking in moral clarity.[51] It is also a way of staking the high moral ground, changing the subject, taking things off the discussion table, or foreclosing certain policy options. Most fundamentally, it arouses passions, invokes images, and invites associations. Whether in linking Saddam Hussein to Al-Qaeda, or otherwise broadening the list of "bad guys," the subtext was clear: "evil leaders do evil things and they do them together." [52] The "axis of evil," which conjoined two well-known historical analogies—Ronald Reagan's reference to the Soviet Union as "an evil empire" and the World War II Axis powers—elicited much criticism overseas, but played well at home. Paul Wolfowitz saw in it a "powerful metaphor" that would grab the headlines and force people to pay attention.[53] White House communications director Dan Bartlett appreciated the "starkness which broke through the clutter." Diplomacy and policy were no longer about nuance. "Good versus evil worked."[54]

Philosophical and theological discussions of evil are certainly legitimate, although one can question the policy relevance of the notion of evil—even more so on matters of money. In the words of columnist Michael Kinsley:

> Calling terrorists "evil" requires no courage and justifies no self-congratulatory puffing. It's just not a problem. But it's also not a solution. Of all the explanations for Sept. 11, 2001, and the subsequent alleged war on terrorism, the least illuminating is that it's all about evil. ... The concept of evil tells you nothing about why—among the many evils wished upon the United States—this one actually happened. Nor does "evil" help us figure out how to stop evil from visiting itself upon us again.[55]

Kinsley further added, with reference to what he called the "All-About-Evil crowd:"

> In order to avoid the danger that understanding terrorism might lead to excusing terrorism, they put understanding itself beyond the pale. This is not just anti-intellectual but actually a hindrance to the war on terrorism. Blocking any deeper understanding of the terrorists' mentality and motives cannot be good for the war effort.[56]

Theologian Kathleen Norris makes a similar point:

> Americans seem to have a very difficult time recognizing that there is a distinction between understanding and sympathizing. Somehow we believe that an attempt to inform ourselves about what leads to evil is an attempt to explain it away. I believe that just the opposite is true, and that when it comes to coping with evil, ignorance is our worst enemy.[57]

Linking evil to finance was somewhat incongruous, and conferred a "magical realism" quality to the terrorist financing literature—a mix of rich detail, surrealism, and fantasy. It is revealing that the neo-conservative tract on terrorist financing, part of an abundant literature on "ending evil,"[58] was titled *Funding Evil: How Terrorism is Financed—and How to Stop It.*[59] As with most works purporting to "reveal the secrets" of terrorist financing, the factual content of the pamphlet was thin at best, yet the projection of theology and metaphysics on matters of finance presented the political advantage of claiming the high moral ground while making groundless accusations.

Numbers are nonetheless necessary, even when invented, if only to lend scientific cachet to reports or analyses, and, to paraphrase Orwell, give the "appearance of solidity to pure wind." In the weeks preceding the Iraqi war, President Bush was very specific about the weapons of mass destruction of Saddam Hussein's regime: 500 tons of mustard gas and nerve gas, 25,000 liters of anthrax, 38,000 liters of botulinum toxin, 29,984 prohibited munitions capable of delivering chemical agents, 18 mobile biological warfare factories, etc.[60] The numbers were of course fictive; they were nonetheless necessary for the public to visualize an "imminent threat"—and believe that policymakers had done the actual counting and knew what they were talking about. Insofar as finance is the realm of numbers, the case for quantifying evil is even more compelling. We saw how the "$300 million Bin Laden personal fortune" story was contrived, how it gained canonic status, and how it provided the foundation for countless financial strikes. Other such figures include the "guesstimate" of a $30 million Al-Qaeda budget.[61]

One of the by-products of the discourse on evil is that the numbers concocted have to be appropriately gigantic. The lawsuit filed on August 15, 2002 against several Saudi princes, banks, charities, etc (Burnett v. Al Baraka Investment and Development Corporation), which came to be called "the lawsuit of the twenty-first century," sought "an amount in excess of $100 trillion" from dozens of defendants.[62] The lawsuit was thoroughly prepared and lavishly financed.[63] Yet on the day after the lawsuit was filed, the attorneys issued a correction, claiming that a "clerical error" had misstated the amount asked: the plaintiffs were "only" asking for one trillion dollars.[64] Perhaps that was the case. Or perhaps the lawyers realized that the initial amount exceeded the GNP of all countries in the world combined. Either way, it reflected the surreal nature of the terrorist financing discourse.

A frequently cited figure places the "economy of terror" at $1.5 trillion.[65] To understand how such figures are contrived, one needs to keep in mind that terrorist financing was a late addition to the massive money laundering edifice.[66] And as Jeffrey Robinson wrote: money laundering (disguising the illegal origin of money) "is all about sleight of hand. It is a magic trick for wealth creation. It is, perhaps the closest anyone has ever come to alchemy."[67] In 1999 Michel Camdessus, the former head of the International Monetary Fund, estimated it at somewhere between 2 and 5 percent of the world's gross domestic product, or $800 billion to $2 trillion.[68] It was a guess, and a not a terribly significant one, since it included so many disparate elements—drug dealing, financial fraud, tax evasion, prostitution, etc—and was at times used interchangeably with the informal sector (non-declared economic activities). Some claimed that money laundering had become the third largest industry in the world (after currency exchange and automobile manufacturing).[69] According to R.T. Naylor, of McGill University:

> All that those frightening statistics about a deluge of "narcodollars" or a burgeoning world Gross Criminal Product really prove is that it is not necessary to take the square root of a negative sum to arrive at a purely imaginary number. But the objective was not to illuminate the shadowy world of crime so much as to enlighten politicians about the need for larger law enforcement

budgets and more arbitrary police powers. Therefore, those magic numbers assumed the status of religious cant and were rarely revised, except heaven-ward.[70]

As terrorist financing came to displace money laundering in the hierarchy of financial crimes and the two started being used interchangeably, the truly stratospheric numbers associated with international money laundering were projected on to the much smaller amounts known to be involved in terrorist financing.[71] Exercises in accounting one-upmanship logically followed. If we are to look at the frequently cited $1.5 billion "economy of terror" figure, we learn that it is, conveniently, "evenly divided into three sectors: $500 billion in capital flights, money which moves illegally from country to country, undetected and unreported; $500 billion in what is commonly known as the Gross Criminal Product, money generated primarily by criminal organizations; and $500 billion in the New Economy of Terror—money produced by terror organizations—of which as much as one-third is represented by legal businesses and the rest comes from criminal activities, primarily the drug trade and smuggling." [72]

In sum, the conflation of unrelated phenomena has resulted in gigantic, though utterly meaningless, figures. An October 2005 *Forbes* magazine cover story illustrates the confusion. Splashed across the cover was the ominous title "Financing Terror." The subtitle—"Why the U.S. Can't Stop the Flow of Billions to Drug Lords, Smugglers and Al Qaida"—suggested the disparate components of the category. A central focus of the article was Al-Barakaat—a company that was actually cleared of terrorist financing.[73] Such a tabloid approach is common. It certainly adds to misconceptions about terrorist financing.

Tropes and blinders of the financial warriors

The financial war gave rise to a new class of "financial warriors," in the United States and overseas—political officials and bureaucrats in charge of waging and promoting the financial war. They operate on the basis of their own axioms, assumptions, "facts," and biases. More specifically, innate tendencies towards "groupthink" are exacerbated by "trained incapacity" and "knowledgeable ignorance."

As will be discussed in Chapter 3, the Bush administration had been bent at the time of the September 11 attacks on implementing an agenda of financial deregulation which included dismantling much of the existing anti-money laundering apparatus. The attacks caused a sharp policy U-turn. With the zeal of the newly converted, those very people who were intent on dismantling the anti-money laundering legislative apparatus found themselves hastily and vigorously expanding it. Countless dysfunctions appeared

as part of this considerable expansion of this anti-money laundering apparatus. The very circumstances of the abrupt and massive shift of resources
towards terrorist financing did not allow for a drastic retooling of competen-
cies and missions.

The bureaucratic antecedents of the financial war have resulted in what
Thorstein Veblen called "trained incapacity"—when habits of mind, overspe-
cialization, and indeed success in one mode of thinking produce the inability to understand the true nature of a problem. Indeed, the law enforcement
mindset had been shaped by earlier wars against organized crime and drug
traffickers, and by an era pre-dating the "democratization" of technology.
The dominant belief was that "organized crime can be isolated and dealt
with simply by giving more power and resources to law enforcement agencies."[74] This has obscured the fluid nature, as well as the ideological and
political character, of radical Islamic terrorism. Crime had to be "organized"
and "for-profit." In the words of a government publication, "With few exceptions, criminals are motivated by one thing—profit. Greed drives the criminal, and the end result is that illegally gained money must be introduced
into a nation's legitimate financial system."[75]

Throughout the war on terror, "organized crime" analogies came easily to
law enforcement agencies steeped in the battle against the mafia, as well as
influential pundits. Thus Michael Ledeen of the American Enterprise Institute, one of the most influential intellectuals in the early days of the war on
terror, described Usama Bin Laden as "the CEO of a multinational terrorist
corporation" who "has been very imaginative at finding ways to make money
from his terrorist ventures."[76] Ledeen asserted: "The best way to think of
the terror network is as a collection of mafia families."[77] In other words,
terrorist financiers functioned somewhat like the "five families" (Bonanno,
Colombo, Gambino, Genovese, and Lucchese) that controlled the New York
criminal empire.[78] The task of law enforcement was to identify the cartel and
drive it out of business.

In the 1980s the focus shifted to the Central and Latin American drug
lords. Following the September 11 attacks, the war on drugs was overshadowed by the threat of Islamic fundamentalism. The massive shift of resources
resulted in a substantial mismatch. Those government agents who did have
some international experience and cultural-linguistic skills were typically
fluent in Spanish and had no experience of the Islamic world. This dysfunction was aggravated by the ideological context of the post-September 11
environment, which aggravated the problem of "knowledgeable ignorance."
The notion was popularized by British historian Norman Daniel when he
described the unfounded yet well-entrenched certitudes held by medieval
Europe about the Islamic world.[79] Despite plenty of contrary evidence, such

certitudes have gelled over the centuries into familiar stereotypes. Knowledgeable ignorance is a distinguishing characteristic of those who held forth
on terrorist financing without knowing much about either the root causes of
terrorism, or the actual workings of the financial world and underworld. The
parallel universe of terrorist financing gave rise to a brand of experts who
fit the description of management scholar Henry Mintzberg: "An expert has
also been defined as someone who knows more and more about less and less
until finally he or she knows everything about nothing. Perhaps this means
that if you understand only certain discrete chunks, ultimately you understand nothing." [80]

The failure to come to grips with the reality of terrorist financing
may indeed be related to the propensity to look at terrorist financing as
a "discrete chunk" divorced from its broader political setting. The various
memoirs published since by many of the principals of the war on terror
are in that respect especially revealing. According to Daniel Benjamin and
Steven Simon, who were then staffers at the National Security Council, at
the time of the August 1998 bombings, "the intelligence community largely
accepted the notion that Bin Laden financed terror out of his own pocket,
using either his family money or cash flow from his Sudan businesses." [81]
(It will be remembered that four years earlier the personal fortune of Bin
Laden had been seized, and that two years earlier, his Sudanese business
holdings had suffered the same fate.) The hard charging counter-terrorism
czar Richard Clarke wrote about the response to those bombings: "One
of our few important victories against criminal financing had come a few
years earlier when the President had invoked the International Emergency
Economic Powers Act against the Cali drug cartel. Now we were going to
take the same approach to al Qaeda." [82] But when it came to figuring out
where that money was, Clarke's assistant William Wechsler came up empty
handed: "This is insane ... [there] are no formal assessments at all, no understanding of the whole picture of where the money is coming from." [83] Later,
led by Richard Newcomb, the head of the Treasury Department's Office of
Foreign Assets Control (OFAC) and architect of the effort against the Cali
cartel, top government officials worked on what they called the "new theory
of the case." The theory now stated that terrorism is big business and had
to involve more than Bin Laden's wealth. The list of "usual suspects" was
very broad, and included every possible source of funds, legitimate and illegitimate. [84] Clarke remarked: "Some of the specifics were still uncertain, but
the 'theory of the case' looked very solid." [85] One thing the group had hit
upon was "continuous fundraising," [86] since money always seemed to appear
miraculously. But the money warriors missed the political and ideological
dimension of terrorism, which they saw exclusively through the lens of finan-

cially motivated organized crime. All this did not do much to improve the understanding of terrorist financing. Nor did it matter much. With the end of the Clinton administration, interest in those matters dissipated, only to reappear following the September 11 attacks.

Between fiction and non-fiction

Since none of Bin Laden's alleged $300 million fortune was traceable, a whole industry appeared purporting to reveal the secrets of its whereabouts. Some of its practitioners were partisan hacks with a transparent political agenda; others were imaginative writers eager to produce scoops. Former Foreign Service officer Marc Sageman described the process by which misinformation, disinformation, outlandish accounts, and stories that are "too good to check" find their way into the public consciousness: "There is a strong tendency to fill in the gaps between facts in order to construct a better narrative, a practice that leads to many inaccuracies when the fillers assume lives of their own in later accounts." [87] Repeating the same allegations and interviewing the same people led "to a false sense of confirmation and a rehash of the rumor mill." [88] Those who made up the original allegations retrospectively appear well informed, and are asked for more revelations. Thus Steven Emerson, who had become one of the most ubiquitous "terrorist experts," said that in the days following September 11, "he has fielded 1,000 calls, many from news organizations." [89]

Another supplier of founding myths was Jack Kelley, the star reporter of USA Today, America's largest circulation daily, who until the discovery by his paper in 2004 of a "pattern of lies and deceit," had produced countless "scoops." Not surprisingly, he found it easy to write about terrorism and terrorist financing. Hiding behind confidential and anonymous sources, he broke many of the stories which have since entered the journalistic bloodstream: the "eyewitness account" of young Palestinian suicide bombers and their culture of death;[90] the revelation that prominent Saudi businessmen "worth more than $5 billion ... continue to transfer tens of millions of dollars" to Bin Laden as "'protection money' to stave off attacks on their businesses in Saudi Arabia;"[91] and the discovery of computer records in Afghan caves showing links between Chicago-based Islamic charities and Al-Qaeda.[92]

Kelley later justified those fabrications by the pressure to produce scoops and compete for major journalistic prizes. (For his suicide bombing "eyewitness account," he was a Pulitzer Prize finalist.) At the time of the revelations about Kelley's practices, there was a veritable epidemic of journalistic scandals. In explaining how outlandish tales can get past fact checking, New Republic editor Charles Lane said that such stories usually "revolve around stereotypes": "They fit into the preexisting grooves that are already etched into everybody's heads, things we think or are predisposed to believe are true." [93]

Since at least the mid-1970s, pulp fiction had also played a role in promoting and perpetuating stereotypes. According to historian Douglas Little, "Beginning in 1975 with the publication of Thomas Harris's *Black Sunday*, which revolved around a Palestinian plot to commandeer the Good-year blimp and terrorize the Super Bowl, a slew of paperback potboilers with titles such as *Jihad*, *Phoenix*, and *On the Brink* routinely depicted Arabs as either ruthless and brutal thugs or greedy sheiks eager to bankroll their bloodthirsty brethren." [94] Ideological fantasies also seemed to confirm the truth of the most extreme assertions about Islam. [95] Since the waning days of Soviet communism, Islam had emerged as a serious contender as a substitute threat. The growing visibility of radical Islamists led many theorists of the New World Order to assert that Islam was on an inevitable collision course with the liberal values of the West. [96] A number of academics, pundits, and policy experts posited the fundamental incompatibility between Islam and Western values. The theme of Islam as a new, larger-than-life global enemy soon became fashionable in certain policy circles. [97]

With the September 11 attacks, the lines between fact and fiction were further blurred. The sheer "unbelievability" of the attacks looked like the stuff of fiction, [98] and gave credence to many of the wildest assertions about Arabs and Muslims. David Frum, a leading figure of neo-conservatism, who in his days as a White House speechwriter had helped coin the "axis of evil" phrase, wrote: "The September 11 attacks had broken the country's heart; anthrax shook its nerve. Nobody then knew much about al-Qaeda and Osama bin Laden. Americans were ready to believe he was a real-life Dr. No: infinitely resourceful and cunning." [99] Comparisons with James Bond villains came easily: they were evil as well as "infinitely resourceful and cunning"—indeed so rich that they could fund their own wars.

Most people's views of organized crime, the drug trade, and more recently Islamic terrorism had been shaped by novels, films, and television series. Significant figures of the war on terror were also part-time novelists, among them Richard Clarke, Robert Baer, Richard Perle, or L. "Scooter" Libby (who was indicted for telling fables under oath in the "Plamegate" scandal). Oliver North, of Iran–Contra fame, now a media star and a participant in the military-industrial-security complex, wrote novels on Islamic terrorism, just as novelists such as Ken Follett or Tom Clancy wrote terrorism-related non-fiction. Highly publicized "non-fiction" books about the Islamic world turned out to be fictional. [100] A notable phenomenon was the huge success of the *Left Behind* series, the politically and religiously charged novels about the

Apocalypse that are extremely popular among those Christian fundamentalists who believe in an imminent Apocalyptic final battle in the Middle East.

It was said about *The Sopranos*, the TV series about a crime family, that it "looks, feels, and sounds like real life." [101] Verisimilitude can easily pass for veracity. Indeed, on the topic of terrorist financing, works of fiction and non-fiction are easily interchangeable. The subject of the hidden wealth of Bin Laden has captured the imagination of many novelists. Chris Ryan's *Greed* (according to the book cover a number 1 bestseller) bears more than a passing resemblance to much of the "non-fiction" genre purporting to reveal the secrets of terrorist financing. One character says:

> Al-Qaeda has a lot of money. Its roots are in Saudi Arabia, and that's a rich place. But it has a lot of support right across that region. There are contributions coming from everywhere—Jordan, Egypt, Pakistan, Malaysia. That's what makes them so deadly. Fanatics we can handle. Fanatics with cash are a different story. Overall, we estimate the organization has at least five billion dollars at its disposal. They hide their money, and they are good at it. So it could be a lot more. [102]

The novel suggests, as did many others, [103] that Al-Qaeda's wealth has been converted into gold and diamonds—"the world's oldest, most internationally accepted currency." Not surprisingly, countless articles and at least one "nonfiction" book on terrorist financing have made a comparable argument—with just about as much empirical evidence. [104]

It could be said, to use satirist Stephen Colbert's terminology, that there is much more "truthiness" than truth in much of the terrorist financing discourse, with "truthiness" defined as "what you want the facts to be as opposed to what the facts are," or "what feels like the right answer as opposed to what reality will support." [105] In that respect, the parallels between Bin Laden's hidden stash and Saddam Hussein's alleged weapons of mass destruction are striking. They caused, respectively, the financial war against global terrorism, and regime change in Iraq. The usual suspects of terrorist financing—rich Arabs, the Saudis, Islamic charities, hawalas, etc—became as familiar as the "smoking guns"—mobile labs, aluminum tubes, and Niger uranium—that helped sell the invasion of Iraq to the American public. Both wars ended up creating a new and very real problem through pursuing an imaginary one.

PART II
RULES OF FINANCIAL
ENGAGEMENT

2

Framing the Guilty: The Financial Terrain

"When I use a word," Humpty Dumpty said, in rather a scornful tone, "it means
just what I choose it to mean—neither more nor less."
"The question is," said Alice, "whether you can make words
mean so many different things."
"The question is," said Humpty Dumpty, "which is to be master—that's all."
Lewis Carroll

Laws that target 100% of the population to control the behavior of 0.001% are also
seldom productive, not least because they tell the 0.001% how not to get caught.
Wall Street Journal

Most people have a magnified impression of the intelligence of those who live in
intimate association with large sums of money. This is an erroneous belief, as
the ultimate reckoning so readily reveals.
John Kenneth Galbraith

B y the time the war on terror started, the rules of financial engagement had been thoroughly transformed. This chapter, which maps
the evolution of the financial theater of war, is divided into three
parts. The first introduces the role of finance in the prosecutorial arsenal.
The belief that "following the money" could resolve crime is well entrenched
in the law enforcement community. RICO statutes enacted in 1970 to fight
organized crime provided further tools essentially devised to "frame the
guilty." At the same time, the Bank Secrecy Act requiring banks to preserve
a financial paper trail and inform the government of their customers' suspicious transactions provided an abundance of "financial footprints." This
arsenal was steadily expanded with the "drug wars" of the 1980s and the

criminalization of money laundering. Of special import to the financial war on terror is the practice of seizing and forfeiting "dirty money."

The second part of this chapter focuses on the transformation of finance in the last couple of decades, and more specifically on the implications of the globalization of finance and law enforcement. The nature of the financial sector, dominated by the dollar and functioning according to rules set under the unquestioned leadership of the United States, gave considerable reach if not effectiveness to financial controls.

The third part of the chapter discusses the advent of the economic sanctions "reflex" following the end of the Cold War. Insofar as financial attacks are perceived as "no body bags" confrontations, they are politically safe—a way of showing resolve and "doing something," without arousing any significant domestic opposition.

The prosecutorial arsenal

1. Evening the scales of justice

At various times in American history, constitutional constraints designed to protect citizens from unfair prosecution were perceived as shielding criminals and political subversives. Since the late nineteenth century, corrupt political machines and organized criminals, though highly visible, seemed beyond the reach of the law. Their vast profits allowed them to manipulate the system, outgunning and outwitting law enforcement agencies. Crime "families" could afford the best "consiglieri" and "fixers" who were in a position to tie the legal system in knots. Organized crime also enjoyed home turf advantage: ethnic homogeneity combined with a system of favors and ruthless retaliation against snitches ensured the prevalence of omertà (code of silence) and other practices which made it nearly impossible for prosecutors to prove that crimes were ever committed. As legendary Boston political boss Martin Lomasney advised his associates: "Never write when you can talk; never talk when you can nod; never nod when you can wink." [1]

The frustrations of law enforcement agencies and the public's impatience with the slow wheels of justice lent support to a steady expansion of prosecutorial tools. Especially at times of war, whether real or metaphorical, fairness standards, the presumption of innocence, the right to due process, and other constitutional protections get weaker. Successive "wars"—on crime, on drugs, and more recently on terror—have given rise to questionable practices essentially designed to "frame" designated "bad guys." Public support for such policies stemmed from the view that they evened the scales in favor of the "good guys," since "bad guys" by definition don't play fair. Controversial laws and prosecutorial practices have had varied fortunes: some were overturned by higher courts, others fell into disuse, and others still took on lives of their own as they were put to new, imaginative uses.

Especially effective as prosecutorial tools were the RICO statutes. When he signed, on October 15, 1970, the Organized Crime Control Bill (also known as the Racketeer Influenced and Corrupt Organizations (RICO) Act), President Richard Nixon turned to his Attorney General John Mitchell and FBI Director J. Edgar Hoover, and said: "I give you the tools. You do the job." [2] The draconian law contained powerful weapons, among them secret "special grand juries" empowered to subpoena and interrogate anyone about virtually anything, and "use-immunity laws" which required complete and total cooperation with the government. Uncooperative witnesses could be jailed for up to 18 months. Congress had written an intentionally vague and sweeping law designed to be used against organized crime. It allowed the federal government to seize the assets of any organization deemed to be a criminal conspiracy, and created new penalties and policing powers over the use of explosives, as well as 25-year-long sentences for "dangerous offenders." Civil provisions included triple damages and the opportunity to present someone as a racketeer. Financial provisions allowed the freezing of assets even before conviction, which could be used to force damage settlements and force the cooperation of certain individuals. The law made it easy to prove a conspiracy. All it took to show a "pattern of racketeering activity" was two violations, even trivial offenses, over a period of ten years.

As prosecutors expanded their reach and ability to target a whole range of derivative and unrelated crimes (perjury,[3] obstruction of justice, money laundering, tax evasion, etc), the financial realm proved especially inviting. With the war on terror, immigration-related infractions, such as overstaying visas, etc, also became derivative crimes of choice.[4]

2. Following the money

"Follow the money" was the advice allegedly given by the mysterious informant "Deep Throat" to journalists Bob Woodward and Carl Bernstein as they investigated the Watergate scandal. Money used to finance the burglary could, according to Deep Throat, be traced to a Mexican bank account, which in turn would lead to the White House.[5] More generally, the Nixon administration had been adept at hiding both the origin and the destination of financial contributions.[6] Disentangling money puzzles did indeed prove useful in uncovering a long list of "high crimes and misdemeanors" which eventually led to the resignation of Richard Nixon. The promise of the money trail has been perpetuated in law enforcement lore by two celebrated cases going back decades. In October 1931, Al Capone, perhaps the best-known gangster of his time, was convicted for tax evasion and sent to jail. The FBI had been unable to nail him despite his many crimes; prosecuting him on tax evasion charges proved much easier. His partners in crime refused to incriminate him, but the testimony of a tax accountant got him convicted. Then in 1932 the abduction and murder of aviator Charles Lindbergh's infant son aroused the passions of Depression-era America. For more than two years, in its search for the perpetrators, the FBI, under the leadership of J. Edgar Hoover, focused almost exclusively on the money trail—the serial numbers of gold certificates paid as ransom. To this day, there is heated disagreement as to the guilt of Bruno Richard Hauptmann, the man who was found in possession of some of those certificates, but the belief that the money trail is invaluable in cracking criminal cases lives on.[7]

The money trail can yield invaluable clues and unmask vast conspiracies. Finance is subject to detailed and arcane regulations, and different rules of evidence make financial crimes easier to prosecute. From a law enforcement standpoint, "fishing expeditions" hold the tantalizing prospects of nailing the bad guys for minor regulatory infractions—even better, of using such infractions as a way of hooking bigger fish. "Al Caponing" a suspected criminal by investigating unrelated financial infractions has since become a venerable law enforcement tradition. In 2000 Treasury Secretary Lawrence Summers declared: "Tackling dirty money gives us more weapons to fight the underlying crimes. As is often noted, it took an accountant to catch Al Capone."[8] And in the financial war on terror, the weapon was liberally used.[9] The main problem with the use of the money weapon to "frame the guilty" is that it hinges on the designation of public enemies. At various times, anarchists, communists, mobsters, drug dealers, and terrorists have been designated as such—alongside ethnic, religious, and other "profiling."

3. The "3 Fs": Finding, freezing, and forfeiting assets

Prior to the passage of the RICO statutes, the government seldom used its prerogative to seize assets related to crime. The Fifth Amendment—which states that no person "shall be deprived of life, liberty, or property, without due process of law; nor shall private property be taken for public use, without just compensation"—made forfeiture laws that were on the books difficult to enforce.[10] Even in the immediate aftermath of RICO, the government made sparing use of forfeiture: between 1970 and 1979, only $30 million were seized from defendants. A 1981 report by the General Accounting Office even criticized the federal government for not making "asset forfeiture a widely used law enforcement technique."[11]

All this changed dramatically with the passage in 1984 of the Comprehensive Crime and Control Act (CCCA), which made it possible for law enforcement agencies to conduct in rem (against the thing) proceedings in a civil court. An ancient practice was thus resurrected.[12] The guilt or innocence of the owner was irrelevant. Since the property itself was being targeted, constitutional objections were sidestepped. And civil (as opposed to criminal) proceedings presented two major advantages: protections afforded to defendants under criminal law, such as the presumption of innocence and the right to counsel, did not apply; in addition, civil cases were decided on a "preponderance of the evidence," whereas in criminal court guilt had be "proven beyond reasonable doubt."

Other factors turned the new law into a powerful law enforcement weapon. Assets could be seized in a civil proceeding without even the need to file criminal charges. The new law also allowed for streamlined, out-of-court "administrative seizure" of assets valued less than $100,000. Prior to the enactment of the CCCA, all revenue generated by federal, civil, or criminal asset forfeiture was deposited into the US Treasury General Fund. The 1984 law transformed the incentive system of law enforcement: federal agents could keep the proceeds from confiscated property and share them, through the Department of Justice Assets Forfeiture Fund, with their counterparts at the state and local levels. Thus local police were able to seize cash, as well as cars, boats, real estate, and other personal property that were presumably purchased with the proceeds of crime (or used to facilitate crime) without even going to court—and keep a large part of the proceeds. New forfeiture laws thus marked a further step in the federalization of the drug wars: state and local police agencies had the option of trying narcotic cases in federal courts (where by the late 1980s, sentences tended to be longer) in exchange for as much as 80 and in some cases 90 percent of all the "drug tainted" property they seized.[13]

In Ronald Reagan's America, asset forfeiture seemed like a win–win proposition, reconciling the tough-on-crime rhetoric with the ideology of reduced government spending: stripping felons from their ill-gotten gains would finance further law enforcement efforts, and such illicit gains would be put to use against those very criminals from whom the funds were forfeited in order to reduce future crime. In the words of former US Attorney General Richard Thornburgh, "It is truly satisfying to think that it is now possible for a drug dealer to serve time in a forfeiture-financed prison, after being arrested by agents driving a forfeiture-provided automobile, while working in a forfeiture-funded sting operation."[14] Later there would be frequent proposals for the further extension of asset forfeiture. The International Narcotics Control Strategy Report released in 1994 by the Department of State advocated "greater asset seizures, not just of bank accounts, but also corporate assets and even corporate entities."[15] The policies had bipartisan support, and only small if increasingly vocal groups within the political mainstream—

most prominently the libertarian wing of the conservative movement, which generally favored drug liberalization and was concerned with the infringements of property rights—found fault with their underlying logic.

Following the criminalization of money laundering, banks that were caught were also subjected to an assortment of forfeitures and fines. The highest-profile case was the federal indictment in Tampa, Florida, in 1988 of two BCCI agencies and nine bank officials on charges of laundering $32 million in drug profits. The bank later pleaded guilty to reduced charges and forfeited $14 million. Five bank officials were later found guilty and sentenced to prison terms ranging from three to 12 years.[16] (Around the same time, a string of Wall Street scandals resulted in confiscation of ill-gotten gains and countless fines.[17] As a result, government agencies in charge of financial regulation, among them the Securities and Exchange Commission, gained considerable financial resources alongside power and autonomy.)

It did not take long, however, before law enforcement agencies became "addicted" to drug-related seizures. The new incentive system was bound to result in abuses: forfeiting property was both easy and lucrative. In many instances, the evidential standard was exceedingly low. Property could be confiscated based on nothing more than probable cause. The accused were considered guilty and had to prove otherwise to get their property back. There were further hurdles: the process was costly and protracted; the victims had only 20 days from the date of seizure to post a non-refundable bond worth 10 percent of the value of the property seized. Justifiably the victims felt that the odds were stacked against them, and only the most persistent (and those with the deepest pockets) pursued the limited recourses still allowed under a "confiscate first, ask questions later" system.

Under those circumstances, a "bounty-hunter" mindset was bound to prevail.[18] It extended beyond law enforcement agents to others, among them private companies hired to assist in the drugs war, and informers who could get as much as 25 percent of the bounty. A number of investigative journalists looked into the matter and discovered rampant abuses: arrests were often motivated primarily by the desire to forfeit property, and it was not uncommon for overeager police officers to make false statements to obtain a warrant. A 1991 investigation by the *Pittsburgh Press Gazette* revealed that in 80 percent of the cases where property was seized, victims were never charged with a crime. In 1989 cash was confiscated from 83 percent of the drivers stopped, but only 19 percent were arrested for alleged crimes. Over a three-year period, the Volusia County (Florida) Sheriff's Department took in $8 million in cash from motorists. Writer Christian Parenti noted that rather than "taking the profit out of drug dealing, the laws merely [dealt] law enforcement into the game." The evidence also showed that those actions were rarely aimed at major drug dealers, but tended to affect the "small fry," the "non-violent, mom-and-pop pot farmers, or independent run-of-the-mill dealers." [19] For one thing, major dealers may be too wily to be caught, and if caught, they are likely to have the resources to fight protracted legal battles. Small dealers are easier to intimidate, and their assets may be seized under the streamlined administrative proceedings. More importantly, such broad sweeps tend to take in innocent bystanders, especially in those communities where ethnic profiling is a common practice.

Those abuses came to be widely recognized. In the words of Michael F. Zeldin, former director of the US Department of Justice's Asset Forfeiture Office, "We had a situation in which the desire to deposit money into the asset forfeiture fund became the reason for being of forfeiture, eclipsing in certain measure the desire to effect fair enforcement of the laws." And according to Gary Schons, former California Deputy Attorney General, "Much like a drug addict becomes addicted to drugs, law enforcement agencies have become dependent on asset forfeitures. They have to have it." [20]

In 1993 Representative Henry Hyde, the Illinois Republican who chaired the House Judiciary Committee, introduced legislation designed to reform asset-forfeiture laws. In a book titled *Forfeiting Our Property Rights*, published by the libertarian Cato Institute, he catalogued the abuses of the system. [21] The law enforcement community strongly opposed the legislation, and in particular the provision that the government would have to prove "by a preponderance of the evidence that the property is subject to forfeiture." Indeed, under the low "probable cause" standard, prosecutors could rely on hearsay to confiscate property. Otherwise they would have to go to court to prove their case. In the words of Gordon Kromberg, the Assistant US Attorney for the Eastern District of Virginia, "When you want to change the burden of proof, you're cutting the throat, eviscerating asset forfeiture as a tool." [22] The gist of his argument was that prosecutors should be allowed "to punish individuals they believe are guilty, even if they can't prove that guilt in a court of law." More specifically, "Prosecutors are busy. Way too many bad guys are running around for them to help catch with stings and convict in court. Some outlaws are even pretty smart." He admitted that he currently had ten money laundering cases in which he couldn't figure out how the people were washing the dough. But still, he knew these people were guilty and was certain they needed to be punished. Should we let these people get away, he asked, before answering in an illuminating way: "Not if we can punish them through other means." [23]

In 2000 the Civil Asset Forfeiture Reform Act was finally passed by Congress. Under the new legislation, federal prosecutors were required to show "a substantial connection between the property and the crime." The cost-bond requirement was eliminated, and under circumstances where the confiscation resulted in serious hardship, the property could be released by a federal court pending final disposition of the case. The new forfeiture system did not get much of a chance to be tested. After September 11 law enforcement was given an even broader range of prerogatives to seize assets and "frame the guilty." Not only did the USA PATRIOT legislation make forfeiture easier than ever; it could now be done preemptively.

Global reach

Throughout the Cold War, there were few politically driven attacks on the financial terrain. A 1986 book on the subject of terrorist financing noted that "the Israelis now realize that, by concentrating on the military aspects of the PLO, they have allowed the organization to blossom. No incisive military action can affect the Swiss bank accounts or the Wall Street investments, and as long as the PLO maintains its financial strengths, it will be listened to, because money still talks." [24] In both the United Kingdom and Israel, it was only in 1989 that sweeping legislation criminalized terrorist funding. [25]

Why was the financial terrain immune to political attacks? The principal reason is that, well into the 1980s, financial regulation was mostly national, and foreign governments and international organizations had little leverage over individual countries. National sovereignty on money matters made law enforcement cooperation difficult. "Politically exposed" individuals and groups worried little about the seizure of their money. All this changed significantly in recent years. Three aspects of the transformation are noteworthy: the globalization of finance and law enforcement, the blurring of the lines between high and low politics, and the growing politicization of finance.

For most of the post-World War II era, national financial regulators enjoyed wide autonomy. They could devise rules and practices with minimum interference from the outside world. In 1944 John Maynard Keynes, who was then actively involved in shaping the postwar financial order, stated the rationale:

> We are determined that, in future, the external value of sterling shall conform to its internal value as set by our own domestic policies, and not the other way round. Secondly, we intend to retain control of our domestic rate of interest, so that we can keep it as low as suits our own purposes, without interference from the ebb and flow of international capital movements or flights of hot money. Thirdly, whilst we intend to prevent inflation at home, we will not accept deflation at the dictate of influences from outside. [26]

In later years, "embedded liberalism" allowed governments otherwise committed to a liberal economic order to reserve the right to control capital movements.[27] Then came the revolution, with the United States at its epicenter, and which spread first to the industrialized nations and then to the rest of the world.[28] The worlds of banking and finance were increasingly "Americanized,"[29] and regulation was increasingly globalized. All these changes occurred against a backdrop of international political change, and can be understood as the result of a combination of ideological hegemony, unilateral policies, and multilateral rules and agreements.[30]

With the lifting of restrictions on capital movements, financial markets became increasingly interconnected, and "financial market regulators no longer held full sway over their regulatory territory."[31] National regulators were robbed of much of their autonomy as they were bound to apply new global rules devised by international bodies, such as the Basle Committee on Banking Supervision, the Bank of International Settlements, the International Monetary Fund, the World Bank, and the World Trade Organization.

The end of the Cold War also brought with it the blurring of the lines separating high and low politics which had until then been neatly compartmentalized. High politics related to issues of war and peace; it was the domain of statesmen, military leaders, and diplomats. In contrast, the realm of low politics was that of economics, trade, culture, etc. It was far less visible to the general public and was generally the preserve of specialized bureaucracies.[32] Insofar as it dealt with vital issues, high politics was at the top of the policy hierarchy, and the two realms tended to operate on separate tracks. In the final years of the Cold War, the two categories were increasingly blurred. As the superpower confrontation ended, economic issues seemed to move to the foreground. National defense lost its saliency, and foreign policy was increasingly preoccupied with economic matters.[33] "Economic warfare," defined by the Department of Defense as the "aggressive use of economic means to achieve national objectives," took new forms and increasingly grew in importance. A turning point occurred in 1986 following the Philippines' "people revolution." At the time, much of the wealth of Ferdinand Marcos, looted from the Philippines, was said to be salted away in Swiss bank accounts. The United States started a long battle to force Switzerland to change its bank secrecy laws. In this and other battles, the United States dangled the threat of closing down the operations of Swiss banks in the United States.[34] The United States was now at the political and economic center of the new system of global regulation. Globalization soon became the new buzzword, with finance playing a pivotal role. "The markets"—the bond markets in particular—with their permanent plebiscite on policies seemed to be the new kingmakers. Threats to the system seemed to come from economic crises. To be sure, there were some "peacetime wars," but they were narrowly confined and small in scope. Then came the September 11 attacks and the dramatic comeback of security concerns. By then, however, the world of finance was largely globalized and national policymakers had lost much of their autonomy. The economic terrain became open to politically motivated attacks, and military offensives were accompanied—or preceded—by a financial strike.

Three aspects of the US leverage are noteworthy. One noted at the time by Susan Strange was structural power, "the power to shape and mould the structures of production, knowledge, security and credit within which others have no choice but to live if they are to participate in the world market economy."[35] The other is the leverage provided by controlling access of foreign companies to the American market. Finally, one of the prerogatives of a superpower is the power to designate or label: defining "terrorism" of course, but also "designating" "rogue states," "certifying" or "decertifying" nations based on how "cooperative" or "uncooperative" they are. Typically, as the next section shows, such designations usually trigger a range of economic sanctions.

Weapons of first resort

In the post-Cold War era, economic sanctions became the foreign policy tool of choice of the United States, the punishment of first resort, an almost automatic reflex. A notable prerogative of the superpower in a unipolar world is the ability to define what constitutes a punishable transgression and mete out punishment. Throughout the 1990s the scope and harshness of sanctions were steadily expanded. They became increasingly broad in their coverage and indiscriminate in their targets. Two pieces of legislation in 1996—the Helms–Burton Act and the Iran–Libya Sanctions Act—broadened the principle of extraterritoriality: third-country firms operating in Cuba, Iran, or Libya would be reached by the long arm of American law. More sanctions were imposed in the Clinton years than had been imposed between the end of World War I and 1992.[36] As of 1998, more than 70 nations with more than half the world's population were subjected to, or living under the threat of, such sanctions. At the time, US laws authorized 21 different sanctions targeting 27 different kinds of foreign conduct, from nuclear non-proliferation to human rights, and from drug trafficking to religious freedom.[37]

The logic of sanctions mirrored the new rules of post-Cold War warfare. The First Gulf War (1990–91) occurred shortly after the 1989 fall of the Berlin Wall and created the new paradigm of sanitized high-tech warfare. The small number of US casualties, the "invisibility" of enemy victims, and the large number of allies, many of whom financed the cost of the war, created new expectations. Later wars caused even fewer casualties, culminating with the zero-casualty Kosovo War. Such lopsided wars would invariably have strong domestic support. In the words of political analyst Kevin Phillips, "So long as actual U.S. war casualties—the stuff of evening news reports—remained minimal, the public could be counted on to cheer the 'cruise missile diplomacy' and clandestine operations that had superseded the old gunboat diplomacy of U.S. Marines pouring ashore to restore order in Santo Domingo or Nicaragua." [38] In the same vein, Joseph Stiglitz, formerly chief economist at the World Bank, wrote: "Modern high-tech warfare is designed to remove physical contact: dropping bombs from 50,000 feet ensures that one does not 'feel' what one does. Modern economic management is similar: from one's luxury hotel, one can callously impose policies about which one would think twice if one knew the people whose lives one was destroying." [39]

The political attractiveness of sanctions for the nation imposing them is obvious: they make governments appear decisive, politicians seem principled, and public opinion feel good. In the words of Mikael Barfod of the European Commission Humanitarian Organization (ECHO), sanctions are "politically tempting instruments for governments to satisfy domestic constituencies by demonstrating an ability for action, that the government can do something." [40] Politicians can stand before cameras, expressing their outrage, and making impassioned pleas for change. For the public at large, imposing unilateral sanctions can be gratifying since it fits with the moralistic view that sinners should receive their just desserts. Indeed, empirical work on the impact of US sanctions has shown that "punishing an offender's behavior makes Americans feel good." [41]

A British government memorandum described sanctions as "cheap and a low-risk alternative to war": "Sanctions are the only coercive measure available to the international community, other than the threat or use of force, to respond to challenges to international peace and security. If diplomacy fails there needs to be a third choice between doing nothing and military intervention." [42] And in the words of former US Defense Secretary James Schlesinger, unilateral American economic sanctions "appear to be a costless way of expressing our disapprobation of the behavior of other governments without incurring the risks of military action. For this reason, sanctions have become a weapon of first rather than last resort for many in Congress and the Administration eager to send a message to those governments whose actions we disapprove or, at least equally importantly, to satisfy the demands of the ever growing number of single-issue domestic interest groups." [43]

The asymmetry of power made the powerful oblivious to the effects of sanctions, despite their potentially devastating effects on certain countries. In Congress, unilateral sanctions have consistently commanded rare bipartisan support. Indeed, votes to impose sanctions were often close to unanimous. Following an overwhelming Congressional vote (94 to 1 in the Senate,

418 to 2 in the House of Representatives) to bar all Burmese exports to the United States in an effort to punish the country's ruling junta, the news merited barely a passing mention in the US media. The Burmese government in contrast called the sanctions "weapons of mass destruction," and argued that they "are imposed on target countries by the rich and powerful nations mainly with the intention to create havoc and bring hardship on the mass population of the people who need to work to live and require basic human needs to survive." [44]

3

The Flawed Money
Laundering Template

There is always an easy solution to every human problem—neat, plausible and wrong.
H.L. Mencken

Even a good idea can be a little frightening when it is the only idea a man has ever had.
Louis Hartz

*Politics is the art of looking for trouble, finding it, misdiagnosing it, and then
misapplying the wrong remedies.*
Groucho Marx

In 1986 the United States became the first country to criminalize money laundering. Under the landmark Money Laundering Control Act, disguising the illegal origin of funds became a crime—separate from the crime that produced those funds. Thus what is peculiar about money laundering is that unlike underlying offenses (say, drug trafficking or armed robbery), it consists of a set of actions, each of which may by itself be innocent, but taken together amount to an attempt to hide the proceeds of an unlawful act. The anti-money laundering apparatus has since kept expanding, domestically and internationally, driven by its own momentum. In the era of globalization, money laundering controls became the notable exception to the rule of steady liberalization of capital flows. The contradiction between liberalization and controls came to the fore in the final years of the Clinton administration, when new attempts at expansion of anti-money laundering controls were strongly resisted.

The conservative and libertarian alliance that managed to block such expansion was well represented among George W. Bush's economic advisers. Indeed, the initial inclination of his administration was to weaken, if not gut, the existing anti-money laundering apparatus. But the September 11 attacks brought about an abrupt about-face. The circumstances of the attacks were such that very little serious thinking went into the wisdom of applying the money laundering template to terrorism. The shock of the attacks against the World Trade Center and the Pentagon called for a swift and forceful response. The money laundering apparatus was there, highly visible and ready to strike. The Bush administration embraced money laundering controls with a vengeance, and those controls formed the central template of the financial war. An administration otherwise characterized by its unilateralism and its distrust of international organization threw its weight behind the FATF (Financial Action Task Force), the Paris-based organization dedicated to combating money laundering. In October 2001 its mandate was expanded to include the fight against terrorist financing.

One of the central arguments of this book is that the use of a money laundering approach to combat terrorist financing is at the origin of many dysfunctions of the financial war. The logic of money laundering is in many ways the exact opposite of that of the funding of ideologically driven terrorism. One is about hiding the proceeds of crime in the financial system; it assumes a crime-for-profit logic. The other is, in the overwhelming majority of cases, about clean money being "soiled." Yet for bureaucratic and political reasons money laundering and terrorist financing have, since September 11, 2001, become interchangeable.

The money laundering paradigm

There is a plausible, but in all likelihood apocryphal, explanation for the origin of the phrase "money laundering." It supposedly originated in the United States in the 1920s, when street gangs used cash-based retail businesses to disguise their revenues from illegal activities such as bootlegging, gambling, prostitution, and protection rackets. One such cover was the coin-operated laundromat, where at the end of the day legal and illegal cash would become indistinguishable.[1] Thus, in more ways than one, money was laundered and gangsters could distance themselves from their crimes, establish a plausible explanation for their wealth, and over time gain respectability. More likely, the phrase was a straightforward description of cleaning dirty money.

The phrase first appeared in print in 1973 in connection with the Watergate scandal. But it was during the "war on drugs" that money laundering became a household term. In 1982 it was used for the first time in legal proceedings.[2] The goal of criminalization was to create yet another weapon against drug traffickers. The war on drugs, begun by the Reagan administration, was expanded in the George H.W. Bush and Clinton years. Although the increasingly harsh methods (confiscation of assets, mandatory sentencing, etc) occasionally clashed with constitutional protections and with the prevailing ideological mood, it continued unabated. The ravages of drugs in American cities justified transgressing the principle of financial liberalization. The money laundering component of the war on drugs, largely invisible to the general public, imposed new reporting and regulatory requirements on financial institutions. It also gave rise to a burgeoning bureaucracy, funded in part by the seizure of assets derived from criminal activities.[3]

The consequence of criminalization was that individuals and financial institutions would be held responsible for handling funds of dubious origin. If, as Balzac wrote, "behind every great fortune there is a crime," then crime and the ensuing wealth could, until recently, be neatly compartmentalized. A number of celebrated businessmen built business empires by hiding illegal endeavors under legitimate fronts.[4] Famous business dynasties were often created by disreputable characters. The taint faded away as the link between the initial crime and subsequent investments became tenuous, and as dubious characters laundered their reputation through well-publicized philanthropy.[5]

Striking at the financial end of crime was meant to deal a fatal blow to mafias and drug dealers and bring morality to the world of finance. Anti-money laundering controls were also a response to the excesses of the globalization of finance. New technologies combined with financial liberalization made instant, no-questions-asked, global movement of funds exceedingly easy. Deregulation was a boon to anyone involved in illicit activity. Secrecy, anonymity, and speed created a veritable financial revolution, fostering a free-wheeling and widely celebrated financial culture. In such an environment, ill-gotten funds could easily find their way into the nooks and crannies of the international financial system. The drug trade was a case in point. The war on drugs occurred in a new financial environment characterized by technological innovation, deregulation, and internationalization, and called for an appropriate law enforcement arsenal. Huge profits were being generated, and the bankers were, wittingly or not, complicit in their recycling. In that environment, targeting the financial sector appeared like a much-needed silver bullet to achieve two goals at once: eliminating the drug scourge, and appeasing the critics of financial liberalization.

Moneymaking was the criminals' motivation, and the "3 Fs" (finding, freezing, and forfeiting) would at once starve criminals of revenue, prevent "dirty money" from entering the system, and fund law enforcement agencies. The financial logic seemed unassailable: by "taking the profit out of crime" there was no more reason why the criminal activity should continue.[6] In the words of one writer, "This drug money is the lifeblood of cartels, necessary for the operation and growth of their vast black market. It is used to pay their private armies and assure the complacency, if not outright complicity, of the nations that shelter them. With illicit profits politicians, judges, police and journalists are regularly bought or silenced by hired assassins." [7]

A veritable corpus of knowledge—some even spoke of a science of money laundering[8]—took shape, alongside the substantial bureaucracy and the equally substantial private sector industry dedicated to training, explaining, circumventing, and lobbying. Virtually every financial institution is currently required to have a substantial money laundering compliance program, which typically consists of the following: designating a money laundering compliance officer, setting up a complete set of anti-money laundering compliance rules and procedures, and subjecting all employees to regular and comprehensive training.[9] This translates into considerable costs in staff, training, and suspicious transaction detection software. In parallel to public bureaucracies, a veritable private sector infrastructure sprouted to provide those services. In sum, considerable vested interests appeared, all sustained by or dedicated to the fight against money laundering.

This corpus of knowledge has its history, its canon, and its heroes and villains. One mythical innovator was Meyer Lansky, often called the "mob's accountant," who made ingenious use of the international banking system, and especially of anonymous Swiss bank accounts. He popularized the "loan back" technique, whereby an illegal deposit becomes collateral for a loan that is not intended to be repaid. Other techniques have involved stocks and commodity brokers, who would engineer back-to-back transactions (buying spot and selling forward, or the reverse) and then destroy the record of the losing transaction, leaving the launderer with an apparent capital gain. A similar technique involved horseracing or lotteries: winning tickets would be bought at a premium, thus providing plausible justification for sudden enrichment. All these techniques were greased by variable combinations of commissions and hush money involving countless intermediaries.[10]

A plausible and internally consistent though tautological discourse, with attendant theories, methods, and taxonomies, kept reality and common sense from intruding too much. The fact that no dent was made in the selling and consumption of drugs seldom called into question that logic. Failure to achieve stated goals was interpreted as proof that laws and their applications needed strengthening. In that as in many other respects, the financial front of the war on drugs offered a preview of the war on terror.

At the core of the paradigm are the "three stages of the money laundering process": placement, layering, and integration. In the initial or placement stage—presumably the easiest to catch—the launderers introduce their illegal profits into the financial system. The theory is that "networks of drug cartels are highly vulnerable, especially at the point just before illegal money enters the international banking system, and that these networks can be attacked in a systematic and effective manner." [11] Drug dealers can either smuggle cash, or convert their revenues into bank deposits or other financial instruments, often away from where they were obtained. Given the provisions of the 1970 Bank Secrecy Act, banks should be able to detect such operations.[12] In reality, money launderers have learned to escape the notice of banks. "Smurfing" or "structuring" is a technique which consists in spreading cash across accounts or over time to remain under the $10,000 threshold. A 1991 amendment to the Bank Secrecy Act took notice and asked banks to look out for such practices. Another technique consists in purchasing a series of monetary instruments (checks, money orders, etc) which are then collected and deposited into accounts at another location.

The second stage is layering, which consists of a series of conversions and movements designed to mask the source, ownership, and location of funds. Globalization, deregulation, and technological innovation have opened boundless possibilities to those who seek to obscure the money trail and confuse investigators. Multiple transactions involving shell or "brass plate" companies in tax havens, nominee directors, and impenetrable financial instruments are prized by launderers. Creating distinct layers between the original crime and the ultimate financial instruments presents numerous advantages. Every step of the way there is plausible deniability, helped by the fact that many of the intermediaries involved in the process may not even be aware of the origin or destination of the funds.

The third and final stage is integration, which happens when the funds re-enter the legitimate economy. Once the money has found its way to a place and form in which it can safely be spent or invested in real estate, luxury assets, or legitimate business ventures, the origin of the funds can be deemed legitimate.

Money laundering has been called the "crime of the 1990s." [13] Between 1986 and 2000, money laundering laws and regulations grew exponentially. Legislators, eager to prove their tough-on-crime credentials, periodically passed new anti-drug laws—often in time to coincide with electoral cycles. The 1988 Anti-Drug Abuse Act, the 1992 Annunzio–Wylie Anti-Money Laundering Act, the 1994 Money Laundering Suppression Act, and the 1998 Money Laundering and Financial Crimes Strategy Act, all broadened definitions and increased penalties. Beyond drug dealing, the range of predicate crimes expanded over time to include over 150 crimes, among them corruption, financial fraud, illegal arms sales, drug trafficking, illegal prostitution, embezzlement, insider trading, bribery, computer fraud, trafficking in endangered species, stolen or smuggled art and antiquities, and, most important for our purpose, terrorism.

National and international bureaucracies soon proliferated. The Financial Crimes Enforcement Network (FinCEN), located in Vienna, Virginia, was set up in April 1990 as the financial-intelligence gathering arm of the US Treasury to track money laundering and other financial crimes.[14] It was given computerized access to data from a variety of government agencies, such as the FBI, the Drug Enforcement Agency, the Secret Service, and Customs. Under the Bank Secrecy Act, FinCEN requires financial institutions to preserve the paper trail behind transactions and file currency transaction and suspicious activities reports. Its importance has steadily grown, with its budget for 2002 reaching $46 million (double that of 1997).

In parallel, the United States engaged since the late 1980s in an effort to internationalize its anti-money laundering laws and practices. The internationalization of the battle against money laundering was epitomized by the creation in 1989 by the G7 of the Financial Action Task Force (FATF) to ensure that no country could serve as a haven for dirty money. The Paris-based FATF, with its "naming and shaming" approach, played in this respect a significant role in forcing countries to adopt appropriate legislation. Since that time, a growing number of countries came to criminalize money laundering. Every major international organization, from the United Nations and the International Monetary Fund to the World Bank, got actively involved in the anti-money laundering fight.

U-turns

The year 2001 saw two significant U-turns on money laundering matters. The Clinton administration's policies were characterized by the expansion of the money laundering controls. The Clinton administration worked closely with the Organization for Economic Cooperation and Development (OECD) and the FATF to impose a major crackdown against tax havens on the grounds that they assisted corrupt dictators, drug lords, and tax cheats. Related arguments were that tax havens distorted trade and cheated governments of legitimate revenues. All signs—from the backgrounds of the Bush nominees to their official and unofficial declarations—indicated that the Bush administration, which took office on January 20, would undo many such controls. The financial sector had been the largest contributor to Bush's presidential campaign and Texas bankers had been especially generous.[15] Lawrence Lindsey, the principal economic adviser of candidate Bush and incoming head of the National Economic Council, was on the record with scathing attacks on money laundering laws. In a 1999 article titled "Invading Financial Privacy," Lindsey argued that the reports that banks had to fill out were like the "proverbial needle in a haystack" with a ratio of 25,000 reports to one case brought, and 0.2 percent convictions. He saw a clear contradiction between the Fourth Amendment of the Constitution (prohibiting unreasonable searches and seizures) and regulatory requirements, adding: "It would seem clear that the current money-laundering practices are the kind of blanket search that the writers of the constitution sought to prohibit. Somehow 'probable cause' does not seem to mesh with the one-in-25,000 odds that the currency transactions reports provide." [16]

Other key Bush appointees were committed to a business-friendly and somewhat unilateralist economic agenda, consisting principally of financial deregulation and tax reduction. Even those who had not previously given much thought to money laundering seemed to think that the previous administration had gone too far and that its policies were burdensome, ineffective, and detrimental to American competitiveness. Paul O'Neill, the new Treasury Secretary, expressed serious reservations about the cost-effectiveness of money laundering rules and regulations. Treasury figures initially estimated at $1.1 billion (the figure was later reduced to $700 million) the amount the government spent on money laundering, with very little to show for it.[17] Another non-negligible factor was the desire to undo, inasmuch as it was politically and bureaucratically feasible, whatever could be undone from the Clinton legacy.

Upon taking office, the new administration ordered a "top-to-bottom" review of anti-money laundering policies, and recommended delays in Clinton-era regulations so that "cost-benefit analyses" could be run—all the while continuing to pay lip service to the need for strong anti-money laundering laws, even expressing support for extending the reporting requirements to include for the first time securities dealers. This was perceived as "a classic Beltway ploy for slowing down and killing rules," [18] especially since the review was led by Dina Ellis, previously a senior lawyer on the Senate Banking Committee under Phil Gramm, the most effective opponent of money laundering regulations.[19]

The first major initiative dealing with financial regulation concerned a reversal on the Clinton initiative aimed at imposing strict controls on tax havens. In May 2001 the Treasury Department announced that the United States would break ranks with other industrial nations and not support OECD efforts to tighten the screws on offshore financial centers. The official argument for refusing to join the global crackdown on criminal and terrorist money havens was two-fold: first, financial markets did not need new controls; second, competition from tax havens—used by many US firms to reduce their tax bills—exerted a beneficial pressure for lowering taxes in the United States.

In an official statement, the Treasury Secretary said he was "troubled that

low tax rates are somehow suspect" and expressed concern about "potentially unfair treatment" of some countries. The Bush administration favors
tax competition between nations, he said, and "it will not participate in
any initiative to harmonize world tax systems." [20] Signals from Washington
in turn emboldened those tax havens that had been threatened with sanctions.[21] The global attempt at reform seemed dead. Many former government
officials expressed dismay over the fact that years of international cooperation had come to naught. A bipartisan group of former Internal Revenue
Service Commissioners who had served in the Kennedy, Johnson, Nixon,
Ford, Carter, and Clinton administrations expressed their displeasure with
the policy of the new administration. In a letter to President Bush, they
warned that "with increasing globalization and the use of the internet, U.S.
taxpayers seeking to evade U.S. taxes will have an increasing ability to transfer assets to tax havens further afield." "These tax havens," the letter said,
"are even less likely to bend to U.S. unilateral pressure. Conversely, they
may well cooperate where 30 OECD countries, some of which have close
historical ties in addition to geographical proximity, act in concert." [22] As for
William Wechsler, the former White House official in charge of money laundering policy, he warned that if the United States weakened or withdrew its
support for the international effort to combat financial abuses, "the entire
effort will be grievously—perhaps irreparably—harmed." [23]

In short, on the eve of September 11, 2001, a significant dismantling
of international financial controls—in particular anti-money laundering controls—seemed on track. When on September 3, 2001 Senator Phil
Gramm, the man who had single-handedly sunk the most ambitious money
laundering legislation, announced that he would not seek re-election, he
justified his decision by saying, "the things I came to Washington to do are
done." [24]

Money laundering is one area where the all-purpose cliché about "September 11 changing everything" is certainly true. The attacks brought about a
180-degree shift in policies and attitudes. Late to get on board, Treasury
Secretary Paul O'Neill (whose independence and candor would later cost
him his job) was still, as late as September 19, expressing his strongly held
belief that the battle against money laundering was a gigantic waste of money.
He declared:

> For the last 15, maybe even 25 years, this nation has had a program aimed at
> so-called money laundering, which is trying to get at evildoers who are moving
> cash around the world economy. And there has been an enormous amount
> of activity upwards of $700 million a year spent on this subject. And when
> I began asking the question of what have we gotten for the money we spent,
> I must say I was very disappointed that over this period of time, there's one

famous case that produced a significant amount of money that was caught. We should insist that we get value for money spent.[25]

A few days later, however, when President Bush announced the "first strike" in the war on terror, it was Paul O'Neill who would find himself at the helm of an unprecedented anti-money laundering crusade.

On October 26, 2001, Congress overwhelmingly passed the USA PATRIOT Act (Uniting and Strengthening America by Providing Appropriate Tools Required to Intercept and Obstruct Terrorism), whose Title III—the International Money Laundering Abatement and Financial Anti-Terrorism Act of 2001—dealt specifically with financial matters. The sweeping legislation expanded the definition of money laundering, lowered the evidence bar, toughened penalties, and greatly increased the global reach of US law enforcement. Notable provisions include the authority to seize terrorist assets, both foreign and domestic, if the property (or its owner) is involved in, related to, or used in support of acts of domestic or international terrorism. Other important provisions expanded law enforcement ability to prosecute unlicensed money transmitters, made the smuggling of bulk cash unlawful, and added terrorism and other offenses to the list of racketeering offenses. The new law also furthered the extraterritorial powers of US law enforcement in the tracing, freezing, and forfeiture of funds suspected of supporting terrorism. It provided a mechanism to obtain foreign bank records through administrative subpoenas. It also gave prosecutors the authority to seize money subject to forfeiture in a foreign bank account by authorizing the seizure of such a foreign bank's funds held in a US correspondent account.

Even though certain provisions of the USA PATRIOT law would later come under assault, opposition to the financial component of the law remained relatively muted. Only a handful of financial institutions, privacy advocates, and hardcore libertarians protested its financial provisions.

Money laundering and terrorist financing

Throughout the 1980s and 1990s, financial liberalization accelerated the free flow of goods and services, but it also facilitated the flow of dirty money. In those years, money laundering became a convenient catch-all concept, over time encompassing dozens of illegal activities, such as dirty money generated by any form of organized crime, foreign corrupt practices, extortion, fraud against financial institutions, export crimes, kidnapping, trafficking in endangered species, and—way down the list—terrorism.

The distinct characteristics of terrorist financing were occasionally recognized before September 11. The shock of the World Trade Center attacks did not allow for much sober thinking about the merits of deploying the substan-

tial money laundering apparatus to fight terrorist financing. Though terrorist financing constituted only a sliver of the money laundering category, it
soon came to occupy much of the "dirty money" universe, displacing in the
process most financial crimes.

In law enforcement circles, the transitions from the war on organized
crime to the war on drugs, and later to the war on terror, were relatively
smooth. The wars against organized crime and against drugs overlapped
significantly. Drug dealing was one of the trades of mafia families, and the
two "law and order" issues were organically linked: in both cases, a small
number of "evildoers" were engaging in criminal, money-making activities
that corrupted society and politics. When he informed the nation that
drug trafficking had been targeted as "public enemy number 1," Richard
Nixon explained that addicts "turn to shoplifting, mugging, burglary, armed
robbery, and so on" to feed their habits.[26] "Drugs and thugs" became a single
policy category whose components were largely interchangeable. By the 1980s
the "war on drugs" had of course greatly escalated, and took on a life of its
own. Punishments became draconian and often mandatory, as in the "three
strikes and you're out" laws. The criminalization of money laundering was a
direct result of this constant ratcheting up of the war on drugs.

The transition into terrorism was equally seamless. The rhetoric—empha-
sizing evil and threats to society—previously aimed at gangsters and drug
lords shifted to terrorists. Indeed, if nothing else, facing that threat required
an even more urgent and forceful response. Terrorism was of course one of
the predicates of money laundering. The problem, however, was that the
type of terrorism that the anti-money laundering apparatus was equipped to
deal with was "narco-terrorism," which involved violent acts conducted by or
on behalf of drug lords to intimidate and sow fear. That form of terrorism—
terrorism-for-profit, linked to the drug trade and other financial crimes—is
qualitatively different from the other, politically and ideologically driven,
terrorism which appeared in the 1990s. The first World Trade Center attack
in February 1993, which killed six people and injured hundreds, brought
jihadist networks to the attention of American law enforcement. This attack—
which would in retrospect be seen as the first salvo in the war of Islamic radicals against the United States—was soon forgotten. Indeed, when the first
anti-terrorist measures were taken, they were primarily designed to protect
the Middle Eastern peace process initiated with the 1993 Oslo Accords.[27]
In a January 1995 executive order, Bill Clinton released a list of 12 "foreign
terrorist organizations," all of them from the Middle East. The list included
Hamas and Hezbollah. The President's executive order froze their assets and
prohibited "any transaction or dealing by United States persons or within
the United States in property or interests in property of the persons desig-

nated."[28] Significantly, neither Usama Bin Laden nor Al-Qaeda was on the list. In those years, however, the Bin Laden name kept appearing on the radar screen of law enforcement agencies, and he was always referred to as a "financier of terror."[29] In January 1996 the CIA had established a station focused exclusively on Bin Laden and his network within its Counterterrorism Center.[30] On August 23, 1996 Bin Laden issued a fatwa declaring war on the United States, and on August 7, 1998 the near-simultaneous destruction of US embassies in Kenya and Tanzania brought about a major escalation of the anti-terrorist campaign. The involvement of Bin Laden and Al-Qaeda was no longer a matter for conjecture. Earlier that year, he had issued a fatwa calling for attacks on American military and civilian targets anywhere in the world. After the embassy attacks, considerable efforts were made both in the United States and internationally through the United Nations to seize Bin Laden's assets and "disrupt his finances." President Clinton ordered the freezing of assets linked to Al-Qaeda, including the funds of Ariana Afghan Airlines, which found itself the subject of an international boycott.

The financial focus was sharpened with the passage of the Antiterrorism and Effective Death Penalty Act of 1996, a sweeping legislation passed in the wake of the April 29, 1995 Oklahoma City bombing. Although the perpetrator, Timothy McVeigh, was an American militia extremist, many provisions of the new law were aimed specifically at Middle Eastern terrorism. The legislation targeted "material support" and directed the State Department to designate Foreign Terrorist Organizations (FTOs).[31] The law explicitly banned fundraising for groups that supported terrorist organizations and toughened penalties for a range of terrorist-related crimes.[32] The notion of "material support" was broadly interpreted. Prosecutors could obtain convictions without having to prove any intent to engage in or further terrorism. Furthermore, even a small financial donation would qualify.[33] One of the law's little-noticed provisions, included specifically as a result of lobbying by Lockerbie victims and their lawyers, amended the Foreign Sovereign Immunity Act to allow citizens to sue foreign nations for human rights violations, provided that those nations had been officially designated as sponsors of terrorism by the State Department.[34]

During Bill Clinton's second term, terrorism, "the enemy of our generation,"[35] moved up to the level of a strategic challenge. Counter-terrorism spending was doubled across 40 departments and agencies. High-profile presidential speeches as well as G7 meetings were focused on this challenge. Every anti-terrorist initiative had components designed to stem the flow of money to terrorist groups.[36] As the puzzle of terrorist financing started preoccupying policymakers, the task naturally fell to those who had previously been in charge of pursuing drug dealers.[37] With the election of George W.

Bush, the financial war seemed to stall. The new administration, obsessed by Iraq, paid scant attention to Al-Qaeda. And as we saw, it had a strong ideological bias against all types of financial control. It took the September 11 attacks to cause a dramatic U-turn.

Though originating in the fight against drugs, money laundering was assumed to be well suited to the fight against terror. In both cases, money was, or was said to be, central. The logical progression from organized crime to drugs to terrorism created a mindset that made it easy to overlook the fundamental differences between the two. The standard characterization of the money laundering problem—"Money laundering is the lifeblood of international drug trafficking" [38]—has automatically mutated into the first axiom of the financial war—that money is the lifeblood or oxygen of terrorism.[39] Its corollary—"by denying the traffickers the ability to launder this money, we can deny them the ability to properly run their business" [40]—was just as readily transposed to the realm of terrorist financing. "Trained incapacity" explains the reflexive shoehorning of terrorist financing within a money laundering paradigm.

This is how Deputy Secretary of the Treasury William Wechsler, the top anti-money laundering official in the Clinton administration, put it before a House of Representatives subcommittee:

> International drug cartels, criminal organizations and terrorist groups must launder their dirty money in order to receive the ultimate benefit of their crimes, and to finance their ongoing criminal operations. There would be no incentive for the cartels to push drugs on the streets of the United States if they could not launder the profits back into their home countries' financial systems, making their money appear to be legitimate and themselves very wealthy.[41]

Yet the two logics are entirely different, and indeed almost antithetical. Money laundering is the process by which dirty money belonging to drug cartels and criminal organizations gets recycled into clean money.[42] Although certain terrorists did become quite wealthy,[43] neither the financing of the September 11 attacks, nor that of subsequent terrorist operations in Bali, Madrid, Jeddah, Casablanca, Amman, London, and elsewhere, would be recognized in that definition. On the contrary, all the available evidence suggests that "clean money" was used to commit these crimes. Even though some terrorists may have been involved in petty crime, no financial transactions were made to obscure the money trail or to reintegrate dirty money into the financial system. And the ultimate goal was certainly not to gain wealth or achieve financial respectability.

The money laundering paradigm makes sense, in theory at least, under two sets of circumstances: in crime-for-profit situations where the goal is to hide the origin of dirty money, and when a small number of "evil-doers"—whether crime families, drug lords, or terrorist paymasters—handle large amounts of money. Under such circumstances the banking system cannot be bypassed. Indeed, the logic of financial crimes is in the final analysis to legitimize ill-gotten money. Under such conditions, the money trail yields crucial clues, and financial institutions are in a position to spot unusual transactions.

But all empirical evidence[44] suggests that the post-September 11 terrorist financing paradigm is fundamentally different. Terrorist financing is now a small part of a much broader, largely amorphous, and certainly ill-understood support network. The amounts needed to fund terrorist operations are small, and such amounts can easily bypass the formal banking system. Furthermore, terrorist financing is in many ways the opposite of money laundering: it is not about cleaning dirty money, but about soiling clean money. And clean money, by its very nature, is consistent with a customer's profile, and cannot be spotted by financial institutions.[45]

In the more serene days preceding September 11, the limited relevance of the anti-money laundering weapon to the fight against terrorism was occasionally noted. Authors of the FATF 2000–2001 *Report on Money Laundering Typologies* issued in February 2001 expressed doubts as to the relevance of money laundering methods to the fight against terrorist financing, stating that maybe "further refinement of specific anti-terrorism measures should take place elsewhere."[46] More specifically:

> Certain experts brought up the point that, despite the similar laundering methods and differences in motivation, this activity might not constitute money laundering per se if the source of the funding is not from criminal activity (for example, if the funds were derived from contributions or donations). If no connection could be shown between the funds and a criminal act that generated them, then these jurisdictions might not be able to assist the investigation or target the funds using anti-money laundering laws.[47]

And the National Money Laundering Strategy, coincidentally issued by the Treasury Department in September 2001, does not discuss terrorist financing in any of its 50 pages.[48]

As we saw, a combination of factors explains why the financial target was so inviting following the September 11 attacks: there was a politically motivated need for a swift and muscular response; the involvement of Usama Bin Laden and the fact that most of the hijackers came from Saudi Arabia made the financial argument especially compelling; and the softness of the financial front ensured that targets would be plentiful. Like the proverbial hammer in a child's hand, the existing money laundering apparatus made everything look like a nail. Bureaucracies that were often criticized for their

failure in the war on drugs and that were under attack by the new administration embraced the chance of expanding their bailiwick into such promis-
ing territory. Indeed, the global war on terror had opened to them a whole
new vista. Funding would be plentiful, and the very nature of the mission
would largely shield the money warriors from criticism.

The absurdity of this transposition has been largely lost on most financial
warriors and self-proclaimed experts on the subject. The existing regulatory
regime had been designed "primarily for discovering and reporting money
laundering—the efforts of criminals, such as drug traffickers, to filter huge
amounts of cash through the financial system." [49] To be sure, one occasionally finds a passing reference to the difference between money laundering
and terrorist financing—but it is typically to conclude that those differences
justify a "more intense application of existing anti-money laundering instruments as well as the use of supplementary mechanisms." [50] By the same token,
soon after the September 11 attacks, a few policymakers had brief epipha-
nies, suddenly realizing that "they had been looking at the world through
the wrong end of the telescope," and that acts of terror could be financed by
"clean money." [51] Such misgivings were almost instantaneously swept aside.
Islamic terrorism would be made, by assertion, indistinguishable from financial crimes. As a money laundering "expert" put it: "So what is the difference
between a terrorist, a drug trafficker, a narco-terrorist, a revolutionary and a
member of an organized crime group? I suggest that there is no difference;
that all of the above are one and the same." [52]

Acronyms were devised—MLTF or AML/CFT for Anti-Money Laundering (AML) and Combating the Financing of Terrorism (CFT)—as if to
certify that the two phrases were now synonymous. [53] In an extraordinary
meeting in Washington DC on October 29 and 30, 2001, the mission of
FATF was formally expanded beyond money laundering to cover terrorist
financing. FATF added to its 40 recommendations nine new ones dealing
specifically with terrorist financing. [54] It called upon all countries to criminalize the financing of terrorism and terrorist organizations, freeze and confiscate terrorist assets, report suspicious transactions linked to terrorism, and
impose anti-money laundering controls on non-traditional banking systems,
such as hawalas. The FATF set forth a timetable for action, which required
the development of additional guidance for financial institutions on the techniques and mechanisms used in the financing of terrorism. As with money
laundering, FATF would "name and shame" countries lacking adequate rules
and impose sanctions against them. [55] Most regions of the world (including
Asia-Pacific, the Caribbean, Latin America, Eastern and Southern Africa,
and the Middle East) now have FATF-Style Regional Bodies (FSRBs) whose
role is to facilitate the adoption, implementation, and enforcement of inter-

nationally accepted standards to combat money laundering and the financing of terrorism.

Financial crime soon came to be dominated by the terrorism question. By 2002 the International Symposium on Economic Crime held in Cambridge had abruptly shifted from issues such as counterfeiting, smuggling, and piracy on the high seas to a near-exclusive focus on terrorist financing.[56] The title of that year's symposium—"Putting the Crooks out of Business!"—reflected the new consensus that terrorist financing was just another type of financial crime, albeit the most important one.

In the name of the global war on terror, the reach of the anti-money laundering apparatus kept expanding, reaching new financial sectors and new industries (such as travel agencies, car dealerships, and jewelry businesses)— without much evidence to support such expansion.[57] As Peter Reuter and Edwin M. Truman have written, "The fact is that, to date, an elaborate system of laws and regulations that affects the lives of millions of people and imposes several billion dollars in costs annually on the American public has been based to a substantial degree on untested assumptions that do not look particularly plausible."[58] At various times, it looked like a backlash was near—that the inadequacy of the money laundering template would be brought to the political fore. In every instance, a new act of terror would silence the critics.[59] The breadth of the new "Money Laundering/Terrorist Financing" category was such that it provided ample bait-and-switch possibilities. The fight against terrorism would furnish the pretext, and minor financial irregularities or petty crime would help obtain convictions. As the September 11 Commission terrorist financing monograph noted, "Nickel-and-dime fraud cases turned into terrorist cases."[60]

PART III
NARRATIVE
AND DYNAMICS

4

Money and the War on Terror Narrative

We're your worst nightmare—white trash with money!
Roseanne Barr Arnold

Where facts are few, experts are many.
Donald R. Gannon

Those that know do not talk. Those that talk do not know.
Taoist maxim

I n the months following the September 11 attacks, and for a period of over two years, the range of acceptable discourse was exceedingly narrow. In the words of former counter-terrorism czar Richard Clarke,

> After the shock of September 11, Americans rallied around the flag in support of the country and their government. Unfortunately, that commendable sentiment brought a blind loyalty, an unquestioning willingness to accept whatever the leadership said was necessary to fight terrorism. By suppressing our natural skepticism, turning off our analytical filters, we participated in *a major national mistake*, the invasion of Iraq.[1]

The Bush administration "did everything possible to portray the United States as a blindsided innocent victim,"[2] and any attempt to understand terrorism was reviled as excusing or justifying it. It was politically incorrect within the mainstream media to talk about the blowback effect or draw any connection between the September 11 attacks and foreign policy.[3] Neither was it acceptable to mention security lapses or the failures of intelligence.[4] Essayist Joan Didion wrote eloquently:

> Many opinions are expressed. Few are allowed to develop. Even fewer change.

53

We have come in this country to tolerate many such fixed opinions, or national pieties, each with its own baffles of invective and counterinvective, of euphemism and downright misstatement, its own screen that slides into place whenever actual discussion threatens to surface.[5]

Ideology and the politically correct discourse

A conventional narrative emerged about the causes of the attacks and the best way for the United States to respond, which would come to determine the course of the war on terror. It was to a large extent shaped by the neo-conservatives within the Bush administration.[6] Having more or less "hijacked" US foreign policy following the September 11 attacks, they launched preemptive strikes against alternative explanations and policies, and wrapped themselves in the flag while stifling dissent. Their worldview had the merit of internal consistency and plausibility. It also meshed with a public sentiment characterized by fear and a yearning for forceful action. The central question, repeatedly asked by the President of the United States, was "why do they hate us?" In his address to Congress on September 20, Bush gave a first answer: "They hate our freedoms: our freedom of religion, our freedom of speech, our freedom to vote and assemble and disagree with each other." The *National Review* elaborated further: "The United States is a target because we are powerful, rich, and good. We are resented for our power, envied for our wealth, and hated for our liberty."[7] President Bush foreclosed any discussion of US foreign policy when he uttered another famous line: "if you're not with us, you're with the terrorists." Who "they" are was never made clear. The ambiguity certainly played into the hands of those who advocated an open-ended escalation of the war on terror.

Such was the mood of the country: a number of things were simply unsayable. There was of course an alternative viewpoint, but to find it one had to look outside the political mainstream. Writing in *The Nation* under the title "Blowback," political scientist Chalmers Johnson answered President Bush's "why do they hate us?" question as follows: "The suicidal assassins of September 11, 2001 did not 'attack America,' as our political leaders and the news media like to maintain; they attacked American foreign policy."[8] Unlike most commentators, Johnson knew what he was talking about. In a book published a year earlier, he had envisioned the possibility of blowback from "the unintended consequences of the US government's international activities that have been kept secret from the American people."[9] It would take a long time (roughly until the steady deterioration of the situation in Iraq in late 2003) for comparable analyses to find their way into the mainstream media. Since the beginning of the second term of George W. Bush, dissent was again tolerable. To paraphrase James Wolcott, many of the "attack poodles" recovered their spine.[10] In the run-up to the Iraq war, none of the "counter-powers" functioned properly. The media failed to play its role. To quote media critic Ben Bagdikian, "Our news regularly proclaims its power to remain independent from officialdom. Yet with rare exceptions, the American mainstream news during combat has been much like the hired bards of medieval monarchs: when war has come, our journalists have become propagandists." [11] Prominent journalists played cheerleaders for the war on terror, taking pains to contribute to the government's efforts to silence dissenters.[12]

The rise to global pre-eminence of the United States had paradoxically been accompanied by a declining interest in all things foreign. Throughout the 1990s, neither the media nor academe paid much attention to the outside world. In his study of the period between the end of the Cold War and the September 11 attacks—what was then widely believed to be the advent of a time of peace—David Halberstam noted the increased parochialism and self-absorption of the sole remaining superpower. In 1992 Bill Clinton managed to use George H.W. Bush's expertise and interest in foreign policy against him.[13] In the words of Halberstam,

> As the Soviet threat to the United States receded, so, too, did the political support for any kind of foreign policy issue that was not immediate in its import. A generation was coming of age in the Congress who cared less about foreign affairs, elected by a generation of voters who cared less, and reported on by a media that paid less attention. ... The country, to be blunt, was more powerful and more influential than ever before, but it was looking inward. It was the most schizophrenic of nations, a monopoly superpower that did not want to be an imperial power, and whose soul, except in financial and economic matters, seemed to be more and more isolationist.[14]

Comparable developments had occurred in academe, where social science came to be captured by theorists, and "area studies" fell into disrepute. In 1998 Peter Hall and Sidney Tarrow deplored the "diminishing attention to the cultural, historical, and political context of trends in particular regions." [15] They wrote:

> In one of the great ironies of current American scholarship, programs that support our reservoir of knowledge about other countries are being threatened just as Americans have become intensely aware of how closely their own fate is tied to events abroad. Even the Central Intelligence Agency is complaining that it cannot find recruits with an adequate knowledge of other languages or regions of the world.[16]

The tendency to theorize about other nations with little need to develop specific understanding meshed well with the neo-conservative movement's highly ideological approach to foreign policy.[17] When it came to Islamic and Middle Eastern studies, these problems were compounded by thorough politicization.

Insofar as people with an actual knowledge of the Islamic world were prone to express misgivings about the Iraq adventure, they were sidelined, and the most prominent among them were systematically attacked.[18] In a bizarre way, ignorance of the Islamic world combined with a specific agenda to become the prerequisites for participation in the policymaking process. Being an "Arabist" had long carried a stigma: those State Department officials who spoke Arabic were automatically suspected of a pro-Arab bias.[19] In preparation for the Iraq war, wholesale purges replaced the few remaining experts with ideologues. Karen Kwiatkowski, a lieutenant colonel in the US Air Force who was posted at the Near East South Asia (NESA) directorate at the Pentagon, witnessed the "seizure of the reins of US Middle East policy" and deplored the fact that "there seemed to be little any of us could do about it." She wrote: "From May 2002 until February 2003, I observed firsthand the formation of the Pentagon's Office of Special Plans and watched the latter stages of the neoconservative capture of the policy-intelligence nexus in the run-up to the invasion of Iraq." She added that "the expertise on Mideast policy was not only being removed, but was also being exchanged for that from various agenda-bearing think tanks, including the Middle East Media Research Institute, the Washington Institute for Near East Policy, and the Jewish Institute for National Security Affairs." [20] In academe, as Sara Roy wrote, there was "a wider determination to monitor, report, defame and punish those individuals and institutions ... whose views the right finds objectionable." [21] One such effort was Campus Watch, a McCarthyite effort by Daniel Pipes to monitor what educators said about US policy in the Middle East—even inviting students to report politically incorrect statements by their professors. After the Iraq war, Pipes said: "I flatter myself perhaps in thinking that the rather subdued academic response to the war in Iraq in March and April may have been, in part, due to our work." [22]

Former Defense Undersecretary Douglas Feith, a leading neo-conservative, justified the cultural incompetence prerequisite in terms of a "greater truth":

> There's a paradox I've never been able to work out. It helps to be deeply knowledgeable about an area—to know the people, to know the language, to know the history, the culture, the literature. But it is not a guarantee that you will have the right strategy or policy as a matter of statecraft for dealing with that area. You see, the great experts in certain areas sometimes get it fundamentally wrong. ... George W. Bush has more insight, because of his knowledge of human beings and his sense of history, about the motive force, the craving for

freedom and participation in self-rule, than do many of the language experts and history experts and culture experts.[23]

Everything that was said about Iraq—that it would be a "cakewalk," that no postwar planning was necessary because the Iraqis would "welcome us with flowers," that a model secular democracy would be created and have a domino effect in the region, that elections would bring moderates to power and marginalize Islamic extremists, etc—turned out to be flat wrong.[24] Yet this did not cause much soul searching among neo-conservatives. Indeed, students of failed prophecies have noted that "when people are committed to a belief or a course of action, clear disconfirming evidence may simply result in deepened conviction and increased proselytizing."[25]

Money, evil, and the "clash of civilizations"

The ideological advantage of the money argument is that it obscured the question of political grievances. Combined with the rhetoric of evil and hatred, it provided what seemed like a powerful explanation for political violence. For many specialists, terrorism boils down to a simple equation: "motivation + capability = terrorism."[26] Indeed, if evil covered, powerfully if not plausibly, the motivation side of the terrorism equation, financial resources provided the capability. It is no surprise that one of the bedrock neo-conservative beliefs was that "terrorism needs to be a multibillion-dollar business,"[27] and that both the themes of evil and that of money loom so large in the neo-conservative literature.[28]

In a Congressional testimony, Jonathan Levin and the ubiquitous Steven Emerson explained: "Terrorism depends upon the presence of three primary ingredients: indoctrination, recruitment and financing. Take away any one of those three ingredients and the chances for success are geometrically reduced."[29] Not only was financing pronounced central to terrorism, but the question of funding was also closely associated with "indoctrination" and "recruitment." A few exotic words would soon easily roll off the tongues of every commentator on terrorism: madrassas, the little-known Koranic schools; Wahhabism, the austere Islamic sect that dominates Saudi Arabia; and Al-Jazeera, the Qatar-based news network, which soon stood accused of propagating an ideology of hatred.[30] Funding fueled hatred and this justified the open-ended expansion of the financial war: anyone connected to Wahhabism or Saudi Arabia could be a suspect; any Islamic charity financing a madrassa could find itself accused of funding terror. One could frequently find statements such as this: "Countries like Saudi Arabia sponsor terror directly because the State school system is run along the principles of Wahhabi Islam which preaches fundamentalism, terror, and the destruction of Western civilization."[31]

Conspicuously absent from the "primary ingredients" of terrorism in Levin's and Emerson's analysis are political grievances. In the aftermath of September 11, anyone who brought up political grievances had to fend off accusations of being anti-American or a "blame-America-firster." [32] Neo-conservative writers launched preemptive strikes against such arguments. As repeatedly explained by Bernard Lewis, Islamic political grievances were grounded in irrationality. Indeed, the essence of Islam was an atavistic hatred of, and rage against, the West.[33] This hatred springs from a succession of defeats by Islam in its millennial confrontation with the West. Others have argued that "claims of 'root causes' are distractions from the real work at hand." [34]

In sum, for many constituencies, Islam was the enemy, and by implication, funds associated with Islam could only be suspect. And the financial argument often justified the most outrageous policy suggestions. Thus Fred Iklé, former Undersecretary of Defense and respected Washington elder statesman, wrote in the *Wall Street Journal*: "Those who out of cowardice use their wealth to pay Danegeld to the preachers of hate and destruction must be taught that this aggression will boomerang. A nuclear war stirred up against the 'infidels' might end up displacing Mecca and Medina with two large radioactive craters." [35]

The first Bush doctrine: Connecting dots and the "six degrees of separation" logic

A few days after September 11, in what may be considered the first "Bush doctrine," President George W. Bush said that "those who 'support or otherwise associate' with terrorists are just as guilty as those who commit the acts of terror themselves." [36] Terrorist financing and other forms of support thus became indistinguishable from the acts of terror themselves—which spurred the hunt for people, groups, and countries with "alleged links to terror." [37] A massive hunt was under way for terror financiers, yet facts were scant, and speculation, misinformation, and disinformation ran rampant.

The vast "dot-connecting" enterprise, amid near total ignorance of the shadowy Al-Qaeda network, was a politically charged exercise. As noted by the September 11 Commission terrorist financing monograph, "the line between rumor-mongering and intelligence was thin." [38] The neo-conservatives within the administration, eager to implicate Iraq and many others in the Muslim world, seized the agenda.[39] There were more than enough self-proclaimed experts eager to peddle evidence of links to terror. Indeed, many "terrorist experts" and policy entrepreneurs specialized in the imaginative connecting of often imaginary dots.[40] The dot-connection enterprise was made quite easy by the "six degrees of separation" logic. A famous 1990 John

Guare play by that title built on the insight that everyone on the planet is connected to any other randomly chosen person by a chain of no more than six mutual acquaintances.[41] It was based on empirical work by psychologist Stanley Milgram about the small world of social networks.[42]

The mother of all "alleged links" was of course that connecting Saddam Hussein to Al-Qaeda. The connection was called "bulletproof" by Vice-President Dick Cheney. Top officials repeatedly spoke of "deep, long-standing ties" of a "sinister nexus," of them "working in concert, with al-Qaeda [becoming] an extension of Saddam's madness and his hatred and his capacity to extend weapons of mass destruction around the world."[43] According to University of Chicago political scientist John Mearsheimer, "Bush did a brilliant job of bamboozling American people that Iraq was directly involved with events of 9/11. There's no good evidence Saddam and Osama bin Laden were linked in any meaningful way. But there's no question most Americans don't see it that way."[44]

For staunch ideologues, the lack of evidence mattered little.[45] To quote Defense Secretary Donald Rumsfeld, "the absence of evidence is not evidence of absence."[46] Using the subtext of evil, William Safire, the columnist for whom a Saddam–Bin Laden alliance was a foregone conclusion, criticized the September 11 Commission's conclusion:

> Think about that. Do today's groupthinkers believe that Osama bin Laden would sit down with Saddam in front of the world's cameras to sign a mutual assistance pact, establishing a formal relationship? Terrorists and rogue states don't work that way. Mass killers collaborate informally, without a photo op, even secretly.[47]

Though the thesis was clearly discredited, the rumors were kept alive, and 70 percent of the American public still believed, two years after the event, that Saddam Hussein was involved in the September 11 attacks.[48]

The logic could of course backfire. Online magazine *Slate* occasionally publishes updates on its "Six Degrees of Adnan Khashoggi" game. In the words of writer Timothy Noah, "To play, you build a chain linking the shadowy international arms merchant to any scandal that occurred during the past 40 years. Players rarely need more than one link." He was "able to link Khashoggi to Iran–Contra, Wedtech, the Marcos Philippine kleptocracy, BCCI, the death of Princess Diana, the Kennedy assassination, Watergate, and the breakup of the Beatles."[49] The writer does emphasize that "Khashoggi's proximity to these events does not demonstrate criminality on his part. But it does illustrate Khashoggi's ubiquity in the noir environment where shocking events tend to take place."[50] In due course, the wheeler-dealer crossed paths with leading Iraq hawk (and strong critic of Saudi Arabia) Richard Perle. As revealed by Seymour Hersh, the two met for lunch when

Perle, then chairman of the Defense Policy Board, an influential group of advisers to the Pentagon, was seeking investors for a venture capital fund investing in security and defense companies. (Perle denied the charge, calling Hersh "the closest thing American journalism has to a terrorist.")[51]

By the same token, many critics of President Bush, most famously filmmaker Michael Moore, had long played up the ties between the Bush family and the Saudis, including the Bin Laden Group (either directly or through their common investment in the Carlyle group).[52] The spurious nature of alleged links can be found in Craig Unger's words: "horrifying as it may sound, the secret relationship between these two great families helped to trigger the Age of Terror and give rise to the tragedy of 9/11." [53]

In the financial war, links were often distant, circumstantial, and inconsequential; they became believable by dint of repetition.[54] As already discussed, the financial argument has always been plausible in the post-September 11 context. A number of "connected dots" were widely publicized. Princess Haifa al-Faisal, wife of Prince Bandar bin Sultan, the Saudi ambassador in Washington, sent money to a woman she did not know for medical treatment. That woman's husband was a friend of another Saudi who happened to befriend, and may have provided financial support to, Khalid Al-Midhar and Nawaf Al-Hazmi, two of the September 11 hijackers.[55] Does that make the Saudi princess a terrorist financier? Authors of the 9/11 Commission Report said they "found no evidence that Saudi Princess Haifa al-Faisal provided any funds to the conspiracy, either directly or indirectly." [56] But anti-Saudi literature kept suggesting otherwise.[57] Writing in the *Weekly Standard*, Stephen Schwartz explained:

> There is no mystery, and there is no need for complicated theorizing, about the scandal. ... Now, the royal family's apologists in the U.S. government and media are engaging in contortions to help the Saudis explain away the money trail. But the relationship between Prince Bandar, his wife, and the world of Saudi "charities," "relief workers," and "Islamic missionaries," in which diverse Saudi functionaries serve as donors, recruiters, protectors, and simple enthusiasts of terror, is elementary.[58]

Making allegations was exceedingly easy, although many terrorist financing accusations crumbled in court. In the words of the September 11 Commission terrorist financing monograph:

> [T]hese initial designations were undertaken with limited evidence, and some were overbroad, resulting in legal challenges. Faced with having to defend actions in courts that required a higher standard of evidence than was provided by the intelligence that supported the designations in the first place, the United States and the United Nations were forced to "unfreeze" assets. The difficulty, not completely understood by the policymakers when they

instituted the freezes, was that the intelligence community "linked" certain entities or individuals to known terrorist groups primarily through common acquaintances, group affiliations, historic relationships, phone communications, and other such contacts. It proved far more difficult to actually trace the money from a suspected entity or individual to the terrorist group, or to otherwise show complicity, as required in defending the designations in court.[59]

The second Bush doctrine: Money and the question of preemption

In the months following the September 11 attacks, a new "Bush doctrine" took shape, which revolutionized strategic thinking, and was put to the test when the war on terror escalated to include Iraq. The second Bush doctrine came to refer to a far broader strategic doctrine of prevention (though it was sold as a doctrine of preemption). In contrast to his predecessors who reserved the right to strike preemptively an enemy preparing an imminent attack, George W. Bush said that he would apply "the concept of imminent threat" to nations or groups developing "capabilities" that might one day threaten America. The second doctrine, first presented in President Bush's graduation speech in West Point on June 1, 2002, became official strategy with the publication of the National Security Strategy on September 17, 2002. Two lines from the President's speech were particularly memorable: "If we wait for threats to fully materialize, we will have waited too long," and "The war on terror will not be won on the defensive."

The new Bush doctrine meshed seamlessly with the axioms of the financial war. The parallels between the justifications for the war in Iraq and the case for preemptive financial war are many. In the case of Iraq, a key argument against waiting too long for evidence was that "the smoking gun" would be "a mushroom cloud."[60] Former Treasury Secretary Paul O'Neill deplored the fact that "we don't know where [the money] is until long after it has been located and spent. By then, it's too late."[61] If indeed money is the "oxygen of terror" and the "mother of intent," then the sheer possession of cash spells danger, and financial preemption, or more accurately prevention, is justified. The quest for terrorist cash was to be aggressive, and low standards of evidence were justified by the nature of the threat. Indeed, most influential "experts" on the subject have consistently harped on "the critical need to preemptively deny terrorists the funds they need to conduct their attacks."[62] New York prosecutor Robert Morgenthau put it best: "If that money can be identified, isolated and seized before it buys what terrorists need, they will be crippled."[63]

5

The Usual Suspects

"I am shocked, shocked to find that gambling is going on in here."
Captain Louis Renault in *Casablanca* (1942)

"Major Strasser has been shot. Round up the usual suspects."
Captain Louis Renault in *Casablanca* (1942)

*"Realizing the importance of the case, my men are rounding up
twice the usual number of suspects."*
Captain Louis Renault in *Casablanca* (1942)

As so much else in the financial war, the list of usual suspects is rooted in the unshakable belief in the $300 million Bin Laden hidden fortune.[1] Days after the 1998 African bombings, an influential piece appeared in the *Wall Street Journal* purporting to reveal the whereabouts of that stash. In it, journalist Steven Emerson, whose primary claim to fame until then had been his assertion that the 1995 Oklahoma City bombing could only have been perpetrated by Middle Eastern terrorists, offered clues:

> Terrorists have become very sophisticated in laundering and disguising their funds. They use a variety of financial vehicles—front companies, charitable organizations, third-party bank accounts—to disguise the location of their assets. Osama bin Laden's most impressive achievement has been his ability to shield from scrutiny and seizure his $300 million financial empire, held in a financial labyrinth of world-wide shell companies, co-investors, governmental entities, bank accounts, religious "charities" and plain old blue-chip investments. A portion of Mr. bin Laden's "portfolio" is held in U.S. and British banks under third-party names and transferred to Islamic religious charities operating under false cover.[2]

Comparable guesswork by other "experts" and "investigators" resulted in similar lists. Certain allegations and factoids were repeated so often that the echo-chamber effect created a sense of self-evidence. Though based on speculation, misinformation, and disinformation, a veritable canon of terrorist financing soon developed. With every new terrorist attack, the usual suspects were trotted out. Broad allegations built upon a scintilla of truth cannot be disproved. Yet as a basis for law enforcement they are pernicious. By implying that each category is, in its entirety or its majority, linked to terror, they have sent the financial warriors on many a wild goose chase. They have invited witch-hunts and systematic profiling, in the process causing considerable collateral damage.

Consider the conclusions of a widely quoted study by the Council on Foreign Relations, which attempted to answer the question "Who funds Al-Qaeda?" First, there is Bin Laden's own personal fortune "whose estimates go up to $300 million." Then there are other sources, legal and illegal; some donated voluntarily, others extorted:

> Some of al-Qaeda's money comes from wealthy, sympathetic Muslims, many of whom helped bin Laden fund the resistance to the 1980s Soviet occupation of Afghanistan. These patrons often own companies, have extensive assets in global financial centers, and use sophisticated techniques to camouflage their transfers of money to al-Qaeda. Al-Qaeda extorts money from wealthy Saudis and Muslims in other countries, sometimes by threatening businesses or individuals. More funds reportedly come from illegal activities conducted by al-Qaeda or on its behalf, including smuggling, drug trafficking, and illicit trade in diamonds and precious metals. A wide array of businesses and other organizations divert some proceeds from otherwise legitimate economic activity. The Yemeni honey trade, for instance, has reportedly been used both to raise funds and to serve as a cover for transporting drugs, weapons, and operatives for al-Qaeda. Other terror funds come from illicit charities that raise money from unsuspecting people and divert donations to terrorists.[3]

Most stories and allegations survived contrary empirical evidence. They were largely debunked by the August 2004 9/11 Commission Report and the accompanying terrorist financing monograph. In just about every respect, the reality of September 11 funding differed from the commonly painted picture. No rogue states were involved. The amounts were small and financing was tight. The report identified two Al-Qaeda operatives, Ali Abdul Aziz Ali and Mustafa al Hawsawi, respectively from Pakistan and Saudi Arabia, as the principal "paymasters." In addition to wiring money from the United Arab Emirates to the hijackers, they played a central role in the plot. No charities, Islamic banks, front companies, or rich Saudi merchants were involved. Contrary to what had been widely reported, no hawalas were used, including in wiring back, a few days prior to the attacks, "surplus" funds in the range of $26,000. In the case of most post-September 11 terrorist attacks, tiny amounts and self-financing by the terrorists themselves was the rule.

This chapter looks at some of the frequently designated "usual suspects": the Saudis, rich Arabs, drugs and crime, gold and diamonds, hawalas and Islamic banks. Islamic charities, perhaps the most commonly mentioned "usual suspects," are discussed separately in Chapter 9.

The Saudis, rich Arabs, charities, and front companies

Allegations about Bin Laden's $300 million dollar inherited wealth were inextricably linked to broader allegations about rich Arabs, the Saudis, Islamic charities, and front companies. Broad allegations were fleshed out in countless news stories. Perhaps the most consequential was the much quoted article by Jack Kelley, the one-time star reporter of USA Today, later revealed to be a "serial fabricator." In an article dated October 29, 1999, he had written about "how prominent businessmen in Saudi Arabia continue to transfer tens of millions of dollars to bank accounts linked to indicted terrorist Osama bin Laden." Quoting "intelligence officials," Kelley stated that "the businessmen, who are worth more than $5 billion, are paying bin Laden 'protection money' to stave off attacks on their businesses in Saudi Arabia."[4]

Durable stereotypes have deep roots. Well before the rise of the neo-conservative propaganda machine, the sudden enrichment of Saudi Arabia in the 1970s had been regarded as both illegitimate and dangerous. Hans Morgenthau, then the most prominent scholar of international relations, wrote:

> The control of oil, the lifeblood of an advanced industrial state, by potentates who have no other instrument of power and who are accountable to nobody, morally, politically, or legally, is in itself a perversity. It is a perversity in the sense that it defies all rational principles by which the affairs of state and the affairs of humanity ought to be regulated to put into a few irresponsible hands power over life and death of a whole civilization.[5]

At the time, policy circles and influential publications did not rule out the idea of "taking over Arab oil fields" as a solution to all economic and political problems.[6]

Other criticisms have focused on the generous funding by the Saudis of Palestinian organizations,[7] and on Saudi influence in the United States. Steven Emerson purported to disclose, in his book The American House of Saud, "how Saudi Arabia and its influential corporate supporters, cultivated through the allure of money, have changed American foreign policy, manipulated the American public, and generated an impact in numerous other ways on American society." [8]

After September 11, allegations and accusations became far more extreme. David Aufhauser, a former general counsel to the Bush Treasury Department who was also chairman of the National Security Council's committee on terrorist financing, called Saudi Arabia "the epicenter of terrorist financing." [9] A Council on Foreign Relations report on terrorist financing had this to say:

> It is worth stating clearly and unambiguously what official U.S. government spokespersons have not. For years, individuals and charities based in Saudi Arabia have been the most important source of funds for Al Qaeda, and for years the Saudi officials have turned a blind eye to this problem. [10]

This is why "the Saudis" as a broad, undefined category came to assume a place of choice among the usual suspects of terrorist financing. Accusations against the Saudis went hand in glove with another equally broad and ill-defined category: Islamic charities. The Saudis and the charities became the evil twins of terrorist financing. The first provided the money, the second served as the conduit.

On July 10, 2002, Richard Perle invited Laurent Murawiec, a Rand Corporation analyst who had been a writer for conspiracy theorist Lyndon LaRouche's publications, to brief the Defense Policy Board, the Pentagon's advisory committee. In the briefing, which came as a shock to the Saudi regime, and an embarrassment to the US, Murawiec called Saudi Arabia "the kernel of evil, the prime mover, the most dangerous opponent." The Saudis were "active at every level of the terror chain, from planners to financiers, from cadre to foot-soldier, from ideologist to cheerleader." [11] The recommendations made to the audience of luminaries were drastic: the United States had to issue an "ultimatum" to the House of Saud, ordering them to "stop any funding and support for any fundamentalist madrasa, mosque, ulama, predicator anywhere in the world," as well as "all anti-U.S., anti-Israeli, anti-Western predication, writings, etc, within Arabia," shut down all charities and confiscate their assets, and "prosecute or isolate those involved in the terror chain, including in the Saudi intelligence services." [12] In case of non-compliance, the analyst said that the United States should invade the country, seize its oil fields, and confiscate its financial assets.

Such views, common among influential neo-conservatives, [13] struck a chord with the public. After September 11, Saudi Arabia had become the country everybody loved to hate. A public opinion survey found that neutral or very negative American views of Saudi Arabia jumped from 63 percent in 1994 to a whopping 81 percent in 2002. [14] In such an environment, criticisms of the Saudis in Congress and in the media came at no political cost. In the burgeoning literature on the Saudis and Wahhabism, the most highly publicized books—typically written by people who had never set foot in the kingdom and possessed neither the language skills nor the religious knowledge—emphasized the themes of hatred and evil.[15] Books with titles such as *Sleeping with the Devil*[16] or *Hatred's Kingdom*[17] were frequently cited. Another striking feature of the anti-Saudi criticisms is that they could be found across the political spectrum. Although the most virulent attacks have come from the neo-conservatives, criticisms could be found from the extreme right to the radical left, and much of it came, despite the close alliance between the two countries, from the mainstream—both Democratic and Republican—of American politics. In Congress, both supporters and critics of the Bush administration have routinely criticized it for cozying up to the Saudis or treating them with "kid gloves." [18]

Based on that logic, some influential commentators have held top Saudi officials—indeed the ruling family itself—politically and financially responsible for the September 11 attacks. Building on Jack Kelley's 1999 article, some argued that "senior princes [used] hundreds of millions of dollars [of] official Saudi money to pay off bin Laden to cause trouble elsewhere but not in the kingdom." [19] Daniel Pipes demanded that the Saudi government disburse $100 billion to compensate the victims' families.[20] The administration of George W. Bush was especially touchy on the subject of Saudi influence. There was of course the matter of the special relationship between the two countries: cheap oil in exchange for military protection. But there was also the issue of the special ties between the Bush family (and in particular, George W. Bush in his days as a Texas oilman) and Saudi financial interests.[21] The government's official position on Saudi Arabia struck a middle ground. As summarized by White House spokesman Ari Fleischer, "Saudi Arabia is a good partner in the war against terrorism but can do more." [22]

A passing reference by an Al-Qaeda defector to the fact that honey production was one of the businesses owned by Bin Laden in his Sudanese years, combined with the freezing after September 11 of three Yemeni businesses involved in honey, turned the honey business into yet another front for Bin Laden,[23] and books on terrorist financing took to explaining how honey, as a "dual use" business, could be used to smuggle money and weapons.[24]

The allegations of great wealth, financial sophistication, and penetration of world markets lent credence to rumors that Bin Laden, his associates, or even the September 11 terrorists had made money from the attacks. In the days preceding the tragedy, there had been seemingly unjustified declines of those stocks that were bound to be the most affected—airlines, investment banks, and insurance and reinsurance companies—by the attacks on the twin towers of the World Trade Center. Short selling of stocks of the two airlines whose planes were hijacked—United Airlines and American

Airlines—had increased by 40 and 20 percent respectively from a month earlier. Investment banking stocks, in particular Morgan Stanley, one of the main tenants of the World Trade Center, and neighboring Merrill Lynch were similarly shorted, as were most insurance and reinsurance companies later affected by attack-related claims. The stock of Germany's Munich Re, which stood to pay out nearly $1 billion in claims from the destruction of the World Trade Center, fell 12 percent in the four days prior to the attacks and another 15 percent on September 11. Another puzzling case was that of Bermuda-based XL Capital, a property-casualty insurer with heavy exposure to aviation losses. The company, whose fundamentals were solid, had just reported strong earnings and had bright future prospects, yet short sales of the company stock had tripled in the previous month.[25]

All this fed accusations that people with foreknowledge of the attacks were behind much of the suspicious short selling. Italian Defense Minister Antonio Martino declared: "I am convinced that the person who organized the attacks in New York has a lucid mind and knows very well that money gives power. It is no exaggeration to think that terrorist organizations were among those who speculated on international markets. Those who acted certainly tried to cover the tracks of their operations." [26] The symbolic targeting of the heart of global finance led further credence to the theory: in addition to human casualties and physical destruction in the heart of global capitalism, the financial attacks would have attempted to cause colossal disruption and massive losses.

Regulatory authorities on three continents immediately opened investigations.[27] But after a few days, the US Securities and Exchange Commission (SEC) and its British, German, Dutch, Italian, French, and Japanese counterparts, after analyzing massive amounts of trading data, came out empty handed. They all announced that there had been no evidence of concerted speculation, insider trading, or stock manipulation.[28]

The short selling of specific stocks could indeed have been the result of more straightforward and less sinister explanations. For about 18 months, the stock market had been in the doldrums, raising the specter of a serious recession. Investors were especially bearish on sectors such as insurance and investment banking, whose performance was directly related to that of the overall stock market. In September 2001 the monthly NYSE short interest activity hit its seventh straight record. There were also specific reasons, widely publicized in the business press in the days preceding the attacks, for certain airline and financial stocks to be battered.[29] One may also argue that, from the standpoint of the attacks' masterminds, suspicious financial transactions could have called attention to the plot, perhaps to the point of foiling it. As later evidence suggested, the number of people in the know must have been extremely small. Some of the hijackers seemed to have learned of their exact mission only after they boarded their planes. And despite a massive manhunt, US law enforcement agencies seem to have been unable to find a single person on the US territory with a direct foreknowledge of the plot.[30] The 9/11 Commission Report also expressed skepticism that such financial manipulation occurred, stating that there was "no evidence that anyone with advance knowledge of the attacks profited through securities transactions."[31] More specifically: "The SEC and the FBI, aided by other agencies and the securities industry, devoted enormous time to investigating this issue, including securing the cooperation of many foreign governments. These investigators have found that the apparently suspicious consistently proved innocuous."[32] Yet the belief in massive speculation proved durable, and references to that episode are commonly found in the literature on terrorism.[33]

Drugs and crime

The association between drug trafficking (and other criminal activities) and terrorism came naturally to those who looked at terrorist financing exclusively through a mercenary lens. The law enforcement community was conditioned to think of "drugs and thugs"—a view further internalized as money laundering tools were systematically extended to fight terrorist finance.[34] It is not surprising that most of the conventional explanations for the financing of September 11 attacks give a central role to drugs and crime. A book purporting to explain "what one needs to know about terror" asserted "a deep, symbiotic relationship between terror and the drug trade."[35] William Weschsler, the top Clinton official in charge of terrorist financing, considered drugs, and crime in general, as one of the principal ways in which Al-Qaeda generated money. He wrote: "Afghanistan is the world's leading producer of opium, and virtually all of it comes from Taliban-controlled territory, despite the fact that the Taliban claim to oppose drug production on religious grounds. Given Al Qaeda's key role in financing the Taliban, there is reason to suspect that it, too, may be involved with drug smuggling."[36] A Center for Defense Information (CDI) primer on terrorist finances stated: "Criminal activities, such as smuggling, counterfeiting and the narcotics trade, account for another large portion of terrorist funding. For instance, al Qaeda and the Taliban reportedly reaped millions of dollars a year through the production and sale of opium from Afghanistan."[37]

The connection between Al-Qaeda and the drug trade was routinely asserted yet never established empirically. In May 2001 Secretary of State Colin Powell announced $43 million in humanitarian aid to Afghanistan, including $10 million specifically in recognition of the Taliban's promise to ban poppy production.[38] It is now clear that even if they derived some income from it, the drug trade actually diminished under the Taliban—this may be perhaps the only good thing to say about their rule. Those who from a political standpoint were classified as "good guys" may in that respect have a worse track record. Indeed, a November 2004 United Nations report argued that since the fall of the Taliban, Afghanistan had become a "narco-economy."[39] The *Financial Times* wrote: "Britain, the lead nation in the anti-narcotics drive in Afghanistan, admitted that there was a risk of the opium boom re-creating the conditions that the 'war against terror' was supposed to eliminate."[40]

The 9/11 Commission Report provides the most reliable evidence to date. It states that "while the drug trade was a source of income for the Taliban, it did not serve the same purpose for al Qaeda, and there is no reliable evidence that Bin Ladin was involved in or made his money through drug trafficking."[41] As for crime and drugs as a means of financing the September 11 attacks, the report concludes: "There is no evidence to suggest that any of the hijackers engaged in any type of criminal activity to support themselves."[42]

Such evidence has done little to modify perceptions. Former "drug czar" Barry McCaffrey explained the "move toward criminal funding" in the "complimentary [sic] capabilities" of terrorists and common criminals.[43] Indeed, the first needed money, while the other generated it. The association came to be logically accepted through the very nature of the discourse on evil.[44] And whether or not the two were connected mattered little to many prosecutors, who often took advantage of a broad prosecutorial arsenal to deal with a variety of petty crimes as if they were terrorist-related.[45]

Gold and diamonds

On May 15, 2002, a United Nations report suggested a new hypothesis: "Al Qaeda may be diversifying financial aspects of its logistics support by converting parts of its assets into gold, diamonds and other precious stones, for example lapis lazuli and sapphires."[46] The report, issued by a committee set up to monitor the application of a Security Council resolution pertaining to terrorist financing,[47] was trying to elucidate an enigma: if the spigots of money destined for Al-Qaeda operatives had been shut down, how could acts of terror still occur? More specifically, there had been continuing attacks on American-led forces in Afghanistan by Taliban and Al-Qaeda fighters who could "no longer rely exclusively on stockpiles stored in caves and other places, since much of it has been seized or destroyed over the past six months."[48]

The report was careful to insist that claims related to gold and diamonds still needed to be substantiated (though it made specific recommendations to restrict the illicit transfer of money from the diamond trade, which "might be abused to provide a vehicle for money-laundering and moving financial assets around the world" [49]). Still, later references to the UN report dropped all such caveats, and the hypothesis became fact. This is how "lapis lazuli and sapphires" entered the canon of terrorist financing.[50] In fact the hypothesis of connections between the infamous "blood diamonds" and Islamic terrorism, and corrupt officials from such countries as Liberia and Sierra Leone and Al-Qaeda officials had been a staple of post-September 11 pulp fiction,[51] and had been investigated by US law enforcement and counter-terrorism officials. No evidence was ever uncovered. The September 11 Commission argued that such assertions were not plausible:

> Trafficking would unnecessarily expose al Qaeda operatives to risks of detection or arrest. Moreover, established traffickers have no reason to involve al Qaeda in their lucrative businesses; associating with the world's most hunted men would attract unwanted attention to their activities and exponentially increase the resources devoted to catching them. Furthermore, al Qaeda neither controls territory nor brings needed skills and therefore has no leverage to break into the sector.[52]

Yet the story was kept alive, if only because it fitted perfectly with the master assumption of terrorist financing—that there was a vast stash of cash being hidden somewhere.[53] Every anonymous source quoted in support of the hypothesis would offer the same analysis: "Diamonds don't set off alarms at airports. They can't be sniffed by dogs. They are easy to hide, and are highly convertible to cash. It makes perfect sense." [54] Douglas Farah, a *Washington Post* journalist, who happened to be based in Africa, and on his own admission had scant knowledge of either terrorism or the Islamic world,[55] made a new career peddling that story. He wrote: "Al-Qaida, perhaps anticipating its accounts would be frozen after the Sept. 11 terrorist attacks, sought to protect its money by sinking it into gemstones, a commodity that is easy to hide, holds its value and is almost untraceable." A variation is that the conversion from cash to precious metals took place in 1998, when Bin Laden was designated as "public enemy number 1."

Hawalas

The Money Laundering Suppression Act of 1994 required money transmittal businesses to register with the government. And according to William Wechsler, who chaired the National Security Council's working group on terrorist finances, unregulated money transfers had at least since January 1999 been identified as "a really significant problem." [56] Yet by the time of the September 11 attacks, no regulations had been issued. Regulatory agencies seemed to have little interest in the matter, and Patrick Jost, the one specialist in the subject (who had contributed to a primer on alternative remittance systems), had left government service in 2000. He later said that his superiors at the agency "did not want FinCEN to pursue this line of work."[57]

In the days following the World Trade Center attacks, there was a predictable scramble to make up for past inattentiveness to the issue. According to journalist John Cooley, "There were so few experts on hawala that a lone British former policeman, now a private detective, has flown to the US at Washington's expense at least three times to brief investigators on the system."[58] The media was full of instant and generally confused explanations of the system,[59] generally presenting it, as *Time* did, as "a banking system built for terrorism." The news magazine went on to describe hawalas as "an international underground banking system that allows money to show up in the bank accounts or pockets of men like hijacker Mohamed Atta, without leaving any paper trail. There are no contracts, bank statements or transaction records, and yet those who use the hawala networks can move thousands of dollars around the world in a matter of hours."[60] (In fact, Atta received funds through bank transfers and not hawalas.) Purported depictions were appropriately sinister:

> In the labyrinthine depths of old Delhi, where the lanes are too narrow even for a rickshaw, men drink tea and chat in shabby offices. Nobody seems to be doing any work, until the phone rings. Then, numbers are furiously scribbled, followed by some busy dialing and whispered instruction. Although it's far from obvious in the innocuous setting, these men are moving money to exporters, drug traffickers, tax evaders, corrupt politicians. And terrorists.[61]

Another characterization went as follows:

> The systems, which are also associated with graft, drug payments, and money laundering, have broad acceptance in much of South Asia and the Middle East. Because these nonbank entities have virtually no record-keeping, investigators have virtually no trail to follow. Hawala systems usually charge less than banks, and they don't maintain extensive transaction records. They keep their costs low by not requiring customer identification, conducting background checks, or reporting large or suspicious transactions to authorities.[62]

Even the basics of hawala were mangled. The *New York Times*, after running a few articles on the subject, had to issue a correction to clarify the origin and meaning of the term.[63] Creative license was never absent. Some gave the remittance system the religiously suggestive name of *hawallah*.[64] One author repeatedly called it *halawa* (which actually means sesame paste).[65]

For a while, hawalas appeared like the solution to the puzzle of terrorist financing.[66] When British officials put together a task force designed to find out the secrets of the underground hawala system, they did not hesitate to see in it a "modern-day Bletchley Park" where, in what is often considered as one of history's greatest intelligence breakthroughs, the Nazis' Enigma code was cracked.

Hawalas and other informal remittance systems had in fact long been studied by anthropologists and development scholars, and they were far less mysterious than they were made out to be. The origin of the word comes from an Arabic root meaning to change or transform (it has later been adopted into both Hindi and Urdu). Many features of hawala were described in sinister tones—"transferring money without physically moving it," "using codes," or settling periodically—although these are common features of all financial transactions. Although operating mostly within certain communities, especially when banking is too expensive, too primitive, or non-existent, they were not necessarily secret. The quest for an ideal or "pure" form of hawala[67] led to abusive generalizations. In fact, hawalas differ from place to place. They exist primarily to help expatriate workers send their paychecks home, although they do have a potential for abuse.

In reality, the role of hawalas is not different from that of money remitters such as Western Union or MoneyGram, who collect money from an individual at one point and pay it to another in another location, charging a fee for the service. Staunch free-marketeers see hawalas as exemplars of a friction-free economic system arising in response to government regulation. They point out that they are faster, cheaper, and more reliable than bank transfers. Many in financial circles noted that the hawala system "might not exist if rules and regulations didn't discourage informal-economy participants from using the banking system."[68] While better regulation and transparency are certainly called for, most attempts have been too clumsy to be successful. Most countries having extensive informal remittance systems were pressured to regulate them.[69] The bureaucratic position was that "even at its most benign, hawala cheats governments of legally owed taxes, customs duties, and other fees that are the rightful income of nations—money desperately needed, especially in the countries where it is practiced, to improve those countries' economic conditions."[70] The ensuing quasi-criminalization of the system has led it further underground, which defeated the purpose of a stringent regulation.

The September 11 Commission recognized that "some of their characteristics allow criminal activity to flourish: little formal record keeping, lack of government controls, and settling transactions that do not go through formal financial channels." Incidentally, hawalas were not involved in the funding of the September 11 plot.[71]

The rushed crackdown against Al-Barakaat,[72] the Somali company wrongly accused of being a terrorist front, stemmed from the kinds of descriptions that gained currency in the weeks after September 11, which emphasized the shady nature of hawalas. Allegations made by the President of the United States when he announced the closure of the company—that no records of transactions were kept, and that hawalas were storefront side businesses fronting for wealthy banks[73]—proved wrong: the later inquiry showed that ample documentation was kept, and that hawalas were actually a large (by Somali standards), above-board business, since remittances from expatriate labor were the largest source of revenue for the country.[74]

Islamic banks

To those who were quick to associate anything Islamic with terrorism, Islamic banks and financial institutions provided a logical target. In a climate of generalized suspicion, Islamic banks—and more generally banks from the Islamic world—were considered guilty until proven innocent. Virtually every work in the "secrets of terrorist financing" genre made such allegations.[75] The *Wall Street Journal* reported that the US Treasury had asked foreign bank regulators, including the Saudi Arabian Monetary Authority, to place Islamic banks under close surveillance.[76]

The general level of ignorance on the subject is epitomized by a statement made by former National Security Adviser Sandy Berger shortly after September 11. The top official in charge of the surveillance of Bin Laden's networks during his tenure at the White House (1996–2000) casually stated that it would be difficult to track down Bin Laden's money because it was hidden in "underground banking, Islamic banking facilities."[77] And it took six months for Treasury Secretary Paul O'Neill, the official in charge of the financial war on terror, to "learn," in March 2002 following meetings in Saudi Arabia, Kuwait, and Bahrain, that Islamic banking is "a legitimate way of doing business."[78] Since that time, the US Treasury has established a scholar-in-residence position to provide better understanding and awareness of Islamic finance,[79] and a growing number of regulators within the United States have expressed their "openness to Islamic financial products"—which in the Islamophobic literature was promptly called "playing into the hands of bin Laden."[80]

The blow to the Islamic finance industry was considerable, since it had been, prior to September 11, well integrated into the global economy, and had been generally regarded as an effective way of countering Islamic extremism.[81] At a November 2001 Islamic Banking Conference in Bahrain, two of the most prominent figures in Islamic finance expressed dismay at the smear campaigns against their institutions. Prince Muhammed Al-Faisal declared: "We all condemn the September 11 attack on the World Trade Center and Pentagon as a heinous crime, which has nothing to do with Islam or Muslims as a whole. The West is raising various questions. But these questions are not raised with us, but with 'experts' who do not know anything about this." Asked about the freezing of assets of some Islamic institutions, he said: "If they wanted to do it merely on the basis of suspicion let them do it. Of course, it is fair to freeze anyone's assets if there is proof and there should be remedy if they do so without any proof." As for Sheikh Saleh Kamel, founder of the Al Baraka Group, and chairman of the General Council for Islamic Banks and Financial Institutions (GCIBFI), he declared: "The concept of Islamic banking is one of the creative methods of Islam to serve the economic and social welfare of Muslims. But some circles tried to use the September 11 attacks to launch a campaign under the false pretext that these Islamic banks are the source for financing terrorism." [82]

6

Dynamics of the Financial War

The ceremony of innocence is drowned;
The best lack all conviction, while the worst
Are full of passionate intensity.
W.B. Yeats

Urbane guerrillas in dark suits, they fought not with AK-47s but with memos,
position papers, talking points, and news leaks. It was unrestricted
warfare; there was no rule book.
Richard Perle

Let's pick on the Saudis for a moment. I loooove to pick on the Saudis.
Ron Motley

George W. Bush told journalist Bob Woodward of his reaction when, on the morning of September 11, 2001, he was informed that a second plane had hit the World Trade Center: "They had declared war on us, and I made up my mind at that moment that we were going to war."[1] War connotes seriousness of purpose; it stifles dissent and turns the world into a battleground; it also provides ample legal cover (as in classifying prisoners of war as "enemy combatants," and engaging in constitutionally dubious practices in the name of the war effort).[2] "We're at war" and "we have been attacked" became all-purpose justifications. The good vs. evil rhetoric further raised the stakes. As noted by Andrew Bacevich, such rhetoric "exempts [leaders] from the moral ambiguity inherent in the exercise of power. It exempts them from rules to which others must adhere. In the pursuit of exalted ends, the use of questionable means becomes permissible."[3] The "new kind of war" was constantly invoked but seldom defined. Former Senators Warren Rudman and Gary Hart, who led the Commission on National Security/21st Century, which in 1999 had warned against a major attack on US soil, wrote: "we face a threat that is neither conventional war nor traditional crime, and that combating it requires new government structures, new policies and new thinking."[4] In July 2005 serious consideration was given to retiring the global war on terror slogan, but top advisers were overruled by President Bush, who insisted: "We're still at war."[5]

The financial war has involved numerous government agencies and countless constituencies. Its multiple dynamics—political, bureaucratic, legal—were all dominated by martial overtones.

Martial finance

Days after the World Trade Center and Pentagon attacks, Donald Rumsfeld wrote that "the uniforms of this conflict will be bankers' pinstripes and programmers' grunge just as assuredly as desert camouflage."[6] It was revealing that such a statement was made by the Defense Secretary, since the Pentagon took on the lead role in all aspects of the war on terror—indeed of foreign policy—including some unlikely ones, such as the Iraqi reconstruction.[7] From the start of the war on terror, the realm of finance had taken on martial overtones.[8] When the Financial Action Task Force (FATF) was asked to supervise the worldwide effort against terrorist financing, its president, Claire Lo, vowed to "strangle" terrorist funding networks and announced grandly: "We all know that the stakes are high. We all know that the world is watching. And we all know that we must deliver."[9]

Martial finance was perpetuated by the emergence of a powerful military-industrial-security complex, driven by unprecedented defense and homeland security spending,[10] a growing militaristic culture,[11] and, last but not least, the vested interests of many cheerleaders of omni-directional belligerence, such as Richard Perle and James Woolsey, whose business ventures and interests stood to benefit handsomely from militarization.[12]

Journalists took to describing the financial warriors in swashbuckling terms. One could frequently come across statements such as this:

> As U.S. soldiers gird for an airborne assault on Osama Bin Laden's strongholds in Afghanistan, another army has set about breaching the Saudi renegade's defenses on another front—his finances. The terrain that this global alliance of forensic accountants, banking experts, and spies must reconnoiter is, in many ways, as forbidding as the mountainous hinterland of Afghanistan. A maze of front organizations, shell companies, and underground banking networks shields the money from view, say investigators.[13]

Much has been said about the new elites that have come to dominate US foreign policy and wage the "war on terror" in the wake of September 11, and the extent to which they differ from the genteel post-World War II establishment.[14] One aspect that has generally been ignored has to do with attitudes towards economics and finance. The "wise men" who shaped the post-World War II order were typically products of the establishment—investment bankers and Wall Street lawyers—with a practical understanding of finance and economics.[15] In contrast, the post-September 11 foreign policy establishment was dominated by "defense intellectuals" who tended to view the world through martial lenses.[16] Their main characteristics are a highly ideological view of the world, a dogmatic belief in the role and utility of raw military power, and a dismissive attitude towards diplomacy and soft power.[17]

Martial tropes shaped decision making on matters of finance, and military metaphors were routinely used. There was constant talk of "disrupting financial networks." The appropriateness of "disruption"—which is "a preemptive, offensive form of counterterrorism," a means of harassing terrorists around the world, "of [flushing] them out of hiding so that cooperative police forces or secret services can then arrest and imprison them" [18]—to the realm of finance is questionable. It does, however, conjure up another image, one that flourished in the early days of the Iraq invasion, that of "shock and awe." In a book of that title written in 1996 by military strategist Harlan Ullman and co-author James P. Wade, it is defined as "very selective, utterly brutal and ruthless and rapid application of force to intimidate"—certainly an apt description of sudden financial blitzes.[19]

The financial war was conceived as a vast "search and destroy" mission. Addressing some of the world's top bankers, David Aufhauser, General Counsel at the US Treasury, suggested they model their approach to catching terror money on the military. Just as 24-hour aerial surveillance can allow American troops to detect, home in on, and bomb terrorists on the basis of a clue as tiny as a tire-track in a desert, banks ought to use the same technology on their customers.[20] On other occasions, Aufhauser referred to section 311 of the USA PATRIOT legislation, which can require US financial institutions to take special measures with respect to "primary money laundering concerns" as the "smart bomb" of terrorist financing, which can be directed against a country, an institution, or a practice, and require special measures, ranging from increased record keeping and reporting obligations, to enhanced due diligence, to termination of banking relationships.[21] By the same token, former counter-terrorism czar Richard Clarke called the ability to freeze dollar accounts of foreign banks "the nuclear bomb of the international finance industry" since it "effectively kills a financial institution." [22] Financial initiatives were actually patterned on military expeditions. The commitment of ground forces in Afghanistan—"boots on the ground" [23]— was paralleled by the Treasury Department promptly dispatching dozens of "jump teams," consisting of technicians, legal experts, and senior officials, to foreign countries to help "identify, disrupt, and defeat" terrorist financing networks.[24]

Politics

The financial war, though usually discussed in a technical and politically neutral manner, was from the start thoroughly politicized. The Bush administration clearly understood the political and electoral advantages of the language of the war on terror.[25] The constant invocation of the terrorist threat reinforced the executive and stifled dissent. And the war on terror undoubtedly helped the "war president" and his party in the 2002 and 2004 elections. As the 2006 elections approach, the low standing of the President and the Republican Party in the polls led them to ratchet up the fear factor. Security alerts suddenly became more frequent. Following the disclosure of a London plot to blow up ten aircraft over the Atlantic, George W. Bush declared: "This nation is at war with Islamic fascists who will use any means to destroy those of us who love freedom." Voters were constantly reminded that the threat was comparable to that posed by fascism and communism, that critics of the Iraq war were "appeasers," and that Democrats were "soft on terror."[26] And as already mentioned, the very nature of the financial front made it irresistible for politicians eager to project forcefulness and decisiveness—or to change the subject. Most significant financial strikes had some hidden political significance. The "first strike" of September 24, 2001 is a case in point. What happened behind the scenes, and which only transpired following the publication of insider memoirs, reveals political maneuvers belied by official declarations.

The context is well known. Despite repeated warnings of an impending devastating attack on US soil,[27] little had been done by way of prevention by an administration then fixated on Iraq.[28] The unheeded intelligence indicated that Al-Qaeda had organized the attacks. Yet the network was shadowy and the whereabouts of Usama Bin Laden were unknown. A military strike against Afghanistan was not immediately feasible.[29] Chaos and confusion reigned in the White House, yet there was an urgent need to show resolve and clear headedness. A New York Times editorial summarized the popular mood: "In the days ahead, Mr. Bush ... must show that he knows what he is doing."[30]

The financial front was thus, by default, where the first show of force would take place. Unlike military operations against the Taliban regime, which required further logistical and political preparation,[31] the financial war could be started right away, since there was an off-the-shelf, ready-to-use set of anti-money laundering policies that had been used, unsuccessfully by most accounts, against drug traffickers.[32] An existing template along with a considerable bureaucratic apparatus could be instantly deployed—never mind that those who would lead the money laundering offensive had been previously bent on dismantling these financial controls.[33]

According to Bob Woodward's fly-on-the-wall account of presidential decision-making, the idea of a "scorecard" was first floated during a meeting of the National Security Council in the White House the day after the attacks. President Bush said that he wanted "a realistic scorecard" and "a list of thugs" to be targeted. "The American people want a big bang," he said. "I have to convince them that this is a war that will be fought with many steps."[34] On Friday, September 21, at a Camp David meeting of the National Security Council, "the scorecard" took center stage. The mood was bleak. There was a pressing need to show progress, despite the fact that "the intelligence was thin gruel" and that George Tenet, the head of the CIA, "had nothing of consequence." Woodward writes: "The president told them about the need to find a way to show visible progress in the war on terror, on their terms. ... He wanted to talk results. He wanted something up on the scoreboard. 'I want the people involved with the operations to know that I am going to be watching.'"[35] Throughout the meeting, George W. Bush kept returning to the issue of terrorist financing: "Disruption of financial networks needs to be a tool in our arsenal. It's important. We must use it." The political resonance of the issue was not lost on him. Unlike a military strike, the financial strike "was something that could be done immediately."[36] International cooperation was needed "to disrupt the networks of funding." He advised the participants: "Look, if countries are reluctant, let us know. Put it on my call list."[37]

The following day, when the President inquired about the "scorecard," he was told that 417 people had been arrested and 331 others placed on watch. So as many as 15 times the number of terrorists who carried out the September 11 attacks had been in the US, perhaps ready to strike. This would not be disclosed to the public. The need to change the subject led once more to the financial terrain. Treasury officials worked frantically to establish a list of terrorist accounts to be frozen. Author Ron Suskind, in his book *The Price of Loyalty*, which is based on Treasury Secretary Paul O'Neill's recollections, describes the mood: "Since the President needed some assets to point to ... all there was to do was seize some assets, and quickly."[38] In the words of General Counsel David Aufhauser, "It was almost comical. We just listed out as many of the usual suspects as we could and said, Let's go freeze some of their assets."[39]

The initial plan was to have the Treasury Secretary announce it in a press conference. But on Sunday, September 23, a "snappy" George W. Bush called Communications Director Karen Hughes to express his displeasure:

"You all don't get it." Her draft statement "missed the point. This was no ordinary bit of business ... —it was big news, and they had to make it so. This is the first bullet in the war against terrorism. This is the first strike. It's not with guys in uniform. It's guys in pinstripes. This will hone in on the fact that this is a completely different kind of war. I should be making this announcement." [40] Not surprisingly, the practical impact on terrorist financing was virtually nil. [41] The intended impact was political and symbolic. It had the effect of reassuring the public that forceful action had been taken and that the terrorist threat had been reduced.

Bureaucratic dynamics

At the time of the September 11 attacks, the Bush administration was bent on shrinking the anti-money laundering apparatus. [42] A 1997 government estimate by the State Department's Bureau of Narcotics and Law Enforcement Affairs estimated that "nearly 5,000 personnel—from at least 75 agencies—are directly involved at the federal and state levels in the prevention and detection of money laundering and the enforcement of anti-money laundering laws." [43] In 2001 some $700 million went to the collection and management of data from financial institutions around the globe and to the screening of such data for irregular activities. In the words of former Treasury Secretary Paul O'Neill, "These huge data grabs and enormous resources had yielded very little. We've invested a lot in this technique, but it doesn't mean it works." [44]

The September 11 attacks caused a sharp policy U-turn: instead of dismantling money laundering bureaucracies, the Bush administration reinvigorated them. They were put in charge of terrorist financing, and the new mission soon crowded out their primary role of fighting financial crime. As we saw earlier, the "trained incapacity" phenomenon created countless dysfunctions. Not only was the money laundering logic ill suited to the new task, but the functional, linguistic, and cultural skills of existing bureaucracies, all geared towards Latin America, were of little use in dealing with an issue involving the Islamic world. [45]

Students of bureaucracies would easily recognize what happened next. Over a period of weeks, new inter-agency teams, as well as new programs and agencies, such as Operation Green Quest, the Foreign Terrorist Asset Tracking Center (FTAT), the Terrorist Financing Task Force, the Terrorist Finance Tracking Program, etc, were created to "identify, disrupt and defeat" terrorist financing networks. [46] The same phenomenon occurred at international and regional levels. The Financial Action Task Force (FATF), the Paris-based organization that had been "naming and shaming" nations into adopting anti-money laundering rules, was now entrusted with doing the same for terrorist financing. Every country was pressured to adopt new laws to create new "anti-money laundering and combating the financing of terrorism" (AML/CFT) bureaucracies. At regional levels, FATF-like organizations proliferated, driven by political and financial inducements.[47]

At a time of continued downsizing of the public sector, where government agencies had to fight hard to justify their funding, the financial war was a boon to bureaucracies. In 2003 no fewer than 20 government entities in the United States were in charge of deterring terrorist financing.[48] Inter-agency fights were greatly complicated by the creation of the Department of Homeland Security (the greatest government reorganization since World War II) and the restructuring of intelligence. In some ways, the war on terror was a worthy successor to the war on drugs, which was described by T.D. Allman as "another entitlement program for the Washington policy-spinners—grabbing appropriations and generating comforting press releases year after year."[49]

The bureaucratic propensity for mission creep went almost unchecked as agencies expanded their domestic and international roles. Thus, while fighting accusations about intelligence lapses in the days before September 11, the FBI could announce in October 2002 that the global war on terror made it necessary to open a liaison office in China.[50] Missions expanded in line with the escalation of the war on terror. As Iraq became the central front of that war, the money warriors embraced this expansion of their mission to a massive "asset recovery mission" with gusto—just as Iraq evolved into what was called a "free fraud zone."[51] Mission creep turned into mission inebriation. In the words of Juan Zarate, Assistant Secretary Terrorist Financing and Financial Crimes at the Treasury Department,

> The identification, freezing, and transfer of Iraqi assets remains a priority for this Administration for several reasons. It is critical that the Iraqi people have access to funds that are rightfully theirs—so that they can rebuild a country burdened by a dictator's decades of neglect. This is also essential to prevent any such former regime assets from being used to fund the Iraqi insurgency and to keep them out of the hands of terrorists both within and outside Iraq. The international community cannot permit these assets to be used against our troops, coalition partners, and innocent civilians in Iraq, or potentially to support the nefarious activities of terrorists around the world. Moreover, the efforts of the international community to identify and repatriate assets stolen by Saddam Hussein and his former regime serve as a strong warning to other tyrants and kleptocrats, who might seek to loot their countries and hide the stolen assets in the international financial system. Lessons learned by the U.S. and the international community in the hunt for Iraqi assets will serve as a model, both for the U.S. Government and for the international community, on how to respond and identify, trace, freeze, and repatriate national patrimony stolen by corrupt despots in the future.[52]

The new bureaucratic environment was an odd mix of the old and the new, of the normal and the exceptional: turf battles among agencies, self-perpetuation, power grabs, hoarding of information, etc,[53] coexisted with the injunction to "think outside the box" and an unprecedented political visibility, which also drove an unceasing quest for "trophies"—evidence that something was being done about terrorist financing. Further, the war on terror being a matter of vital interest, the financial warriors had a somewhat privileged status: no cost-benefit analyses were involved in assessing the usefulness of bureaucracies and their decisions were seldom subjected to second guessing.

The desire to act aggressively and "think outside the box" led to the appointment to high political positions of many alumni of the Iran–Contra scandal and of the Central American "dirty wars" of the 1980s.[54] Shortly after the September 11 attacks, Elliott Abrams who in 1987 had pleaded guilty to two misdemeanor counts of unlawfully withholding information from Congress, was appointed Senior Director for Near East and North African Affairs at the National Security Council. At the start of George W. Bush's second term, he was promoted to be his deputy national security adviser, in charge of the "global democracy strategy." [55] John Negroponte, who as ambassador to Honduras in the 1980s had been involved in the covert funding of the Nicaraguan Contras, was named ambassador to the United Nations, then ambassador to Iraq, before becoming in Febuary 2005 the first Director of National Intelligence, a position created following a recommendation of the 9/11 Commission. One of the most illustrious architects of the Iran–Contra scheme, retired Admiral John Poindexter, who served as national security adviser to President Ronald Reagan and was sentenced to six months in jail for lying to Congress (a conviction overturned on appeal), was named Director of the DARPA (Defense Advance Research Projects Agency) Information Awareness Office.[56] These appointments led Calvin Trillin to write: "So Elliott Abrams (the felon) is back, And Poindexter's now a big cheese, High level appointments now favor the guys, With rap sheets instead of CVs." [57]

DARPA's vocation was to come up with unusual ideas, but Poindexter's initiatives, both half-baked and grandiose, may have exceeded the agency's mission. At first came a massive computerized surveillance project, known as the "Total Information Awareness" program, a Big Brother-like project meant to collect information about potential terrorist threats by tapping into computer databases to collect financial data, and medical, travel, and credit records. Dossiers would thus be compiled on millions of US citizens. After criticisms in the media and in Congress over invasions of privacy issues, the project was modified and its name changed to the "Terrorism Information

Awareness" program with a pledge not to snoop on citizens.[58]

What proved too much was the creation of a "market in terrorism." The project which appeared under a DARPA division called FutureMAP, or "Futures Markets Applied to Prediction," was designed to enhance the work of intelligence agencies, perhaps even helping foil terrorist attacks. Traders would buy and sell one-year futures contracts based on what might happen in Egypt, Jordan, Iran, Iraq, Israel, Saudi Arabia, Syria, and Turkey in terms of economics, civil and military affairs, or specific events, such as terrorist attacks, coups, or assassinations. Examples given were the overthrow of the King of Jordan or the assassination of Yasser Arafat. Anyone could trade, according to the website, provided they registered and deposited funds in a trading account.[59] Organizers were especially keen to attract people with special knowledge or interest in the Middle East. According to the project's now defunct website, "Whatever a prospective trader's interest ... involvement in this group prediction process should prove engaging and may prove profitable." [60] Based on the view that markets "are extremely efficient, effective and timely aggregators of dispersed and even hidden information ... often better than expert opinions," such a market would be a sensible way of predicting acts of terror, as well as the evolution of the political situation in a very dangerous part of the world.[61]

Little thought was given to the fact that such a scheme could create a new class of terrorists, who would foment acts of terror for speculative gain. Terrorists could also disseminate disinformation while distracting attention from their real target. A public outcry followed the disclosure of the project, which was shelved, also leading to the departure of Poindexter.

Enter the lawyers ...

"Terrorists who might be undeterred by the threat of American military force must now weigh the possibility of retaliation by the world's largest contingent of lawyers." Thus wrote attorney Allan Gerson in *The Price of Terror*, the account of his protracted legal battle against Libya following the Lockerbie explosion of PanAm flight 103.[62] Along with lead attorney Ron Motley, famous for forcing asbestos companies, and later tobacco companies, to pay billions of dollars to settle massive lawsuits, Gerson filed what he called "the lawsuit of the twenty-first century"—another attempt at using US courts to redress the problem of global terror.

On August 15, 2002, a 258-page complaint, filed in the US District Court in Alexandria, Virginia, sought "an amount in excess of $100 trillion" from some 80 defendants.[63] (A correction was later issued: because of a "clerical error," the actual amount sought was only $1 trillion.)[64] The list of defendants included three Saudi princes (former intelligence chief

Turki bin Faisal al-Saud, second Deputy Prime Minister, and Defense Minister Sultan bin Abdul Aziz al-Saud, and banker Mohammed bin Faisal al-Saud[65]), the government of Sudan, the Saudi Binladin Group, a number of Middle Eastern financial institutions, and eight Islamic foundations. They were accused of racketeering, wrongful death, negligence, and conspiracy.[66] Calling themselves "The 9/11 Families United to Bankrupt Terrorism," the plaintiffs alleged that Saudi money had "for years been funneled to encourage radical anti-Americanism as well as to fund the al Qaida terrorists." The suit, modeled on the successful legal action against Libya, aimed "to force the sponsors of terror into the light and subject them to the rule of law" by seeking unprecedented damages.[67]

The government-funded victim compensation fund created following the September 11 tragedy had shielded certain parties such as airlines from lawsuits, but not terror financiers. In the words of one World Trade Center widow, "It was stated very specifically that we couldn't sue anything domestic. But anything that had to do with funding terrorism, any terrorist nation, terrorist financers, we could go ahead and sue." [68] True to "Sutton's Law," [69] the deep pockets of individuals, organizations and states accused of funding terror created an irresistible opportunity. Following the September 11 attacks, a number of lawyers (who stood to pocket one-third of the settlements) canvassed the survivors of the victims of the tragedy and devised strategies for hard-hitting, high-profile lawsuits.

The first post-September 11 lawsuit in New York against Afghanistan (as well as Usama Bin Laden and Al-Qaeda)[70] was filed before the passage of the USA PATRIOT Act, and went nowhere, because Afghanistan was not on the State Department's list of countries supporting terrorism. But the passage of the USA PATRIOT legislation[71] further eased the ground for massive lawsuits—in effect for the internationalization of American tort law. Addressing the questions posed by the "lawsuit of the twenty-first century" journalist Jennifer Senior wrote:

> Assuming the answer [to the question of the sponsorship of terror] is Saudi Arabia, what does that make Motley's case, exactly? A glorified, globalized tort suit? Or an example of a new wartime jurisprudence, one that fights terrorism with lawyers as well as guns and statesmen? The answer, in a sense, is both, and it could be the new way of the world. Those who take a dim view of Motley's work, dismissing it as nothing more than worldwide ambulance chasing, will be startled to learn that it is theoretically possible, in today's borderless society, to follow a screaming siren all the way to Riyadh.[72]

Many copycat suits inevitably followed. Another trillion-dollar suit, filed on September 4, 2002, was noteworthy because it focused on Iraq's alleged role in the September 11 attacks.[73] The suit was brought by the firm Kreindler

& Kreindler, a New York law firm specializing in aviation disaster litigation, in the US District Court in Manhattan, and charged that Iraqi government officials knew about plans for the attacks. It sought more than a trillion dollars in damages, naming as defendants Iraq, the Iraqi intelligence agency, Saddam Hussein and his sons, Al-Qaeda Islamic Army, Usama Bin Laden, the estates of the hijackers, the Taliban, and organizations that financed the attacks. According to the suit, "Since Iraq could not defeat the U.S. military, it resorted to terror attacks on U.S. citizens." The complaint traced what it termed "close contacts" between Al-Qaeda and the Iraqi regime over a ten-year period. According to attorney James P. Kreindler, "This is a seething network of murderers who have penetrated Iraq and Middle Eastern countries, and it couldn't have happened without the approval of Saddam Hussein." [74]

Other lawsuits against alleged sponsors and financiers of terror were filed by specific industries or companies. And many more are likely to be filed by lawyers lured by the possibility of a windfall. A $300 billion lawsuit was brought by insurance companies against terrorist groups, companies, and countries supporting terrorism.[75] Cantor Fitzgerald Securities, a bond trading firm which lost 658 of its 1,050 employees on September 11, sought in a $7 billion lawsuit filed in US District Court in Manhattan to hold the Saudi government along with dozens of defendants accountable on the grounds that the kingdom "knew and intended that these Saudi-based charity and relief organization defendants would provide financial and material support and substantial assistance to al-Qaeda." [76] The country was accused of materially supporting Al-Qaeda by helping to raise money for it, by knowingly and intentionally employing Al-Qaeda operatives, by laundering its money, and by providing Al-Qaeda with safe houses, false documents, and ways to obtain weapons and military equipment, and engaging in a pattern of racketeering as it participated directly or indirectly in al-Qaeda's work through its "alter-ego" charities and relief organizations, which it funded and controlled.[77]

On the surface, the lawsuits related to the sponsoring or financing of terror pursue the same agenda as the administration. In the words of attorney Allan Gerson, "If you hit people in the pocketbook, it will have a deterrent effect. If you pay a lot of money, you won't sponsor terrorism in the future." [78] Indeed, by aiming to strike a fatal blow at the abettors of acts of terror, they are in line with the view that such abettors are just as guilty as the perpetrators. Some of the lawyers have also trumpeted their desire to get to the bottom of the question of terrorist financing. According to Gerson, "We're trying to expose the extent, the depth, the orchestration, the financial support that terrorist organizations have received for perhaps a decade from various Saudi interests." [79]

In reality the administration was critical of the highest-profile lawsuits, leading to sharp exchanges. It even tried to argue that those who were party to such lawsuits might forfeit their right to compensation from the Victim Compensation Fund. Attorney Ron Motley went as far as accusing the government of protecting its "gangster" friends in Riyadh.[80] The official position of the American government had always been that such private initiatives would stand in the way of US diplomatic efforts. In this particular instance, the heavy emphasis on Saudi Arabia was unwelcome. It risked upsetting the traditionally good US relations with that country; it placed the spotlight on the necessary yet controversial alliance; and it raised yet again the touchy issue of the close business and personal ties between the Bush family and the Saudi elites.[81] Another issue, although many prominent Republican lawmakers favored the suit,[82] is the support of many in the administration for a reform of a tort system which allows for such mammoth lawsuits.

In parallel, the "six degrees of separation" logic unleashed by the financial war made it possible to file lawsuits against banks that held accounts of people or organizations "linked" to terror. The Jordan-based Arab Bank found itself sued because it held accounts of Islamic charities, which were accused of organizing funding drives for families of suicide bombers whose houses were destroyed by the Israeli government.[83]

Perhaps the main problem with such lawsuits (which some defendants have called extortion pure and simple[84]) is that they lead to further disinformation. Considering the highly charged cases and the considerable stakes involved, the quest for truth takes a back seat to a winning-at-all-costs strategy. In straining to connect dots, the temptation to cut corners is great. As a result, the fog of financial war can only get thicker. Celebrity attorneys seeking sensationalism know how to play on emotions and on general ignorance of a complex subject. Media-savvy attorneys write op-ed pieces,[85] and plant stories in the media to further their case. They can put forth crackpot theories and dubious experts.[86] The anti-Saudi lawsuit used a sensation-seeking writer as "chief investigator,"[87] and focused heavily on the controversial Defense Policy Board briefing by Laurent Murawiec to prove the nefarious role played by the Saudis.[88] The overarching theme was that the Saudis tolerated, even sponsored, the export of terror in exchange for leaving the Saudi regime alone.[89]

In the "lawsuit of the twenty-first century," the stated objective is to convince juries of an oversimplified storyline which has been repeated so often that it has become utterly plausible. Addressing families of victims, attorney Ron Motley explained his strategy against a screen showing heaving smokestacks and tangled pipes:

Here's how I would explain to a jury all this legal mumbo jumbo. This is a terrorist factory. Let's call it Al Qaeda Inc. And those smokestacks are spewing out terror, hatred, jihad, suicide bombers. So who's liable if you've lost a loved one to Al Qaeda Inc.? It's the bank that loaned the money. It's the architect who designed the factory, knowing it was going to be spewing out hatred. It's the suppliers who supplied the factory with ingredients to manufacture terrorist acts. They're all responsible, each and every one. That's the law of the United States.[90]

Most likely, the case will never go to trial, but the lawyers, who as of early 2004 had sunk $12 million into the case, gamble that the size of out-of-court settlements will justify the expense.[91]

As for the lawsuit against Iraqi leaders, it was based on a theory about links between Iraq and Al-Qaeda that has been thoroughly discredited. The most specific accusations were based on an article which appeared in an obscure Iraqi newspaper.[92] In May 2003 US District Judge Harold Baer ordered a number of defendants, including Usama Bin Laden, Al-Qaeda, the Taliban, Saddam Hussein, and the former Iraqi government to pay nearly $104 million to families of two September 11 victims.[93] In his ruling, the judge concluded that the lawyers, who had relied heavily on "classical hearsay" evidence, "have shown, albeit barely ... that Iraq provided material support to bin Laden and Al Qaida" and collaborated in or supported the September 11 attacks. So not only was there a contradiction between the judge's ruling and all the available evidence, but there was also a clash between the ruling and stated US policy, which was that frozen Iraqi funds would be earmarked for the country's reconstruction.

PART IV
WAR AND CONSEQUENCES

7

Targets and Collateral Damage

To be sure of hitting the target, shoot first, and call whatever you hit the target.
Ashleigh Brilliant

When a particular problem is intractable, enlarge it.
Donald Rumsfeld

The strong do what they can; the weak suffer what they must.
Thucydides

This chapter addresses two related themes that have been largely absent from the discussion of the war on terror: the disconnect between guilt and retribution, and the collateral damage caused by the financial war. Although financial strikes can cause considerable economic, political, and psychological damage, such damage is easy to ignore. Money warriors reap high bureaucratic and political rewards from their actions, and have little sense of the damage they inflict on distant lands. Abusive classifications and false positives go unnoticed. The nature of the financial front has turned it into a favorite punching bag, a favorable terrain for punitive expeditions, where the many are punished for the sins of the few. The case of Al-Barakaat, the Somali remittance company wrongly accused of being a secret financier of Al-Qaeda, vividly illustrates the asymmetry: the high-profile closure of the company was presented as a triumph, yet it brought further devastation to one of the world's poorest countries.

Prevention, retribution, and punitive warfare

On the morning of September 11, the President of the United States report-edly told the Vice-President: "We're at war. ... Somebody's going to pay." [1] When Defense Secretary Donald Rumsfeld cautioned George W. Bush that international law allowed the use of force only to prevent future attacks and

not for retribution, this is how, according to counter-terrorism czar Richard
Clarke's account, the President reacted: "Bush nearly bit his head off. 'No,'
the President yelled in the narrow conference room, 'I don't care what the
international lawyers say, we are going to kick some ass.'" [2] Rumsfeld himself
would soon drop any such objections. A few days later, he advocated bombing Iraq for the simple reason that "there aren't any good targets in Afghanistan. And there are lots of good targets in Iraq." [3]

Such views soon permeated the top echelons of the administration. In his
book Bush At War, journalist Bob Woodward describes how Deputy Defense
Secretary Paul Wolfowitz, a leading neo-conservative, pressed Bush as early
as September 15, 2001 to attack Iraq rather than Afghanistan because it
would be easier: "He worried about 100,000 American troops bogged down
in mountain fighting in Afghanistan six months from then. Iraq was a brit-
tle oppressive regime that might break easily. It was doable." [4] Douglas J.
Feith, the third-ranking Pentagon official and also a neo-conservative, went
one step further. In a September 20 memo revealed by the 9/11 Commission
Report, he "expressed disappointment at the limited options immediately
available in Afghanistan and the lack of ground options," suggesting instead
"hitting terrorists outside the Middle East in the initial offensive, perhaps
deliberately selecting a non-al Qaeda target like Iraq." Feith's views were
notable because he even suggested hitting targets far removed geographically
from the perpetrators' base. He wrote: "Since U.S. attacks were expected in
Afghanistan, an American attack in South America or Southeast Asia might
be a surprise to the terrorists." [5]

One of the most influential right-wing ideologues, Michael Ledeen, holder
of the American Freedom Chair at the American Enterprise Institute, alum-
nus of Iran–Contra, and author of a guide to winning the war against the
"terror masters," [6] summarized his view as follows: "Every 10 years or so, the
United States needs to pick up some small crappy little country and throw it
against the wall, just to show the world we mean business." [7] In the days after
September 11, the mood in the country was amenable to such attitudes, and
neither the elites nor the general public seemed very discerning when it came
to targets. Popular right-wing talk-radio host Michael Savage took to railing
against "Turd" World immigrants.[8] On September 16, the Sikh owner of
a gas station was killed in Mesa, Arizona. Countless attacks, physical and
verbal, were reported against Arab Americans, South Asian Americans,
and other people, Muslim and non-Muslim, who looked "Middle Eastern." [9]
Representative John Cooksey, Republican of Louisiana, declared: "If I see a
guy come in that's got a diaper on his head and a fan belt wrapped around
the diaper on his head, that guy needs to be pulled over and checked." [10]

On September 12, neo-conservative intellectual Robert Kagan, who would soon emerge as one of the most influential theorists of unilateralism and the systematic use of force, wrote in the *Washington Post*: "Let's not be daunted by the mysterious and partially hidden identity of our attackers. ... Congress should immediately declare war. It does not have to name a country." [11] The same day, Democratic Senator Zell Miller of Georgia declared, "I say, bomb the hell out of them. If there's collateral damage, so be it." Throughout the 1990s, collateral damage had been a popular euphemism to account for the fact that even "surgical" strikes could hit innocent bystanders. It became the vague and sanitized reference to an ugly by-product of war, where innocents were killed and maimed alongside the intended target, and sometimes instead of it. Sanctions routinely hit the wrong target. An *Oil & Gas Journal* editorial summarized the logic as being akin to "kicking the household cat because a stray mongrel bites a pedestrian down the road." [12]

After September 11, causing collateral damage was precisely the point. Thomas Friedman, the *New York Times* foreign affairs columnist, who had been on every possible side of the Iraq war, came to the conclusion that "the 'real reason' for this war, which was never stated, was that after 9/11 America needed to hit someone in the Arab-Muslim world." "[Go] into the heart of the Arab-Muslim world, house to house, and make clear that we are ready to kill," was the message, one addressed among others to those "who thought allowing Muslim charities to raise money for ... 'martyrs' was O.K." The columnist concluded: "And don't believe the nonsense that this had no effect. Every neighboring government—and 98 percent of terrorism is about what governments let happen—got the message." [13]

The Al-Barakaat case

The highest-profile case in the financial war on terror was undoubtedly that of Al-Barakaat. On November 7, 2001 President George W. Bush, flanked by Treasury Secretary Paul O'Neill, Secretary of State Colin Powell, and Attorney General John Ashcroft, announced: "Today, we are taking another step in our fight against evil." Simultaneous police raids in the United States—Massachusetts, Minnesota, Washington, and Ohio—and overseas—Canada, Italy, Switzerland, and the United Arab Emirates—had shut down Al-Barakaat, a Somali remittance network headquartered in Dubai. In addition, 62 organizations and individuals had their assets frozen.[14] The moves were the result of "solid and credible" evidence that the organizations named were operating "at the service of mass murderers." President Bush added: "By shutting these networks down, we disrupt the murderers' work." More specifically, "Today's action interrupts Al-Qaeda's communications, it blocks an important source of funds, it provides us with valuable information." [15] A long list of accusations followed: Al-Barakaat was skimming money from transactions to fund Al-Qaeda; it provided Internet services, and was even involved in shipping weapons to terrorists. Prosecutors in Boston also charged two brothers, Muhamed and Liban Hussein, with running an unlicensed money-transmittal business, Al-Barakaat North America, in Massachusetts. The first was arrested and held without bail and in solitary confinement. The second happened to be in Canada where he was held in custody before a possible extradition to the United States.

President Bush reiterated his "clear message to global financial institutions: You are with us, or you are with the terrorists. And if you're with the terrorists, you will face the consequences." Treasury Secretary Paul O'Neill described the company as the "the quartermasters of terror" and called it "a pariah in the civilized world."[16] All the specific characteristics of the company—its modest storefront operations, its involvement in telecommunications, etc—were made to fit within the broader terrorist-financing narrative. In the feeding frenzy that followed, more alarming details surfaced. It was suggested that the company was founded and partly owned by Usama Bin Laden himself.[17] The scale and scope of the alleged fundraising efforts were said to be substantial: officials said that 5 percent of every transaction was skimmed, thus providing $15–25 million annually to Al-Qaeda.

Shutting down Al-Barakaat was hailed by the government and the media as a resounding success. Administration officials asserted that it had made a significant dent in Al-Qaeda's finances, and that it was "a shining example of what President Bush's financial campaign against terrorism is aimed at: an organization with the patina of legitimacy that is siphoning money to terror groups."[18] According to David Aufhauser, US Treasury Department General Counsel, "This is our model of what we say is unacceptable."[19] Documents seized would furnish a treasure trove to law enforcement. Jimmy Gurule, Undersecretary of the Treasury for enforcement, said: "From what I've learned, this has had a major effect on bringing down, dismantling a major network used by Mr. bin Laden to move money and to communicate."[20] And Deputy Treasury Secretary Kenneth Dam declared: "We believe from our intelligence channels that Al-Qaeda and other terrorist organizations are suffering financially as a result of our actions."[21] The operation boasted a number of firsts: the first major operation of Operation Green Quest; the first involving the closure of American establishments; the first global operation involving simultaneous shutdown of US and foreign offices. The only negative comments came from those who criticized the government for not acting earlier against the company.[22]

In reality, after the initial euphoria, the Al-Barakaat case became an embarrassment for the financial warriors. It came to illustrate many of the dysfunctions of the financial war—the power of rumor and innuendo, the flimsy nature of what passed for evidence, and the unaccountability of bureaucrats. It highlighted the asymmetry of the financial war, showing how self-aggrandizing mid-level bureaucrats could inflict further misery on one of the world's poorest countries. The media, while giving huge play to the news of the initial closure of Al-Barakaat, barely covered the epilogue of the story—the exoneration from charges of terrorist financing. In Somalia in contrast, every aspect of the case was widely known. As a result, there was a strong sense of the injustice done to the company and the country.[23] The Al-Barakaat case also was a blow to international cooperation, as it eroded much of the pre-existing goodwill, and generated great cynicism towards the process of terrorist designation and asset seizure.

The Al-Barakaat (literally meaning "blessings") network of money remitters, headquartered in Dubai in the United Arab Emirates, was set up to address the needs of Somali immigrants who sent, on a weekly or monthly basis, a significant part of their earnings to their families. Founded by Ahmed Nur Ali Jumale in the late 1980s,[24] the company focused initially on remittances from Somalis working in the Persian Gulf. Following the 1991 collapse of the Somali government and banking system, Al-Barakaat assumed a significant role in the Somali economy. Its biggest asset was the large Somali diaspora in the US and Europe, who used it to send money to Somalia via Dubai, where Emirates Bank International (EBI) facilitated the transmission of money. Al-Barakaat provided a real service to a country devastated by war and famine. Even the United Nations used the Al-Barakaat network to transmit funds for its relief operations in the country.[25]

At the time of the September 11 attacks, Al-Barakaat was the largest business group in Somalia, with subsidiaries involved in banking, telecommunications, and construction. It had 60 offices in Somalia and 127 abroad in 40 countries, mostly involved in wiring money from expatriate Somalis to their families at home. Yet it was not the kind of conglomerate that the description implies—more like a franchise system of loosely connected, independently owned firms, not unlike large US remittance companies such as Western Union or MoneyGram.

As the East African country descended into further disintegration, a number of Somalis settled in the United States. Minneapolis had the largest number of such immigrants, and, as the terrorist financing monograph of the 9/11 Commission reveals, the operations of Al-Barakaat soon attracted attention. The local community, suddenly confronted with the influx of a relatively large and "different" community,[26] was predictably suspicious. Somalia evoked the ignominious retreat of American marines in 1993—one of those foreign policy setbacks which in the eyes of leading neo-conservatives projected the sort of weakness that invited the World Trade Center attacks. Since 1996 there had been a number of suspicious activity reports (SARs) filed by Minneapolis banks. The activities of Al-Barakaat could indeed seem unusual, or in the parlance of the anti-money laundering paradigm, "inconsistent with normal banking activity." The estimated $2 million a month found to be moving from Somali "collectors" in the city through the money-transfer system seemed too large for such impoverished communities.[27] Furthermore, the multiplication of small cash transactions that would converge into a single account in the United Arab Emirates (UAE) could easily pass for an attempt at "structuring" or "smurfing"[28] large, illegally obtained funds. By 2001 SARs numbered in the hundreds.[29]

Law enforcement agencies sought out informants within the Minneapolis Somali community. Tips and rumors—that Al-Barakaat was "closely associated with or controlled by the terrorist group Al-Itihaad Al-Islamiya (AIAI), and that a percentage of Al-Barakaat's proceeds went to fund AIAI, which in turn gave a portion to Usama Bin Ladin"—were dismissed by intelligence professionals, and attributed to political and business rivalries within the community.[30] Minnesota police, US Customs, and the Internal Revenue Service had all investigated the company at one time or another. In early 1999 the FBI had developed an intelligence case; by 2000 it had opened a criminal one. Especially mysterious was the role and importance of Al-Itihaad Al-Islamiya (AIAI): for some, the organization was dormant if not defunct; for others it was active and dangerous. Similar confusion reigned on the subject of ties with Al-Qaeda. Significantly, Al-Itihaad Al-Islamiya was not listed by the State Department as a terrorist organization.

In the days and weeks following September 11, there was a renewed political interest in Somalia, a failed state where Al-Qaeda could find sanctuary, and which was seriously considered as a possible military target.[31] Warlords who controlled most of Somalia and were based in Baidoa seemed eager to place themselves under American protection and induce the return of US troops. They promoted the view that the weak UN-sponsored government, under the leadership of Abdiquassim Salad Hassan, was overrun by terrorists. Using the idiom of the war on terror, Abdullahi Sheikh Ismail, the acting chairman of the loose alliance of warlords, asserted that "approximately 20,480 armed extremists" in Somalia and "85% of the government is al-Itihaad." He told American envoys that with a little bit of help, he would be ready "to liberate the country from these evil forces."[32] At the same time, however, other reliable sources suggested otherwise—that the Islamist party was primarily a nationalist one, with no significant ties to Al-Qaeda. If we are to believe Al-Barakaat executives, there was another aspect to the rumor mill—an attempt by rivals to eliminate the remittance "giant."

The post-September 11 surge of interest in both Somalia and hawalas, combined with the generalized paranoia that "terrorists are among us," breathed new life into the sputtering Al-Barakaat investigations.[33] According to the 9/11 Commission Report, reliable evidence was scarce, but there was a great deal of pressure to "show results." In their quest for a prize trophy, law enforcement officials cut many corners.[34] Since the shutdown, the company denied any wrongdoing. Few believed Ahmed Nur Ali Jumale, the Al-Barakaat chairman, when he said that the accusations were "all lies."[35] In his words, "There is at this time no Al-Ittihaad Al-Islamiya in Somalia. It is discussed as if it is powerful and existing, when actually it is dead."[36] Company officials repeatedly explained that the operation, far from being a "terrorist front," was merely a system for Somalis working overseas to send money to relatives, "a kind of Western Union for a nation without a functioning central bank."[37] The figures mentioned by the United States were said to be fanciful: the company was accused of transferring $15–25 million annually to Al-Qaeda, at a time when it handled $140 million in hawala transfers yearly, with annual profits totaling $700,000.[38] According to the company chairman, "$20 million is more than we could make in 20 years."[39]

The early investigation failed to help the government's case, and a new theory was soon put forth by law enforcement agencies. A US Treasury official said that the company, earlier described as the "quartermaster of terror," was in fact a "piece of a larger mosaic," one in which Al-Qaeda served as "the umbrella organization for a loose network of single-purpose, fundamentalist Islamic organizations."[40] A US official quoted by the *Financial Times* stated that "there is no reason to make a distinction" between Al-Qaeda and al-Ittihaad, and that Al-Barakaat provided "logistical support," including Internet connection, to the terror network, which only "shows you the broad base of this kind of movement": "Who would have thought such an operation would exist in Somalia? Think ... of what might exist in the rich countries."[41]

But soon the case started unraveling. All countries had fully cooperated in shutting down the company, but a close examination of the records failed to substantiate the accusations. It had been assumed that Al-Barakaat, given the way hawalas had been described, kept no records and that transfers left no trace.[42] But it so happened that both Al-Barakaat and Emirates Bank International, the Dubai bank where the money exchange deposited its money, had kept scrupulous records of all transactions. Their cooperation with the FBI was deemed "exceptional."[43] The records produced were so detailed that the September 11 Commission noted that the recordkeeping was far more extensive than what US investigators had been accustomed to in the United States. In the words of Abdirisak Aden, a partner in the

Swedish operation of Al-Barakaat, "You have to keep careful records in case someone comes back and says their relatives didn't receive the money."[44]

Many countries, which until then had taken US proclamations on faith, started questioning those allegations. In December 2001 a Canadian judge, saying that he found no evidence of a link to terrorism, rejected the US request to extradite Liban Hussein, the chairman of Barakaat North America. The man was freed on a $12,000 bond.[45] A renewed request for extradition was again rejected by Canadian authorities in June 2002, following a "full and thorough investigation of the information collected." "We looked at the evidence," said a Canadian Justice Department spokesman, "and then it became clear there was no evidence." The Canadian Foreign Ministry concurred: "Canada has concluded that there are no reasonable grounds to believe Mr. Hussein is connected to any terrorist activity." In addition to denying Hussein's extradition, Canada dropped all charges, unfroze his assets, and announced that it would ask the United Nations to remove him from its list of terrorism suspects.[46]

The "evidence" furnished by the United States was also questioned in Sweden, where the predicament of the "Somali Swedes" who operated the Al-Barakaat operation was widely publicized. According to the *Wall Street Journal*:

> The Treasury sent Sweden 27 pages of information it said proved the case against the men. Twenty-three pages were news-release material: a packet of background documents on al Barakaat, including a statement by President Bush on al Qaeda and a transcript of a briefing led by Secretary of State Colin Powell. The Somali Swedes were mentioned only in a flow-chart of al Barakaat's structure. The U.S. also sent four other pages [where according to Swedish police, there was nothing] that would warrant criminal charges against the men. Their lawyer paid a visit to U.S. Treasury officials to press their case. He says it was more like an inquisition than a hearing.[47]

Since any transaction with the "Somali Swedes" would be criminal, money was raised by charitable organizations to help them. Similar developments took place in Luxembourg and elsewhere.

In reality, all that US investigators could find was one regulatory infraction, and it was unrelated to terrorism. Mohamed Hussein was found guilty of operating a money-transfer business without a Massachusetts license. In July 2002 he was sentenced to 18 months in prison.[48] (The lack of a license did not seem to reflect any sinister intent. Indeed, records showed that in August 2000, the company tried to obtain a money-transfer license from the Massachusetts Division of Banks, which refused the application a month later as "seriously deficient and illegible" and invited it to reapply.[49]) On the matter of terrorist financing, allegations could not be substantiated. No criminal case was brought against Al-Barakaat in the United States. After the US-based Al-Barakaat offices filed a lawsuit challenging the action, most assets frozen in the United States under executive order (and some assets frozen by other countries under a UN resolution) were unfrozen.

The unfreezing of the Al-Barakaat assets was as discreet as the crackdown had been highly publicized. In the media, it was barely mentioned. More worryingly, many top government officials continued to claim the closure of the Al-Barakaat network as a major victory of the war on terror. One wonders whether top officials of the Treasury Department and even members of Congress were aware of it. Indeed, three weeks after the unfreezing, Kenneth W. Dam, Deputy Treasury Secretary, was presenting before the Financial Services Committee of the United States House of Representatives a progress report on the implementation of the USA PATRIOT Act. In his testimony, he did not fail to repeat what every senior official had been saying for months: "we disrupted Al-Barakaat's worldwide network that, by some estimates, was channeling $15 to $20 million dollars a year to Al-Qaida." [50] Nor did the Financial Action Task Force (FATF), the "international coordinator of the financial war," seem clear on the nature of the case. In a 2004 guide to governments, it uses a mid-sentence bait-and-switch technique to explain that "in the wake of September 11, investigators in the United States identified Al-Barakaat as a funding channel for Al Qaeda, successfully presenting three Barakaat officials for carrying out more than $10 million in illegal fund transfers." [51]

Predictably, no government official admitted to a mistake. OFAC continued to claim that it had met the evidentiary standard for designations.[52] Treasury spokesman Rob Nichols explained that the de-listing occurred because those companies had taken "remedial action to disassociate themselves from the terrorist Al-Barakaat network. They appear, after extensive review, to have been unwitting participants in the network, and their disassociation furthers our goal of dismantling the network." [53] The greatest impact of the case was of course on Somalia proper. Ahmed Abdi Hashi, Somalia's ambassador to the United Nations, said: "Thousands of Somalis had deposits in Al Barakaat. Depositors cannot access their funds. Businessmen cannot do business. Many are going bankrupt. We don't want to be seen as defending anyone linked to terrorism. All we want is to see the evidence." [54]

According to United Nations estimates, annual remittances to Somalia amounted in 2001 to about $500 million, more than it earns from any other economic sector and ten times the amount of foreign aid it receives.[55] The closure resulted in the reduction of such remittances by half, along with other disruptions: the company owed $6 million to depositors in its Mogadishu bank, and another $184,000 in unpaid transfers. Its international telephone service was stopped by US-based Concert Communications, a joint venture between AT&T and British Telecom, cutting off 25,000 subscribers.[56] To be sure, as is typical of informal remittance systems, other underground systems reappeared over time,[57] but not without rising costs to the Somali economy. The targeting of Al-Barakaat had long-term consequences. The company was the country's biggest employer and ran the biggest bank, the biggest phone system, and the only water-purification plant. Closing the company resulted in the layoff of 700 employees.[58] Beyond the economic impact, the symbolic impact—the perception that Somalia was unfairly treated—may have been the most significant and may have played a role in the rise, four years later, of Islamic fundamentalists.[59]

Beyond Somalia, the case was a blow to international cooperation and called into question the competence and reliability of the officials in charge of the financial war. In those countries such as Canada or Sweden, where the case generated extensive coverage, Al-Barakaat was portrayed as an innocent bystander, an unwitting collateral victim of the financial war on terror. A European diplomat assigned to the United Nations Security Council told the *Wall Street Journal*: "In the immediate aftermath of 9/11, there was enormous goodwill and a willingness to take on trust any name that the U.S. submitted." Later, allies grew skeptical as "a re-orientation of the sanctions regime [occurred], focusing on people who weren't even members of guerrilla groups." [60] More generally, as reported by the *New York Times*, "Foreign governments have made it clear that they will not continue to support Washington's call for sanctions unquestioningly, and some allies have pressed for new ways to ensure that future sanctions are well founded." [61] According to Ted Dagne, a Somalia expert with the Congressional Research Service in Washington, the decision to put Al-Barakaat out of business was based on "junk intelligence" and proved to be "a major blunder." [62] Even within the United States government, where the case is often presented as a success, some have questioned the wisdom of the operation. A senior official told the *New York Times*: "This is not normally the way we would have done things. We needed to make a splash. We needed to designate now and sort it out later." [63]

Even otherwise well-informed writers who have covered the Treasury Department and the financial war still refer to the Al-Barakaat episode as a policy triumph.[64] More worryingly, many top government officials continue to claim the closure of the Al-Barakaat network as a major victory of the war on terror.

Abusive designations and false positives

At the time of the September 11 attacks, there were in New York City alone no fewer than 85 people named, like the lead hijacker, Mohamed Atta.[65] One can understand both the trepidation of banks who were asked to match their customers' lists with those of terrorists, and the anticipation felt by law enforcement officials. Banks were faced with a dilemma: law enforcement agencies submitted names, many of them very common, without other identifying information such as addresses and dates of birth, and given the circumstances they were expected to err on the side of caution. The instructions were to "freeze first and ask questions later."[66] Money was presented as the oxygen of terror, and tabloids and policy entrepreneurs were publicizing the view that "terrorists are among us," ready to strike again.[67] Doing otherwise could result in stiff fines, or worse—a "link to terror" label. In the words of banking consultant Bert Ely, "I'm appalled by the sweep that's going on. The FBI is asking banks to run this huge dragnet to compensate for the fact that they got caught with their pants down."[68] Within days thousands of people saw their bank accounts frozen or closed for no reason other than homonymy or erroneous transliteration of names. There were also hoaxes, false tips, malicious rumors spread by people with personal, political, or business agendas,[69] and outright mistakes, which, compounded by overzealous enforcement, resulted in countless "false positives."[70] Companies with names comparable to Al-Barakaat (one example is Al-Baraka, an Islamic bank) were often confused for the Somali money remitter, suffering indignities in the process.

The impact on customers who faced this predicament was significant: they could not pay their bills, or cash their paychecks; their outstanding checks bounced, ruining their credit. They were essentially excluded from the legal payment system. Very few of those people turned out to have any link to terror.[71] Mohammad N. Ahmad, Pakistani-born and an American citizen since 1995, was among the countless people with a personal experience of mistaken identity. A manager in the global telecom division of Lockheed Martin Corporation, he had been a customer of Citibank for ten years when he discovered that his account had been frozen. The reason: as part of the "first strike" of the war on terror, the Treasury Department's Office of Foreign Assets Control had issued a list of 27 suspect organizations and individuals to US financial institutions, and Mustafa Muhammad Ahmad, a name "as common as John Smith in English," was on the list.[72]

As for faulty intelligence, it is not a new probem. Twelve days after the August 7, 1998 bombings of US embassies in Kenya and Tanzania, 13 US cruise missiles launched from ships in the Red Sea destroyed the El Shifa factory in Khartoum. The bombing, part of Operation Infinite Reach, which also destroyed an Al-Qaeda training camp, was based on faulty and outdated intelligence.[73] The claim was that the factory produced dangerous chemicals, and that it was partly owned by Usama Bin Laden. In reality the factory produced pharmaceutical products, and had been bought five months earlier by Salah Idris, a Saudi Arabian businessman. The bombing was followed by the freezing of $24 million in Idris's bank accounts in the United Kingdom, under a US regulation covering "pending investigations of interests of Specially Designated Terrorists."[74] Considering the impact of an attack against a devastated country's largest pharmaceutical company—which many regard as the greatest foreign policy blunder of the Clinton presidency—Paul R. Pillar, the CIA's deputy counter-terrorism chief at the time, wrote that the episode inflicted a "broader blow ... on the perceived integrity of U.S. intelligence and U.S. counterterrorist efforts generally."[75] After a long legal battle, Idris was exonerated and financially compensated for the mistake. But that was before the September 11 attacks.

Since that time anyone accused of a crime is more likely to be presumed guilty. In Donald Rumsfeld's words, "The absence of evidence is not evidence of absence." The law enforcement position was that "with terrorism you do not have the luxury of sometimes waiting to figure out if the guy is truly a terrorist."[76] A related argument was advanced by Treasury Secretary Paul O'Neill: "If we wait until we have 100% evidence, it may be difficult to incriminate them."[77] In sum, the presumption of guilt is so powerful that getting removed from blacklists or exonerated from accusations are uphill and uncertain battles.[78] As noted by Marc Sageman, a former foreign service officer who worked closely with the Mujahideen, "Although arrests are front-page news, there is rarely any fanfare about exoneration."[79]

As more blacklists are drawn, cases of mistaken identity multiply. One list which is notoriously riddled with such cases is the "no fly" list, which bars certain individuals from boarding airplanes.[80] Senator Edward M. Kennedy, Democrat of Massachusetts, tells about how between March 1 and April 6, 2004 his name appeared on no-fly lists (because it resembled an alias used by a suspected terrorist) and on five occasions, airline agents tried to block him from boarding airplanes. The Senator tells about this exchange with one agent:

> "You can't buy a ticket to go on the airline to Boston."
> "Well, why not?"
> "We can't tell you."[81]

In early April, Homeland Security Secretary Tom Ridge called the Senator to apologize and promise that the problem would be resolved, but two days later another airline agent tried to stop him once again from boarding a plane, leading Kennedy to wonder how ordinary citizens—and one might add, those belonging to categories singled out for profiling—could navigate the tangled bureaucracy if a well-known and easily recognizable senator had so much trouble.[82]

An additional problem is that politicians, law enforcement officials, and prosecutors seldom admit mistakes. Victims of abusive designations and false positives are often forced to plead guilty to lesser charges, something that is very common in the financial realm, where complex and contradictory rules give discretion to prosecutors and law enforcement officials: the wrongly accused will always be found guilty of something, no matter how trivial.[83] One famous case was that of Captain James Yee, a Muslim chaplain at Guantanamo Bay, who risked the death penalty when he was initially charged with six criminal counts of mishandling classified information and suspected of leading a ring of subversive Muslim servicemen. He was held in solitary confinement for 76 days. Though exonerated of those very serious charges, he was nonetheless found guilty of non-criminal charges of adultery and downloading Internet pornography.[84]

The arrest and jailing of people based on false, and usually anonymous, tips has become increasingly common, often resulting in deportations, prison terms, and at the very least financial expense.[85] Clearing one's name and reputation is an uphill battle with no guarantee of fair treatment. Even after full exoneration, the impact lingers, and old charges can always be dredged up or otherwise resurface. Although top officials now claim more sensitivity to the problem of damaging reputations,[86] the financial terrain presents far too many incentives for muscle flexing and overkill. Such projections of force always leave in their wake substantial collateral damage. As shown by the issue of the Iraqi weapons of mass destruction and the link between Saddam Hussein and Al-Qaeda, accusations made repeatedly have a way of sticking in the public mind long after they have been discredited.[87] The association with terror is especially damning for any individual or any business. In a climate of fear, no one likes to "take chances."[88] A story from American political lore illustrates this mindset. As told by journalist Chris Matthews: "An elderly woman tells a reporter that she intends to vote against Senator Barry Goldwater, the 1964 Republican candidate for president: 'He's the guy who's going to get rid of TV.' 'But, madam,' interrupts the reporter, 'I think you're making a mistake. Senator Goldwater is talking about getting rid of the Tennessee Valley Authority, TVA.' 'Well,' the elderly woman persists, 'I'm not taking any chances.'"[89]

8

"Gated Finance" and Other Contradictions of the Financial War

Ninety percent of everything is crud.
Theodore Sturgeon

The greater the ignorance the greater the dogmatism.
Sir William Osler

We cannot solve the problems that we have created
with the same thinking that created them.
Albert Einstein

The war on terror is fraught with dilemmas and contradictions—between the grand strategic objective of spreading democracy worldwide and alliances with undemocratic nations; between massive defense spending and economic development; between civil liberties and public safety; between the requirements of intelligence and those of law enforcement; between strategy and tactics.[1] This chapter explores those contradictions that are specific to the financial war. The bulk of the chapter discusses the clash between liberalization and criminalization, which gave rise to logic of "gated finance." Later sections discuss the contradictions between "following the money" and systematic exclusion, escalation and diminishing returns, soft power and unilateralism, and courting Islamic moderates while simultaneously targeting them. The final section discusses the risks of financial blowback.

Between liberalization and criminalization: the logic of gated finance

The dominant economic doctrine in the years between the fall of the Berlin Wall and the September 11 attacks was undoubtedly that of "market fundamentalism."[2] The idea of the unquestioned superiority of the market over state intervention, combined with the assertion that "the rules have been changed forever,"[3] was embedded in most of the "big ideas" about a presumed epochal transition—from the "end of history" to the "new economy" to "globalization." Openness was a dogma,[4] and globalization, to quote columnist Thomas Friedman, one of its most fervent promoters, meant "the spread of free-market capitalism to virtually every country in the world."[5]

The need to liberalize and deregulate financial markets—to end "financial repression"[6]—was part and parcel of this new economic ideology. Freeing up capital flows was imperative, and served as justification for a vast movement of financial deregulation and liberalization, which started in the United States, and spread first to advanced industrial economies and later to the rest of the world.[7] In the words of Federal Reserve Chairman Alan Greenspan, "The accelerated opening up in recent years of product and financial markets worldwide offers enormous benefits to all nations over the long run."[8] Even countries with a rudimentary financial sector were told that by deregulating their financial sectors and opening them to international competition, they would achieve a more efficient mobilization of savings, more equitable and just distribution of resources, more responsible and profitable lending, less volatile business cycles, and more stable economic systems. Financial controls were dismissed as either unworkable or as adding intolerable costs to national and international economies.[9] In contrast to the huge inefficiencies generated by controls, the anonymity and speed of financial transactions would bring forth an efficient allocation of resources at the global level. As noted by Steven Clemons, during that "high trust era," "America believed that it was moving its political economy a notch closer to the theoretical constructs of frictionless capital flows and investment, efficiently directed by high levels of quality information, good institutional governance and feedback loops."[10]

The attacks on the World Trade Center and the Pentagon brought to the fore the dark side of global financial freedom. The freedom of capital movements happens to benefit illegal as well as legal activities.[11] As noted by Senator John Kerry in his 1997 book dealing with "the web of crime that threatens America's security:" "The opening of borders to international commerce and the information highway have benefited terrorists every bit as much as they have helped legitimate businesspeople and criminals."[12] Classical political economists had recognized the flip side of economic freedom—though they left it for others to worry about, since their role was to explain and encourage wealth creation.[13] In contrast, contemporary cheerleaders of globalization and the information age oversold their argument: the problems generated by the unfettered capital flows were to be solved through the magic of omniscient markets. Walter Wriston's book, *The Twilight of Sovereignty*, the first of a genre that thrived in the 1990s,[14] asserted that in the new era, "There can be no more Pearl Harbor-like surprises."[15]

Of course, the September 11 attacks showed that such surprises could still occur. There was an initial period of shock, confusion, and questioning of existing orthodoxies. But soon afterwards, market fundamentalism made a dramatic comeback. Addressing Asian leaders gathered in Shanghai in October 2001, President Bush reaffirmed his unwavering commitment to the free market. He said: "Terrorists want to turn the openness of the global economy against itself. We must not let them."[16] Officially, there would be no trade-off between openness and security. In reality, market fundamentalism now had to coexist with "national security fundamentalism."[17] The two logics were absolute yet contradictory: one insisted on the need for unhindered capital movements; the other called for constant vigilance. The contradiction was resolved through the logic of gated finance. As in gated communities, for a community to enjoy all freedoms, it had to be walled off from its messy surroundings. Outside those gates, ceaseless scrutiny would prevail.

It should be said that the foundations for a two-tiered logic had been established with the emergence of global financial regulation since the mid-1980s. First came the "too big to fail" doctrine, which essentially insulated the largest financial firms—those whose collapse could have devastating consequences on the economy as a whole—from failure.[18] A paradoxical situation followed: just as rules were increasingly formalized and codified, regulators at the national and international levels were given greater discretion to make arbitrary decisions about the life or death of financial institutions.[19] Another significant development was the imposition of capital adequacy ratios to be imposed on a worldwide basis: the first Basle ratios were initially designed to exclude inadequately capitalized banks from international finance. Following the 1991 collapse of the Bank of Credit and Commerce International (BCCI), further principles of global regulation appeared. An additional criterion was imposed for full participation in the global economy, based on the quality of national regulation. Thus the 1991 Federal Deposit Insurance Corporation Improvement Act (FDICIA) segregated banks on the basis of two major criteria. For domestic banks, capital adequacy determined the nature of supervision: well-capitalized institutions were subjected to a light regulatory regime, whereas the others would be subjected to tight controls. As for foreign banks operated in the United States, they were subjected to an

additional layer of controls, and had to show that their home country regula-
tor had an effective system of "comprehensive consolidated supervision." [20]
This and other new regulatory norms were soon enforced on a worldwide
basis by the Basle Committee on Banking Supervision and other international organizations.

One of these norms was "self-regulation," which authorized certain
companies, but not others, to engage freely in certain types of financial innovation. This new approach, propounded by the Group of Thirty, a New York
based association of the world's leading financial institutions, provided for
regulators to divide firms into two groups. The largest ones were allowed to
develop their own risk management models and tools. Their regulation would
focus on the accuracy of models, and the quality of internal risk controls and
disclosure policies. In contrast, the smaller financial institutions would be
subjected to much tighter supervision and would be prohibited from engaging in certain risky activities. [21]

After September 11, the clash between the two absolutes—market fundamentalism and national security fundamentalism—was resolved in practice
through systematic profiling. The gated financial community which enjoyed
the privileges of a free and open system of finance consisted by and large
of the financial institutions of the main industrialized countries. The rest
of the world was generally left outside. The Islamic world in particular was
subjected to constant scrutiny. Some countries already slapped with the
rogue label had been subjected to financial sanctions and faced a de facto
exclusion from the global financial system. What was new was that countries
and businesses that had been well integrated in the global economy now
faced major hurdles and restrictions. [22]

The most visible ones were the financial controls instituted after the
September 11 attacks (primarily those included in the USA PATRIOT legislation). The Treasury Department was given the power to cut off any use of
the US financial system by a bank, business, or country that did not exercise
adequate control over terrorist financing and money laundering. The tightening of "know your customer" rules resulted in banks making unreasonable demands on broad categories of customers to ensure that they were free
of "alleged links to terror." [23] New rules on correspondent banking, which
required that banks ensure that none of their correspondents was, wittingly
or unwittingly, involved in financing terror, led to a systematic review by all
financial institutions of their correspondent relationships. Banks from the
Islamic world were required to prove a negative, and many could not pass
muster. [24]

There were also many less visible or invisible barriers. In the tense climate
following the 2001 terrorist attacks, the frequent tendency to equate Islam

with terrorism spread to the financial sphere: institutions associated with the Islamic world were presumed guilty until proven innocent.[25] The metaphorical walls took a number of forms including the systematic surveillance directly, or through home country regulators, of designated institutions,[26] and the disproportionate filings of suspicious activities reports for transactions with certain parts of the world. Gated finance amplified perceptions of exclusion and double standards: whereas many developed countries could flout with impunity global rules on terrorist financing and money laundering,[27] no such forbearance was shown to those outside the gated community. The integration of many Islamic countries and institutions into the global economy took a giant step backward. Significant amounts were withdrawn from the United States, driven by fears of confiscation and general unease. Many institutions and individuals felt like sitting ducks, ready to be accused of links to terror, and open to the possibility of lawsuits, press campaigns, or vast fishing expeditions by regulatory agencies. They chose to sell their holdings in the United States and other Western countries.[28]

Many international financial institutions came to the conclusion that they would rather not do business with certain individuals, firms, or countries.[29] Many customers have had the unpleasant experience of receiving letters from their bank announcing, without further explanation, that their accounts had been closed.[30] Although such customers could in theory go to another bank, "Know Your Customer" investigations by other institutions would create suspicions, turning them into "high-risk customers," and effectively shutting them out of the banking system. Even wealthy people who in an earlier era would have been courted by most financial institutions have received that type of treatment—people at risk of having ties to terrorism, people whose bona fides cannot be verified, or "politically exposed individuals" whose assets were at risk of future confiscation. The banks' reasoning is easy to understand: whatever income such accounts generate may not justify possible regulatory and law enforcement headaches. (A number of international banks had in the past to trace and seize fortunes of deposed leaders such as Ferdinand Marcos in the Philippines, Joseph Mobutu in Zaire, and Sani Abacha in Nigeria.) In order to avoid costly information requests and seizure orders from law enforcement agencies, a few banks have even refused to deal with leaders from the Islamic world, including for a time members of the once much-courted Saudi royal family.[31]

In 2004 the Sudanese embassy in Washington had to shut down for three weeks because it was unable to find a bank willing to take its money. When Riggs Bank in Washington found itself embroiled in a money laundering scandal[32] and closed down its embassy practice, no other bank wanted to deal with the Sudan, a country often associated with terror. US State Department officials found themselves reduced to begging certain banks to accept Sudan as a client. The matter took on national security overtones, since the United States could have been found in violation of the "full facilities" clause of the Vienna Convention on Diplomatic Relations. After the Sudanese threatened to retaliate by cutting off banking services to the US mission in Khartoum, Treasury Secretary John Snow and Secretary of State Colin Powell jointly asked Federal Reserve Bank of New York President Timothy Geithner to take the rare step of opening an account for the African country.[33]

No such diplomatic considerations would apply to individuals, corporations, or for that matter banks that would often find themselves shut out of the financial system. Even the largest and most established businesses from the Islamic world have been victim of campaigns attempting to link them to terror. When Investcorp, an $8.6 billion private equity firm based in Bahrain, tried to enter New Jersey's lucrative garbage industry, it was promptly and very publicly investigated by the state's counter-terrorism office over allegations that its Middle Eastern investors "might have ties to terrorists and their financiers."[34] Many deals involving well-known investors were actually sunk by rumor and innuendo.[35]

The best-known example is the political uproar that followed the acquisition by Dubai Ports World of Britain's Peninsular & Oriental Steam Navigation (P&O) in February 2006. In Congress and in the media, the deal, as a consequence of which freight terminals at six US port facilities would fall under the control of Dubai, was presented as a threat to national security. Though the United Arab Emirates was deemed a crucial and solid ally in the "war on terror," and a Muslim country which embraced modernity and fought fundamentalism, a steady drumbeat kept repeating that "two of the hijackers in the Sept. 11 attacks came from the United Arab Emirates and laundered [sic] some of their money through the country's banking system."[36] President Bush insisted that "it would send a terrible signal to friends and allies not to let this transaction go through," and vowed to veto (for the first time in his presidency) any legislation blocking the deal. Convinced that the political battle could not be won, the Dubai company agreed to cede control of the US ports to another entity.

Commenting on the flap, columnist David Ignatius wrote:

> It sent a message that for all the U.S. rhetoric about free trade and partnerships with allies, America is basically hostile to Arab investment. And it shouldn't be surprising if Arab investors respond in kind. One could blame it all on craven members of Congress, if the opinion polls didn't show that Americans are overwhelmingly against the deal—and suspicious of Muslims in general. Those poll numbers tell us that America hasn't gotten over September 11, 2001. If anything, Iraq has deepened the country's anxiety, introspection and foreboding.

Ignatius added:

> The ironic fact is that the UAE is precisely the kind of Arab ally the United
> States needs most now. But that clearly didn't matter to an election-year
> Congress, which responded to the Dubai deal with a frenzy of Muslim-bashing
> disguised as concern about terrorism. And we wonder why the rest of the
> world doesn't like us.[37]

Smaller companies can seldom survive the mere hint of a link to terror.
Ptech, an innovative Massachusetts software company, would have been an
unquestioned American success story were it not for a distant and inconsequential link to a blacklisted Saudi investor. The company had been
co-founded in 1994 by Oussama Ziade, a Lebanese immigrant. It counted
among its clients such firms as IBM, Aetna, Motorola, and Sprint, as well
as government agencies such as the FBI, the Air Force, the Navy, and the
Department of Energy. It was all but destroyed when a former employee
informed the FBI that Yassin al-Qadi, a man who headed a charity accused
of having links to terror, had invested some money in the company. Insofar
as he was on a Treasury Department list of "blocked persons," all US entities were prohibited by law from doing business with him.[38] A December
2002 raid on the company's offices triggered a media frenzy, which instantly
turned the company into a pariah. Top Ptech executives were told by their
bank that their accounts were closed. Many "terrorist experts" were eager to
"connect dots" in order to show a link to Al-Qaeda.[39] Some even suggested
"the possibility that terrorists may be using their money to buy into our
national infrastructure in order to undermine our economy and security
from within."[40]

Placing entire countries and broadly defined business sectors outside
the walls of the gated financial community is politically significant, since
such policies clash with the official long-term strategy of the United States
to encourage the Arab and Islamic world to reform and integrate into the
global economy. Indeed, "inclusion" is said to be the secret weapon against
terror,[41] and economic reform cannot be dissociated from democratization
and integration in the global economy. Most blueprints for long-term reform,
such as the the Greater Middle East Initiative (GMEI) or the Middle East
Partnership Initiative (MEPI), were premised on such ideas.[42]

Even those institutions that were destined to play a central role in the
future development of the Middle East and the Islamic world were victim-
ized by the financial war. Organizations whose vocation was to build bridges
found themselves on the wrong side of gated finance, in the process "compli-
cating the Bush administration's push for political and economic change
in the region."[43] The predicament of Arab Bank, which was the target of
potentially crippling lawsuits, is a vivid illustration of the contradictions

of the gated finance system. The lawsuits were a direct consequence of the "six degrees of separation" logic unleashed by the financial war. One of the bank's customers was the Saudi Committee for the Relief of the Palestinian People. The charity, created by the Saudi government, organized funding drives for Palestinians, and particularly the families of suicide bombers whose houses were destroyed by the Israeli government. Because some of those payments had transited through Arab Bank accounts, the bank was subjected to highly publicized lawsuits filed on behalf of relatives of US citizens killed or injured in violence in the Middle East.[44] The bank, founded in Palestine in 1930 and now based in Amman, is the third largest lender in the Arab world; it has $32 billion in assets, and 400 branches on all five continents. The Arab Bank's biggest stockholders include the governments of Jordan and Saudi Arabia and wealthy Arab investors, including the heirs of late Lebanese Prime Minister Rafik Hariri, who had a 9 percent stake. Most significantly, its 22 branches in the West Bank and Gaza Strip made it a key player in the Oslo peace process. Its close ties to Israeli banks, Arab governments, the European Union, and international organizations such as the World Bank made it an important interlocutor of the United States government. It was at the request of US State Department officials that it moved to open several branches in Iraq.[45]

Reporting rules are complex, contradictory, and subject to arbitrary and capricious enforcement. The American Banking Association recently complained to the government that "no standard appears to exist" for a proper compliance program.[46] Although other banks, such as Citibank and Israel Discount Bank, had also served as conduits for the funds of the charity, Arab Bank was singled out by US regulators for punitive action on the grounds that it had "inadequate controls." Despite interventions at the highest political levels, little could be done to stop the legal and regulatory steamrollers. Despite the fact that the bank has consistently received high marks from US regulators on money laundering and other compliance issues, the US Office of the Comptroller of the Currency (OCC) said it determined that the bank's branch had internal control weaknesses, especially in its international funds transfer activities.[47] The bank agreed to downgrade its presence in New York, converting the branch it had operated since 1982 to an agency office (which meant it could no longer receive deposits, though it was allowed to continue activities in trade and corporate finance).[48] In August 2005, without acknowledging wrongdoing, the bank agreed to pay a $24 million fine. It released a statement accusing US regulators of enforcing "confusing and constantly evolving" money laundering laws, and complaining that the $24 million fine was "unreasonably high."[49] The State Department condemned the regulators' action, and Amin Haddad, chairman of the Palestinian Monetary Authority, called it a "violation of all agreements with Israel and the US concerning the Palestinian banking system."[50] Similar dynamics have led many Arab banks in the United States to scale back their operations, or exit the market altogether.

It is questionable whether those outside the gates deserve their banishment, or whether gated finance can reduce terrorism. In most of the post-September 11 attacks, Islamist terrorists did not even come straight from Islamic countries, and some were not even nationals of Islamic countries.[51] Nor did they seem to use banks headquartered in Islamic countries. There is no empirical evidence that banks belonging to the Islamic world are more exposed to terrorist financing or criminal money. It may be that those intent on committing acts of terror are well aware that such institutions are subjected to greater scrutiny. And those who are in the business of hiding needles prefer larger haystacks. It has also been noted that "traffickers look for an area which is politically stable, financially stable, and with financial credibility because they feel that their deposits or their transactions are going to be safer or more professionally handled."[52] Whatever the causes, most of the large money laundering scandals of the past few years have involved the establishment of gated finance—banks such as Citibank, Bank of New York, or Riggs Bank. And virtually all of the financial transactions of the September 11 terrorists transited through American banks.[53]

"Following the money" and the consequences of exclusion

There are also other consequences to "gated finance" and systematic exclusion. The conventional law enforcement justifications for going after the terrorists' money consist of two main reasons: one is to "disrupt" financing to prevent further attacks; the other is to "follow the money trail,"[54] which can yield valuable clues and unmask broader conspiracies. In the words of Treasury Secretary Paul O'Neill, "The money trail doesn't lie. … It could yield an awful lot about who [the terrorists] were dealing with—when and where."[55] So far, however, the money trail has mostly helped connect the dots of terrorist attacks that have already been committed.[56] Even the shadowy September 11 terrorists left a paper or "electronic" trail: the money they received and spent, the flight tickets they purchased, and the cash they withdrew from automatic teller machines (ATMs) could be traced and yielded clues about their identities and whereabouts in the days leading to the attacks.

In their desire to act forcefully to "dismantle terror networks" and "disrupt" terrorist financing, money warriors have gone overboard in freezing funds and taking vigorous measures against a variety of institutions and countries. Judging from the increase in acts of terror, it is doubtful that "disrupting" financing or "raising the cost of terrorist fundraising" had the intended effects. At the same time, however, such policies have greatly hampered the pursuit of the money trail. Indeed, the age-old dilemma of the police—should a suspected lawbreaker be arrested early on, or should he be trailed until all necessary evidence is gathered?—has taken on a new dimension. The disclosure on August 10, 2006 of a London plot to bomb ten airliners heading for the United States by mixing liquid explosives highlighted the dilemma: British officials wanted to delay the announcement in order to keep the surveillance of the suspects going, whereas their US and Pakistani counterparts seemed eager to reap political gains from an immediate announcement.[57] Though the plot had, according to one senior police chief, the potential of bringing about "mass murder on an unimaginable scale," the timing of the announcement raised questions. Craig Murray, former British ambassador to Uzbekistan, wrote: "None of the alleged terrorists had made a bomb. None had bought a plane ticket. Many did not have passports. It could be pretty difficult to convince a jury that these individuals were about to go through with suicide bombings, whatever they bragged about on the net."[58] Abusive profiling combined with the financial warriors' desire to exhibit trophies, trumpet accomplishments, and exclude wide swaths of potential terrorists from the system produced unintended consequences. Well before revelations about the Terrorist Finance Tracking Program, terrorists were given ample notice to avoid using legal channels when transferring money across borders.[59]

The quasi-criminalization of a number of activities and endeavors (hawalas and Islamic charities come to mind), in addition to other heavy-handed policies, had the effect of driving considerable financial flows—of which criminal funds are probably just a small percentage—underground. The underground economies of developing countries had been receiving mixed signals. Prior to September 11, the goal was one of double integration—of underground economies into legal national economies, and of national economy into the global system. Peruvian economist Hernando de Soto has been a strong advocate of ending the system of "legal apartheid" by bringing the poor, heretofore confined to the informal sector, into the legal economy. The influential economist also argued that this would offer a chance to resolve the problem of terrorism.[60] Yet on the other hand, as the previous section suggested, pressures to remain or go further underground have greatly increased. It is not clear that the raft of laws and regulations, especially in developing countries, where people are accustomed to breaking cumbersome and "absurdly impractical" regulations,[61] had the intended effect. Many felt threatened and unduly singled out by national and international authorities, recreating a justification for going underground. In de

Soto's words, many people "do not so much break the law as the law breaks them—and they opt out of the system."[62]

The policy of systematically driving questionable groups underground has other consequences as well. In the words of Israeli counter-terrorist expert Boaz Ganor:

> Outlawing a terrorist organization will simply make it harder to foil terrorism because in practice it will drive the group's activists underground and prevent their public activities, making it harder for the security forces to follow their actions, movements, and intentions. Penetrating an underground organization is considerably harder than penetrating an open organization holding public activities. Furthermore, outlawing the terrorist organization will cause it to become more extreme: it will strengthen the radicals among its ranks, who will soon go over to the use of violence, escalating the group's violent activity. In practice, from the moment it is outlawed all the group's resources will be directed towards planning and carrying out attacks. Even those resources that were previously used to finance non-violent and legal activities will be used for terrorism from now on. Outlawing will also block all channels of dialogue with the organization and its members, which will prevent the possibility of moderating its position and solving the dispute peacefully.[63]

When Sudanese leader Hassan Turabi was pressured by American officials to expel Bin Laden from his country in 1995 following an assassination attempt against Egyptian President Husni Mubarak, he initially tried to convince them that they would be better off leaving the terrorist in the Sudan, where he could be kept under constant surveillance.[64] Indeed, following his 1996 expulsion, whatever trails existed went cold. Failure to understand the true nature of terrorist financing is no doubt related at least in part to the preference of money warriors for strategies of "running and gunning," and bombastic announcements, which provide terrorists with loud and clear messages on how not to get caught. The opposite approach—what Jonathan Randal called the "needlework, that time-consuming, patient, dull, but professional accumulation of detail"[65]—holds much more promise to get to the bottom of terrorist financing.

Escalation and diminishing returns

The first financial strike, launched on September 24, 2001, set in motion open-ended escalation mechanisms.[66] It was presented as a mere opening salvo, with many more strikes to be expected. As President Bush put it: "And, by the way, this list is just a beginning. We will continue to add more names to the list. We will freeze the assets of others as we find that they aid and abet terrorist organizations around the world."[67] A week later, the President announced the freezing of 50 new accounts "linked to terrorist activity," 30 of them in the United States and 20 of them overseas. In the weeks following the September 11 attacks, such announcements—dubbed by the President's advisers "the Rose Garden Strategy"[68]—became routine.

Less visible but equally consequential were actions taken by national and international bureaucracies. Since the beginning of the financial war, they had been put on notice: more was expected of them. Numerous control mechanisms, public and private (politicians, interest groups, the media, etc), kept up the pressure. At the October 2001 emergency meeting of the Financial Action Task Force (FATF), during which the anti-money laundering organization saw its role expanded to include terrorist financing, Treasury Secretary Paul O'Neill urged the participants to provide monthly updates on their progress.[69] By the same token, the United Nations Monitoring Committee was constantly asking member states to add more names to lists of terrorist financiers.[70] Such blacklists were only the tip of the iceberg. Armed with new powers, rapidly expanding "money laundering and terrorist financing" bureaucracies kept imposing new rules and new enforcement and coordination mechanisms. In turn, financial institutions had to show progress, which took the form of constant increases in suspicious transactions reported and accounts closed.

Combining those pressures with the financial war discourse opened the door to perverse consequences. If money is truly the "oxygen of terror," then the persistence of acts of terror was proof that the task was far from completed. The money warriors would then stand accused of being insufficiently aggressive, and pressured to exhibit more trophies—which could only be done by a further stretching of the "alleged link to terror" notion, and a further lowering of standards. Most measures were motivated not by new information about terrorist financing but by a constant broadening of the dragnet and a concomitant lowering of standards.

Initially only "terrorists with global reach"[71] were being targeted, but the financial war soon broadened and deepened. The initial focus on Al-Qaeda was diluted with an attendant loss of effectiveness. As the financial war escalated beyond those networks posing a direct terrorist threat to the United States, attitudes changed from taking US statements on faith to cynicism about US methods and intentions.[72] On November 7, the crackdown reached Al-Barakaat, the Somali money remittance company, and Al-Taqwa, an investment group based in Switzerland and linked to the Muslim Brotherhood.

On December 4, following a suicide bombing in Israel, Hamas was targeted, along with the Holy Land Foundation, the largest Islamic charity in the United States. President Bush justified stretching the "global reach" argument by explaining: "Hamas is guilty of hundreds of other deaths over the years, and just in the past 12 months, it killed two Americans. And today we act." [73] As for the Holy Land Foundation, it was targeted because it provided financial support to schools that "indoctrinate children to grow up into suicide bombers," and to suicide bombers and their families.[74] The extension of the war beyond "terrorists with global reach," and to groups such as Hamas and Hezbollah, which had no connection to the World Trade Center attacks, and whose nationalist grievances were regarded as defensible by most countries, created further cracks in international cooperation. The international community was deeply divided, and serious discrepancies appeared between the US and UN lists (which focused on Usama Bin Laden and Al-Qaeda).

On December 14, 2001, the FBI raided the offices of two other prominent Islamic charities in the United States, the Global Relief Foundation and the Benevolence International Foundation, both Illinois-based, freezing the assets of the former.[75] By hitting the most visible Islamic charities in the United States, the Bush administration opened itself to accusations that it was waging a war on Islam, which would later greatly complicate the task of "winning hearts and minds" in the Islamic world.[76]

In January 2002 came the controversial designation of the "axis of evil." The widely supported war in Afghanistan was to be only "phase 1" of a much broader war.[77] The March 2003 attack on Iraq, which was deeply unpopular internationally, was, it will be remembered, accompanied by countless actions on the financial front.[78] Later financial attacks were no longer directly linked to terrorism, but to an ever broadening set of foreign policy issues.[79]

As noted in the terrorist financing monograph of the September 11 Commission, "Policymakers, many newly thrust into the world of intelligence, were sometimes surprised to find that intelligence assessments were often supported by information far less reliable than they had presumed." [80] Many law enforcement decisions could simply not be defended in court. More specifically, "designations were undertaken with limited evidence, and some were overbroad, resulting in legal challenges. Faced with having to defend actions in courts that required a higher standard of evidence than was provided by the intelligence that supported the designations in the first place, the United States and the United Nations were forced to unfreeze assets." Part of the problem was that the "alleged link to terror" was slapped on all too liberally, and, as we saw, the "six degrees of separation," combined with the mood in the immediate post-September 11 period, could make spurious links look bulletproof.[81] As the next section shows, international cooperation suffered as a consequence of the open-ended escalation of the war.

Unilateralism and soft power

While able to dictate policies, the United States was unable to obtain desired outcomes. In the words of Roula Khalaf, "A heavy hand can galvanize reluctant countries to adopt tougher measures, but when the purpose, efficacy and price of the policy are so suspect, it may also produce deep resentment from vitally important friends."[82]

In his book *The Paradox of American Power*, Joseph Nye argued that despite overwhelming military and economic power, the United States was heavily dependent on others to solve a wide range of issues.[83] The financial war is certainly one such issue: results on that front can only be achieved through genuine international cooperation and "soft power." In Nye's words, "The United States lacks both the international and domestic prerequisites to resolve conflicts that are internal to other societies and to monitor and control transnational transactions that threaten Americans at home. We must mobilize international coalitions to address shared threats and challenges. We will have to learn better how to share as well as lead."[84] Instead, the financial front, though occasionally cloaked in a rhetoric of cooperation and consensus, was mostly dominated by blunt coercion and unilateral measures.

For reasons discussed in the early chapters of this book, the financial terrain was particularly vulnerable to punitive expeditions and gratuitous displays of raw power.[85] Where quiet, unspectacular, and long-term actions were needed, heavy-handedness and bluster dominated, with shining "trophies" exhibited to score easy political points. Since the days following the September 11 attacks, the mood was one of unabashed unilateralism, defined by Charles Krauthammer as seeking "to strengthen American power and unashamedly deploy it on behalf of self-defined global ends."[86] The United States money warriors, though ill prepared for the task,[87] were keen on micro-managing the global financial war. As representatives of the aggrieved party and sole superpower, they had little patience with advice from other countries and operated in "broadcast only" mode. Although European countries had had substantial experience dealing with Islamic extremists, they were largely excluded by US money warriors from decision-making.[88] One example was the prompt dispatching of American advisers, on the grounds that the Europeans "needed additional expertise" in following the money trail.[89] Yet as a general rule, foreign countries are in a better position to know about their local extremists and infiltrate their networks.[90]

Rather than genuine cooperation, mutual manipulation prevails. In the political realm, the pattern is familiar. Consider the case of Uzbekistan, one of the early practitioners of that art. This is how Jackson Diehl describes Islam Karimov, that country's strongman, and, at least until 2005, a key strategic ally of the United States:

> Although he may have been raised on the politics of the Soviet politburo, Karimov is quickly learning the art of American clienthood, as practiced by friendly dictators. First, be quickest among your neighbors—Karimov's are Afghanistan and the former Soviet republics of Central Asia—to volunteer bases and staging areas to the Pentagon. Next, serenade Washington with speeches about your love of capitalism and democracy, while releasing a political prisoner or two to appease the State Department. Finally, sit back and count the US aid money that rolls in ... while quietly sustaining the repression that keeps you in power." [91]

In the financial realm such games are even easier to play, with cynicism prevailing on all sides. Virtually all countries—the exceptions being a few "rogue states"—agreed in principle to join in the financial war, and change their legislations accordingly. The US has been constantly prodding others to "do more" about terrorism, using the carrot of financial aid and the stick of sanctions. Agreements on money laundering and terrorist financing are typical illustrations: American and international money warriors can display trophies, and open up opportunities for bureaucratic "busyness" as they are called to play central advisory and training roles. Those on the receiving end, while often appropriately cynical about such agreements, also have things to gain, as generous financial incentives are usually part of the package. Over time, most make the best of it: countries boast of how strict and comprehensive their money laundering apparatus is. Prodded to show results, in the forms of frozen accounts or blacklisted individuals or groups, many learn to use the war on terror as a cover for their own agendas. Slapping domestic enemies with the "terrorist" label, even linking them to Al-Qaeda, provides protection from criticism over human rights abuses. Early on, Ariel Sharon labeled Yasser Arafat "our Bin Laden," and India stressed the connection between Al-Qaeda and Kashmir separatists. Russia linked its Chechnya problem to global terror, and China tied its support for the US-led war on terrorism to its own efforts to suppress Muslim separatists of the Uighur ethnic group in its western Xinjiang Province. Elsewhere, as in Uzbekistan in 2005, brutally repressed domestic opposition groups were labeled Islamic terrorists.

Moderates and extemists

The idea that the triumph of "moderate Islam" over extremism would provide a long-term solution to terrorism was frequently articulated following the September 11 attacks, and took center stage during Bush's second term with "a comprehensive strategy to discredit and demystify extremists' ideology and promote moderate Islamic voices." [92] Indeed, for a time, the "global war on terror" (GWOT) slogan seemed to have been retired and replaced by that of "global struggle against violent extremism" (GSAVE).[93]

But there had been from the start a central contradiction in the thinking of many of those neo-conservatives who shaped the conventional wisdom on terrorism. Many who advocated the need for moderation and democracy regarded Islam as intrinsically inimical to such values. In Judith Miller's 1996 book *God Has Ninety-Nine Names*, which purports to explain "militant Islam," a telling quote reflects the mistrust of moderates. Tracing the political evolution of Sudanese Islamist leader Hassan Turabi, Miller saw a pattern:

> Turabi had been tolerant in opposition when a democratic outlook was useful. Out of office, Turabi had spoken the language of reform and pluralism; ... ruling, however, was something else. Martin Kramer, the Israeli analyst of militant Islam, argued that as a rule, an Islamic militant's "moderation" was inversely correlated to his proximity to power; the farther away from power Turabi had been, the greater his so-called moderation. Bernard Lewis, another fierce critic of Islamic absolutism, had put it this way: "Moderation," or "pragmatism," in a radical fundamentalist movement usually reflected a lack of alternatives. An Islamic "moderate," he quoted Arab friends as saying, was one who had "run out of ammunition." [94]

In sum, moderation was merely a tactical ploy by extremists to attain power. It is revealing that both the author of the above quotation and the "experts" cited played a significant role in shaping the war on terror narrative. Judith Miller is the star *New York Times* journalist who served as a conduit for much of the disinformation that preceded the 2003 Iraqi invasion. Her stories about Iraqi "defectors" and about Saddam Hussein's weapons of mass destruction made the front page of her newspaper and were picked up by the rest of the media, greatly contributing to building up support for the war. Miller also played a bit part in the administration's attempt to discredit Ambassador Joseph Wilson, an early critic of the Iraq war. As for Martin Kramer, he is known mostly for his jihad against the Middle Eastern Studies Association, the principal academic organization of scholars who study that region. His campaign to discredit area experts (alongside with Daniel Pipes' "campus watch"), which was greatly amplified by the echo chamber of the neo-conservative media (*The National Review*, *The Weekly Standard*, *The New York Post*, *The New York Sun*, etc), was certainly a factor in excluding most of the academics with an actual knowledge of the Middle East and the Islamic world from the policy process.[95] And Bernard Lewis is of course the unquestioned "doyen of Middle Eastern experts," who "explained Islam" to Vice-President Dick Cheney and other top officials in the aftermath of the September 11 attacks.[96]

Moderates were disproportionately affected by the financial war. The very logic of economic sanctions, as already mentioned, is often about "kicking the household cat because a stray mongrel bites a pedestrian down the road,"[97] and money measures hit those whose money was within the reach of money warriors. Considering that the financial offensive had started in earnest in the mid-1990s, it is unlikely that those intent on committing acts of terror would still keep their money exposed to confiscation. More generally, it is not unreasonable to assume that those Muslims whose investments reflected a vote of confidence in the United States and in the global economy were more likely to be moderates.

Many people experienced various forms of vexation, ranging from finding themselves on no-fly or other interdiction lists, to having their accounts closed, or more generally to being treated as suspects. Indeed, many in the banking community have noted "the danger of institutional racism, of making life hard for customers of Middle Eastern origin."[98] In many instances, entire communities were under siege.[99] In the soft front of finance, the tendency to equate Islam with terrorism has spread to the financial sphere: financial flows associated with the Islamic world were often suspect, and bankers enjoyed the privilege of refusing to conduct certain operations without the need for an explanation.[100] A great number of Islamic voices friendly to the United States expressed their disappointment at being badly treated simply because of their religious or ethnic background.

Consider the case of Fouad Siniora, a moderate Sunni who was Minister of Finance of Lebanon (later Prime Minister), when he was told that his US visa would be canceled because of a $660 donation he had made to Al-Mabarrat Islamic Charity Society[101] during an *iftar* (the fast-breaking meal during the holy month of Ramadan) in 2000. Such cases, though often resolved, tend to leave a bitter taste. Writing under the title "How to Lose Friends and Win Enemies," commentator Adib Farha noted the self-defeating character of such actions:

> According to the American logic, a contributor to [Sayyed Mohammed Hussein] Fadlallah's charity is, by definition, a co-financier of terrorism. It did not matter that the charity is reputed to be one of the most transparent charities in Lebanon, and runs various educational and social projects that serve thousands of orphans and other needy Lebanese. It did not matter either that Fadlallah is not on good terms with Hizbullah, whom the US considers to be a terrorist organization, or with Iran, who is on the US list of state-sponsors of terrorism. America must understand that despite its double standards in its approach to the regional conflict, its principles and its values have many friends among us. Unfairly alienating its natural friends is counter productive to the cause of international peace, regional stability, and the fight against extremism and terrorism.[102]

Financial blowback

Soon after the September 11 attacks, there was a frenzy of covert operations all over the world. Competition between the CIA and the Defense Department resulted in massive expenditures. Judging the CIA understaffed, slow moving, and risk averse, the Pentagon started encroaching on its turf.[103] In January 2005 the Pentagon acknowledged that the Defense Intelligence Agency (DIA) was sending out special clandestine teams called "strategic support teams" to a number of "emerging target countries" in order to gather intelligence, but also penetrate and destroy shadowy organizations such as Al-Qaeda.[104] A Pentagon memo stated that "recruited agents may include 'notorious figures' whose links to the US government would be embarrassing if disclosed." [105]

The lessons of the blowbacks from the Cold War era were not learned.[106] Of special interest to us is financial blowback. At the time of the anti-Soviet Afghan jihad, as the United States and Saudi Arabia lavished money and weapons on unsavory and otherwise unreliable characters, a secular Afghan warned them: "For God's sake, you're financing your own assassins." [107] It is indeed ironic that the two countries that were the principal bankrollers of the jihad (to the tune of $3 billion each) later became the main targets of offshoots of that jihad. In the index to Steve Coll's authoritative account of the Afghan war, under the entry "CIA funds given to Ahmed Shah Massoud" (who was not even among American intelligence's favorite warlords), there are no fewer than 50 references.[108] One lesson was that although loyalty was for rent, it was not for sale. As Michael Scheuer, who served as the chief of the Bin Laden "virtual station" at the CIA from 1996 to 1999, put it: "Afghans can't be bought off with bribes. Plying them with money usually guarantees that they will do the opposite of what the United States asks." [109]

Focusing on a proximate threat breeds "mission myopia"—an inability to consider the big picture and anticipate fallouts. Working in little-understood and often war-torn areas, where political agendas are inscrutable and alliances tangled, this can result in the provision of valuable resources for friends who may later turn into foes. Ahmed Chalabi is a good case in point. An Iraqi exile, he was the driving force behind the creation of the Iraqi National Congress in 1992, an exiles' organization dedicated to the overthrow of Saddam Hussein. Styling himself a friend of the US in a hostile region, he channeled large amounts of US government funds (for which he refused to provide proper documentation) in exchange for a steady stream of highly questionable "intelligence" on the regime. After the invasion he was exalted by the Bush government. Then his Baghdad headquarters were raided in March 2004 and information was revealed that indicated he has been feeding intelligence about the Americans to the Iranians.[110] Chalabi subsequently re-invented himself as an anti-American populist.

Chalabi's Iraqi National Congress had received since 1992 over $100 million from the United States.[111] From the Bush administration alone, Chalabi and his political organizations had received at least $39 million.[112] One of those organizations, the Information Collection Program, kept receiving until June 2004 a payment of $340,000 a month.[113] At a time when terrorist operations are conducted on a shoestring, the amounts being spread worldwide in support of questionable allies are mind-boggling. The amounts involved in the Information Collection Program may look like small change. For some perspective: the monthly stipend exceeded the total $304,000 outlays of the September 11 attacks.[114]

9

The Question of Islamic Charities

No good deed goes unpunished.
Clare Boothe Luce

Things turn from truth to lie when a partial truth is used to explain everything.
Dennis Praeger

By the time a social theory is formulated in such a way that it can be tested,
changing circumstances have already made it obsolete.
Charles Issawi

On September 11, 2001, David Aufhauser, General Counsel of the Treasury Department, happened to be in Britain, attending the annual meeting of the International Symposium on Economic Crimes. As usual in such circumstances, the mood was self-congratulatory. Chief justices, attorneys generals, and regulatory chiefs from around the globe were taking stock of their successes in combating money laundering, when news of the World Trade Center attacks broke. Ron Suskind described the scene in vivid terms: "Then a murmur went through the crowd of nearly three hundred. In a moment, a thirty-foot screen—which seconds before had carried bullet points of victories—filled with images of the trade towers burning." [1] This is when Aufhauser experienced his *eureka* moment. In his words:

> You intuitively knew what everyone was thinking: that we had been looking at the world through the wrong end of the telescope. That the chief enemy of peace was not criminal proceeds seeking a way to launder in a place of hiding. But, actually, what you might otherwise describe as clean money—actually money given to charities—which had been spirited around the globe to kill people. [2]

Three months later, following the dramatic announcement of the crack-down on Al-Barakaat, President Bush warmly congratulated Treasury Secretary Paul O'Neill: "You've done a great job, Paul. ... I really feel progress here." "Yes, it's a start,' O'Neill replied, "but we know there's a lot more money out there that we just can't seem to get to. It's clean money, in charities, and we don't know where it is until long after it has been located and spent. By then, it's too late." [3]

If money is the residual explanation of choice for acts of terror, then Islamic charities—sprawling, mysterious, and ubiquitous—became the favorite "usual suspect"—an ill-defined, all-purpose explanation for the inability to track and seize terror money. Soon after the September 11 attacks, sweeping statements about charities, usually combined with references to "the Saudis," became a staple of the terrorist financing debate. *Funding Evil*, the neo-conservative tract on terrorist financing, characteristically misidentified Al-Barakaat, the Somali remittance network, as a "Saudi charity." [4]

Reflexively connecting Saudi Arabia's Islamic charities and terrorism had become so common that in his infamous 2002 briefing to the Defense Policy Board, Laurent Murawiec hammered on the need to "dismantle, ban all the kingdom's 'Islamic charities,' [and] confiscate their assets." [5] It was not just a few fraudulent or corrupt charities, but every single Islamic charity, which stood accused. Rather than simply reforming the charity system through greater transparency, an ideologically driven recommendation was pushed by people who either never heard of *zakat* (the religious obligation of almsgiving) or else were eager to provoke a confrontation against Islam as a whole. If "money given to charities" was the indeed the "chief enemy of peace," then drastic action was justified.

As with other "usual suspects," the charge contained a kernel of truth. Charities—and more generally Islamic non-governmental organizations (NGOs)—seemed active wherever terrorist acts occurred. And using charities as a cover for terrorist acts fits nicely with the rhetoric of evil. When he targeted three Islamic NGOs in the "first strike" in the war on terror on September 24, 2001, George W. Bush declared: "Just to show you how insidious these terrorists are, they oftentimes use nice-sounding, non-governmental organizations as fronts for their activities." Much of the terrorist financing literature stressed the "deliberately commingled legitimate activities with illegitimate ones," [6] which was just another proof of the cunning and duplicity of "evildoers." The reflexive equation of Islamic charities with terrorism was so hammered into the public consciousness that it even provided fodder for popular comedians. [7]

Charity, Islam, and the war on terror

Prior to September 11, 2001, the world of Islamic NGOs and charities was little known. In the investigations into the 1993 World Trade Center attacks, charities were peripherally mentioned. With the 1998 African bombings, it became clear that charities could wittingly or unwittingly be involved in acts of terror: a few fraudulent charities had been set up with the specific goal of providing cover for the preparation of the attacks; even some of the main-stream charities were unwittingly penetrated by terrorists. In the Palestinian occupied territories, charities had been very active and accused of providing financial aid to families of suicide bombers.

American law enforcement agencies had their own encounters with polit-icized charities. Non-governmental organizations with ties to the Middle East, Ireland, Central America, and other parts of the world, whose osten-sible purpose was to alleviate suffering in war zones, were at various times accused of providing cover to terrorist groups. FBI agents have noted strik-ing parallels between the Holy Land Foundation for Relief and Development and the New York based Northern Ireland Aid Committee, or Noraid.[8] The Holy Land Foundation, the largest Islamic charity in the United States, had long been suspected of funneling money to Hamas, the Palestinian militant group designated as terrorist by the United States in 1995. Similarly, Noraid had, since its creation in 1970, raised considerable amounts of money in the Irish-American community, yet was widely believed to divert money intended for widows and orphans to the Irish Republican Army (IRA).

In every instance, two discourses fought for acceptance: one arguing that charities existed as a cover for political activities, and that any separation between the political and the social wings of "terrorist" organizations was spurious; the other arguing that the separation between violent militancy and social action was watertight. Clearly, people view such matters through pre-conceived ideological and political lenses: sympathy or dislike for a cause tends to determine perceptions, making impartial assessments nearly impos-sible. For one thing, in trouble spots where law and order are absent, distinc-tions are by definition blurred: guerrillas and insurgents operate from the shadows and intermingle with civilian populations, and money collected for humanitarian uses can easily be diverted for military purposes. Furthermore, the relief provided by philanthropic organizations where the state is weak or hostile can be a tool to generate political support,[9] and humanitarian acts, such as aid to political prisoners and their families, can have significant political implications.[10] In the final analysis, money is fungible, and using it for relief frees up funds for other purposes.

Another set of arguments concerns the legal implications for donors. The very act of donating money to certain organizations was long regarded as a political statement, a form of free speech covered by First Amendment protections. But in recent years, financiers have come to be regarded as enablers: by aiding and abetting terrorists, they make acts of terror possible. As we saw, in his September 11 address to the nation, President Bush emphatically stated that all forms of support would be indistinguishable from the acts of terror themselves.[11]

All these considerations help explain the frustrations of law enforcement agencies. One precedent in particular, involving the Committee in Solidarity with the People of El Salvador (CISPES), had a chilling impact on investigations of non-profit groups. Between 1981 and 1985, the FBI had aggressively investigated CISPES, a Chicago-based group sympathetic to Salvadoran Marxist rebels fighting that country's US-backed government, but the investigation backfired. CISPES successfully fought back in court, and in 1997 the FBI agreed to pay $190,000 in legal fees to settle the case. A number of agents were disciplined for "inadequacies" in the probe, and the government agreed to make an extraordinary apology in court. Following that episode, law enforcement, despite an ever-growing arsenal, had reservations about going after groups claiming a legitimate political and humanitarian agenda. Since the mid-1990s, there had been numerous investigations of Islamic charities but none went anywhere. For one thing, the evidence gathered was inconclusive and would not stand up in court. Also, in the post-Watergate environment, government agencies tended to err on the side of caution.[12]

Following the September 11 attacks, the pendulum suddenly swung in the other direction. Unsubstantiated allegations gained credibility, law enforcement was granted new tools, and the political climate was highly conducive to turning Islamic charities into targets of choice. The dual logics of finance as residual explanation and of the "six degrees of separation" made it possible to reduce the complex world of Islamic NGOs to the funding of terror.[13] Intent and consequence, the legitimate and the illegitimate, the deliberate and the unwitting, were all blurred. Donors were penalized for the sins of recipients. If a sum had been diverted to benefit a terrorist group, or if an employee had crossed the line from humanitarian work to militancy, then the entire charity—indeed, every one of its donors—could be held accountable. Countless charities were branded as "terrorist fronts." Prosecutors would go on fishing expeditions in search of infractions—often innocent mistakes or unrelated irregularities—to justify increasingly harsh punishments. With every new terrorist attack, the question of Islamic charities would arise anew, and there would be pressure for more crackdowns, and calls for yet stricter controls.

One day after the August 10, 2006 announcement of a foiled plot to bomb airplanes flying from the United Kingdom to the United States, there was already speculation that money from an Islamic charity, Crescent Relief, which had been founded to collect money for Kashmir earthquake victims, had been funneled back to the plotters. Predictably, though the claims were not substantiated—according to a Pakistani foreign policy spokeswoman, it was "speculation and fabrication"—the charity's funds were frozen.[14]

What makes the clash between the law enforcement logic and the religious logic politically significant is that almsgiving or *zakat* (literally, purification) is a religious obligation for all Muslims. It is one of the five pillars of Islam,[15] which in the hierarchy of religious duties ranks third, after the profession of faith and daily prayers. The Koran specifies the proper recipients of *zakat*: the poor and the needy, *zakat* collectors, travelers in difficulty, and captives (9:60).[16] The *hadith* (sayings and deeds of the Prophet) delves into the matter in great detail and a complex jurisprudence later took shape. Over time, elaborate rules were laid down as to rates, proper recipients, collection practices, exemptions, and the like.

Insofar as Islam looks favorably upon commerce, private property, and wealth, *zakat* has always played a role of religious purification in addition to its basic central socio-economic functions.[17] For with wealth comes responsibility towards the needy and others—hence the religious connotation of all philanthropy. *Zakat* structures the welfare system, providing mechanisms to achieve some measure of income redistribution and deal with the problem of poverty.[18] Above a certain amount of income and assets, every Muslim is expected to contribute. Since every Muslim is either required to pay *zakat* or entitled to receive it, *zakat* is at the core of Islamic solidarity.[19] Many well-to-do Muslims offer a supplemental charitable contribution, above and beyond the religiously required amount, known as *sadaqa*. Such contributions are typically associated with long-term projects and broader solidarity schemes, such as building hospitals, orphanages, or schools, or with encouraging the propagation of the faith. Finally, no understanding of Islamic philanthropy would be complete without reference to pious endowments known as *awqaf*,[20] institutions created in perpetuity and which enjoy wide autonomy, although they fall in certain countries under the control of the government.

The contrast between the role of *zakat* in the Islamic tradition—a pillar of the faith, a religious obligation for all Muslims, a central part of the Islamic welfare system—and the way it has been portrayed in much of the terrorist financing canon—as a ploy to fund terror or as a "collection plate in radical mosques"[21]—is quite striking.

Geopolitics and Islamic charities

The next few pages explain the evolution of charities from a geopolitical standpoint. The first modern transnational Islamic charities appeared in the context of the Cold War, and came to play a significant international role as a result of the oil boom of the 1970s. The year 1979—which saw the Iranian revolution, the Mecca uprising, and the Soviet invasion of Afghanistan—marked a turning point for Islam and the beginning of a new, overtly political role for Islamic charities. The mid-to-late 1980s were characterized by a stepping up of the anti-Soviet jihad in Afghanistan and a fiscal crisis in Saudi Arabia. The period was marked by an all-out effort to help the Afghan resistance, and the rise of private and uncontrollable charities. Following the Soviet withdrawal from Afghanistan in 1989, the role of Islamic charities could be explained in terms of two sets of political developments: the ensuing chaos, and the position of Islam in the post-Cold War "new world order."

1. 1962–79: The Cold War and the internationalization of Islamic charities

Until the oil boom, Islamic charity had a distinctly local character. Religious foundations and well-to-do Muslims would typically distribute money to the needy within their communities. The amounts involved were generally small and their political impact was negligible. The appearance of global Islamic charities is a recent phenomenon and an indirect consequence of the "Arab cold war," which was nested within the broader superpower confrontation, and pitted Saudi Arabia against Gamal Abdul Nasser's Egypt. As a way of trumping Nasser's pan-Arabism, Saudi Arabia proclaimed the doctrine of Islamic solidarity.[22] It founded in 1962 a pan-Islamic movement, the Muslim World League, whose missions were "to fulfill God's obligation by propagating his message and spreading it all around the world" and to "unify the world of Muslims."[23] The early efforts were relatively modest, given that the kingdom was barely solvent.

As Egypt's fortunes declined, in particular following the 1967 Six Day War defeat, Saudi Arabia's rose. The year 1970 further increased the stature of the kingdom. That year saw Nasser's death (and his replacement by Anwar Sadat, who would cultivate close ties with Saudi Arabia) and the creation of the Organization of the Islamic Conference (OIC), which provided under the de facto leadership of Saudi Arabia a permanent forum uniting all Islamic countries.[24] Equally dramatic changes took place on the economic front. Between October 1973 and January 1974, the price of oil quadrupled, suddenly transforming the international position of Saudi Arabia, the world's largest producer of oil.[25] As a result, between 1970 and 1974, the oil revenues of Saudi Arabia grew tenfold in inflation-adjusted terms,[26] and the government's five-year budget went from $9.2 billion in the 1969–74 period to $142 billion in the next five years.[27] This sudden windfall provided a boost to the

fledgling pan-Islamic movement—and to Islamic non-governmental organizations.

Although it was not known at the time, Saudi Arabia became actively involved, well before the Afghan jihad, in the last battles of the Cold War. Indeed the years of the oil boom were also marked by the end of the Vietnam War, the Watergate scandal, and economic turmoil. More specifically, in the conduct of its foreign policy, the United States was hobbled by two sets of constraints. One had to do with domestic political factors: in the wake of Vietnam and Watergate, and revelations of high-profile Congressional hearings (in particular the Church committee hearings), the US Congress, which also holds the power of the purse, tried to rein in the executive's proclivity for unauthorized foreign adventures. The other was economic: the United States, in the midst of stagflation and other economic problems, was no longer in a position to finance many of its more expensive foreign policy operations. This is where the Saudis stepped in. In a February 2002 speech at Georgetown University, his alma mater, Prince Turki Al Faisal, the former Saudi chief of intelligence discussed the role of the "Safari Club:"

> In 1976, after the Watergate matters took place here, your intelligence community was literally tied up by Congress. It could not do anything. It could not send spies, it could not write reports, and it could not pay money. In order to compensate for that, a group of countries got together in the hope of fighting communism and established what was called the Safari Club. The Safari Club included France, Egypt, Saudi Arabia, Morocco, and Iran. ... The main concern of everybody was that the spread of communism was taking place while the main country that would oppose communism was tied up. Congress had literally paralyzed the work not only of the US intelligence community, but of its foreign service as well. And so, the Kingdom, with these countries, helped in some way, I believe, to keep the world safe at the time when the United States was not able to do that.[28]

The various members of that group contributed in different ways. Saudi Arabia's contribution was by and large limited to providing money. Under such "checkbook diplomacy," the Saudi government would finance, with no questions asked, covert operations in countries such as Angola and Nicaragua.[29] Acknowledging such discreet help, President Jimmy Carter declared in 1977 that there "has not been any nation in the world that has been more cooperative than Saudi Arabia."[30] During the Reagan years, foreign policy cooperation was stepped up to such a degree that Prince Bandar, Saudi Arabia's ambassador to the United States, confided to a journalist that, "if you knew what we were really doing for America, you wouldn't just give us AWACS, you would give us nuclear weapons."[31]

In the wake of the oil boom, there was increasing talk of a New International Economic Order (NIEO)—of new relations between North and South and of Southern and particularly Islamic solidarity.[32] The massive transfer of wealth was in theory to benefit the world's have-nots, and especially the Muslims among them. A by-product of these developments was the transformation of Islamic charities. The government opened its bountiful treasury to Islamic NGOs. As Steve Coll explained:

> [Wahhabism] was a determined faith, and now overnight an extraordinarily wealthy one. Saudi charities and proselytizing organizations such as the Jedda-based Muslim World League began printing Korans by the millions as the oil money gushed. They endowed mosque construction across the world and forged connections with like-minded conservative Islamic groups from southeast Asia to the Maghreb, distributing Wahhabi-oriented Islamic texts and sponsoring education in their creed.[33]

Among the organizations created in the years of the oil boom was the IIRO (International Islamic Relief Organization), founded in 1978, which soon became the world's largest Islamic charity.

2. 1979–84: The new politics of Islam

The year 1979 was an *annus horribilis* for both the United States and Saudi Arabia. In both countries, long-held beliefs were challenged by political developments in Iran, Saudi Arabia, Pakistan, and Afghanistan. In the United States, the view that Islam was a quiescent, politically benign religion was abruptly refuted. The communist threat was then stronger than ever, and Islam was now regarded as a potentially destabilizing force. In a sudden reversal, Washington policymakers drew a distinction between "good" and "bad" Muslims.[34] The Ayatollah Khomeini's brand of revolutionary Islam was to be fought, whereas the alternative Islamic model, that of conservative Saudi Arabia, was to be given full support.

The Saudis were challenged on three fronts. Iran, now ruled by Shia clerics, questioned their legitimacy while proclaiming its ardent desire to export its own brand of Islamic fundamentalism.[35] The Iranian propaganda, denouncing those regimes that were friendly to the West and attacking "the Sultan's clerics" (in reference to those religious sects subservient to their conservative governments) reached far beyond the Shia world into the Sunni mainstream.[36] On the domestic front, the Saudi rulers were greatly embarrassed by the Mecca uprising, which they perceived to be a direct challenge to their religious authority: not only were they accused of impiety, corruption, and profligacy, but they had proven unable to quash the rebellion on their own. Indeed, the regime had to bring French special forces—"infidels"—into the holy city of Mecca. Then there was the fear that the hated Soviet communists would, by way of Afghanistan, close in on their oil fields.[37]

One prong of the Saudi response to those events was to placate the conservative religious establishment. In many respects, the Saudi society was re-Islamicized. A number of Westernizing trends (for example, those involving the emancipation of women) were rolled back.[38] Another prong was a new emphasis on national security and intelligence matters. It took the form of further consolidation of the alliance with the United States, along with massive purchases of weapons, and a build-up, virtually from scratch, of a powerful intelligence apparatus under the leadership of Prince Turki bin Faisal. The apparent contradiction between the close cooperation between Saudi Arabia and the United States on the one hand, and the promotion of a radical, sectarian brand of Islam was seized on by Saudi-bashers as proof of Saudi duplicity. In reality, there was a logical if myopic calculation behind such a policy. In the words of one specialist, King Fahd's "close association with the United States and his increased involvement in U.S. covert operations around the world required Islamic steps on behalf of the kingdom to offset the Western orientations of the kingdom's foreign policies."[39]

The third prong, the promotion of jihad in Afghanistan,[40] brought together political and religious calculations. The Saudi government generously bankrolled the anti-Soviet insurrection. It encouraged its youth to join the Afghan Arabs. (Among the financial inducements were cut-rate airfares, plus a variety of generous stipends.) Perhaps more significantly for our purpose, the government encouraged all Saudis—indeed all Muslims— to make financial contributions. Members of the Islamic community were under siege, threatened by an ideology promoting atheism. The arguments for support were many: it was a holy war; there was considerable need for relief; and it was an opportunity to engage in *daawa* (proselytism) and the promotion of the Saudi brand of Islam. The religious weapon was a potent if dangerous one. Indeed, in authoritarian societies where avenues for political activity are limited, religion can provide useful cover. But such long-term, hypothetical considerations were overshadowed by the urgent need to support the Mujahideen.

Islamic NGOs were central to that effort, which involved all of the Persian Gulf rulers, as well as the businesses and citizens of those countries. In sum, charitable work became inseparable from *daawa* and broad geopolitical objectives.

3. 1984–89: Financial, military, and religious escalation

The year 1984 marked a turning point in the Afghan war. In Washington, the initial, rather modest rationale for supporting the Afghan resistance— "bleeding the Soviets"—soon gave way to more ambitious goals. For the first time, the view that the Soviets could actually be defeated was entertained.

Soon it would be widely held. Such defeat required a substantially stepped-up financial and military aid. Political maneuvers in Washington resulted in a quantum leap in such aid.[41] Equally significant for our purpose was the new focus on religion. Two mutually reinforcing elements were at play: one was the view that a "holy war" against the Soviets would have a powerful mobilizing impact among the Mujahideen; another was the belief that reviving Islam within the Soviet Union would greatly weaken the Soviet Union.[42]

There was also an economic rationale for the greater involvement of charities. Oil revenues had declined from a high of $120 billion in 1981 to $17 billion in 1985.[43] The Saudi Treasury was also depleted by the rapid growth of foreign-policy-related expenditures, which included the funding of Saddam Hussein's war against Iran. An earlier Saudi commitment to match dollar-for-dollar the American outlays in Afghanistan[44] meant that they had to follow the American escalation. Given the general discontent of the population over declining economic standards, there were limits to the Saudi government's checkbook diplomacy. This is where the private sector and Saudi society were called on to contribute further to the Afghan jihad. Wealthy merchants, some of whom had created their own foundations, responded generously, while people of more modest means took to making anonymous donations in ubiquitous collection boxes. Groups with dubious political (and sometimes financial) objectives could easily blend in.

Religion was a powerful way of mobilizing Saudi society. As described by Steve Coll:

> Middle-class, pious Saudis flush with oil wealth embraced the Afghan cause as American churchgoers might respond to an African famine or Turkish earthquake. Charity is a compulsion of Islamic law. The money flowing from the kingdom arrived at the Afghan frontier in all shapes and sizes: gold jewelry dropped on offering plates by merchants' wives in Jedda mosques; bags of cash delivered by businessmen to Riyadh charities as *zakat*, an annual Islamic tithe; fat checks written from semiofficial government accounts by minor Saudi princes; bountiful proceeds raised in annual telethons led by prince Salman, the governor of Riyadh; and richest of all, the annual transfers from GID [Saudi intelligence] to the CIA's Swiss bank accounts.[45]

Fundraising was thus constant: from foreign pilgrims in Saudi Arabia to worshippers in foreign mosques, everyone was expected to contribute. Comparable dynamics led other oil-rich states such as Kuwait and the United Arab Emirates to do the same.

Islamic NGOs and charities were the logical conduits for all those funds. The all-out effort to mobilize the Islamic world provided a windfall, but came at the cost of a significant loss of control by governments over the origin and destination of funds. In hindsight, there is much criticism of the failure to control charitable donations. But the point at the time, whether for religious or geopolitical reasons, was to maximize the aid that would reach Afghanistan. In the pursuit of such goals, one could be neither too picky nor too careful.

4. 1989–2001: NGOs and failed states

The Soviet withdrawal from Afghanistan led the country into deeper chaos. In the words of Robert Gates, "We expected post-Soviet Afghanistan to be ugly, but never considered that it would become a haven for terrorists operating worldwide."[46] In 1992 the communist regime in Kabul fell, and a civil war, pitting various Mujahideen warlords against one another, ensued. Following the Soviet withdrawal, the United States, now preoccupied by other developments (such as the fall of the Berlin Wall and the disintegration of the Soviet Union) lost interest in Afghanistan. By 1994 US assistance to that country had all but ended.[47]

Two noteworthy developments occurred in 1996. One was the capture of Kabul by the Taliban, the "students in religion" who longed for a pure unadulterated form of Islam. They had the support of Pakistan and Saudi Arabia. Pakistan's control of neighboring Afganistan, through its sponsorship of such Islamic extremists, increased its leverage over arch-rival India, especially with regard to the disputed Kashmir region where a jihadist movement was brewing.[48] As for Saudi Arabia, it was eager to expand its influence over distant Islamic lands. Many outside the government, and especially in the Saudi religious establishment, were attracted to the Taliban vision of authentic Islam, and had undertaken their own initiatives to provide support for the new regime.[49] The general attitude of the United States toward the Taliban was characterized by Steven Coll as one of "indifference."[50] Retrograde policies, on issues such as women's education, were certainly a cause for worry. But there was another perspective, one focusing on the stabilizing, "cleansing" side of a regime that would unite the Pashtuns, reduce factional bloodshed, curtail the drug trade, and provide opportunities for an oil pipeline.[51] The year 1996 also saw the arrival in Afghanistan of Usama Bin Laden, who had been expelled from the Sudan by a government now eager to curry favor with the United States.[52] Afghanistan, then the quintessential failed state, became a haven for jihadi groups, and Al-Qaeda in particular.[53]

Although Saudi Arabia was by far the main bankroller of the country, the government had lost control over financial flows. After years of encouraging individual Saudis to contribute to the jihad, private contributions had found their own channels. In 1990–91, amidst a fiscal crisis caused by low oil prices, the Saudis had been asked to foot much of the bill for the First Gulf War.[54] The gathering of threats (alongside the ample opportunities for fat commissions and the desire to show gratitude to the United States and the many participants to the anti-Iraq coalition) also sent the Saudis on a gigantic shopping spree for ever more sophisticated weapons at a time of falling oil prices and steadily declining personal incomes.

Most significantly, in the decade preceding the September 11 attacks, Islam was a religion under siege. Many in the US foreign policy establishment saw Islam as a fitting substitute for communism, and marked Islamophobic tendencies appeared throughout the Western world.[55] In various parts of the Islamic world, most notably in Bosnia, Kosovo, and Chechnya, Muslim populations came under attack, creating more refugees, and more humanitarian crises.[56] The American withdrawal from Afghanistan had left many former allies bitter. Many Mujahideen felt that they had been used and were now being left to their own devices just as foreign assistance was most needed to stabilize the country and rebuild it.[57] This, plus the stationing of US troops in Saudi Arabia, soon turned the United States into the principal enemy of many jihadis.[58]

Tragedies call for humanitarian aid, and, as was noted in the United States in 2005 in the wake of Hurricane Katrina, "fake charities and business opportunities abound in the wake of a tragedy:" "Armed with emotional appeals to donate to relief efforts or invest in humanitarian technology—and often mimicking the names of legitimate organizations—these crooks siphon millions that could be used to aid disaster victims."[59] Another endemic problem is the hidden political agenda of many charitable organizations.[60] In Afghanistan in the 1990s, and to some extent in Bosnia, Kosovo, and Chechnya, those problems were greatly amplified by a context of civil strife, religious tensions, and failed states.

Since the early 1990s it became clear that in all those failed states, charities (or what passed for charities) were out of control. Many NGOs came to reflect the chaotic environments within which they operated, and became heavily politicized. Even government-controlled charities saw some of their overseas branches infiltrated by terrorist groups.[61] Indiscriminate proselytizing combined with the surrounding anarchy was conducive to the appearance of an informal charitable system, fed by donation boxes and itinerant money collectors (often referred to in the terrorist financing literature as "financial facilitators"). Fraudulent, fly-by-night charities also proliferated. Some were crude financial scams; others little more than terrorist fronts.[62]

By 1994 Saudi Arabia and other oil-rich states, now acutely conscious of the problem, tried to do something about it. That year, the Saudi government undertook a number of initiatives to regain control over Islamic charities, and more generally rein in indiscriminate religious proselytizing: Usama Bin Laden's assets were also confiscated, and he was stripped of his citizenship.[63] Following the 1998 bombings of US embassies in Kenya and Tanzania, there were more closures of fraudulent charities. But the genie was out of the bottle. The idea of transnational jihad was by then well incubated. If mainstream charities were by and large kept on a short leash, control over informal charities proved slippery: they would instantly resurface under different guises.

Hitting at mainstream charities

Fraudulent charities were elusive and largely beyond the reach of governments: they were part of a broad, informal, and amorphous support system; they thrived in failed states; and following closures they had a way of resurfacing under new names and guises. Yet following the September 11 attacks, the generic notion of "Islamic charities" came under attack. In an overheated political climate the money warriors were constantly taunted: why are Islamic charities allowed to operate in the United States? Those attacks were amplified by systematic Saudi-bashing. Given the dynamics of steady escalation,[64] it was only a matter of time before the main Islamic charities, including those that were strictly controlled and enjoyed worldwide respectability, would be caught in the dragnet. Vast fishing expeditions were undertaken in the name of the war on terror, though charges were unrelated to terrorism and had to do with financial irregularities,[65] immigration violations, past links to the Afghan jihad (when Bin Laden was fighting on the good side of the Cold War) or the Arab–Israeli conflict.[66] In due course, the largest Islamic charities in the United States, the Global Relief Foundation (GRF), the Benevolence International Foundation (BIF), and the Holy Land Foundation, came under attack.

Mainstream charities were vulnerable on many levels. They were particularly susceptible to a "six degrees of separation" logic,[67] since the numbers of both donors and recipients were extremely large. Since the main charities had substantial bureaucracies and multi-country operations, it was relatively easy to go in search of financial irregularities or the unavoidable bad apple. In turn, entire charities—or anyone peripherally connected to them—could find themselves slapped with the "terrorist financier" label. Prominent public figures such as philanthropist Yusuf Islam (formerly the pop singer Cat Stevens) and basketball star Hakeem Olajuwon thus found themselves "linked" to terror.[68]

1. Afghanistan blowback

The Benevolence International Foundation (BIF), a charity in suburban Chicago, had its origins in the Afghan jihad. In 1992 Syrian-born American Enaam Arnaout launched Benevolence's operations in Bosnia, ostensibly to distribute relief supplies to civilians and soldiers.[69] Over the years, it sent millions of dollars to Muslim countries.

On December 14, 2001, as part of an investigation into terrorist financing, the government froze the charity's assets. The same day, the assets of
the Global Relief Foundation, another leading Islamic charity, were seized.[70]
Both charities fought back with civil lawsuits attacking the secret use of
evidence, and arguing that their constitutional rights to due process were
being violated. In an affidavit, Arnaout said his group had never aided
anyone "known to be engaged in violence, terrorist activities, or military
operations." But on April 30, 2002, the government struck back, filing a
criminal perjury charge against Arnaout, who had stated under oath that
his charity did not support terrorism and violence. The government charged
that he and his charity had had intimate ties with Al-Qaeda for years, and
helped funnel money and equipment to its operatives on three continents.
Arnaout was held without bail on the grounds that he was a flight risk.

Prosecutors filed a 35-page FBI affidavit alleging that Benevolence International and Arnaout were linked to terrorists and had knowingly supplied
aid to Al-Qaeda. A computer disk at a Benevolence International Foundation
office in Bosnia contained minutes of the founding meeting of Al-Qaeda as
well as pictures of Arnaout, posing with weapons such as missile launch-
ers and anti-aircraft guns. Also seized were undated handwritten messages,
using code names, between Bin Laden and Arnaout. Most significantly, the
charity was accused of sending as much as $685,000 to Muslim fighters in
Chechnya in 2000. For US Attorney Patrick Fitzgerald (who would later gain
fame as the "Plamegate" prosecutor), "This is all part of a mosaic" proving
close ties between Al-Qaeda and Arnaout: "They keep an archive of old bin
Laden photographs in their offices. It tells you something." [71]

In response, the charity's lawyers argued that the government's case was
based on tenuous and outdated links: incriminating photos and messages
dated to the 1980s or early 1990s when the US and Bin Laden were aiding
the Afghans in their war against the Soviet Union. One of the lawyers
declared: "There's nothing in these photos that depicts anything inappropriate." He accused prosecutors of filing the photos as evidence just to "get
them into the newspaper." [72] The government's aggressive tactics were seen
as an effort to intimidate the organization, which had dared challenge the
asset freeze. Indeed, perjury prosecutions were extremely rare in pending
civil cases. Jason Erb, a spokesman for the Council on American Islamic
Relations in Washington, declared: "You're going to be charged with perjury
for declaring your innocence? I think it really makes American Muslims feel
that they are not going to get a fair shake in the justice system." [73] Arnaout
consistently denied that he had sent any money to Al-Qaeda, or that he had
supported terrorism.

It became a *cause célèbre* in the Muslim-American community. The case alarmed Muslim-American civil rights groups and gave rise to protests and demonstrations alleging that the charity was singled out because it was Islamic. Mujeeb Khan, a political coordinator for a Chicago-based group called Muslim Voters of America, called Arnaout a political prisoner and said that the government's affidavit was "based on innuendo and guilt by association."[74] The conditions of his detention—he was held in solitary confinement and "locked up like a dog" according to his attorneys—and the fact that his treatment was "markedly different" from that of other pre-trial detainees added to perceptions of discrimination.[75]

Days before the trial was to begin in February 2003, US District Judge Suzanne B. Conlon expressed doubts about the way prosecutors had drawn up the indictment, saying they had failed under the rules of evidence to show why many of the accusations should be brought to a jury. Only hours before the trial was set to begin, Enaam Arnaout pleaded guilty to the less serious charge of racketeering. He admitted that he had misled donors by fraudulently diverting funds. While donors thought the money was destined for widows, orphans, and the poor, Benevolence International was actually sending boots, blankets, uniforms, tents, and other goods to militants in Bosnia and Chechnya. Whereas US attorney Patrick Fitzgerald argued that Arnaout had lied about his ties to Al-Qaeda and should receive a 20-year sentence, defense attorneys suggested he receive two to five years in jail, in part because Arnaout cooperated with prosecutors in their investigation into Al-Qaeda, and also because of the good works of his charity. The sentencing judge refused to add as much as a dozen years to his sentence, saying his racketeering offense wasn't a crime of terrorism, and that the materials sent to Bosnia and Chechnya were not shown to be for terrorist uses. In her words: "The government has not established that the Bosnian and Chechen recipients of BIF aid were engaged in a federal act of terrorism. ... Nor does the record reflect that he attempted, participated in, or conspired to commit any act of terrorism. ... The government failed to connect the dots." Arnaout's alleged ties to Al-Qaeda were "ambiguous and innocuous," and there was no evidence that he "identified with or supported" terrorism.[76] Indeed, the archives discovered in Benevolence's Bosnia offices did not implicate Arnaout. Federal Judge Conlon duly noted that although Arnaout had a personal association with Usama Bin Laden, it came during the Afghan war against the Soviet Union in the 1980s, "when this country wasn't necessarily opposed to bin Laden."[77] Arnaout's attorney, Joseph Duffy, said the decision "pretty much vindicates what the defense has claimed from the inception, and that is that neither he nor his charity had anything to do with terrorism."[78]

Defenders of Enaam Arnaout stress that he was a victim of shifting alliances of the last two decades. He had been involved in the anti-Soviet jihad of the 1980s, when the Mujahideen were, in Ronald Reagan's words, "freedom fighters." Saudi journalist Jamal Ahmad Khashoggi, who had accompanied both Arnaout and Usama Bin Laden in Afghanistan in the late 1980s, had this to say:

> Most Americans are aware that, despite their support for the Afghan jihad against the Soviets, they had no men on the ground in Afghanistan. The large amounts of arms and aid they provided, in cooperation with Saudi Arabia and Pakistan, used to be stocked in Pakistani warehouses. They relied on brave and motivated individuals to run guns to the mujahideen. Arnaout was one of those. Now though, the FBI, as evidence against him, is using photos of Arnaout carrying an AK-47 and posing with Afghan warlord Gulbuddin Hekmatyar. Had he known what the future had in store, Arnaout would undoubtedly have had his picture taken with the countless US congressional representatives who used to visit the region.[79]

Though exonerated of charges of terrorism, the original accusation was kept alive. On June 10, 2005, in a speech delivered at the National Counterterrorism Center in Northern Virginia, President Bush boasted that investigators had "helped close down a phony charity in Illinois that was channeling money to al Qaeda."[80]

2. The Palestinian connection

The September 11 Commission's financial monograph took note that, although no link existed between Hamas and Al-Qaeda,[81] "cases involving Hamas or certain other terrorist groups are easier to prosecute because the fundraisers are more open about supporting causes that have legitimacy in certain circles and, therefore, are more likely to make incriminating comments on wiretaps or to informants.[82] Anyone raising money in the United States for al Qaeda or groups affiliated with al Qaeda is likely to be extremely secretive and do everything possible to ensure the funds cannot be traced back to him or her."[83] It is ironic that Hamas was first classified as a terrorist organization in January 1995 because of its opposition to the Oslo peace process, which was then at the top of the foreign policy agenda of the Clinton administration. In late 2001, not only was the peace process all but dead, but the foreign policy apparatus was largely controlled by neo-conservative hawks who, since at least 1996, had been trying, from the opposite side of the spectrum, to derail the Oslo peace process.[84]

Throughout the 1990s, the Holy Land Foundation for Relief and Development was the subject of constant political scrutiny. With its primary focus on the Gaza Strip and the West Bank, the charity, based in Richardson,

Texas, was from its early days plagued by accusations that it had close ties to Hamas—indeed that it was a front for that organization. In October 1993, one month after the historic White House handshake between Itzhak Rabin and Yasser Arafat, FBI agents had infiltrated a two-day gathering of the Islamic charity at the Marriott Courtyard hotel in Philadelphia. The meeting revealed a desire to torpedo the Oslo process by undermining the leadership of Arafat and continuing the resistance movement. According to the agents' account of the gathering, "It was decided that most or almost all of the funds collected in the future should be directed to enhance the Islamic Resistance Movement and to weaken the self-rule government [that later became the Palestinian Authority]. Holy War efforts should be supported by increasing spending on the injured, the prisoners and their families, and the martyrs and their families." [85]

Israeli authorities outlawed the Holy Land Foundation's operations in the occupied territories in 1997 and confiscated its funds. Despite a steady stream of information passed along to US authorities by the Israeli government and pro-Israel groups in the US such as the Washington Institute for Near East Policy, proving a direct link between the Holy Land Foundation and Hamas was elusive.[86] The FBI was in favor of outlawing the Foundation but the Justice Department disagreed. According to FBI agent Robert Blitzer, "We all figured just logically some of that [Holy Land money] was being siphoned off for bad stuff, and the Israelis told us that. But the Israelis 'couldn't separate a good dollar from a bad dollar, and neither could we.'" But more senior Justice Department officials would ask them, "How can you prove to us this money isn't saving children's lives?" [87]

Following the September 11 attacks, the proclaimed goal of the Bush administration was to concentrate on "terrorists with global reach"—those who were a direct threat to the United States. President Bush, initially seeking to create a broad coalition against terrorism, resisted repeated Israeli demands to include various Palestinian groups such as Hamas as well as the Lebanese Hezbollah in that category. But with the growing convergence of views on terrorism issues between the Israelis and the Americans, it was only a matter of time before Hamas would be targeted.

On December 4, 2001, following suicide attacks in Israel which resulted in 25 deaths and over 200 casualties, the United States added Hamas to the list of terrorists with a "global reach," and froze the assets and accounts of the Holy Land Foundation, along with those of Beit el Mal Holdings, an investment company in East Jerusalem, the West Bank, and Gaza, and Al Aqsa Islamic Bank. That morning, FBI and Treasury agents raided Holy Land offices in four states. President Bush explained: "Money raised by the Holy Land Foundation is used by Hamas to support schools and indoctrinate children to grow up into suicide bombers. Money raised by the Holy Land Foundation is also used by Hamas to recruit suicide bombers and to support their families."[88] In response, the Foundation said it had "never provided funds, services, or any other form of support to Hamas or any other group that advocates, sponsors, or endorses terrorism, terrorist acts, or violence in any form or for any purpose."[89] Shukri Abu-Baker, the foundation's chief executive, declared: "We are a charity. We're not in a position to fight political wars against anyone. We have always denied that accusation, and the administration did not produce any qualitative evidence. The foundation is strictly a humanitarian organization, and we have never supported Hamas." He said that about half of the $5 million the charity disbursed in the previous year had gone on clothing, food, and medicine for Palestinian refugees in the occupied territories, while the other half went to a variety of other recipients, ranging from Turkish earthquake victims, refugees in Chechnya, Kosovo, Jordan, and Lebanon, food pantries in New Jersey and Texas, and a fund for the victims of the terrorist attacks on the World Trade Center and the Pentagon.[90] Following the freeze, eight American Muslim organizations asked President Bush to reverse his decision and accused him of capitulating to the demands of the Israeli government and the pro-Israel lobby.[91]

A long legal and political battle ensued. On July 26, 2004, the Holy Land Foundation for Relief and Development and seven of its top officials were indicted on charges of funneling $12.4 million to individuals and groups associated with Hamas between 1995, when President Clinton labeled Hamas a terrorist organization, and its closing in late 2001. The 42-count federal indictment said that the Foundation had been set up in the late 1980s "to provide financial and material support to Hamas" and that several of its top officials are related to senior leaders of Hamas, which sponsors suicide bombings against Israel. The charity's lawyer, John Boyd, said that the FBI had relied on "materially misleading" information, such as falsified or mistranslated documents, and asked the inspector general's office at the Justice Department to investigate the FBI. In his words, "Holy Land not only had nothing to do with Hamas, it assiduously avoided Hamas. The result of the FBI's conduct is that an apparently innocent organization is destroyed."[92]

In the United Kingdom, the Palestinian Relief and Development Fund, or Interpal, had been subjected to comparable scrutiny. Allegations of ties to Hamas go back to 1996, when a first investigation was conducted by the Charity Commission. Then in 2003, following pressure from the United States, another investigation was undertaken. President Bush ordered the US Treasury to "block and freeze" all Interpal's assets, on the grounds that the charity was a "specially designated global terrorist." The US allegations were that Interpal, based in Kilburn, north London, was "the fund-raising coordinator of Hamas" and "a principal charity utilized to hide the flow of funds to Hamas."[93]

In August 2003 the United Kingdom followed suit. But a month later, investigators closed the inquiry and lifted the freeze, allowing the charity to resume its operations. The Charity Commission said that the US authorities were unable to substantiate claims that Interpal channeled money to Hamas for terrorist and political activities. All that US officials produced to support their claim were newspaper clippings.[94] The episode nonetheless left a bitter taste. Ibrahim Hewitt, the chairman of Interpal's trustees, said: "The biggest problem was the effect of the action on the confidence our donors had that we could get help through—now we can get back to concentrating on that."[95] Hewitt also expressed disappointment that "such unsubstantiated allegations can be made so flippantly."[96]

The clash between the religious and law enforcement logics

The *zakat* system, with its anonymity, imprecise rules, and lack of centralized control, can easily be manipulated and abused. *Zakat* donations, though "obligatory" from a religious standpoint, are voluntary. In addition, though often regarded as a "religious tax," *zakat*—even in those few countries where it is administered by the state—lacks the transparency and record-keeping requirements of modern tax systems. As in the Christian tradition,[97] the act of donating to the poor is supposed to be discreet.[98] Despite set rates, *zakat* is often distributed in a haphazard way in response to solicitations or specific events (a war, an earthquake, etc), or at specific times of the year (most donations occur during the holy month of Ramadan). Often, money would be given to unknown panhandlers or deposited in donation boxes outside mosques or in public places. Though ostensibly meant for specific causes or recipients, there is no way of knowing whether the money actually reached its intended beneficiaries. Nor would the donors be, at least in the pre-September 11 era, overly preoccupied with that. According to Abdel-Rahman Ghandour, "For a long time, the world of Islamic charities was guided by the religious view that what mattered was the act of giving. There was no point in verifying that the recipients actually put the money to its intended use, since God would call them to account on Judgment Day."[99] Such an attitude made it relatively easy for people to raise funds, say for the building of a new mosque, only to divert the funds to another purpose. The lackadaisical attitude of donors was reinforced both by cultural traits—such as the value of generosity that is so central to Bedouin culture—and by the sudden enrichment of oil-producing countries. For some of the immensely wealthy potentates, saying no to a request desined to benefit the poor—or the

Muslim faith—was simply not an option.

In recent years, the question of the proper recipients of charitable donations had undergone a significant evolution. There is still of course a strong
emphasis on the needy and deprived (the orphans, the widows, the disabled,
the aged, the sick). But three additional categories of recipients have assumed
greater importance. First are refugees, the modern-day equivalent of two of
the traditional recipients of *zakat*, namely captives and stranded travelers,
which are increasingly important for the simple reason that a majority of
the world's refugees are Muslim.[100] Second are prisoners and their depen-
dents—a rapidly growing category.[101] The third is the broadly defined effort
to promote and protect Islam. As Muslim communities have found themselves under attack, the *daawa* effort, which involves proselytizing among
non-Muslims as well as deepening the faith of Muslims, has assumed greater
importance.[102] With all three of these categories overlapping and over-repre-
sented in trouble spots and "failed states," the notion of a "humanitarian
jihad"[103]—an ambiguous concept with mostly spiritual but possibly militaristic connotations—was embraced by a growing number of Muslims.

The ubiquity of Islamic charities in places such as Afghanistan, Somalia,
Bosnia, Chechnya, and Israel's occupied territories has led many self-styled
specialists in Islam or terrorism to draw a straight line between the presence
of charities and terrorist acts. In reality, in war zones, relief, whether Islamic
or not, is badly needed, and charities have little choice but to have some
contacts with outlawed groups. Asia Foundation executives William P. Fuller
and Barnett F. Baron explained the situation they have encountered in Sri
Lanka:

> [Organizations] trying to provide assistance to the millions of Sri Lankans in
> areas controlled by the Tamil Tigers, a named terrorist organization, have little
> choice but to "deal with" this group, at least to provide safe passage for person-
> nel and materials. Likewise, in many countries, local human rights NGOs and
> election monitors are regularly—and falsely—accused by their political oppo-
> nents of supporting radical organizations or violent opposition groups, and
> therefore may be "implicated in questionable activity."[104]

Hence the clash between law enforcement logic and religious logic.
The first logic would impose, Israeli-style, a systematic policy of collective
punishment: following a suicide bombing, the perpetrator's family's home
is destroyed, and other punishments are visited upon his survivors.[105] The
religious logic in contrast holds that charity should not be subjected to any
political or other litmus test. In the words of Ibrahim Hooper, spokesman
for the Council on American Islamic Relations, "I think that Muslims have
a duty to feed the orphans and the needy and it's not our obligation to ask
that orphan who was your father or what did your father do. The only ques-

tion we should ask is, are you hungry." [106]

The Holy Land Foundation for Relief and Development acknowledged that orphans of suicide bombers may have received some of its funds, though not as part of a policy to encourage suicide bombings. It said it gave aid "without regard to the political, religious, or social views of the residents who receive this aid." [107] According to Israeli records, Muhammed Anati, head of the Foundation's Israeli branch, told investigators that "families of so-called martyrs" did not receive any better treatment than other recipients. "We have about 700 orphans, and only 1% of them belong to Hamas families. If it is the orphan of a martyr or not of a martyr, it is not important to the organization." [108]

With the escalation of the war on terror, the contradiction between the two logics was accentuated. What happens when people and charities are forbidden by law to help legally blacklisted, yet religiously deserving recipients? Given the religious, or indeed the humanitarian imperative, such help, even when forbidden by law, is likely to occur, albeit through underground or informal channels. One example of this occurred in Sweden, in connection with the crackdown on the Al-Barakaat network.[109] When three Somalis living in that country were caught in the international law enforcement dragnet and found themselves unable to make a living, their widely publicized plight elicited considerable sympathy, and a charity fund was set up, collecting $25,000 in small donations. When a far-right Swedish political party demanded the charity fund be frozen and its organizers prosecuted for violating UN sanctions, Sweden's government rebuffed the demand.[110] As sanctions multiply against groups, individuals, and especially charities in the Islamic world, one can simply imagine the creative ways in which the law can get circumvented.

Impacts and consequences

Reforming the Islamic charities system was long overdue, yet post-September 11 policies proved mostly counterproductive: they weakened mainstream, "controllable" charities, while building up informal, unchecked, and potentially dangerous charitable and donor networks. Most significantly, the relentless attacks against Islamic charities provided considerable ammunition to all those who argued that the war on terror was above all a war against Islam. To quote Lebanese Shia cleric Mohammad Hussein Fadlallah, the head of one such foundation:

> Since the events of September 11, the American policies toward Islam and Muslim countries in general have posed certain cultural and political challenges and created a global environment hostile to Muslim charity work. Under the pretext of fighting terrorism through targeting its financial resources, the

U.S. has in fact dismantled most of the world's Islamic charity organizations and forced many Arab and Muslim states to restrict charity work.[111]

The effort to control Muslim charities was led by Washington bureaucrats lacking in religious and cultural knowledge. Failing to understand the nature of *zakat*, or the political, financial, and regulatory environment within which charities operated, they imposed money-laundering-style controls which only succeeded in driving charities and donor networks underground.[112] Many reforms, such as the removal of anonymous deposit boxes, were impractical and actually impossible to implement.[113] Muslim donors caught in the dragnet and seeking to avoid future harassment repeatedly asked the US Treasury to release lists of acceptable charities.[114] Instead of such lists, the US Treasury issued voluntary guidelines,[115] which were as vague as they were impractical. The guidelines warned against funding organizations that may "deal with" named terrorist organizations, organizations that may be "otherwise associated with" terrorists, or anyone who "is or has been implicated in any questionable activity." Little assurance was given to prospective donors, since following the guidelines did not preclude future legal or regulatory action.[116]

The crackdown happened at a time when non-Islamic charities enjoyed unprecedented government support. Private philanthropy had always played an important role in the United States,[117] but an equally strong, constitutionally mandated tradition of separation of church and state had placed strict limits on government promotion of religious charities. With the rise of the religious right, a movement aimed at tearing down that wall was able to tip the balance. Marvin Olasky,[118] a Marxist turned Christian fundamentalist, was especially influential. His view that a combination of hard work, private charity, and morality provided the best way of dealing with social problems was seductive to radical conservatives eager to further dismantle the welfare state. In his 1996 book *Renewing American Compassion*, Olasky argued that America should "put welfare entirely in the hands of church—and community—based organizations." [119] From shelters to soup kitchens to job training, private organizations would fill the vacuum left by the elimination of social programs. From Newt Gingrich to George W. Bush, prominent political figures embraced the idea that religious and charitable organizations would more than make up for the disengagement of the state.

The idea provided the basis for George W. Bush's "compassionate conservatism"—a theme which instantly struck a chord in the Islamic community. Indeed, considering the future turn of events, a bitter irony is that the principle of Islamic charities fitted almost perfectly in the political-economic vision of the White House ideologues who placed "faith-based initiatives" at the center of their domestic agenda. Many Islamist thinkers had long advocated the "privatization of welfare" and its replacement by zakat, philan-thropy, and other religiously based redistribution schemes.[120] This was actu-ally a key selling point in the aggressive efforts of veteran Republican activist Grover Norquist to court the Muslim-American vote in the 2000 election. The outreach campaign was so successful that George W. Bush obtained 81 percent of the Islamic vote.[121]

Shortly after he took office, Bush created the White House Office of Faith-Based and Community Initiatives, whose goal was to promote part-nerships between the government, at the federal and state levels, and reli-gious groups (including Muslims). But soon after September 11, every single Islamic charity came under a cloud of suspicion, and sweeping fishing expe-ditions were undertaken by the money warriors. Charities, whether secular or religious, are often plagued by weak financial controls and financial irreg-ularities.[122] In the case of Islamic charities, comparable irregularities took on a sinister character. News headlines would suggest "links to terror." Yet one would have to read much farther in such news stories to discover either that the link was most tenuous, or that non-terrorist-related abuses were involved. For example, an article titled "Charity Said to Have Paid Terrorists" turned out to be about directors "believed to have diverted large sums of money to buy cars, houses and other personal items." [123]

The fallout from the offensive against charities fall under two catego-ries—injury and insult. Shutting down major American Muslim charities and indicting or detaining several prominent Muslim donors had a chill-ing impact on donations. Many potential donors feared doing anything that might bring scrutiny from the FBI. In the words of a Muslim entrepreneur from California, "I have children to raise, I have a business to run, and I don't want to take any chances." [124] Most mainstream charities saw a big drop in donations, and, as a result, their intended recipients suffered.[125] A vicious circle was in place: just as welfare and humanitarian relief needs were most needed, in part because of the consequences of the war on terror, funds were dwindling. At a time when poverty, hopelessness, and despair are widely acknowledged as factors in breeding terror and sustaining terror networks, this is certainly a worrying development.

But the element of insult—gratuitous actions, perceived slights, double standards, etc—was equally significant. Crackdowns seemed timed to offend and embarrass, as they typically took place at the time of the holy month of Ramadan.[126] Forcing certain charities to engage in expensive legal battles to defend themselves against accusations of funding terrorism was perceived by many as a backhanded way to strip them of their assets.[127] Many critics also contrasted the weakening of Islamic charities with the vast offensive by Christian charities in Islamic lands.[128] The attacks on mainstream Islamic charities were intended to show resolve and send a message to "terrorist financiers." The blow to such charities seems to have produced the opposite effect—it drove certain charities underground, strengthened informal networks, and broadened the potential support system of terrorists.[129]

PART V
ASSESSMENTS AND
RECOMMENDATIONS

10

"Catastrophic Successes": Assessing the Financial War

The hardest thing of all is to find a black cat in a dark room, especially if there is no cat.
Confucius

There is no success like failure, and failure is no success at all.
Bob Dylan

One more such victory and we are lost.
Pyrrhus

The financial war has been subjected to very little critical scrutiny. Most assessments of the financial war took official statements at face value. The 100-day progress report issued by the White House following the September 11 attacks announced that "the United States and its allies have been winning the war on the financial front" and assured that "denying terrorists access to funds is a very real success in the war on terrorism." [1] There was no reason to question it at the time, yet in later years, as most aspects of the war on terror were widely and openly criticized, the financial front remained immune to scrutiny. When President Bush, in his September 14, 2005 address to the United Nations announced that "terrorist financing has been drained," [2] the statement was so uncontroversial that it was barely noticed by the media. The view that the financial war was a success was reaffirmed in December 2005 when the bipartisan September 11 Commission assigned letter grades to the government based on the implementation of the panel's 41 key recommendations[3]—the best grade was awarded to the effort against terrorist financing. In an otherwise dismal "report card," the government received an A-minus, for its "vigorous effort against terrorist financing." [4]

To be sure, amid the generally uncritical reporting of the "pseudo-events" of the financial war, and announcements that terrorist funding had been "halted,"[5] criticisms occasionally surfaced. They focused, however, almost exclusively on arguments which bolstered rather than questioned the existing paradigm—that the financial war was not pursued aggressively enough, or that foreign countries were not providing the needed help.[6] A resurgence of attacks led to questioning whether terror had really been starved of its "oxygen." Thus, in September 2002, a United Nations report concluded that the US-led effort on terror financing had failed to dent the resources available to Al-Qaeda. And following a spate of worldwide attacks—on a French tanker off the Yemeni coast, on US Marines in Kuwait, on a discotheque in Bali—CIA director George Tenet told the Joint Intelligence Committee on October 17, 2002 that the risk of a new terror attack inside the United States was as grave and immediate as it was before September 11, 2001: "It is serious, they've reconstituted, they are coming after us, they want to execute attacks. They plan in multiple theaters of operation. They intend to strike again."[7] Political opponents and others seeking to outflank the administration saw in the financial war a safe target: the Bush administration was too timid or "slothful."[8] In the run-up to the 2004 presidential election, Democratic candidate John Kerry repeatedly urged the Bush administration to "get serious" on terrorist financing.[9]

The German philosopher Friedrich Nietzsche observed that "the most common form of human stupidity is forgetting what one is trying to do."[10] The measurement of success should be the end of terrorism, or at the very least a steep decline in acts of terror. But in the parallel universe of the financial war, rules and processes have taken on a life of their own, and the measure of success is no longer a reduction in the number of acts of terror, but rather the multiplication of rules and the hyperactivity of process. The much touted "aggressiveness" of the financial war[11] was seen as synonymous with effectiveness. The empirical evidence is troubling. Not only is there a disconnect between actions and results, but the propensity of the financial war to overkill has become counter-productive.

It is true that the first 100 days saw a flurry of activity on the financial front, with frozen accounts, high-profile initiatives, and a highly publicized broadening and deepening of the financial war.[12] But there was little evidence that such efforts starved terrorists of financing. Indeed, the September 11 Commission's terrorist financing monograph, released in August 2004, stated that precisely at the time of the 100-day progress report (which coincided roughly with the end of the military offensive in Afghanistan), there was an actual increase in terrorist funding. According to the report, "there is evidence that donations increased substantially after the United

States attacked al Qaeda in Afghanistan, suggesting considerable anti-U.S. sentiment among the donors." [13] By the same token the very day of President Bush's September 2005 speech to the United Nations was marked by a resurgence of terrorist acts in Iraq.[14] And almost simultaneously with the awarding of "A-minus" to the financial warriors, a report by the Government Accountability Office, the investigative arm of Congress, came out which was sharply critical of the government's financial war effort.[15] If nothing else, these developments suggest that money is not the oxygen of terror.

Catastrophic successes

During the 2004 presidential election, the closest the Bush administration came to acknowledging mistakes in Iraq was to call the war a "catastrophic success." [16] The financial warriors measured success in terms of the multiplication of controls and initiatives affecting the international financial system. In one of his statements about Al-Qaeda's finances, former Treasury General Counsel David D. Aufhauser boasted that what "matters is the impact we're having on their cash flow, which has slowed." As evidence, he cited widespread reports that Al-Qaeda was fleeing the heavily scrutinized Western banking system, switching to couriers to convey cash, gold, diamonds, and other commodities. "That's slower, costlier, and easier to catch," he said.[17] Although such a shift may have slowed down Al-Qaeda's resource flows, the idea that it has made them "easier to catch" is optimistic. Once resources have left the formal banking circuits, they become nearly impossible to catch, whatever form they are in.

In March 2005 Robert Werner, the head of the Treasury Department's Office of Foreign Assets Control, boasted that the United States had limited terrorists' ability to move and store funds by freezing almost $150 million and blocking the financial transactions of roughly 400 people since the September 11 attacks. He declared: "That's always been the counterpoint, that if you drive people out of the formal system, they are harder to find. However, it also shows that our actions can disrupt and impede corrupt financial flows in a very, very significant way. If people are deprived of the banks and non-banks, whether it's broker-dealers, or money remitters, or insurance companies, it gets very difficult." [18] On May 4, 2005, Undersecretary for Terrorism and Financial Intelligence Stuart Levey told two sub-committees of the US House of Representatives: "We are seeing terrorist groups avoiding formal financing channels and instead resorting to riskier and more cumbersome conduits like bulk cash smuggling. And, most importantly, we have indications that terrorist groups like Al-Qaeda and Hamas are feeling the pressure and are hurting for money." [19]

Many such "successes" have proven catastrophic. The financial war came

at a very high price. As discussed elsewhere, among many other contradictions, "gated finance" has clashed with other goals of the war on terror,
and has forced terrorists into "Neanderthal" conduits such as gold bars and
sacks of cash.[20] This has further complicated the task of law enforcement.[21]
Indiscriminate financial measures, especially those affecting Islamic charities, played a big role in fostering the view that the war on terror was a war
on Islam, which in turn has increased active and passive support for terrorism.

In early May 2005, news headlines announced yet another major breakthrough in the global war on terror: "Al Qaeda's Number 3" had been
captured. President George W. Bush called the capture of Libyan national
Abu Farraj al-Libbi in Pakistan—a "top general" and "a major facilitator and
chief planner for the Al-Qaeda network"—"a critical victory in the war on
terror."[22] Pervez Musharraf, Pakistan's military ruler, boasted that the arrest
was a fatal blow to Al-Qaeda. "We have broken their back. They cease to
exist as a cohesive, homogenous body under good command and control,
vertical and horizontal."[23] A few days later, however, the Sunday Times
revealed that the event was of far less significance than initially thought. The
arrested terrorist "was not the terrorists' third in command, as claimed, but
a middle-ranker derided by one source as 'among the flotsam and jetsam' of
the organization."[24] He had been neither on the FBI's most-wanted list, nor
on the State Department's "rewards for justice program." It may have been
a case of mistaken identity.[25] The story may have been "cynically hyped by
both Pakistan and the United States to distract attention from their lack of
progress in capturing Bin Laden, who has now been on the run for almost
four years."[26] (Incidentally, a suspiciously large number of captured terrorists
were said to be "Al Qaeda's number 3"—a shadowy position, considering that
only the top two officials of the organization—Usama Bin Laden and Ayman
Al Zawahiri—are known with any certainty.)[27]

Another explanation was that the story was designed to drown out—
successfully, it turned out—another more significant one that had appeared
a few days earlier: unreleased State Department statistics had shown a threefold increase in "significant" terrorist attacks (from 175 to 655) between 2003
and 2004.[28] In the words of Larry C. Johnson, a former senior State Department counter-terrorism official: "Last year was bad. This year is worse. They
are deliberately trying to withhold data because it shows that as far as the
war on terrorism goes internationally, we're losing."[29]

Tampering with the annual statistics on terrorism had become something
of a ritual. When it was first released in April 2004, the 2003 "Patterns
of Global Terrorism" report had offered a glowing assessment of the war
on terror. It announced that worldwide terrorism dropped by 45 percent

between 2001 and 2003, and boasted that the previous year had seen the lowest annual total of international terrorist attacks since 1969.[30] Deputy Secretary of State Richard Armitage said: "You will find in these pages clear evidence that we are prevailing in the fight." And Ambassador Cofer Black, State Department Coordinator for Counterterrorism, explained: "There have been fewer victims because the community of nations is collaborating more efficiently and effectively. We have had a tremendous amount of help and we are very grateful."[31]

But it turned out that despite the considerable resources marshalled in putting together the most authoritative study on the subject, the report was little more than an exercise in creative writing. The numbers had been crudely massaged. Omissions, simple mistakes in arithmetic, a wrong cutoff date, were only some of the problems. The conclusions of the report were also at odds with the information contained in its body. Following questions by outside researchers and members of Congress, the report was corrected and reissued in June 2004. The revised number of people killed or wounded in international terrorist attacks in 2003 turned out to be twice what was originally reported: there had been a 56 percent increase from 2002, and the number of "significant" attacks reached its highest level in more than 20 years.[32]

The following year, the State Department decided, just as significant terrorist attacks had tripled, to stop altogether the inclusion of such statistics in its "Patterns of Global Terrorism." In a letter to Secretary of State Condoleezza Rice, Representative Henry A. Waxman, a California Democrat, commented that "the large increases in terrorist attacks reported in 2004 may undermine administration claims of success in the war on terror, but political inconvenience has never been a legitimate basis for withholding facts from the American people."[33]

Considering the ambiguities of the very notion of a war on terror,[34] measuring success was tricky. At the same time, however, one of the reasons behind the early focus on the financial front was that it lent itself to a scorecard logic[35]—"metrics" to use Defense Secretary Donald Rumsfeld's word. (Another measurement, reminiscent of the Vietnam War, was the use of the enemy body count as a measure of success.[36]) The truth of the matter is that most of the proclamations of "victory" and "progress" were not very significant. Since the September 11 attacks, President Bush's line had been that "because America has led, the forces of terror and tyranny have suffered defeat after defeat, and America and the world are safer."[37] Throughout the 2004 presidential campaign, the "talking point" repeated to show the success of Bush as a "war president" was that there had been no attack on US soil since September 11, 2001.[38] On July 11, 2005, four days after the terrorist attacks in London, President Bush told graduates of the FBI Academy: "We're fighting the enemy in Iraq and Afghanistan and across the world so we do not have to face them here at home." [39] (Democratic Senator Carl Levin remarked, "Tony Blair must absolutely have blanched when he heard that." [40])

Triumphalism came easily to the financial warriors. Top officials claimed that since 1997, they had Bin Laden's financial network almost "completely mapped," [41] and that the measures taken after September 11 had "made a dent in al-Qaeda's fundraising operations and that the group [had] not found new ways to raise money." [42] As he toured the Financial Crimes Enforcement Network, President Bush called it the "the front line of our war." [43] Top Treasury officials took to portraying themselves as "the greatest enemies of the terrorists." [44] The very occurrence of financial strikes was assumed to reduce the "stash of cash" available to terrorists. The first strike of the war on terror, against "the financial foundation of the global terror network," suggested the permanent disabling of financial networks. [45] A week after the first strike, when he announced that 50 new accounts would be frozen, Bush proclaimed that this constituted "progress on the financial front." [46] Every subsequent announcement came with great fanfare: there had been "inroads in isolating funds"; Al-Qaeda was "crippled," "severely disrupted," and "unable to move funds for terrorist operations." [47]

Following the disclosure of the controversial monitoring of the massive Swift (Society for Worldwide Interbank Financial Telecommunications) system, Treasury Secretary John Snow said that the program was the thing he was "proudest of" in his tenure: "It's really government at its best. It's responsible government. It's effective government." [48] Vice-President Dick Cheney called the program "absolutely essential" to protecting the country from further attacks. [49] Yet the specifics were far from convincing. According to Stuart Levey, Treasury Undersecretary for Terrorism and Financial Intelligence, the program helped in the probe of the July 7, 2005 London bombings, and helped lead investigators to "a key facilitator of terrorism in Iraq." [50]

How could there be such a gulf between rhetoric and reality? One reason was that the financial dimension of terror was isolated, and within this parallel universe a peculiar logic prevailed, whereby process becomes divorced from outcome.

Another distorting factor is that definitions of terror were broadened to the point of meaninglessness. According to Juliette Kayyem, a former Clinton administration Justice official who heads the national security program at Harvard University's John F. Kennedy School of Government, "What we're seeing over time is the equivalent of mission creep: Cases that would not be terrorism cases before Sept. 11 are swept onto the terrorism docket. The problem is that it's not good to cook the numbers. ... We have no accurate assessment of whether the war on terrorism is actually working."[51] Bruce Hoffman, who heads the Washington office of Rand Corporation, also commented: "For so many of these cases, there seems to be much less substance to them than we first assume or have first been told. There's an inherent deterrent effect in cracking down on any illicit activity. But the challenge is not exaggerating what they were up to—not portraying them as super-terrorists when they're really the low end of the food chain."[52]

President Bush often asserted that "federal terrorism investigations have resulted in charges against more than 400 suspects, and more than half of those charged have been convicted."[53] Yet the *Washington Post* investigative reporters who looked into the matter found out, first, that 39 people—not 200—had been convicted of crimes related to terrorism or national security, and, second, that most cases had no connection to terrorism at all. Convictions were essentially for relatively minor crimes such as making false statements and violating immigration laws.[54] Indeed, as another *Washington Post* investigation concluded, "immigration charges are being used much as they have been for years against drug traffickers—as a tool to lock up suspects, gain informants and obtain search warrants."[55] Following the investigation of the World Trade Center attacks, 768 suspects were secretly processed on immigration charges. Most were deported after being cleared of connections to terrorism.

Finally, financial warriors are prompt at adding names and amounts, but are slow at subtracting them when suspects are exonerated of links to terror. As noted by James Bovard, "Federal officials continually bragged of the total amount of alleged terrorist assets frozen. But there were no press releases confessing that much of the money was later returned after no evidence of wrongdoing could be found."[56]

Needles and haystacks

If true victories in the financial war consist in finding proverbial needles, much of what passes for great strides in the financial war boils down to the creation of new haystacks, or the enlargement of existing ones. Broadening reporting rules, creating new databases, subjecting more companies to reporting requirements and similar initiatives have typically been unveiled with great fanfare and breathless anticipation. Unfortunately, initiatives designed to create haystacks as a way of uncovering needles usually complicates the task.

The information revolution has made it very easy to compile gigantic databases, while artificial intelligence software has held out the prospect of finding terrorists through the miracle of technology. To say the least, results so far have been disappointing. Ron Suskind had this to say about the government's vast "search and seizure" machine: "As this machine searched the landscape, it swept up the suspicious, or simply the unfortunate, by the stadiumful and caught almost no one who was actually a danger to America." [57] One crimimal information project known as Matrix (Multi-state Anti-Terrorism Information Exchange) tried to use a "high terrorism factor" scoring system incorporating such factors as age, sex, ethnicity, credit history, "investigational data," information about pilot and driver licenses, and connections to "dirty" addresses known to have been used by other suspects. It resulted in a gigantic haystack of 120,000 people who showed a statistical likelihood of being terrorists. Their names were given to the US authorities. [58]

Similar haystacks are generated by the proliferation of useless or misleading tips. Between September 11 and November 6, 2001, law enforcement authorities have fielded no fewer than 435,000 tips in response to Attorney General John Ashcroft's call for Americans to report any suspicious activities. As a result, during that period, 1,100 people were detained, and the Justice Department drew up a list of 5,000 Middle Eastern men it wanted to question further. [59] It was a useful reminder that "when people are looking for something suspicious, almost anything can start to look fishy." [60] Although virtually all people ensnared in the program had nothing to do with terrorism, the initiative was judged "helpful" by the bureaucracies involved, and further tips were invited. [61]

There are countless examples of such open-ended accumulation of haystacks—and still, law enforcement agencies and foreign governments are constantly pressed to furnish more names. [62] Between 2003 and 2005, the number of international terrorism suspects or people who allegedly aid them, maintained by the National Counterterrorism Center, has more than quadrupled, reaching 325,000 names. [63] Another example is the exponential growth in suspicious activity reports, or SARs. The system had long been criticized for its cost and inefficiency: in 1998, out of 96,900 SARs filed, there were only 932 money laundering convictions (none for terrorist financing), representing a cost of more than $10 million per conviction; yet the number of reports kept increasing, jumping to 156,931 in 2000. [64] In 2001 it was estimated that 250,000 SARs had been filed, although most of them were probably never read. [65] With the start of the war on terror, banks wanted above all to avoid accusations that they were being lax, or that they did not take the "Know Your Customer" requirement seriously. (One author wrote: "'Know your customer' rule. Bankers call it KYC. I call it CYA, which stands for 'Cover your ass,' because that's what most of them are really doing." [66])

In 2004, following a $40 million fine levied against AmSouth, an Alabama bank, for failing to file suspicious activity reports, and a $25 million fine against Washington's Riggs Bank, many banks stepped up their strategy of "defensive filings" to avoid fines (or worse, crippling criminal indictments) for failing to flag suspicious transactions.[67] Subsequent developments revealed the absurdity of the system. Following its problems with regulators, Riggs Bank went overboard in its filings of SARs. Any large cash transaction was treated as inherently suspicious. Among those reported to regulators for possible money laundering were Washington luminaries such as Bob Dole, the long-time Washington senator and 1996 Republican presidential candidate, and former Defense Secretary Frank Carlucci.[68] The *Wall Street Journal* reported that Senator Dole, whose withdrawals since 1997 averaged $12,000 a week, kept a wad of $100 bills in the breast pocket of his shirt for walking-around money. In his words, "I probably use a credit card four or five times a year. I don't even have a wallet."[69] Both Dole and Carlucci say they belong to a generation which has an aversion to debt and credit cards.

In 2005 it was estimated that 700,000 SARs would be filed by banks in the United States, an increase of more than 37 percent over 2004.[70] In the United Kingdom, numbers of suspicious transactions reported increased fivefold between 2001 and 2005, from 30,000 to 150,000.[71] According to John J. Byrne of the American Banking Association's center for regulatory compliance, "Banks are filing on anything remotely possibly illegal. It's the 'when in doubt, file' syndrome." According to Byrne, banks worry about being prosecuted, and want to "stave off unwanted criticism or second guessing."[72] Even the head of the Treasury Department's Financial Crimes Enforcement Network (FinCen) recognized that such "defensive filings" "have little value, degrade the valuable reports in the database and implicate privacy concerns."[73]

In early 2005 an organized effort by the international financial community was aimed at reducing the number of SARs filed by banks. The Financial Services Roundtable, which represents many of the largest US banks, insurance, and securities firms, warned that a flood of such reports was costing the industry nearly $11 billion on money laundering compliance in 2005, up 50 percent since 2002.[74] In a letter to Treasury Department officials, 52 banking associations around the country said that a "lack of clarity" by the government in explaining what is expected of them in complying with regulations to deter terrorist financing and money laundering has "complicated, and in some cases undermined" those efforts.[75] In the words of Charles A. Intriago, a former federal prosecutor who runs Money Laundering Alert, "This strikes me as a fruitless exercise, an impossible task. This risks further burdening the industry, and it's tough to see how it will produce much if any useful data for the government in tracking terrorist financing." [76]

As for the secret Terrorist Finance Tracking Program, Treasury Secretary John Snow has given assurances: "It is not 'data mining,' or trolling through the private financial records of Americans. It is not a 'fishing expedition,' but rather a sharp harpoon aimed at the heart of terrorist activity." [77] Yet as such emergency programs become institutionalized, and as comparable dragnets are considered,[78] privacy advocates and financial institutions alike have reason to worry.

11

Rethinking Money and Terror

It is not that they cannot see the solution. It is that they cannot see the problem.
G.K. Chesterton

Rebellion must have an unassailable base, something guarded not merely from attack, but from the fear of it: such a base as the Arab revolt had in the Red Sea ports, the desert, or in the minds of men converted to its creed.
T.E. Lawrence

O would some power the gift give us
To see ourselves as others see us.
Robert Burns

The general understanding of the problem of terrorism has evolved quite a bit since the early days of the war on terror—except on matters of terrorist financing. Financial warriors still have a tendency to go around in circles in search of a magic bullet. Consider the case of UK Chancellor of the Exchequer Gordon Brown, who in October 2001 had announced the creation of a modern-day "Bletchley Park" to "crack the code" of terrorist financing.[1] Over four years later, in February 2006, he promised, in almost identical words, yet again another Bletchley Park: "As Chancellor, I have found myself immersed in measures designed to cut off the sources of terrorist finance. And I have discovered that this requires an international operation using modern methods of forensic accounting as imaginative and pathbreaking for our times as the Enigma codebreakers at Bletchley Park achieved more than half a century ago."[2] Terrorist finance was a code to be cracked. Salvation would come from technology, or from the mind of a brilliant mathematician.

Other aspects of the war on terror have undergone significant change. Many of the unsayables of the post-September 11 era have become an acceptable part of the mainstream discourse. The once taboo theme of intelligence failure has long been broken. Countless books and reports have amply documented two colossal failures—the inability to prevent the September 11 attacks despite repeated warnings, and the weapons of mass destruction fiasco which furnished the pretext for the Iraq war.[3] Another taboo concerned the "why do they hate us?" question. The politically correct answer was that "they hated us because of our freedoms." Acknowledging that "they hate us because of our policies" has now become commonplace. Since the start of George W. Bush's second term, there has been a new emphasis on multilateralism and public diplomacy. The new approach aimed at a more genuine engagement of the United States with the rest of the world, repairing frayed ties with allies, and, above all, winning "hearts and minds" in the Muslim world, as evidenced by the high-profile appointment of Karen Hughes, one of George Bush's most trusted aides, to the position of Undersecretary of State for Public Diplomacy.

Examples abound of the new public skepticism over the conduct of the global war on terror. On November 24, 2004, the Pentagon released a report by the Defense Science Board, an advisory committee to the Defense Secretary, composed of top military commanders and intelligence figures, on the subject of "strategic communication." The report was sharply critical of the Bush administration and ran counter to the dominant narrative. In answer to the "why do they hate us?" question, the report said that "Muslims do not 'hate our freedom,' but rather they hate our policies," adding that "when American public diplomacy talks about bringing democracy to Islamic societies, this is seen as no more than self-serving hypocrisy."[4] It stated that the resentment in the Islamic world was due to US support for Israel and for Arab dictatorships, and not to a hatred of Western values themselves.[5]

It was the first of a series of official reports and statements critical of the war on terror. In January 2005 Robert Hutchings, director of the National Intelligence Council (NIC), the official research arm of the entire US intelligence community, presented "Mapping the Global Future," the Council's latest report on long-term global trends, which stated that Iraq had become "a magnet for international terrorist activity."[6] The report suggested that the Al-Qaeda generation that trained in Afghanistan would soon dissipate, "to be replaced in part by survivors of the conflict in Iraq."[7] The following month, CIA chief Porter Goss told the Senate Intelligence Committee that the United States was less secure than it had been before the Iraqi invasion. In his words, "Islamic extremists are exploiting the Iraqi conflict to recruit new anti-U.S. jihadists. These jihadists who survive will leave Iraq experienced and focused on acts of urban terrorism. They represent a potential pool of contacts to build transnational terrorist cells, groups and networks in Saudi Arabia, Jordan and other countries." [8] The Director of Defense Intelligence, Vice-Admiral Lowell E. Jacoby, concurred: "Our policies in the Middle East fuel Islamic resentment. Overwhelming majorities in Morocco, Jordan, and Saudi Arabia believe the U.S. has a negative policy toward the Arab world." [9]

Such revisionist views had some impact on policies. Indeed, with the formal start of the second Bush administration in January 2005, a broad review of the "global war on terror" was initiated. In July 2005, recognizing that the fight against Al-Qaeda was more of an ideological battle than simply a military one, a number of top administration officials announced that the "global war on terror" (GWOT) policy would be retired and replaced with that of "a global struggle against violent extremism" [10] (GSAVE).[11] Hints of a clash of civilizations were dropped in favor of an embrace of moderate Islam, which would be an equal partner in what Donald Rumsfeld called the "global struggle against the enemies of freedom, the enemies of civilization." [12] National Security Adviser Steven J. Hadley explained: "It is more than just a military war on terror. It's broader than that. It's a global struggle against extremism. We need to dispute both the gloomy vision and offer a positive alternative." [13] As for General Richard B. Myers, chairman of the Joint Chiefs of Staff, he had "objected to the use of the term 'war on terrorism' before, because if you call it a war, then you think of people in uniform as being the solution." In his words, the solution is "more diplomatic, more economic, more political than it is military." [14]

To be sure, there were still supporters of the earlier militaristic and unilateralist approach. Although most of the leading neo-conservatives (such as Paul Wolfowitz, Douglas Feith, and Richard Perle) had left the administration, a few (most notably Elliott Abrams, promoted to Deputy National Security Adviser in February 2005) were still part of the second Bush term, and many of their ideas had been injected into the political bloodstream. The Christian fundamentalist constituency, which claimed credit for helping the President win re-election, still made its voice heard. And hardliners still dominated cable television and talk radio, and their presence was still felt in the print media. President Bush himself seemed unsure of the path to follow. Some of his policies and statements reflected a sharp departure from the course taken during his first term, playing down the bravado and the gratuitous slights to allies. Yet at the same time, he often seemed incapable of shedding his "war president" persona. After many of his top advisers had officially dropped the "war on terror" rhetoric, he characteristically insisted on "staying the course," stating: "Make no mistake about it, we are at war. We're at war with an enemy that attacked us on September the 11th, 2001. We're at war against an enemy that, since that day, has continued to kill." [15]

In contrast, no reassessment was undertaken in connection with the financial war. Frantically making rules domestically and internationally, still living within their own parallel universe, and insulated from empirical challenges, the financial warriors "stayed the course." They no doubt felt vindicated by the "A-minus" grade awarded to them by the September 11 Commission.[16] Unlike other public officials, their statements reprised, often word for word, the immediate post-September 11 discourse.[17]

The unexamined paradigm

Terrorist financing "facts," axioms, and assumptions born in the immediate aftermath of September 11 have hardened into hard-to-shake myths and urban legends. The centrality of money and other commonly held beliefs on terrorist financing have been debunked by the September 11 Commission. All recent terrorist attacks have cost very little money, yet every act of terror is invariably followed by expert disquisitions on the central role of money, and by calls for stricter financial controls. The axiom that money is the lifeblood of terror is unquestioned, as is the underlying assumption of a finite stash of terrorist money hidden somewhere in the global financial system. Thoroughly discredited "facts" and allegations keep resurfacing in articles and books about terrorist financing.[18]

In the deluge of books and articles on the post-September 11 world, the conventional wisdom on terrorist financing is usually repeated uncritically.[19] Only a couple of books, both dealing with broader aspects of the war on terror, are notable for directly criticizing the fallacies of the financial war. One is *Through Our Enemies' Eye*, published anonymously by Michael Scheuer, who served as the chief of the Bin Laden "virtual station" at the CIA from 1996 to 1999, and argued convincingly that the focus on Bin Laden's money obscured the more fundamental issues of politics and ideology.[20] The other is James Bovard's *Terrorism and Tyranny*, which saw in the financial war a power grab by bureaucrats who brought all sorts of unrelated crimes under the terrorist financing umbrella.[21]

The dichotomy between new thinking on various aspects of the terror threat and old thinking on terrorist financing can be seen in two recent documents—one a "blueprint for action" published three years after the World Trade Center attacks by a who's who of top former government officials under the chairmanship of former counter-terrorism czar Richard Clarke,[22] and the other published almost simultaneously under the title "Update on the Global Campaign against Terrorist Financing"[23] by the prestigious Council on Foreign Relations. The Clarke report acknowledges "the strong consensus among experts that the ranks of the jihadists have increased significantly since 9/11,"[24] and the fact that the war in Iraq "has been deeply counterproductive to the greater effort" since it has "alienated crucial allies in the battle against jihadists, made friendly Muslims into skeptics, turned skeptics into radicals, and created a new battleground for itinerant jihadist insurgents." [25] It calls for a sharp departure from the hard-headed militarism and unilateralism that have characterized the first term of George W. Bush, and for a new focus on multilateralism and international cooperation.[26] More specifically, it emphasizes the need to stress long-denigrated soft-power issues, such as the battle of ideas and the need to reach out to Muslims.[27]

In contrast, on the subject of terrorist financing, the Clarke report proves that there had been no learning curve. In its recommendations on "the elimination of terror financing," the report had this to say:

> The next president should designate a special assistant to the president for combating terrorist financing at the National Security Council, with the specific mandate to lead U.S. efforts on terrorist financing issues. Congress should pass and the president should sign legislation requiring the executive branch to submit to Congress on an annual basis a written certification detailing the steps that foreign nations have taken to cooperate with American and international efforts to combat terrorist financing.[28]

In other words, none of the early assumptions of the financial war had been questioned. The only solutions lay in doing more of the same—only more forcefully. "Eliminating terror financing" would occur through the creation of more bureaucracy-intensive schemes, both domestically and internationally. Finance was still regarded as an autonomous realm, based on the axioms and assumptions of the immediate post-September 11 environment.[29] According to Clarke et al:

> As long as al Qaeda maintains a lucrative financial network, it remains a lethal threat to the United States. And al Qaeda still has money to fund terrorist operations. The financial network that currently supports al Qaeda is diverse and ever-changing, taking advantage of unprotected or undetected opportunities to raise, hold, and move funds. Yet there is a central "theory of the case" that characterizes U.S. understanding of the al Qaeda financial network and guides U.S. actions to disrupt it and track it back to specific terrorist cells and leaders.[30]

Characteristically, although the "blueprint for action" to "defeat the jihadists" puts "eroding the support" for extremists at the center of its proposals,[31] it fails to draw any connection between the financial war and the issue of support.

The Council on Foreign Relations report, chaired by controversial insurance tycoon Maurice Greenberg,[32] offered "specific strategic and tactical recommendations," which failed to question any of the principles underlying the financial war. Again, the report's summary was: let's do more of the same, only more forcefully. More specifically, the report recommended, on the domestic front "centralizing authority for policy formation and implementation on these issues within the White House," and on the international front, the creation of a new multilateral organization to facilitate international cooperation." Another recommendation was to place "issues regarding terrorist financing front and center in every bilateral diplomatic discussion with every 'front-line' state in the fight against terrorism." [33]

The next section suggests that the established axioms and assumptions that have guided the financial war ought to be seriously examined in the light of new empirical evidence. The concluding part of this chapter makes suggestions for reform, based on the alternative paradigm of terrorist financing. [34]

The empirical evidence

One of the certainties of the post-September 11 environment is that following every terrorist attack, money will re-appear as an all-purpose residual explanation. Pundits will bring up the need to cut off terrorist funding, and the financial terrain will be where forceful action will be instantly taken by governments. Just as predictably, subsequent inquiries will disclose that terrorist attacks involve very small amounts—which no broadening of the financial dragnet can prevent.

It has happened after the New York and Washington attacks. It also happened after Bali, Madrid, Istanbul, and London. And it will happen again. The soft terrain of finance is where governments can take action and show resolve before knowing anything of substance about the circumstances of the attacks. The notions that deadly terrorist attacks can be conducted with very little money, that cross-border fund transfers may not be necessary, that plotters can be local, etc, have yet to sink in.

A paradox is that while the actual cost of terrorist attacks is one of the few things investigators can determine with any degree of confidence, the financial warriors still operate on the basis of fanciful assumptions. After the September 11 attacks, a number of thorough investigations traced with some precision the flow of money received and disbursed by the 19 hijackers. While movements of funds transiting on bank accounts did not exceed $304,000, it is assumed that there might have been some unrecorded cash transactions, although—considering the modest lifestyle of the hijackers—such amounts were probably quite small. Another reason for possible discrepancies is related to what should fall under the "cost" rubric of the operation, i.e. whether costs should be limited to the actual preparation of the attacks—flight lessons, scouting, and practice flights—or whether living expenses of the hijackers in the US in 2000 and 2001 should be included.[35]

A breakdown of income and expenses as evidenced by the paper and electronic trail (credit card and ATM transactions, rental payments, purchase of airline tickets, and other items) yielded a fairly accurate picture of the hijackers' lives as well as the logistics of the operation. Deposits into bank accounts held by the hijackers, which included several accounts at SunTrust Banks Inc. in Florida, totaled $303,481.63, while $303,671.62 was disbursed to the hijackers. Some of the hijackers also "maxed out" on their credit cards. Most deposits ($143,000, or 47 percent of the total) were made in cash. Next ($103,200, or 34 percent of the total) came from wire transfers, which included transfers from the United Arab Emirates via Citigroup in New York. There were also small deposits in travelers' checks and in personal checks. Most withdrawals ($128,000, or 42 percent) took place through ATMs. About $45,550, or 15 percent of the total, was spent on airline tickets, and $39,500, or 13 percent, was spent on "aviation," which included flight lessons. Checks written to individuals accounted for about $36,440 (12 percent). About $33,400 (11 percent) was characterized as "miscellaneous," which included some daily living expenses. About $6,000 (2 percent of the total), was spent on cars, and a comparable amount was spent on lodging.[36]

Under the existing money laundering regime, there was no reason for any of the financial transactions to raise any red flags. The amounts were too small to be detected. The hijackers, who claimed student status (some were indeed in flight school), dealt with sums and transfer patterns that were deemed normal: as foreign students, they had a plausible reason for receiving funds periodically from abroad in amounts corresponding to reasonable estimates of tuition and living expenses. The bank involved, SunTrust Banks, was a major regional American bank. It is not surprising that, contrary to persistent media accounts, no financial institution had filed a Suspicious Activity Report (SAR) in connection with any of the 19 hijackers prior to September 11 (although such SARs were filed after the names of the hijackers were made public.)[37] As the September 11 Commission's financial monograph reported: "The failure to file SARs was not unreasonable. Even in hindsight, there is nothing ... to indicate that any SAR should have been filed or the hijackers otherwise reported to law enforcement."[38] And it is not clear that any of the new financial safeguards put in place *in response* to the September 11 attacks would, in and of themselves, have caught the money—let alone prevented the attacks.

In sum, in just about every respect, the reality of September 11 funding differed from the widely believed assertions. No rogue states were involved. No charities, hawalas, Islamic banks, front companies, or rich Saudi merchants were involved. The amounts were small and financing was tight. Two principal "paymasters" or "financial facilitators," Ali Abdul Aziz Ali, a.k.a. Ammar al Baluchi, a.k.a. "Ali," and Mustafa al Hawsawi, had wired most of the funds from the United Arab Emirates.[39] Neither fit the profile of the "usual suspect" literature.[40]

Who if anyone was behind those shadowy paymasters? The question had the quality of a Rorschach test, since different groups with different political beliefs and agendas offered specific answers.[41] The 9/11 Commission Report was unable to be more specific:

> To date, the U.S. government has not been able to determine the origin of the money used for the 9/11 attacks. Ultimately the question is of little practical significance. Al Qaeda had many avenues of funding. If a particular funding source had dried up, al Qaeda could have easily tapped a different source or diverted funds from another project to fund an operation that cost $400,000–$500,000 over nearly two years.[42]

A massive attack such as that of September 11 cost less than half a million dollars. Smaller, albeit highly destructive attacks cost much less. The 1993 World Trade Center attack cost less than $20,000.[43] The twin October 2002 nightclub bombings in Bali, which killed 202 people, cost less than $50,000.[44] The August 1998 twin truck bombings of the US embassies in Kenya and Tanzania, which killed 231 people, cost $10,000.[45] And the November 2003 attacks in Istanbul, Turkey—four suicide truck bombings that killed 62 people—cost less than $40,000.[46] The Madrid bombings of March 2004, which involved ten simultaneous attacks on four commuter trains and killed 191 people, cost $10,000.[47] And according to Mohammed Bouzoubaa, Morocco's justice minister, the May 2003 bombings in Casablanca, which killed 45 people, cost $4,000.[48] The cheapest of all may have been the four coordinated suicide bombings that struck London's public transport system in July 2005, which killed 52 civilians and injured over 700 people: their total cost was under $1,000.[49]

If there is a pattern, it is probably that the cost of mounting an attack keeps decreasing—that far from being the oxygen of terror, money is now a minor aspect of terrorism. This remains to be understood by financial warriors and terrorist experts. Despite ample evidence hiding in plain sight, the financial warriors have learned little if anything. Over four years after the September 11 attacks, the discourse on terrorist financing has remained unchanged. Every official report seems to have the obligatory cliché: "money is like oxygen to terrorists, and it must be choked-off,"[50] or some variation on that theme. In its guide titled "The Financial War on Terror," the Financial Action Task Force explains: "Terrorism is a business ... and like all businesses, terrorism requires money."[51]

It is difficult to see how the current system, with its focus on large sums, international transfers, and paymasters, can catch small, locally funded, and often self-financed operations. Yet the mindset dominated by a money laundering paradigm still prevails, on the basis of a syllogism: "most serious and organised crime is motivated by financial gain;"[52] terrorism is a serious and organized crime; therefore it is motivated by financial gain. As already discussed,[53] differences between the logics of terrorist financing and the crime-for-profit model which includes money laundering (where sums are substantial, where there is a crime-for-profit logic, where the origin of money is criminal and needs disguising, etc), are substantial, yet the money warriors keep pushing for more money-laundering-inspired rules and more reporting requirements in order to get to the bottom of the money trail.

Financial institutions have long been skeptical of the usefulness of much of the paperwork generated first by the war on drugs and later by the war on terror. The exponential growth of Suspicious Activities Reports (SARs) has done little to detect crime, and there is no evidence that a single act of terror had been prevented thanks to such reports.[54] Insofar as thorough "know-your-customer" checks and abundant "suspicious transaction reports"[55] have not stopped the terrorist attacks, more controls were deemed expensive, ineffective, and intrusive. Yet in the aftermath of major terror attacks, especially those of New York, Madrid, and London, banks were under pressure to show that they were doing their part in the war on terror by enthusiastically approving the open-ended expansion of reporting requirements, and devising new ways of detecting terror funding.[56]

Money laundering is still assumed "to be a key element in stopping the financing of terrorist groups, of the type suspected of planning and carrying out" the London bombings.[57] That such statements turn out to be utterly misleading is irrelevant to a financial war ensconced within its own parallel universe. It took almost six months for investigators to determine with some precision the total cost of the attacks. As was the case whenever such information was disclosed, the media gave it little play.

Following the London bombings, a new profiling category known as "backpacker terrorists" was added to the long list of "red flags"—young men who abruptly transfer all their assets to relatives in the expectation of imminent martyrdom. Financial institutions had to reprogram their computer monitoring systems to detect such occurrences.[58] After the full story of the London bombings was uncovered, it became clear that the financial trail would have been of little use in anticipating the attacks.[59] For one thing, the grand total for the attacks was $1,000.[60] Equally significant, the terrorists had none of the characteristics the financial warriors were trained to look out for. Three of them were born and raised in the United Kingdom.

The fourth, a convert to Islam, had been born not in the Middle East or any Islamic country but in Jamaica.[61] There had been no foreign assistance, financial or otherwise, and no complex banking transactions or cross-border financial transfers. And there had been no sudden account closures.[62]

The early war on terror discourse overplayed, in addition to money, the presumed essence of Islam, as well as the role of Koranic schools, the madrassas, which for a while captured the imagination of the chattering classes. Bernard Lewis in particular saw "Muslim rage" at the center of the terrorist phenomenon and "the suicide bomber" as "a metaphor for the entire Middle East."[63] But serious empirical work has debunked these assertions. Robert Pape, a political scientist at the University of Chicago, has studied every suicide bombing and attack around the globe from 1980 to 2003—315 in all. He argued that "there is far less of a connection between suicide terrorism and religious fundamentalism than most people think." For one thing, the leading instigators of suicide attacks are the Tamil Tigers of Sri Lanka. Also, among Muslim bombers, attacks were always linked to foreign occupation: Palestinian suicide attacks only started after the acceleration of Israeli settlement in the occupied territories; Hezbollah attacks in Lebanon started after the 1982 Israeli occupation; there were no suicide attacks in Iraq prior to 2003. Pape concluded:

> What nearly all suicide terrorist attacks actually have in common is a specific secular and strategic goal: to compel modern democracies to withdraw military forces from territory that the terrorists consider to be their homeland. Religion is often used as a tool by terrorist organizations in recruiting and in seeking aid from abroad, but is rarely the root cause.[64]

In his famous memo expressing misgivings about the war on terror, Defense Secretary Donald Rumsfeld had asked: "Are we capturing, killing or deterring and dissuading more terrorists every day than the madrassas and the radical clerics are recruiting, training and deploying against us?" A repeated demand of would-be reformers of the Islamic world has been the replacement of these schools by a modern educational system. Peter Bergen and Swati Pandey looked into the educational backgrounds of 75 terrorists behind some of the most significant recent terrorist attacks against Westerners and found few graduates of those Koranic schools among them. A majority of terrorists were actually college educated, often in technical subjects like engineering. The authors concluded:

> While madrassas may breed fundamentalists who have learned to recite the Koran in Arabic by rote, such schools do not teach the technical or linguistic skills necessary to be an effective terrorist. Indeed, there is little or no evidence that madrassas produce terrorists capable of attacking the West. And

as a matter of national security, the United States doesn't need to worry about Muslim fundamentalists with whom we may disagree, but about terrorists who want to attack us. ... While madrassas are an important issue in education and development in the Muslim world, they are not and should not be considered a threat to the United States.[65]

Towards reform

Despite the low cost of terrorist attacks, money can be a significant facilitator and enabler. Financing, provided it is properly understood, is also a potent intelligence and investigation tool. As terrorists attempt to gain access to weapons of mass destruction, money is bound to assume an even greater role in the future—which is all the more reason to address the issue in an effective manner. The financial war has been botched, and is in need of a complete overhaul, from a review of underlying axioms and assumptions to a reassessment of methods and techniques. This final section is divided into the three parts: the first part attempts to reframe the terrorist financing issue, the second deals with matters of intelligence, culture, and understanding, and the third suggests political and bureaucratic reforms.

1. Reframing the terrorist financing issue

Three of the findings of the September 11 Commission have been barely noticed, and their implications with regard to the financial war have gone unaddressed. One is that there is no hidden stash of cash on which Al-Qaeda can periodically draw, and no "central bank" or central paymaster.[66] Instead, a pay-as-you-go system was sustained by self-financing, and permanent fundraising.[67] The second finding is that frantic rule-making is of little use in trying to starve terrorists of funding. The third is that political developments are a significant—probably the most significant—factor in broadening the support system (including financial support) of the terrorists. Indeed, in the 100 days following the September 11 attacks, there were two parallel developments: the relentless escalation in the financial war under the leadership of the United States,[68] and the war in Afghanistan. The net result, which in effect calls into question the existing financial war paradigm, was that "donations [to Al-Qaeda] increased substantially."[69]

The contention of this book is that in an insurgency, the money issue cannot be separated from politics, and in particular from the issue of popular support. Addressing the financial question in isolation is not only ineffective but counter-productive. The focus should be on ideological commitment and the support system. The University of Maryland political scientist Shibley Telhami put it in terms of supply and demand: "By regarding terrorism as the product of organized groups that could be confronted and destroyed, without regard to their aims or to the reasons that they succeed in recruiting many willing members, the United States pursued a 'supply-side'-only approach."[70] This is clearly not enough. In Telhami's words:

> To succeed, terror organizers, regardless of their aims, need to recruit willing members, raise funds, and appeal to public opinion in pursuit of their political objectives. Public despair and humiliation are often fertile ground for terror organizers to exploit. If this demand side persists, the terrorism phenomenon is unlikely to be contained. For every terror organization that is destroyed, other suppliers will arise to exploit the persistent demand.[71]

Before asking the "where does the money come from" question, other more fundamental questions must be asked about the support network: its characteristics, its motivations, its grievances, etc. Terrorism and insurgency are primarily political phenomena. The more support there is for insurgents or terrorists, the more financing will appear. In fact money is only one element of the support network—and not the most crucial one. Others include logistical, political, and moral assistance (providing safe-houses, hiding places, protection, etc) which do not necessarily involve cash outlays.

Important work has been done on the terror networks,[72] but very little exists on broader support networks. There are different shades of support, from more or less active to more or less passive. There is also a "floating middle"—people who are mostly indifferent, perhaps opposed to terrorists, yet could at some point be swayed by changing circumstances.[73] In contrast to hardcore combatants, who no matter what will always be intent on committing acts of terror, the support network is made up of people whose support will waver according to events and policies. In fighting an insurgency, the primary struggle is political: it consists in winning the support of local populations, and defeating the ideology that fuels the insurgency—in sum, separating terrorists from their support system. The financial front is particularly vulnerable to a common counter-insurgency mistake, the criminalization of the support network, which like all overreactions always plays into the hands of hardcore insurgents. As columnist David Ignatius wrote, "Certain people will never be stopped; they are beyond convincing and integrating. What is in play, however, is the support network."[74] Whereas extreme measures can be justifiable in dealing with hardcore combatants, the broad support network must be approached differently. This is where addressing the root causes of terror, winning over hearts and minds, and using other tools of soft power come into play.

A number of indicators bear this out. One of course is the steady increase of acts of terror, despite—and in large part because of—"vigorous" policies. Another is the steady deterioration of the image of the United States in the Islamic world. One poll conducted in September 2004 shows the following:

only 12 percent of Muslims believe that the United States respects Islamic values, and only 7 percent believe the West understands Muslim culture; only 13 percent of Egyptians, 6 percent of Jordanians, and 3 percent of Saudi Arabians hold a favorable opinion of the United State; and majorities in seven out of eight Muslim countries worry about a military threat from the United States.[75] Any deterioration of sentiment translates into greater support for militant groups: more neutral bystanders will become passive supporters; more passive sympathizers will turn to active support; and more supporters will cross the line to actually committing acts of terror.[76] Needless to say, this will also translate into broader financial support.

The tropes and blinders of the war on terror made it nearly impossible to understand this. The organized crime and drug trafficking lenses,[77] in addition to the nature of the early war on terror narrative, have obscured the fluid character of the terrorist threat. The "if you are not with us, you are with the terrorist" mindset called for a sweeping criminalization of the support system and the systematic use of collective punishment. To quote President Bush, "There is no neutral ground—no neutral ground—in the fight between civilization and terror, because there is no neutral ground between good and evil, freedom and slavery and life and death."[78] As early as September 13, 2001, Deputy Defense Secretary Paul Wolfowitz had pledged a broad and sustained campaign: "It's not just simply a matter of capturing people and holding them accountable, but removing the sanctuaries, removing the support systems, ending states who sponsor terrorism. We're going to keep after these people and the people who support them until this stops."[79] The criminalization of the support network formed the basis of the first Bush doctrine, which stated that those who harbor terrorists or finance acts of terror are just as guilty as those who commit them. The "six degrees of separation logic" did the rest.[80] Punishing the many for the sins of the few was justified on legal and moral grounds by prominent scholars such as Alan Dershowitz.[81]

Another set of blinders could be traced to the legacy of the Vietnam War. It took a long time for the architects of that war to understand that they were facing an insurgency. And soon after the lessons of insurgency were finally learned, they were promptly unlearned. In the neo-conservative worldview, all things objectionable in US foreign policy have their roots in the Vietnam War. "Kicking the Vietnam syndrome" became part of the war on terror ethos, and unlearning the "lessons of Vietnam" became an article of faith. In 1996, in a belated *mea culpa*, Robert McNamara who as Defense Secretary had been one of the architects of the war, revisited many of the errors committed and drew some lessons.[82] Errors included the failure "to adapt our military tactics to the task of winning the hearts and minds of people from a totally different culture," "our misjudgment of friend and foe alike reflected our profound ignorance of the history, culture, and politics of the people in the area, and the personalities and habits of their leaders," and more broadly, the profound misunderstanding of the nature of the conflict and misreading the reality to fit ideological preconceptions. As for lessons learned, they included: "get the data," "be prepared to reexamine your reasoning," and "empathize with your enemy." McNamara and the other "best and brightest" of the Vietnam era had not paid much attention to the conclusions of earlier students of insurgency such as T.E. Lawrence, who had observed that a rebellion could be successful when "two in the hundred were active, and the rest quietly sympathetic to the point of not betraying the movements of the minority to the enemy."[83] Many of Lawrence's writings (which also included the statement that "war upon rebellion was messy and slow, like eating soup with a knife") are directly applicable to today's events in Iraq: "the British in Mesopotamia remained substantially an alien force invading enemy territory, with the local people passively neutral or sullenly against them."[84]

It is only with the onset of President Bush's second term that some within the administration came to terms with the logic of insurgency. The financial implications of that logic have yet to sink in. At the intersection of the shadowy world of terror and the opaque world of finance, terrorist financing remains little understood, and a great deal of research needs to be done on that subject. Any serious empirical work should start by questioning axioms, assumptions, and founding myths, and acknowledging blinders. All the assertions (about the identity between money laundering and terrorist financing, about "dirty money," the drug trade and terrorism, etc) should be working hypotheses and subjected to rigorous examination. Only then would a clear picture of the financial side of insurgency emerge.

2. Matters of intelligence and understanding

British military historian Correlli Barnett wrote:

> Rather than kicking down front doors and barging into ancient and complex societies with simple nostrums of "freedom and democracy," we need tactics of cunning and subtlety, based on a profound understanding of the people and cultures we are dealing with—an understanding up till now entirely lacking in the top-level policy-makers in Washington, especially in the Pentagon.[85]

In the war on terror the abundance of potent tools was accompanied by paucity of understanding and cultural or religious sensitivities. On September 16, 2001, President Bush spoke of a "crusade." In the financial realm, the highest-profile operation was called "Operation Green Quest"—further lending credence to suspicions that the financial war was against Islam.[86] An

ethnocentric perspective transposed the mythology of the Far West on to a
very different part of the world. Announcing that Bin Laden was "wanted
dead or alive," and offering generous bounties yielded scant results.[87] Following the September 11 attacks, the reward for information leading to Bin
Laden's capture was raised to $25 million (up from $5 million in 1998). In
March 2004 the House of Representatives passed, by a unanimous vote, the
Counter-Terrorist and Narco-Terrorist Rewards Program Act, which would
double to $50 million the bounty on Bin Laden.[88] (In Iraq, $25 million
bounties were placed on the heads of Saddam Hussein and his sons. The
capture of the Iraqi dictator was not related to the ransom; that of his sons
occurred under circumstances that have yet to be fully elucidated.) Former
CIA official Michael Scheuer has observed that "despite offering millions in
reward money, not a single Afghan has turned over a "high-value" Taliban or
al-Qaida target to U.S. forces." [89]

A big part of the September 11 failure of intelligence could be attributed to questions of knowledge and understanding. Crucial intercepts which
could have averted the tragedy had gone untranslated. The need for better
human intelligence, for a massive campaign to recruit Arabic translators,
and more generally for the recruitment of officials familiar with the Middle
East, the Islamic world, and international issues was widely recogized. To
cite only one example, FBI Director Robert Mueller had promised Congress
and the American public a top-to-bottom reorganization of his agency, with
a specific focus on these areas.[90] Yet a lawsuit by FBI agent Bassem Youssef
against the agency alleging bias[91] shed a troubling light on those reform
efforts. Youssef, an Arab-American and one of very few agents with appropriate linguistic and cultural skills, had been excluded from the September
11 investigations, and later repeatedly passed over for top-level headquarters
jobs in terrorism. This was part of a broader phenomenon: those people who
could have provided some expertise—Arabists, Muslim-Americans, scholars
of the Middle East—were systematically excluded from policymaking.[92] Sworn
testimonies by top agency officials suggested that lack of counter-terrorism
experience, let alone international experience and linguistic skills, was a near
pre-requisite for such positions. Daniel Byman, a national security expert
who worked on both Congressional and presidential investigations of terrorism and intelligence failures, reviewed the Youssef case for the court, and
concluded that the FBI overall remains woefully weak in expertise on the
Middle East, terrorism, and intelligence liaison: "Many of its officers, including those quite skilled in other aspects of the bureau's work, lack the skills to
work with foreign governments or even their U.S. counterparts." [93] This led
Senate Finance Committee Chairman Charles Grassley, a Republican from
Iowa, to ask: "Why would the FBI hire people to run the counterterrorism

division who don't know anything about counterterrorism?"[94]

Four years later, contrary to what he had promised following the September 11 attacks, FBI Director Robert Mueller was now of the opinion that counter-terrorism supervisors did not need to have a background in Arabic, the Middle East, or international issues.[95] Gary Bald, the bureau's executive assistant director in charge of terrorism, testified that he had to get his terrorism training on the job when he came to headquarters two years earlier. When asked about his grasp of Middle Eastern culture and history, he replied: "I wish that I had it. It would be nice." In his opinion, no counter-terrorism experience was necessary. As for Dale Watson, the FBI's terrorism chief in the two years after September 11, 2001, he declared, "You need leadership. You don't need subject matter expertise." Recognizing in a sworn testimony that he did not know the difference between the Shia and Sunni, he affirmed that there was no need for such knowledge: "A bombing case is a bombing case. A crime scene in a bank robbery case is the same as a crime scene, you know, across the board."[96] When asked about the "skill sets" needed "to better identify, penetrate and/or prevent a future Osama bin Laden-style terrorist attack," Watson answered: "They would need to understand the Attorney General guidelines for counterterrorism and counterintelligence investigation." Pressed on whether "anything else" mattered, he replied "no."[97]

Historian Rashid Khalidi has noted the dangers of ideological biases and cultural ignorance. Since colonial times, important misconceptions have arisen because of the inability of "foreigners to understand what they saw and were told ... since they did not speak the local languages, and their own ignorance and biases were often so debilitating as to blind them to the realities before their eyes."[98] The near total absence of linguistic and cultural skills has led to a phenomenon of overcompensation. One cannot help but think about Justice Louis D. Brandeis warning against "the insidious encroachment by men of zeal, well-meaning but without understanding." Political scientist Larry Diamond, who for a short time advised American occupation forces in Iraq, observed people making decisions "with a high degree of confidence but little knowledge of the country."[99]

On matters of terrorist financing there are further complications, since the money warriors should also have a thorough understanding of regulatory and financial cultures, a complex and little-studied area which posits that banking and financial structures are embedded within a religious, institutional, political, and cultural context that cannot, international prodding notwithstanding, be changed overnight.[100] In failed countries such as Afghanistan and Somalia, the vast majority of people have never been inside a bank. Trying to impose US-style paperwork and disclosure will do little to resolve the terrorist financing issue. One example is the suspicion in the United States of excessive cash, which triggers the filing by banks of Suspicious Activities Reports (SARs). What may make sense in a country where only 32 percent of financial transactions are conducted in cash may not make sense where virtually all transactions are done in cash.[101] Veterans of Central American drug wars are likely to see in every pile of cash proof of criminal intent. Those trained in scrutinizing footnotes in American companies' annual reports complain when sent to distant lands to ply their skills that the records are "indecipherable." [102] Drafting laws and regulations that look good on paper but are disconnected from the realities of those societies they aim to change is counter-productive.[103]

In much of the Islamic world, cash is still king. Ethnocentric assumptions have made it impossible for financial warriors to understand this. Jonathan Randal, one of only a handful of journalists with intimate knowledge of the Islamic world (most others are simply, in the words of Robert Fisk, practitioners of "hotel journalism"), has described vividly "this cultural fixation with cash, ... this abiding fondness for cash, often big bundles of banknotes kept in pockets or desk drawers." Combined with "notoriously porous borders when it came not just to money, but arms, explosives and men on the run," such cash economies were impossible to understand for people lacking appropriate experience: "Cash was cash, and cash was the way business, sub rosa and aboveboard, was done. Formal borders were lines on maps, not realities, and often were not even demarcated." [104] Not only were the financial warriors unable to "see" much of the cash moving in suitcases, envelopes, belts, and pockets, but whenever "honest" cash was found, they invariably assumed the worst. To quote Randal again:

> In Iraq in 2003 American soldiers searching for pro-Saddam Hussein suspects systematically confiscated considerable amounts of cash found in private homes. The soldiers were convinced the cash was proof of payoff money either from—or for—the armed resistance to the American occupation. They could not comprehend that Arabs innocently kept their savings at home in cash as a hedge against the regime's chronic unpredictability, often in dollars correctly seen as less volatile than constantly devaluating Iraqi *dinars*. The confiscations were considered as theft and helped increase Iraqi suspicions of the occupation.[105]

The centrality of cash and its imperviousness to sanctions and financial controls are epitomized by the aftermath of the July–August 2006 war between Israel and Hezbollah, when the Shiite militia promptly set up a financial compensation mechanism whereby families who had lost their homes instantly received $12,000 in cash.[106] Absent necessary knowledge and understanding, as they undergo "on the job training," the financial warriors will be conditioned to swallow whole the entire terrorist financing mythology.[107]

3. Structural reforms

In just about every respect, my recommendations for political and bureaucratic reform differ from those made in the reports of Richard Clarke and Maurice Greenberg.

1. Although the two phenomena have, since September 11, been approached as though they were interchangeable, terrorist financing ought to be completely dissociated from money laundering.[108] As already discussed, the two are fundamentally different: money laundering is about disguising the criminal origin of money; it is based on a crime-for-profit logic, and is usually connected to drugs, corruption, and white-collar crime; terrorist financing linked to Islamic extremism is primarily a political and ideological phenomenon, which usually involves small, undetectable amounts of "clean money." Failing to see the difference between the two has produced the perverse policy consequences discussed in this book. The "money laundering/ terrorist financing" realm became an autonomous, free-standing, and self-perpetuating one, driven by its own bureaucracies and "experts," and largely disconnected from the attempt to reduce the terrorist threat. In such a realm "busyness" and frantic rule-making prevail, making it easy for mushrooming bureaucracies to lose track of their original mission. Not only was the dirty-money approach dysfunctional, but the saliency of terrorist financing resulted in crowding out money laundering and white-collar crime cases.

2. "Blue ribbon" commissions addressing intractable issues are prone to recommending the creation of more bureaucracies, and are especially fond of the notions of "czars." Twenty government agencies dealing with terrorist financing is probably far too many. Rather than further bureaucracy-intensive schemes and more redundancies, inefficiencies, and turf battles, radical streamlining is in order. As for the designation of a White House official in charge of terrorist financing, it would further insulate the financial dimension and politicize it, amplifying in the process existing dysfunctions. Both the Clarke and the Greenberg reports are also squarely in favor of creating more international bureaucracies, with more monitoring and reporting requirements imposed on foreign countries. Money warriors like to think that once all countries have adopted US-style money laundering controls, terrorist financiers will have nowhere to hide, and terrorism will stop. Such a logic cannot possibly be sustained when amounts are small and when terrorists are homegrown or self-financed. It is also questionable

whether the creation of an annual certification process of countries is what the world needs.[109]

3. Both the Clarke and the Greenberg reports favor greater centralization of terrorist financing policies, and of raising the profile of the financial war on terror. By the same token, virtually all writers on the subject like to stress its centrality and importance—with the attendant emphasis on political visibility. There are two main problems with further politicizing the issue: one is that it makes financing issues vulnerable to political hijacking, demagoguery, and grandstanding, and in turn produces counter-productive policies; another is that high-profile announcements give ample notice to those planning acts of terror, allowing them to act in such a way as to elude detection.[110] In reality, issues of terrorist financing are best addressed by low-key policies that are all but invisible to the public. Perhaps the most effective tools are solid intelligence and the ability to infiltrate the support network.[111] Reliance on cooperation and soft power holds much more promise than bombastic announcements, "making splashes," or seeking to project power.[112] More generally, given the alternative, support-based paradigm discussed in the book, where understanding local regulatory and financial cultures is paramount, "subsidiarity" [113]—the notion that officials of individual countries are in a better position to identify terrorist funding, and that the United States should only interfere in a support and coordination capacity, not to dictate policies—is far preferable to the current top-down, hierarchic system, where ethnocentric assumptions prevail.[114]

4. The government agency best suited to play the lead role in terrorist financing matters is the State Department. Although it was marginalized and subjected to unrelenting attacks by neo-conservatives throughout the first Bush term,[115] the State Department is the one bureaucracy which is still somewhat equipped to deal with the bigger picture, and relate financing matters to counter-insurgency and public diplomacy. Equally important, through its Foreign Service, it has an institutional reservoir of country knowledge, along with the language and cultural skills that are sorely missing in those agencies that have an exclusively military, financial, or law enforcement focus.

5. Those in charge of the financial war must possess a number of skills: an understanding of the politics and the financial and regulatory environments of the Islamic world and, perhaps most importantly, linguistic and cultural competence. This should be evident, yet as we saw in the case of the FBI, even years after the September 11 attacks, many in top government positions still consider such skills unnecessary.

The financial war has from the start been fraught with dysfunctions, unintended consequences, and collateral damage. It could be argued that highly publicized financial strikes have made things worse, typically by unnecessarily antagonizing people otherwise well disposed towards the United States and whose support would have been critical in reducing the terrorist threat.[116] In the financial realm, one of the apprehensions expressed by Donald Rumsfeld in his famous October 2003 "long hard slog" memo— that "the harder we work, the behinder we get"—has certainly proved true.[117] Reconsidering terrorist financing and reforming policies are thus urgent matters.

EPILOGUE

The Last Happy Warriors

In politics, what begins in fear usually ends in folly.
Samuel Taylor Coleridge

Money is like water down the side of the mountain.
It will find a way to get around the trees.
Ralph Reed

It is difficult to get a man to understand something
when his job depends on not understanding it.
Upton Sinclair

The November 2006 elections marked a turning point in the politics of fear. In 2002 and 2004, the war on terror had been successfully exploited for partisan advantage.[1] George W. Bush was presented as a forceful "war president" while Democrats stood accused of weakness on national security. In the name of a national effort to counter an existential threat, political dissent was largely stifled. Controversial policies were justified as necessary responses to the September 11 attacks, and a steady stream of terror alerts could be counted on to drown out unfavorable news.[2]

The Republican strategy for the 2006 election was based on the same playbook.[3] The war rhetoric was cranked up, and any criticism of the administration was denounced as "helping the enemy." As President Bush put it a week before the election: "However they put it, the Democrat approach in Iraq comes down to this: The terrorists win and America loses."[4] But by then, the national mood has shifted. Iraq was in the midst of a civil war, and the administration's claims of imminent victory were no longer credible. There was a consensus among intelligence services and policy experts that the invasion and occupation of Iraq had actually fueled radicalism and worsened the terror threat.[5] The war in Iraq, which had been presented as the "central front" of the war on terror, was an unmitigated disaster, and no amount of fear-mongering could prevent the Democrats from gaining control of both houses of Congress.

The day after the "thumping" his party received, and which was largely attributed to the Iraq war, President Bush announced the resignation of Defense Secretary Donald Rumsfeld and his replacement by Robert Gates, a former CIA director. After years of repeating that he would "stay the course," President Bush said that he would undertake a major review of the war in Iraq. An administration that until then had been loath to soliciting outside advice went on a consultation binge. Over a two-month period, policy-making seemed on hiatus—except as discussed in this epilogue, on matters of finance.

The most highly publicized recommendations came from the Iraq Study Group, a bipartisan commission appointed by Congress, headed by former Secretary of State James Baker and former Chairman of the House Foreign Affairs Committee Lee Hamilton. On December 8, the Commission, which included five Democrats and five Republicans (among them Robert Gates), released a sharply critical report. Largely reflecting the attitudes of American public opinion,[6] the Baker–Hamilton report argued that the situation in Iraq was "grave and deteriorating," that the current approach to Iraq was "not working," and that the American ability "to influence events within Iraq (was) diminishing." Asserting that there were "no military solutions" to the crisis, it called for a "new diplomatic initiative" that would involve all of Iraq's neighbors, including Iran and Syria, as well as the international community, and would include attempts at resolving other regional issues, most prominently the festering Arab–Israeli conflict.

President Bush ended up ignoring the advice of the Baker–Hamilton report, choosing instead that of the neo-conservative American Enterprise Institute, which recommended a "surge." On January 10, 2007, President Bush announced that he would be sending 21,500 extra troops to Iraq. The much delayed announcement was anticlimactic and poorly received. Yet confusion and disarray translated into new offensives on the financial front.

The financial exception

The war on terror, presented as a Manichean struggle of good against evil, had been, for much of the post-September 11 era, the overarching political issue. A few trial balloons (or gaffes) showed how politically costly it was to question the wisdom of that war. When Democratic candidate John Kerry said in 2004 that he hoped America would eventually get back to a place where "terrorists are not the focus of our lives, but they're a nuisance," he was roundly attacked—with Vice-President Dick Cheney stating that it was proof that he was unfit for office—and had to backtrack. Around the same time, President Bush, in what columnist Gwynne Dyer called "a brush with the truth," opined that the war on terror could not be won, but that conditions could be changed to make terrorism less acceptable in some parts of the world. This led Democrats to pounce on the President, who soon retracted his statement.[7] In sum, candidates competed on who could show more steadfastness in waging the war on terror, and Republican strategists pulled off a narrow victory by adopting a "stay the course" rhetoric while painting the Democratic candidate as a "flip-flopper" who was soft on terror. But as we saw, there were also subtle shifts in policy. Soon after the 2004 election, as the situation in Iraq worsened, the "war on terror" rhetoric came close to being retired,[8] though it reappeared with a vengeance with the looming 2006 elections.

By then, serious questioning of the very notion of a "war on terror" was no longer taboo. John Mueller, a political scientist at Ohio State University, wrote in a book titled *Overblown: How Politicians and the Terrorism Industry Inflate National Security Threats, and Why We Believe Them*:

> A threat that is real but likely to prove to be of limited scope has been massively, perhaps even fancifully, inflated to produce widespread and unjustified anxiety. This process has then led to wasteful, even self-parodic expenditures and policy overreactions, ones that not only very often do more harm and cost more money than anything the terrorists have accomplished, but play into their hands.[9]

Following a thorough analysis of the price of the war on terror, he concluded that the "chief costs of terrorism derive not from the damage inflicted by the terrorists, but what those attacked do to themselves and others in response."[10] In the same vein, University of Pennsylvania political scientist Ian Lustick wrote in a book titled *Trapped in the War on Terror*:

> The government's loudly trumpeted "War on Terror" is not the solution to the problem. It has become the problem. The War on Terror does not reduce public anxieties by thwarting terrorists poised to strike. Rather, in myriad ways, conducting the anti-terror effort as a "war" fuels those anxieties. By stoking these public fears and attracting vast political and economic resources in response to them, the War on Terror encourages, indeed virtually compels, every interest group in the country to advance its own agenda as crucial for winning the war. As a result, widening circles of Americans are drawn into spirals of exaggeration, waste, and fear.[11]

The "war" itself has become a "more fearsome enemy than the terrorists it was putatively designed to fight,"[12] and the government found itself "trapped" since it could "never make enough progress toward 'protecting America' to reassure Americans against the fears it is helping to stoke." [13]

Many political figures involved in fighting that "war" concurred. In the United Kingdom, Sir Ken Macdonald, the Director of Public Prosecutions, warned against "fear-driven and inappropriate" responses. He denied that Britain was caught up in a "war on terror" and called for a "culture of legislative restraint" in passing laws to deal with terrorism. In his words, "The fight against terrorism on the streets of Britain is not a war. It is the prevention of crime, the enforcement of our laws and the winning of justice for those damaged by their infringement." [14] In the final days of 2006, the Foreign Office had finally recognized the pitfalls of the war rhetoric and instructed ministers to stop talking of a "war on terror." [15] In the United States, Defense Secretary Donald Rumsfeld himself, when asked in the final days of his tenure what he would have done differently, singled out "calling the war a 'war on terror.'" [16]

The financial war was exceptional in that it was mostly immune from such criticisms. Most critics focused on either the Iraqi debacle or on the impact of that war on civil liberties and democratic ideals. In Iraq nothing had gone according to plan. The Iraq war was to be a cakewalk, and was supposed to be followed by "regime change" in Iran and elsewhere. It was envisioned that "less than 5 months" after the invasion only one brigade (some 25,000 to 30,000 troops) would be sufficient to maintain law and order in Iraq and that by 2006 only 5,000 troops would be needed. In parallel, the military under Donald Rumsfeld was undergoing a massive technological and strategic transformation that was supposed to allow it to operate on the basis of a "10-30-30 timetable" to defeat America's enemies: 10 days to topple a rogue regime, 30 days to establish order in its wake, and 30 more days to prepare for the next military undertaking. [17] Those who had envisioned serial wars were bound to be disappointed: American forces were bogged down in Iraq and had little desire for more military interventions.

Critics also focused on the impact of the war on terror on civil liberties and democratic ideals. Following the September 11 attacks, the executive branch was given broad latitude—by the legislative and judicial branches with the strong support of public opinion and the media—to wage the war as it saw fit. Civil liberties and due process took a back seat to the quest for security. A steady stream of revelations—about Guantanamo, Abu Ghraib, extraordinary renditions, warrantless eavesdropping, and a host of other violations of human and civil rights—finally caused a backlash. With legal challenges, media skepticism and an electoral setback, the year 2006 saw, in the words of journalist James Risen, "the American government's system of checks and balances slowly clicking back into place, forcing the Bush White House to confront new limits and more scrutiny." [18]

On the military and human-rights front, reality checks eventually transformed what had been ideologically driven perceptions and debates on the war on terror. According to Ambassador Peter Galbraith, until January 2003 President Bush himself was "unfamiliar" with the terms Sunni and Shia. In Galbraith's words:

> So two months before he ordered U.S. troops into the country, the president of the United States did not appear to know about the division among Iraqis that has defined the country's history and politics. He would not have understood why non-Arab Iran might gain a foothold in post-Saddam Iraq. He could not have anticipated U.S. troops being caught in the middle of a civil war between two religious sects that he did not know existed.[19]

The rapidly escalating death toll in Iraq and the egregious violations of human rights brought about a critical re-thinking of the war on terror in the mainstream media. Policy-makers and many in the educated public strove to gain a better understanding of political, religious and other factors.

Amidst all those changes, the financial front stood apart as the one front with no paradigm shift on the horizon. Axioms posited in the days following the September 11 attacks were still, six years later, taken for granted,[20] and public debate is still mired in fantasy, although, as discussed throughout the book, plenty of contrary evidence is widely available to anyone willing to investigate the matter. In recent months, significant legal decisions have thrown further doubt on much of the founding mythology of terrorist financing.[21] With very few exceptions,[22] the financial front was exempt from criticism. In fact, most of the general criticisms of the war on terror—such as Ian Lustick's warning against "primitive ideas, devoid of any nuance or particularity that might offer clues about the enemy's behavior"[23]—would have been particularly applicable to the financial front. On a slow news day, one can always see an article or two on the financial war, but these typically read like barely rewritten press releases. Such articles typically claim that the financial warriors are succeeding in starving terrorists of funding, but that more remains to be done.[24]

This book has discussed at length those characteristics of the financial realm that help explain its immunity to criticism.[25] The financial warriors also kept flaunting the A-minus grade awarded by the 9/11 Commission in December 2005 to the government's policies against terrorist financing. As the highest score given in a wide-ranging and mostly critical report on federal anti-terrorism efforts based on the panel's 41 key recommendations, it seemed to justify presenting the financial war as the one exception to the rule that the war on terror was not going well. Largely on the basis of that grade, 95 percent of a panel of "foreign policy experts" queried by *Foreign Policy* and the Center for American Progress said that "some or a great deal of progress had been made" on "staunching the flow of terrorist money worldwide." [26] In contrast, 87 percent of those experts said America's public diplomacy was failing, and nearly half said that failure was the result of poor leadership and ineffective policies. Also, 88 percent believed that the war in Iraq was having a negative impact on US national security, 92 percent said that the Bush administration's performance on Iraq had been below average, with nearly 6 out of 10 experts saying the Bush administration was doing the "worst possible job" in Iraq. [27]

Public opinion reflected those attitudes. At a time when President Bush's ratings were plummeting and where a majority of Americans were dissatisfied with most aspects of the war on terror, financial actions were widely praised. In July 2006, when a controversial program to monitor virtually all inter-bank transfers through Belgium-based Swift was revealed, it had the support of 70 percent of the American public. [28] Treasury Secretary John Snow declared that this program, which was called illegal by the European Union, [29] represented "government at its best"—"responsible government, effective government, government that works." [30]

On matters of terrorist financing, there had been no reality checks and thus no learning. Walled inside its own parallel universe, the realm of finance remained "faith-based." [31] The financial warriors' attitude could be summarized as "a terrorist is a terrorist and the law is the law." All sorts of claims could be made, with little concern for accuracy of analysis or proportionality of punishment. Most financial warriors are still unaware of the fundamental differences between terrorist financing and money laundering. [32] Indeed, the lack of scrutiny and the absence of checks and balances have turned the financial war into a realm where there is ample room for bait-and-switch and virtually no accountability. The breadth of the terrain, and as discussed in the following pages, the potential offered by extraterritoriality and secondary boycotts offered an unlimited supply of targets. The conflation of financial crimes and terrorist financing, and the amalgamation of terrorist organizations such as Al-Qaeda with groups such as Hamas and Hezbollah, which mixed political violence, national grievances and social work opened unlimited vistas for the financial warriors. Hence the increase in bureaucratic "busyness" domestically and internationally. [33] More haystacks were assembled in search for increasingly elusive needles, [34] and financial firms were subjected to increased controls. [35] On the legal front, more international banks were sued in US courts for holding accounts of charities "tied to terror." Thus NatWest and Credit Lyonnais stood accused of dealing with Interpal, a British-based charitable organization accused of funding Hamas (though it was twice cleared of such charges in the United Kingdom). [36]

Amidst sober and critical accounts of the war on terror, one memoir published in early 2007 stood out for its giddy enthusiasm and self-congratulatory tone. In *Global Financial Warriors: The Untold Story of International Finance in the Post-9/11 World,* former Treasury Undersecretary for International Affairs John B. Taylor discussed his great successes in "starving terrorists of funding."[37] With no apparent irony, he took credit for bringing "financial stability" to Iraq, and called international cooperation on terrorist financing the "*best* example of international cooperation in the field of international finance since the establishment of the Bretton Woods institutions at the end of World War II."[38]

One can only be puzzled by Taylor's claims that he and his financial warriors managed "to prevent and suppress" the financing of terrorism. Indeed, international terrorist attacks increased by 56 percent in 2003, by 300 percent in 2004 and by 400 percent in 2005.[39] Other relevant indicators are equally worrying: according to a World Bank report, the number of "fragile" countries at risk from terrorism jumped from 17 to 26 between 2003 and 2006,[40] and anti-American feelings have soared to unprecedented levels throughout the Islamic world.[41] All this would suggest either that the financial war was a dismal failure or that money is not the "oxygen" of terror—which would undermine the basic paradigm of the financial war.

The former Treasury Undersecretary clearly failed to heed his boss Paul O'Neill's warning against the bureaucratic tendencies to confuse process and outcome and mistake activity for progress.[42] Indeed, although he maps out in great detail all the committees, taskforces, and evaluation and monitoring mechanisms he created (and shares the secrets of doing it so successfully), he never pauses to address questions of substance, such as the truth of designations and accusations or the effectiveness of policies.[43]

Political crossroads, financial minefields

One of the main conclusions of the Iraq Study Group was that the solution in Iraq, and indeed in the entire Middle East, had to be primarily diplomatic and political—not military. For every flash point of the war on terror, there are disagreements between partisans of conciliation and partisans of military escalation, between advocates of dialogue and advocates of a clash of civilizations. By looking at examples from North Korea, Iran, Israel's occupied territories and Iraq, we can see that financial initiatives have almost always stood in the way of political solutions, and were influenced by (or played into the hands of) the most hawkish elements. In a war increasingly defined as being "against extremists," financial initiatives have had the effect of strengthening extremists at the expense of moderates. Martial methods and attitudes, in particular the propensity for overkill and the lack of concern for the actual consequences of financial strikes, have actually undermined the more positive and effective uses of finance, in areas such as intelligence and law enforcement.[44]

In the case of North Korea, a financial action seemed calculated to derail the landmark denuclearization agreement signed on September 19, 2005 by North Korea, the United States, China, Russia, Japan and South Korea. The Pyongyang regime pledged to "abandon all nuclear weapons and existing nuclear programs" in exchange for a "full normalization" of relations with the United States. Yet four days later, a little-noticed decision by the US Treasury Department torpedoed the agreement: Banco Delta Asia, a small Macao bank was accused of money laundering, counterfeiting and acting as a conduit for cash to and from North Korea, and subjected to drastic sanctions.[45] Further measures were intended to cut off that country's access to the international banking system: international banks were warned to stay away from lending to North Korea or handling transactions involving the country lest they too would be ostracized. Financial sanctions became the principal stumbling block to a new agreement, which was held up for almost another year and a half.[46] Indeed, it was only after those sanctions were lifted that North Korea returned to the bargaining table.[47] In the words of Selig Harrison, director of the Asia Program at the Center for International Policy in Washington, "It was no secret to journalists covering the September 2005 negotiations, or to the North Koreans, that the agreement was bitterly controversial within the administration and represented a victory for State Department advocates of a conciliatory approach to North Korea over proponents of "regime change" in Pyongyang. The chief US negotiator, Christopher Hill, faced strong opposition from key members of his own delegation at every step of the way."[48] In other words, the hardliners chose the financial terrain to win their battle against supporters of a compromise. Not surprisingly, however, after the February 13, 2007 agreement, the spin of the financial warriors was that their sanctions had brought the North Koreans back to the bargaining table and that the same approach would be used to force Iran to change its behavior.[49]

In the bitter standoff between the United States and Iran, financial strikes had by default been the weapon of choice. The preferred policy of hardliners had been to strike Iran militarily soon after the Iraq invasion.[50] The unexpected turn of events in Iraq made such a strategy militarily and politically risky, and hawks had to fall back on financial strikes. Yet insofar as Iran had been subjected to countless financial restrictions since the 1979 revolution, financial action had to be ratcheted up through extraterritorial applications of US law and secondary boycotts. Sanctions were justified on a number of grounds: Iran's nuclear program, the funding of Hezbollah and Hamas, "meddling" in Iraq, etc. On September 8, 2006, the Treasury Department announced that it had cut off Bank Saderat, one of Iran's largest state-owned banks, from the US financial system. Until then, Iranian banks had been barred from doing business directly with US banks. Now payments through foreign banks that involved Iran could not be processed in the United States.[51] The Treasury Department also launched a campaign to force international banks (with a special focus on European and Japanese banks lending money to the oil sector) to stop dealing altogether with Iran: they were warned that they could "inadvertently" be helping Iran infiltrate the international banking system.[52] In December 28, 2006 firms from Russia, China and North Korea were subjected to US financial sanctions because they had sold military equipment to Iran and Syria.[53] A few days later, broad sanctions were imposed against Bank Sepah, another leading state bank, which was designated as a "facilitator" in Iran's nuclear program.[54] Not surprisingly, extraterritorial measures were especially controversial. When a Canadian bank implemented policies preventing Canadians with certain dual citizenships (Iran, Iraq, Cuba, Sudan, North Korea or Myanmar) from having US dollar accounts, a predictable outcry followed.[55]

The strategy of financial strangulation has certainly created economic hardship for average Iranians, but it has helped Iranian hardliners to tighten their grip on power.[56] In the words of Vali Nasr and Ray Takeyh, "Ironically, US policy has buttressed the Iranian regime, which has justified its monopoly of power as a means of fending off external enemies and managing an economy under international duress."[57] And as John D. Negroponte, outgoing Director of National Intelligence, told Congress in January 2007, Iran's influence is growing across the region "in ways that go beyond the menace of its nuclear program."[58] It has become a dominant force in Iraqi and regional politics, and increasingly assumes a financial role once filled by Gulf Arab states.[59]

Financial strikes against Hezbollah also became increasingly frequent following the July–August 2006 war between Israel and the Shia militia. Sweeping actions were taken, even when money was used to run the militia's network of clinics, schools and other services. In the words of Pat O'Brien, Assistant Treasury Secretary for Terrorist Financing, "We don't buy into the frame of mind that you can distinguish between the military and social arms. Money is fungible."[60] Especially controversial was branding Hussein Al-Shami, a micro-lender close to the Shia militia, a "specially designated global terrorist" at the very time when micro-lending was celebrated as a tool for poverty relief in developing countries. Ironically, the staunchest ally of the United States in Lebanon, Prime Minister Fouad Siniora, had himself run foul of the financial warriors: he once had his visa to the United States canceled for making a small donation to an Islamic charity.[61] Neither he nor other political opponents of Hezbollah seemed to approve of the crackdown, which had no visible impact on Hezbollah's finances, since the militia was able to disburse some $180 million to victims of the Israeli attacks. According to cabinet minister Ahmed Fatfat, clamping down on Hezbollah's money, "which comes in suitcases, not through banks," will disrupt its social services but won't limit its military capabilities.[62] The net effect of the US approach, in the words of journalist Andrew Higgins, was that "it has strengthened the view of Hezbollah's supporters, many of whom come from Lebanon's most-impoverished areas, that America wants to keep them poor, not fight terrorism." [63]

In December 2006, the United States also imposed sanctions on what it called a major fundraising channel for Hezbollah in Latin American, in the "tri-border area" linking Brazil, Argentina and Paraguay. But the Brazilian Foreign Ministry issued a declaration on behalf of the three countries, saying that they are "unwilling to place complete trust in US assertions about the war on terror." According to the official statement, "there is no sign of the occurrence in that region of activities linked to terrorism or their financing," nor is there any "new data or evidence that corroborates the accusation by the United States." [64]

In Israel's occupied territories, a succession of financial sanctions had devastating effects. Following the January 2006 elections which brought Hamas to power, a form of collective punishment was imposed against the Palestinian people: Israel stopped paying the tax revenues it collected on behalf of the Palestinian Authority, a total withholding of 75 percent of its budget; American and European withholding of aid made it impossible to pay public employees; teachers went on strike, and health services collapsed. Given that government salaries are the principal source of income, 66 percent of Palestinian families fell below the poverty line. Charities sending money to the Palestinian Authority became particularly vulnerable: with Hamas in power, anyone sending relief money destined for the government could be labeled a terrorist financier. In effect, the six degrees of separation logic was "criminalizing compassion." [65]

Disruptions caused by those policies contributed to bringing Palestinians to the brink of civil war, but the funding gap was in part filled by other sources. A number of private and public sources (including, for example, the government of Qatar) promised to provide their own aid.[66] Iran pledged $250 million to the Palestinian government. Unorthodox methods of transferring money prevailed. Thus, upon returning to Gaza after a two-week trip abroad, Prime Minister Ismail Haniya was carrying $35 million dollars packed in suitcases. (He was held up for seven hours by Israeli forces at the

Rafah border crossing on the Gaza–Egypt crossing. The money stayed in Egypt.)[67]

In Iraq, finance was one area where lack of adequate oversight and public scrutiny allowed ideology and politics to run amok. Rajiv Chadrasekaran, who covered the American occupation of Iraq for the *Washington Post*, reveals that Iraq's $13 billion budget was entrusted to six young gophers who had never been to that part of the world and "had no previous financial management experience." He also tells of 24-year-old Jay Hallen, who was put in charge of the creation of a new Iraqi stock market even though he "hadn't studied economics or finance." The sole qualification of those people was that they had passed an ideological litmus test: they had worked in political campaigns in Washington, were connected to influential neo-conservatives or had worked for agenda-bearing Washington think-tanks.[68]

As for the quest for insurgency funds, the contradiction between claims of success and the continuing insurgency led to tortured and ever-changing explanations. The *New York Times* recently disclosed the contents of a classified United States government report—so secret that it could not even be disclosed to US allies—on the funding of insurgency.[69] The study, which was written in June 2006, was conducted by an inter-agency group led by Juan Zarate, Deputy National Security Adviser for Combating Terrorism, and made up of representatives from the CIA, the FBI, the Defense Intelligence Agency, the State Department, the Treasury Department and the United States Central Command. The central conclusion was that the insurgents have no trouble getting funding. Characteristically, while acknowledging that they knew very little about crucial aspects of the insurgents' operations, the authors of the seven-page report had no qualms about concocting numbers: insurgents raised $70 million to $200 million a year from illegal activities, including $25 million to $100 million from oil smuggling and other criminal activity involving the state-owned oil industry, aided by "corrupt and complicit" Iraqi officials, and $36 million from kidnapping ransoms. Citing "intelligence reporting," the report indicated that 10 to 15 of the 4,000 Islamic charities and NGOs had diverted funds and provided "cover for insurgent recruitment and the transport of weapons and personnel."[70]

Although countless statements by President Bush and other officials have accused Iran and Syria of channeling money to fuel the insurgency, the report acknowledged that "sources of terrorist and insurgent finance within Iraq — independent of foreign sources —are currently sufficient to sustain the groups' existence and operation." Indeed, funds were so widely available that "terrorist and insurgent groups in Iraq may have surplus funds with which to support other terrorist organizations outside of Iraq." In the words

of W. Patrick Lang, a former chief of Middle East intelligence at the Defense
Intelligence Agency, "A judgment like that, coming from a National Security
Council-generated document is not an analytical assessment as much as it is
a political statement to support the administration's contention that Iraq is a
central front in the war on terrorism. It's a statement put in there to support
a policy judgment." [71]

The discussion of the whereabouts of Saddam Hussein's fortune is
equally puzzling. Finding those assets had once been "the top priority" of
the Treasury Department.[72] If we are to believe the report, during the first 18
months of the war, the insurgency was funded by Hussein loyalists who paid
"foreign fighters and couriers." The trail to those funds had "gone cold" in
part because of the American-led international effort to freeze $3.6 billion
in "former regime assets," and in part because erstwhile loyalists have been
spending the money on their living expenses.[73] Still, initiatives to recover
such funds have resurfaced at opportune times. Following the grotesque
execution of Saddam Hussein in December 2006, the financial warriors
unveiled a new initiative: they would intensify the search for the former
dictator's illicit fortune, specifically for some $4.4 billion in illegal profits
allegedly earned between 2000 and 2003 from an oil-for-trade pact with
Syria.[74]

A particularly embarrassing fact is that the disbursement of funds by
the US-led Coalition Provisional Authority may have added to the insurgents' treasure. According to Stuart Bowen, the special inspector general for
Iraq reconstruction, some $8.8 billion in Iraqi funds (from Iraqi oil sales,
seized Iraqi assets and surplus funds from the UN oil-for-food program) were
disbursed "without assurance the monies were properly used or accounted
for." A memorandum prepared by the House Committee on Oversight and
Government Reform stated, "Many of the funds appear to have been lost
to corruption and waste ... thousands of 'ghost employees' were receiving
paychecks from Iraqi ministries under the CPA's control. Some of the funds
could have enriched both criminals and insurgents fighting the United
States." Indeed, nobody seemed to have an idea about the whereabouts of
those $8.8 billion. In a special hearing, Paul Bremer, the former head of the
Coalition Provisional Authority, was surprised about all the fuss. Addressing
Representative Henry Waxman, the Committee Chair, he said, "These are
not appropriated American funds. They are Iraqi funds." [75]

The dynamics of the financial war explain why the decisions of financial
warriors almost always—whether because of heavy handedness or incompetence—play into the hands of extremists, poisoning the atmosphere, compli-
cating international cooperation and reducing the likelihood of a political
settlement. Four aspects are especially relevant. First, the financial war is

ancillary to the broader, mostly military, war on terror. Since September 11, there has been a close alliance between the Treasury Department and the Pentagon, which explains the martial style of the global financial warriors.[76] Significantly, the Taskforce for Terrorist Financing at the Treasury Department was known as the "war room." [77]

Second, the financial realm is also autonomous and self-propelling. Bureaucracies dedicated to "money laundering and terrorism financing" are driven by the desire to broaden their turf. Their ceaseless quest for "trophies" created a perpetual motion effect, kept alive by the thriving "terrorism industry"—"politicians, experts, the media, academics, the bureaucracy, and risk entrepreneurs who profit in one way or another by inflating the threat international terrorism is likely to present." [78] To paraphrase Pierre Bourdieu, the financial war may have been dysfunctional in terms of its effects on the United States, yet it was perfectly functional for its bureaucrats.

Third, the financial terrain was one where hawks of all stripes, and in particular those belonging to the neo-conservative movement, could still weigh in long after they were thoroughly discredited. Many of the most durable myths about terrorist financing were incubated by those circles.[79] But only in the financial realm did their core beliefs—about preventive attacks, about unilateralism, about the malleability of the world, about "evil"—remain unchallenged.

Fourth, and perhaps most significantly, action on the financial front became a substitute for action on other fronts. On the frequent occasions were events did not go according to plan, the role of finance as residual explanation of choice would expand.[80] Also, the impossibility of action on the military front triggered compensating mechanisms: responses could only take place on the financial front. We saw that the first strike in the financial war, which took place on September 24, 2001, was primarily a way of showing resolve at a time when a military strike against Afghanistan was not immediately possible.[81] By the same token, just as the war on terror found its limits on the military and human rights fronts, financial initiatives continued unimpeded—indeed they accelerated.

This formidable array of forces, combined with a near total absence of scrutiny, explains why financial warriors have generally chosen to err on the side of recklessness.

Notes

Introduction. The Fog of Financial War

1. "President Freezes Terrorists' Assets." Remarks by the President, Secretary of the Treasury O'Neill, and Secretary of State Powell on Executive Order, the White House, Office of the Press Secretary, September 24, 2001.
2. Judith Miller, "The Money Track: The 27 Whose Assets Will Be Frozen Are Just the First of Many, a U.S. Official Says," *New York Times*, September 25, 2001.
3. "President Freezes Terrorists' Assets," September 24, 2001.
4. David E. Sanger and Joseph Kahn, "Bush Freezes Assets Linked to Terror Net; Russians Offer Airspace and Arms Support," *New York Times*, September 25, 2001.
5. Statement of G-7 Finance Ministers, Department of the Treasury, September 25, 2001.
6. See Chapter 3.
7. http://www1.worldbank.org/finance/html/amlcf.
8. Ron Suskind, *The One Percent Doctrine: Deep Inside America's Pursuit of Its Enemies Since 9/11* (New York: Simon and Schuster 2006), pp 11–13.
9. Eric Lichtblau and James Risen, "Bank Data Is Sifted by U.S. in Secret to Block Terror," *New York Times*, June 23, 2006.
10. John Willman, Michael Mann, and Richard Wolffe, "US Has Frozen $6m of Assets Linked to Al-Qaeda," *Financial Times*, October 1, 2001.
11. http://www.whitehouse.gov/news/releases/2001/12/100dayreport.html.
12. Tim Golden, "5 Months after Sanctions against Somali Company, Scant Proof of Qaeda Tie," *New York Times*, April 13, 2002.
13. See Chapter 7.
14. Executive Order 12722: Blocking Iraqi Government Property and Prohibiting Transactions with Iraq. August 2, 1990. archives.gov/federal-register/executive-orders/1990.html.
15. "U.S. Announces It Will Seize Iraqi Assets," The Newshour with Jim Lehrer, PBS, March 20, 2003.

16. There were only a few exceptions. See for example http://www.foxnews. com/story/0,2933,81729,00.html.

17. Ibrahim Warde, "Irak: l'eldorado perdu," *Le Monde diplomatique*, May 2004.

18. Ken Adelman, "Cakewalk in Iraq," *Washington Post*, February, 2002; Ken Adelman, "'Cakewalk' Revisited," *Washington Post*, April 10, 2003. See also Richard Perle, "Relax, Celebrate Victory," *USA Today*, May 2, 2003, and Bob Woodward, *Plan of Attack* (New York: Simon and Schuster, 2004), pp 409–10.

19. Hearing on a Supplemental War Regulation, House Committee on Appropriations, March 27, 2003.

20. Testimony of Juan C. Zarate, Deputy Assistant Secretary Executive, Office for Terrorist Financing & Financial Crimes, Department of the Treasury, before the House Financial Services Subcommittee on Oversight and Investigations, March 18, 2004. Department of the Treasury, Office of Public Affairs.

21. *Ibid.*

22. "U.S. Announces It Will Seize Iraqi Assets," The Newshour with Jim Lehrer, PBS, March 20, 2003.

23. David E. Sanger and David M. Halbfinger; "Cheney Warns of Terror Risk If Kerry Wins," *New York Times*, September 8, 2004.

24. Paul Richter, "Poland Adds to Coalition Troop Cuts," *Los Angeles Times*, December 28, 2005.

25. http://www.whitehouse.gov/news/releases/2001/12/100dayreport.html.

26. See Chapter 11.

27. Stephen Valdez, *An Introduction to Global Financial Markets* (New York: Palgrave Macmillan, 2000), p 73.

28. Pseudo-events are events of no intrinsic importance that are staged solely for the purpose of generating press coverage. See Daniel J. Boorstin, *The Image: A Guide to Pseudo-Events in America* (New York: Vintage, 1992), pp 11–12.

29. The Newshour with Jim Lehrer, PBS, September 19, 2001.

30. See Chapter 10.

31. Eric Lichtblau and Josh Meyer, "Crackdown on Terror Funding is Questioned," *Los Angeles Times*, April 7, 2002.

32. *The 9/11 Commission Report: Final Report of the National Commission on Terrorist Attacks upon the United States*, Thomas H. Kean, Chair, and Lee H. Hamilton, Vice Chair, authorized edition (New York: W.W. Norton, 2004), p 260.

33. Bob Woodward, *Bush at War* (New York: Simon and Schuster, 2002), p 25.

34. Suskind, *The One Percent Doctrine*, p 141.

35. Woodward, *Bush at War*, p 112.

36. *Ibid.*, p 49.

37. Ron Suskind, *The Price of Loyalty: George W. Bush, the White House, and the Education of Paul O'Neill* (New York: Simon and Schuster, 2004), p 193.

38. *Ibid.*, p 193.

39. Woodward, *Bush at War*, p 120.

40. William F. Wechsler, "Strangling the Hydra: Targeting Al Qaeda's Finances," in James F. Hoge, Jr. and Gideon Rose (eds), *How Did This Happen? Terrorism and the New War* (New York: Public Affairs, 2001), p 129.
41. Daniel Benjamin and Steven Simon, *The Age of Sacred Terror: Radical Islam's War against America* (New York: Random House, 2003), p 269.
42. *Ibid.*
43. Dana Blanton, "Fox News Poll: Bush Approval Holding," Fox News, June 29, 2006. http://www.foxnews.com/story/0,2933,201573,00.html.
44. Mark Weisbrot, "Financial War against Terrorism Off to a Slow Start," October 10, 2001, Center for Economic and Policy Research, Washington, DC. http://www.cepr.net.
45. "Follow the Money," *The Economist*, May 30, 2002.
46. Robert Fisk, "The double standards, dubious morality and duplicity of this fight against terror," *The Independent*, January 4, 2003.
47. "President Freezes Terrorists' Assets," September 24, 2001.
48. Nicholas Watt, "MI5 team to track terror cash: Money trail 'Bletchley Park' experts target bank network," *Guardian*, October 16, 2001.
49. See, for example, Rohan Gunaratna, "The Lifeblood of Terrorist Organizations: Evolving Terrorist Financing Strategies" in Alex Schmid (ed), *Countering Terrorist through International Cooperation* (Rome: International Scientific and Professional Advisory Council of the UN and the UN Terrorism Prevention Branch, 2001); William F. Welchsler, "Strangling the Hydra: Targeting Al Qaeda's Finances" in Hoge, Jr. and Rose (eds), *How Did This Happen?*
50. Adam Clymer, "Panel Backs House Bill on Monitoring of Finances," *New York Times*, October 12, 2001.
51. Gerald P. O'Driscoll, Jr., Ph.D., Brett D. Schaefer, and John C. Hulsman, Ph.D., "Stopping Terrorism: Follow the Money," Backgrounder #1479, The Heritage Foundation, September 25, 2001.
52. Faye Bowers, "Headway on the Al Qaeda money trail: Top Treasury official claims vast reduction in terrorist cash flow—with long road ahead," *Christian Science Monitor*, October 10, 2003.
53. James Adams, *The Financing of Terror: How the Groups That Are Terrorizing the World Get the Money to Do It* (New York: Simon and Schuster, 1986), p 236.
54. Bowers, "Headway on the Al Qaeda money trail," *Christian Science Monitor*, November 3, 2003.
55. Anitha Reddy, "Terrorists Are Now Targets in Money-Laundering Fight," *Washington Post*, July 25, 2002.
56. See, for example, the glowing assessment of the first 100 days issued by the White House: http://www.whitehouse.gov/response/financialresponse.html.
57. See, for example, Sarah Laitner, Cathy Newman, and George Parker, "Britain Puts Crackdown on Terrorist Financing at the Centre of its EU Presidency," *Financial Times*, July 13, 2005.
58. Ken Adelman, "Cakewalk in Iraq," *Washington Post*, February 13, 2002; Ken

Adelman, "'Cakewalk' Revisited," *Washington Post*, April 10, 2003. See also Richard Perle, "Relax, Celebrate Victory," *USA Today*, May 2, 2003, and Woodward, *Plan of Attack*, pp 409–10.

59. James Fallows, *Blind into Baghdad: America's War in Iraq* (New York: Vintage, 2006), pp 43–106.

60. Much was made of the "$750,000 in hundred-dollar bills" found in his final hideout. See Ambassador L. Paul Bremer III, with Malcolm McConnell, *My Year in Iraq: The Struggle to Build a Future of Hope* (New York: Simon and Schuster, 2006), p 250.

61. Mark Hosenball, "Exclusive: Plane? Found. Cash? Still Missing," *Newsweek*, March 8, 2004.

62. Julie Flint, "Terror funding must be understood and soon," *Daily Star*, December 22, 2003.

63. Eric Schmitt, "U.S. General Says Coalition Is Choking Funds to Insurgency," *New York Times*, December 12, 2003.

64. Eric Schmitt and Thom Shanker, "Rebels: Estimates by U.S. See More Rebels with More Funds," *New York Times*, October 22, 2004.

65. *Ibid.*

66. James Bennet, "Israelis, in Raid on Arab Banks, Seize Reputed Terrorist Funds," *New York Times*, February 26, 2004.

67. Schmitt, "U.S. General Says Coalition Is Choking Funds to Insurgency," *New York Times*, December 12, 2003.

68. Schmitt and Shanker, "Rebels: Estimates by U.S. See More Rebels with More Funds," *New York Times*, October 22, 2004. See also Richard A. Oppel, Jr., "Iraq Accuses Jordan of Allowing Financing of Insurgency," *New York Times*, August 22, 2005.

69. According to Boaz Ganor, among the heavenly rewards, the suicide bomber "will have seventy-two virgins at his beck and call, who will provide for all of his needs." Boaz Ganor, *The Counter-Terrorism Puzzle: A Guide for Decision-Makers* (New Brunswick: Transaction, 2005), pp 77–8.

70. Christopher H. Schmitt and Joshua Kurlantzick, "When charity goes awry: Islamic groups say they may lose control of money they send overseas," *U.S. News and World Report*, October 29, 2001. In Israel, this argument was used to justify the destruction of the homes of suicide bombers.

71. Ganor, *The Counter-Terrorism Puzzle*, p 77.

72. See, for example, Robert Pape, *Dying to Win: The Strategic Logic of Suicide Terrorism* (New York: Random House, 2005); Mia Bloom, *Dying to Kill: The Allure of Suicide Terror* (Columbia University Press, 2005).

73. John Roth, Douglas Greenburg, and Serena Wille, *Monograph on Terrorist Financing*, National Commission on Terrorist Attacks Upon the United States, Staff Report to the Commission, 2004, p 35.

74. See Chapter 11.

75. John Ward Anderson, Steve Fainaru, and Jonathan Finer, "Bigger, Stronger Homemade Bombs Now to Blame for Half of U.S. Deaths," *Washington Post*,

October 26, 2005.

76. *The 9/11 Commission Report*, p 13.

77. David Hunt, *They Just Don't Get It: How Washington Is Still Compromising Your Safety—and What You Can Do about It* (New York: Crown Forum, 2005).

78. The O'Reilly Factor, Fox News, July 7, 2005.

79. *Ibid.*

80. Laitner, Newman, and Parker, "Britain Puts Crackdown on Terrorist Financing at the Centre of its EU Presidency," *Financial Times*, July 13, 2005.

81. David Rennie, "Brown and Straw get tough with EU over terror laws," *Daily Telegraph*, July 14, 2005.

82. Jenny Booth, "EU agrees crackdown on terrorist finances," *The Times*, July 12, 2005.

83. "£20m for terror measures and bomb victims," *Guardian*, July 19, 2005.

84. Laitner, Newman, and Parker, "Britain Puts Crackdown on Terrorist Financing at the Centre of its EU Presidency," *Financial Times*, July 13, 2005.

85. Rennie, "Brown and Straw get tough with EU over terror laws," *Daily Telegraph*, July 14, 2005.

86. Booth, "EU agrees crackdown on terrorist finances," *The Times*, July 12, 2005.

87. Stuart Levey, "The war on terrorist financing must be stepped up," *Financial Times*, September 26, 2005.

88. *Ibid.*

89. Hannah K. Strange, "July 7 bombings 'cost just $1,000,'" United Press International, January 3, 2006.

90. Robert M. Morgenthau, "Cutting Off the Funds for Terror," *New York Times*, October 22, 2001.

91. Strange, "July 7 bombings 'cost just $1,000,'" United Press International, January 3, 2006.

92. Fawaz A. Gerges, *The Far Enemy: Why Jihad Went Global* (Cambridge: Cambridge University Press, 2005), p 270.

93. Jonathan Randal, *Osama: The Making of a Terrorist* (New York: Alfred A. Knopf, 2004), p 42.

94. Gerges, *The Far Enemy*, p 40.

95. Nick Kochan, *The Washing Machine: How Money Laundering and Terrorist Financing Soils Us* (Mason, OH: Thomson, 2005), p 67.

96. Gerges, *The Far Enemy*, p 272.

97. "The Fight Against Money Laundering," *Economic Perspectives*, May 2001.

98. See Chapter 10.

99. Joseph S. Nye, Jr., *Soft Power: The Means to Success in World Politics* (New York: Public Affairs, 2004), pp 1–3; and Joseph S. Nye, Jr., *The Paradox of American Power: Why the World's Only Superpower Can't Go It Alone* (Oxford: Oxford University Press, 2002).

100. "Rumsfeld's war-on-terror memo," *USA Today*, October 22, 2003.

101. *Ibid.*

Chapter 1. Fantasy, Fiction, and Terrorist Financing

1. Michael Lewis, *Liar's Poker: Rising through the Wreckage on Wall Street* (New York: Norton, 1989), p 186.
2. Jack G. Shaheen, *Reel Bad Arabs: How Hollywood Vilifies a People* (New York: Interlink Pub Group, 2001), p 2.
3. *Ibid.*, p 7.
4. Joan Didion, "Fixed Opinions, or the Hinge of History," *The New York Review of Books*, January 16, 2003.
5. See Chapter 5. Some groups with particular agendas would add or subtract from that list. The proponents of the Iraqi war focused particularly on the role of "rogue states." On September 12, 2001, columnist William Safire asked: "What well-financed terrorist organization, under what country's secret protection, slaughtered so many Americans?" William Safire, "New Day of Infamy," *New York Times*, September 12, 2001.
6. *The 9/11 Commission Report.*
7. John Roth, Douglas Greenburg, and Serena Wille, *Monograph on Terrorist Financing*, National Commission on Terrorist Attacks Upon the United States, Staff Report to the Commission 2004.
8. *The 9/11 Commission Report*, p 30.
9. Gerges, *The Far Enemy*, pp 17–22.
10. See Chapter 7.
11. *The 9/11 Commission Report*, p 170.
12. Kenneth Katzman, "Terrorism: Near Eastern Groups and State Sponsors, 2001," (Washington, DC: Congressional Research Service), September 10, 2001.
13. In Peter Bergen's authoritative oral history of Bin Laden, the number of sons was estimated to be at least 25. Furthermore, the father's inheritance was divided according to the Shariah law, which meant that the daughters were not excluded, but received half of the sons' shares. Peter L. Bergen, *The Osama bin Laden I Know: An Oral History of al Qaeda's Leader* (New York: Free Press, 2006), pp 10, 400.
14. On that subject, see Carmen Bin Ladin, *Inside the Kingdom: My Life in Saudi Arabia* (New York: Warner Books, 2004), p 131.
15. Richard Labévière, *Dollars for Terror: The United States and Islam* (New York: Algora Publishing, 2000), p 117.
16. *Monograph on Terrorist Financing*, p 20.
17. *Ibid.*, p 20.
18. Quoted in Anonymous, *Through Our Enemies' Eyes: Osama Bin Laden, Radical Islam, and the Future of America* (Washington, DC: Brassey's Inc., 2002), p 77.
19. The company, as well as a number of members of the Bin Laden family, use different spellings of the name.
20. See Chapter 9.
21. Randal, *Osama: The Making of a Terrorist*, p 125.

22. *Monograph on Terrorist Financing*, p 20.
23. See, for example, *CDI Primer: Terrorist Finances*, Center for Defense Information, October 25, 2002; Kurt Eichenwald, "Terror Money Hard to Block, Officials," *New York Times*, December 10, 2001; Kevin McCoy and Dennis Cauchon, "The business side of terror," *USA Today*, October 16, 2001.
24. Karen DeYoung, David Hilzenrath, and Robert O'Harrow Jr., "Bin Laden's Money Takes Hidden Paths to Agents of Terror," *Washington Post*, September 21, 2001.
25. *The 9/11 Commission Report*, p 170.
26. Randal, *Osama: The Making of a Terrorist*, p 125.
27. Maurice R. Greenberg, Chair, William F. Wechsler and Lee S. Wolosky, Project Co-Directors, "Terrorist Financing: Report of an Independent Task Force" (New York: Council on Foreign Relations, November 14, 2002), p 1.
28. *Monograph on Terrorist Financing*, p 20.
29. Martin Bentham, "Terror chief has global cash machine," *Sunday Telegraph*, September 16, 2001.
30. *Ibid.*
31. Myron Levin, "Terror Exacts High Price at Low Cost Funding: Cutting off the source of money may not shut down groups that operate on shoestring budgets," *Los Angeles Times*, September 25, 2001.
32. Tony Karon, "Al Qaeda's in the Money," http://www.time.com, August 29, 2003.
33. James Risen, *State of War: The Secret History of the CIA and the Bush Administration* (New York: Free Press, 2006), p 10.
34. *Monograph on Terrorist Financing*, p 34.
35. *Ibid.*, p 20. See, for example, "Le rapport du juge Garzon sur Al-Qaida," *Le Monde*, March 17, 2004; Bruce Hoffman, Rohan K. Gunaratna, and Sidney Jones, "Terrorism: International and Regional Dimensions," Regional Outlook Forum 2005, Singapore, Institute of Southern Asian Studies, January 2005, p 4.
36. See, for example, Ron Suskind, "Why Are These Men Laughing?" *Esquire*, January 2003; "Mrs. Hughes Takes Her Leave," *Esquire*, July 2002; and *The Price of Loyalty*.
37. Ron Suskind, "Without a Doubt," *New York Times Magazine*, October 17, 2004.
38. Woodward, *Bush at War*, p 421. A senior official in the first George W. Bush administration told Seymour Hersh that the President said that "God put me here" to deal with the war on terror. See Seymour M. Hersh, "Where is the Iraq war headed next?," *The New Yorker*, December 5, 2005. See also Mark Lawson, "The Maker of US Policy," *Guardian*, October 8, 2005.
39. Suskind, "Without a Doubt."
40. "President Bush Outlines Iraqi Threat." Remarks by the President on Iraq, Cincinnati Museum Center, Cincinnati Union Terminal, October 7, 2002, http://www.whitehouse.gov/news/releases/2002/10/20021007-8.html.

41. Joe Klein, "Why the 'War President' Is under Fire: Bush's anti-terror policies are dangerously simple," *Time*, February 15, 2004.
42. Suskind, "Without a Doubt."
43. Suskind, *The Price of Loyalty*, p 67.
44. *Ibid.*, pp 117–18.
45. Ibrahim Warde, "L'ordre américain, coûte que coûte," *Le Monde diplomatique*, April 2003.
46. Joel Havemann, "Bush's Deficit Plan Is All in the Math," *Los Angeles Times*, February 7, 2005.
47. Suskind, "Without a Doubt."
48. *Ibid.*
49. Glenn Kessler, "War's Rationales Are Undermined One More Time: Revelations May Hurt Bush's Image," *Washington Post*, October 7, 2004.
50. Sam Tanenhaus, "Bush's Brain Trust," *Vanity Fair*, July 2003.
51. William J. Bennett, *Why We Fight: Moral Clarity and the War on Terrorism* (New York: Doubleday, 2002).
52. Richard Cohen, "...Unshakable Faith," *Washington Post*, July 17, 2003.
53. Woodward, *Plan of Attack*, p 93.
54. *Ibid.*, p 94.
55. Michael Kinsley, "Deliver Us from Evil," *Washington Post*, September 20, 2002.
56. *Ibid.*
57. Kathleen Norris, "Native Evil," *Boston College Magazine*, Winter 2002.
58. Most significantly, David Frum and Richard Perle, *An End to Evil: How to Win the War on Terror* (New York: Random House, 2003).
59. Rachel Ehrenfeld, *Funding Evil: How Terrorism Is Financed—and How to Stop It* (Chicago: Bonus Books, 2003).
60. President George W. Bush, State of the Union Address, January 28, 2003, http://www.whitehouse.gov/news/releases/2003/01/20030128-19.html.
61. *The 9/11 Commission Report*, p 170.
62. See Chapter 6.
63. Jennifer Senior, "Intruders in the House of Saud," *New York Times Magazine*, March 14, 2004.
64. Seth Stern, "Can a trillion-dollar lawsuit stop Saudi terror-cash flow?," *Christian Science Monitor*, August 20, 2002.
65. Loretta Napoleoni, "Money and Terrorism," *Strategic Insights*, April 2004. See also Loretta Napoleoni, *Modern Jihad: Tracing the Dollars behind the Terror Networks* (London: Pluto Press, 2003).
66. See Chapter 3.
67. Jeffrey Robinson, *The Laundrymen: Inside the World's Third Largest Business* (London: Simon and Schuster Pocket Books, 1998), p 3.
68. Lawrence Malkin and Yuval Elizur, "The Dilemma of Dirty Money," *World Policy Journal*, Spring 2001.
69. Robinson, *The Laundrymen*, p 16.

70. R.T. Naylor, "Follow-the-Money Methods in Crime Control Policy," in Margaret E. Beare (ed), *Critical Reflections on Transnational Organized Crime, Money Laundering, and Corruption* (University of Toronto Press, 2003), p 263.

71. See Chapter 11.

72. Loretta Napoleoni, "Money and Terrorism," *Strategic Insights*, April 2004. See also Loretta Napoleoni, *Modern Jihad*.

73. Michael Freedman, "Financing Terror: Why the U.S. Can't Stop the Flow of Billions to Drug Lords, Smugglers and Al Qaida," *Forbes*, October 17, 2005.

74. Michael Woodiwiss, *Gangster Capitalism: The United States and the Global Rise of Organized Crime* (London: Constable & Robinson, 2005), p 39.

75. *FinCen Advisory*, The United States Department of the Treasury, Financial Crimes Enforcement Network, March 1996, Volume 1, Issue 1, p 2.

76. Michael Ledeen, *The War against the Terror Masters: Why It Happened. Where We Are Now. How We'll Win* (New York: St Martin's Griffin, 2003), p 41.

77. *Ibid.*, p 41.

78. Selwyn Raab, *Five Families: The Rise, Decline, and Resurgence of America's Most Powerful Mafia Empires* (New York: Thomas Dunne Books/St Martin's Press, 2005).

79. Norman Daniel, *Islam and the West: The Making of an Image* (Edinburgh: Edinburgh University Press, 1962).

80. Henry Mintzberg, *The Rise and Fall of Strategic Planning: Reconceiving Roles for Planning, Plans, Planners* (New York: Free Press, 1994), p 317.

81. Daniel Benjamin and Steven Simon, *The Age of Sacred Terror: Radical Islam's War against America* (New York: Random House, 2003), p 269.

82. Richard A. Clarke, *Against All Enemies: Inside America's War on Terror* (New York: Free Press, 2004), p 191.

83. *Ibid.*, p 191.

84. See Chapter 5.

85. Clarke, *Against All Enemies*, p 192.

86. *Ibid.*

87. Marc Sageman, *Understanding Terror Networks* (University of Pennsylvania Press, 2004), p 67.

88. *Ibid.*

89. Felicity Barringer, "Terror Experts Use Lenses of Their Specialties," *New York Times*, September 24, 2001.

90. Jack Kelley, "The secret world of suicide bombers," *USA Today*, June 26, 2001.

91. Jack Kelley, "Saudi Money Aiding bin Laden," *USA Today*, October 29, 1999.

92. Jack Kelley, "What al-Qaeda left behind keeps the CIA a step ahead," *USA Today*, January 30, 2002.

93. John Gorenfeld, "Blood-thirsty Arabs, vigilante Jews," *Salon*, March 23, 2004.

94. Douglas Little, *American Orientalism: The United States and the Middle East*

since 1945 (University of North Carolina Press, 2002), p 38.

95. Rashid Khalidi, *Resurrecting Empire: Western Footprints and America's Perilous Path in the Middle East* (Boston: Beacon Press, 2004), p 11.

96. Samuel Huntington, *The Clash of Civilizations and the Remaking of the World Order* (New York: Simon and Schuster, 1996), p 70.

97. Fawaz A. Gerges, *America and Political Islam: Clash of Cultures or Clash of Interests?* (Cambridge: Cambridge University Press 1999), pp 52-3.

98. Tom Clancy's 1995 best-selling *Debt of Honor* novels featured a cover drawing of a 747 jetliner crashing into the US Capitol; the plane's Japanese pilot was determined to avenge his family's losses from World War II. See James Bovard, *Terrorism and Tyranny: Trampling Freedom, Justice, and Peace to Rid the World of Evil* (New York: Palgrave Macmillan, 2003), p 60.

99. David Frum, *The Right Man: An Inside Account of the Bush White House* (New York: Random House, 2005), p 177.

100. Ali Abunimah, "A hoax and honor lost for Norma Khouri," *Daily Star*, August 10, 2004.

101. *The New York Times on The Sopranos*, introduction by Stephen Holden (New York: ibooks, 2000), p xi.

102. Chris Ryan, *Greed* (London: Arrow Books, 2004), p 51.

103. Gérard de Villiers, *L'or d'Al-Qaida* (Paris: Gérard de Villiers S.A.S., 2003). Many of the recent books of the prolific pulp fiction author have dealt with terrorists and their money. His most recent work is a two-volume novel revealing the whereabouts of Saddam Hussein's hidden treasure: Gérard de Villiers, *Le trésor de Saddam* (Paris: Gérard de Villiers S.A.S., 2006).

104. Douglas Farah, *Blood for Stones: The Secret Financial Network of Terror* (New York: Broadway Books, 2004).

105. 60 Minutes, CBS News, April 30, 2006.

Chapter 2. Framing the Guilty: The Financial Terrain

1. William Safire, *No Uncertain Terms: More Writing from the Popular "On Language" Column in The New York Times Magazine* (New York: Simon and Schuster, 2003), p 49.

2. Christian Parenti, *Lockdown America: Police and Prisons in the Age of Crisis* (London: Verso, 2000), p 11.

3. A common anti-mob ploy was to bring mob associates before a grand jury and ask them if they knew a certain person. They would deny it, but then the prosecution would produce surveillance photos or other evidence, proving perjury.

4. Mary Beth Sheridan, "Immigration Law as Anti-Terrorism Tool," *Washington Post*, June 13, 2005.

5. John D. O'Connor, "I'm the Guy They Called Deep Throat," *Vanity Fair*, July 2005.

6. Bob Woodward, *The Secret Man: The Story of Watergate's Deep Throat* (New York: Simon and Schuster, 2005), pp 60-1, 70-2.

7. Lloyd C. Gardner, *The Case That Never Dies: The Lindbergh Kidnapping* (Rutgers University Press, 2004).

8. "Combating International Money Laundering," Remarks of Secretary Lawrence H. Summers on International Money Laundering to the BAFT, ABA and SIA, United States Department of the Treasury, Office of Public Affairs, March 2, 2000.

9. Glenn R. Simpson, "U.S. Indicts Head of Charity for Helping Fund al Qaeda: Government Uses 'Al Capone' Tax Charges for This and Other Terror-Financing Cases," *Wall Street Journal*, October 10, 2002.

10. A significant exception occurred during the Civil War with the Confiscation Acts. In 1861 and then again in 1862, the government declared all property belonging to Confederate officers or those who aided the rebels to be forfeitable *in rem*. The US Supreme Court held that the Act was an exercise of the war powers of the government and was applied only to enemies.

11. Parenti, *Lockdown America*, p 50.

12. In medieval England, common law provided for the forfeiture of any inanimate object or animal causing a man's death. Known as a "deodand," the object was declared tainted or evil, held guilty, and forfeited to the feudal lord.

13. Parenti, *Lockdown America*, p 51.

14. Quoted in Michael W. Lynch, "Forfeiture Fury," *Reason*, July 1999.

15. "International Narcotics Control Strategy Report," US Department of State, Bureau Of International Narcotics Matters, April 1994, http://dosfan.lib.uic.edu/ERC/law/INC/1994/11.html.

16. James Ring Adams and Douglas Frantz, *A Full Service Bank: How BCCI Stole Billions around the World* (New York: Simon and Schuster, 1991), p 5.

17. James Stewart, *Den of Thieves* (New York: Simon and Schuster, 1991).

18. Richard Miniter, "Ill-Gotten Gains: Police and prosecutors have their own reasons to oppose forfeiture-law reform," *Reason*, August 1993.

19. Parenti, *Lockdown America*, pp 52–3.

20. Lynch, "Forfeiture Fury," *Reason*, July 1999.

21. Henry Hyde, *Forfeiting Our Property Rights: Is Your Property Safe from Seizure?* (Washington, DC: Cato Institute, 1995).

22. Lynch, "Forfeiture Fury," *Reason*, July 1999.

23. Michael W. Lynch, "Police Beat: In which our man in Washington observes the nation's guardians," *Reason*, July 1999.

24. Adams, *The Financing of Terror*, p 126.

25. Ganor, *The Counter-Terrorism Puzzle*, pp 186, 191–2.

26. In Elizabeth Johnson and Donald Moggridge (eds), *The Collected Writings of John Maynard Keynes, Volume 26: Activities 1943–46: Shaping the Post-war World: Bretton Woods and Reparation* (Cambridge: Cambridge University Press, 1980), p 16.

27. John Gerard Ruggie, "International regimes, transactions, and change: Embedded liberalism in the postwar economic order" in Stephen D. Krasner

(ed), *International Regimes* (Cornell University Press, 1983).

28. Michael Moran, *The Politics of the Financial Services Revolution: The USA, UK and Japan* (New York: St Martin's Press, 1991), pp 2–3.

29. See, for example, Henry Kaufman, *On Money and Markets: A Wall Street Memoir* (New York: McGraw Hill, 2000), pp 113–37; Michael Moran, *The Politics of the Financial Services Revolution*, pp 53–87.

30. Ibrahim Warde, *Islamic Finance in the Global Economy* (Edinburgh: Edinburgh University Press, 2000), pp 180–8.

31. Richard O'Brien, *Global Financial Integration: The End of Geography* (New York: Council on Foreign Relations Press, 1992).

32. Brian White, "Diplomacy" in John Baylis and Steve Smith (eds), *The Globalization of World Politics: An Introduction to International Relations* (Oxford: Oxford University Press, 2001), p 322.

33. Andrew J. Bacevich, *American Empire: The Realities and Consequences of U.S. Diplomacy* (Harvard University Press, 2002), pp 41–2.

34. Ibrahim Warde, *The Regulation of Foreign Banking in the United States* (San Francisco: IBPC, 1997), p 153.

35. Susan Strange, *Casino Capitalism* (London: Basil Blackwell, 1989), p 67.

36. Similarly, between the creation in 1945 of the United Nations and 1990, the Security Council voted sanctions only twice (against Rhodesia and South Africa). Since the end of the Cold War the UN imposed sanctions on no fewer than 12 occasions. See United Kingdom Parliament, Select Committee on International Development Second Report, February 10, 2000.

37. Stuart E. Eizenstat, Undersecretary of State for Economic, Business and Agricultural Affairs, Testimony before the House International Relations Committee, June 3, 1998.

38. Kevin Phillips, *American Dynasty: Aristocracy, Fortune, and the Politics of Deceit in the House of Bush* (New York: Viking, 2004), p 271.

39. Joseph Stiglitz, *Globalization and Its Discontents* (New York: W.W. Norton, 2003), p 24. See also Ibrahim Warde, "Les faiseurs de révolution libérale," *Le Monde diplomatique*, May 1992.

40. United Kingdom Parliament, Select Committee on International Development Second Report, February 10, 2000.

41. Raymond Tanter, *Rogue Regimes: Terrorism and Proliferation* (New York: St Martin's Press, 1999), p 21.

42. United Kingdom Parliament, Select Committee on International Development Second Report, February 10, 2000.

43. James Schlesinger, Introduction to Lee H. Hamilton, "Sanctions, Congress and the National Interest," July 20, 1998, *Nixon Center Perspectives*, Volume 3, Number 3.

44. Glenn Kessler, "Hill Passes Measure to Punish Burma with Trade Sanctions," *Washington Post*, July 17, 2003.

Chapter 3. The Flawed Money Laundering Template

1. See, for example, Chris Mathers, *Crime School, Money Laundering: True Crime Meets the World of Business and Finance* (Buffalo, NY: Firefly Books, 2004), pp 21-2. A variation on the laundering theme is that gangsters used car wash businesses.
2. US v $4,255,625.39 (1982) 551 F Supp.314 (1982 US Dist. LEXIS 15918).
3. See Chapter 2.
4. See, for example, Edward Jay Epstein, *Dossier: The Secret History of Armand Hammer* (New York: Random House, 1996).
5. See, for example, John Cooney, *The Annenbergs: The Salvaging of a Tainted Dynasty* (New York: Simon and Schuster, 1982).
6. There is an abundant literature critical of the assumptions and methods of the "war on drugs." See, for example, Mike Gray (ed), *Busted: Stone Cowboys, Narco-Lords and Washington's War on Drugs* (New York: Thunder's Mouth Press/Nation Books, 2002) and Judge James P. Gray, *Why Our Drug Laws Have Failed and What We Can Do about It: A Judicial Indictment of the War on Drugs* (Temple University Press, 2001).
7. David A. Andelman, "The Drug Money Maze," *Foreign Affairs*, July/August 1994.
8. See Brett F. Woods, *The Art and Science of Money Laundering: Inside the Commerce of the International Narcotics Traffickers* (Boulder, CO: Paladin Press, 1998).
9. Mathers, *Crime School, Money Laundering*, p 137.
10. Robinson, *The Laundrymen*, p 41.
11. http://www.fatf.org.
12. The Bank Secrecy Act created four requirements: (1) a paper trail of bank records to be maintained for five years; (2) a Currency Transaction Report (CTR) to be filed for currency transactions greater than $10,000; (3) a Currency or Monetary Instrument Report (CMIR) to be filed when currency or monetary instruments greater than $5,000 (later raised to $10,000) are taken out of the US; (4) a Foreign Bank Account Report (FBAR) to be filed whenever a person had an account in a foreign bank greater than $5,000 (later raised to $10,000) in value.
13. Robinson, *The Laundrymen*, p 383.
14. http://www.fincen.gov.
15. Lucy Komisar, "'After Dirty Air, Dirty Money,'" *The Nation*, June 18, 2001.
16. Lawrence Lindsey, "Invading Financial Privacy," *Financial Times*, March 19, 1999.
17. Suskind, *The Price of Loyalty*, p 181.
18. Adam Cohen, "Banking On Secrecy," *Time*, October 14, 2001.
19. Edward Alden and Michael Peel, "US may ease stance over money laundering: Coalition is pushing regarding reporting of big cash deposits," *Financial Times*, June 1, 2001.
20. David Cay Johnston, "Former I.R.S. Chiefs Back Tax Haven Crackdown,"

New York Times, June 9, 2001.

21. "Money laundering: Fighting the dirt," *The Economist*, June 21, 2001.
22. Johnston, "Former I.R.S. Chiefs Back Tax Haven Crackdown," *New York Times*, June 9, 2001.
23. William Wechsler, "Follow the Money," *Foreign Affairs*, July–August 2001.
24. Helen Dewar, "Sen. Phil Gramm of Texas Will Not Seek Reelection," *Washington Post*, September 4, 2001.
25. The Newshour with Jim Lehrer, PBS, September 19, 2001.
26. Parenti, *Lockdown America*, pp 9, 52.
27. Bill Clinton, *My Life* (New York: Alfred A. Knopf, 2004), pp 701-3.
28. Douglas Jehl, "Cutting Terrorists' Support; Clinton Orders Assets of Suspected Terrorist Groups Frozen," *New York Times*, January 25, 1995.
29. Clarke, *Against All Enemies*, p 96.
30. Michael Scheuer, the head of that station, would later write two books sharply critical of the US war on terror. See Anonymous, *Through Our Enemies' Eyes: Osama Bin Laden, Radical Islam, and the Future of America*, and Anonymous, *Imperial Hubris: How the West Is Losing the War on Terror* (Washington, DC: Brassey's Inc., 2004).
31. The designation is made every two years by the Secretary of State according to three criteria for designation: (1) the group must be foreign; (2) the group must engage in terrorist activity; and (3) the group's actions must be aimed at US interests.
32. Benjamin and Simon, *The Age of Sacred Terror*, p 228.
33. Attending training camp, for example, would, after September 11, be considered material support.
34. See Chapter 6.
35. Clinton, *My Life*, p 719.
36. *Ibid.*, p 717.
37. Benjamin and Simon, *The Age of Sacred Terror*, p 269.
38. Robinson, *The Laundrymen*, p 1.
39. See Chapter 1.
40. Robinson, *The Laundrymen*, pp 1-2.
41. William F. Wechsler, Testimony before the House Committee on Government Reform, Subcommittee on Criminal Justice, Drug Policy and Human Resources, June 23, 2000.
42. Robinson, *The Laundrymen*, p 3.
43. Adams, *The Financing of Terror*, p 182.
44. See Chapter 11.
45. *The 9/11 Commission Report*, p 53.
46. Financial Action Task Force on Money Laundering (FATF-XII), *Report on Money Laundering Typologies 2000-2001*, February 1, 2001, p 19.
47. *Ibid.*, p 20.
48. *Monograph on Terrorist Financing*, p 38.
49. *Ibid.*, p 53.

50. Peter Reuter and Edwin M. Truman, *Chasing Dirty Money: The Fight against Money Laundering* (Washington, DC: Institute for International Economics, 2004), p 3.

51. Suskind, *The Price of Loyalty*, p 179.

52. Mathers, *Crime School, Money Laundering*, p 112.

53. Paul Allan Schott, *Reference Guide to Anti-Money Laundering and Combating the Financing of Terrorism* (Washington, DC: World Bank Publications, 2006).

54. "Terrorist finance: Don't relax," *The Economist*, May 30, 2002. A ninth recommendation was later added concerning the regulation of cash couriers.

55. http://www.fatf.org.

56. "Terrorist finance: Moving target," *The Economist*, September 12, 2002.

57. Reuter and Truman, *Chasing Dirty Money*, p 7.

58. *Ibid.*, p 8.

59. Tobias Buck and Paul J Davies, "Banks back rules to thwart terror," *Financial Times*, July 27, 2005.

60. *Monograph on Terrorist Financing*, p 74. See also James Bovard, *Terrorism and Tyranny*, pp 81–132.

Chapter 4. Money and the War on Terror Narrative

1. Clarke, *Against All Enemies*, preface to the paperback edition, p xiii.

2. Bovard, *Terrorism and Tyranny*, p 2.

3. Ramesh Ponnuru, "Blame America First," *National Review*, October 15, 2001.

4. There had been considerable "chatter" in the weeks before September 11 about a major terrorist attack in the US, involving hijacked planes. FBI agents had warned that suspicious Muslim fundamentalists were taking flying lessons. On August 6, 2001, an intelligence briefing delivered to President Bush at his Crawford, Texas, ranch was simply titled "Bin Laden Determined to Strike in U.S." Since May 2002, a steady stream of leaks painted a devastating picture of the lackadaisical approach of the intelligence community to pre-September 11 warnings. It took a number of Congressional reports and the detailed account of the September 11 Commission for the full scale of the intelligence debacle to be understood, and finally followed by the greatest reorganization of intelligence in almost 60 years.

5. Joan Didion, "Fixed Opinions, or the Hinge of History," *The New York Review of Books*, January 16, 2003.

6. See, for example, Stefan Halper and Jonathan Clarke, *America Alone: The Neo-Conservatives and the Global Order* (Cambridge: Cambridge University Press, 2004); Anatol Lieven, *America Right or Wrong: An Anatomy of American Nationalism* (Oxford: Oxford University Press, 2004); and Stanley Hoffmann, with Frédéric Bozo, *Gulliver Unbound: America's Imperial Temptation and the War in Iraq* (Lanham, MD: Rowman and Littlefield, 2004).

7. *National Review*, October 1, 2001.

8. Chalmers Johnson, "Blowback," *The Nation*, October 15, 2001.

9.   *Ibid.* See also Chapter 8.

10. James Wolcott, "Flooding the Spin Zone," *Vanity Fair*, November 2005. See also James Wolcott, *Attack Poodles and Other Media Mutants* (New York: Miramax Books, 2004).

11. Quoted in John R. MacArthur, *Second Front: Censorship and Propaganda in the Gulf War* (Berkeley: University of California Press, 1993), p xi.

12. See, for example, John MacArthur, "Everybody Wants to Be at Versailles" in Kristina Borjesson (ed), *Feet to the Fire: The Media After 9/11 – Top Journalists Speak Out* (New York: Prometheus Books, 2005).

13. David Halberstam, *War in a Time of Peace: Bush, Clinton and the Generals* (New York: Scribner, 2001), p 58.

14. *Ibid.*, p 75.

15. Peter A. Hall and Sidney Tarrow, "Globalization and Area Studies: When Is Too Broad Too Narrow?" *The Chronicle of Higher Education*, January 23, 1998.

16. *Ibid.*

17. See Francis Fukuyama, *America at the Crossroads: Democracy, Power, and the Neoconservative Legacy* (Yale University Press, 2006).

18. Zachary Lockman, *Contending Visions of the Middle East: The History and Politics of Orientalism* (Cambridge: Cambridge University Press, 2004), pp 251–67.

19. Robert Kaplan, *The Arabists: The Romance of an American Elite* (New York: The Free Press, 1995).

20. Karen Kwiatkowski, "The New Pentagon Papers," *Salon*, March 10, 2004.

21. Sara Roy, "Short Cuts: On the Silencing of US Academics," *London Review of Books*, April 1, 2004.

22. Zachary Lockman, "Behind the Battles over US Middle East Studies," *Middle East Report*, January 2004.

23. Jeffrey Goldberg, "A Little Learning: What Douglas Feith knew, and when he knew it," *The New Yorker*, May 9, 2005.

24. See, for example, Ken Adelman, "'Cakewalk' in Iraq," *Washington Post*, February 13, 2002; Ken Adelman, "'Cakewalk' Revisited," *Washington Post*, April 10, 2003. See also Richard Perle, "Relax, Celebrate Victory," *USA Today*, May 2, 2003, and Bob Woodward, *Plan of Attack*, pp 409–10.

25. Leon Festinger, Henry W. Riecken, and Stanley Schachter, *When Prophecy Fails* (New York: Harper Torchbooks, 1956), p 12.

26. Boaz Ganor, *The Counter-Terrorism Puzzle.*

27. Halper and Clarke, *America Alone*, p 34.

28. Michael Ledeen, *The War against the Terror Masters: Why It Happened. Where We Are Now. How We'll Win* (New York: St Martin's Griffin, 2003); David Frum and Richard Perle, *An End to Evil: How to Win the War on Terror* (New York: Random House, 2003).

29. "Terrorism Financing: Origination, Organization, and Prevention: Saudi Arabia, Terrorist Financing and the War on Terror." Testimony of Steven

Emerson with Jonathan Levin before the United States Senate Committee on Governmental Affairs, July 31, 2003.

30. Ron Suskind, *The One Percent Doctrine*, p 136.
31. Micah Halpern, *What You Need to Know About: Terror* (New Milford, Connecticut: Toby Press, 2003).
32. Khalidi, *Resurrecting Empire*, p xii.
33. Bernard Lewis, "The Roots of Muslim Rage: Why so many Muslims deeply resent the West, and why their bitterness will not easily be mollified," *The Atlantic Monthly*, September 1990.
34. Edward Rothstein, "Exploring the Flaws in the Notion of the 'Root Causes' of Terror," *New York Times*, November 17, 2001.
35. Fred C. Iklé, "Stopping the Next 9/11," *Wall Street Journal*, May 31, 2002.
36. Tim Golden, "5 Months after Sanctions against Somali Company, Scant Proof of Qaeda Tie," *New York Times*, April 13, 2002.
37. Dan Balz and Bob Woodward, "America's Chaotic Road to War: Bush's Global Strategy Began to Take Shape in First Frantic Hours after Attack," *Washington Post*, January 27, 2002.
38. *Monograph on Terrorist Financing*, p 74.
39. Halper and Clarke, *America Alone*.
40. See Benjamin Wallace-Wells, "Private Jihad: How Rita Katz got into the spying business," *The New Yorker*, May 29, 2006.
41. John Guare, *Six Degrees of Separation* (New York: Vintage, 1994).
42. Malcolm Gladwell, "Six Degrees of Lois Weisberg," *The New Yorker*, January 11, 1999.
43. Eric Schmitt, "Rumsfeld Says U.S. Has 'Bulletproof' Evidence of Iraq's Links to Al Qaeda," *New York Times*, September 28, 2002.
44. Eric Boehlert, "Are We Safer Now?," *Salon*, July 31, 2003.
45. For an especially creative way of linking Saddam Hussein and Al-Qaeda, see Fouad Ajami, "Two Faces, One Terror," *Wall Street Journal*, November 16, 2002. See also Micah L. Sifry and Christopher Cerf, *The Iraq War Reader: History, Documents, Opinions* (New York: Touchstone, 2003), pp 387-91.
46. Bill Keller, "The Year in Ideas: Pre-emption," *New York Times Magazine*, December 15, 2002.
47. William Safire, "The New Groupthink," *New York Times*, July 14, 2004.
48. Dana Milbank and Claudia Deane, "Hussein Link to 9/11 Lingers in Many Minds," *Washington Post*, September 6, 2003.
49. Timothy Noah, More "Six Degrees of Adnan Khashoggi," *Slate*, February 26, 2001.
50. *Ibid.*
51. Late Edition with Wolf Blitzer, CNN, March 9, 2003.
52. Michael Moore, *Fahrenheit 9/11*, Sony Pictures, 2004.
53. Craig Unger, "The Biggest Crime in American History and Planes Are Grounded. Yet the House of Saud Gets Safe Passage Home," *Independent on Sunday*, July 18, 2004. See also Craig Unger, *House of Bush, House of Saud: The*

Secret Relationship between the World's Two Most Powerful Dynasties (New York: Scribner, 2004).

54. Sageman, *Understanding Terror Networks*, p 67.
55. Linda S. Heard, "In Defense of a Princess," *Counterpunch*, December 3, 2002, http://www.counterpunch.org/heard1203.html.
56. *The 9/11 Commission Report*, p 498.
57. Gerald L. Posner, *Why America Slept: The Reasons behind Our Failure to Prevent 9/11* (New York: Random House, 2003), p 138.
58. Stephen Schwartz, "The Princess and Her 'Charities,'" *The Weekly Standard*, December 2, 2002.
59. *Monograph on Terrorist Financing*, p 47.
60. National Security Adviser Condoleezza Rice said: "The problem here is that there will always be some uncertainty about how quickly [Saddam Hussein] can acquire nuclear weapons. But we don't want the smoking gun to be a mushroom cloud." Late Edition with Wolf Blitzer, CNN, September 8, 2002.
61. Suskind, *The Price of Loyalty*, p 199.
62. Statement of Matthew A. Levitt, "The Role of Charities and NGOs in the Financing of Terrorist Activities." Hearing before the Subcommittee on International Trade and Finance, Committee on Banking, Housing, and Urban Affairs, United States Senate, August 1, 2002 (Washington, DC: US Government Printing Office).
63. Robert M. Morgenthau, "Cutting Off the Funds for Terror," *New York Times*, October 22, 2001.

Chapter 5. The Usual Suspects

1. See Chapter 1.
2. Steven Emerson, "How to really fight terrorism," *Wall Street Journal*, August 24, 1998.
3. http://cfrterrorism.org/responses/money.html.
4. Jack Kelley, "Saudi Money Aiding bin Laden," *USA Today*, October 29, 1999.
5. Quoted in Jack Anderson, with James Boyd, *Fiasco: The Real Story behind the Disastrous Worldwide Energy Crisis–Richard Nixon's "Oilgate,"* (New York: Times Books, 1983), p 256.
6. Robert Dreyfuss, *Devil's Games: How the United States Helped Unleash Fundamentalist Islam* (New York: Metropolitan Books, 2005), p 248.
7. Adams, *The Financing of Terror*, p 53.
8. Steven Emerson, *The American House of Saud: The Secret Petrodollar Connection* (New York: Franklin Watts, 1985), p 1.
9. Written Testimony of David D. Aufhauser, General Counsel before the Committee on Banking, Housing and Urban Affairs, United States Senate, September 25, 2003. US Department of the Treasury, Office of Public Affairs.

10. Maurice R. Greenberg, Chair, William F. Wechsler and Lee S. Wolosky, Project Co-Directors, "Terrorist Financing: Report of an Independent Task Force," New York: Council on Foreign Relations, November 14, 2002, p 8.

11. Jack Shafer, "The PowerPoint That Rocked the Pentagon: The LaRouchie defector who's advising the defense establishment on Saudi Arabia," *Slate*, August 7, 2002.

12. *Ibid.*

13. Ledeen, *The War against the Terror Masters*, p 83; Frum and Perle, *An End to Evil*, p 8.

14. As'ad Abukhalil, *The Battle for Saudi Arabia: Royalty, Fundamentalism, and Global Power* (New York: Seven Stories Press, 2004), p 28.

15. See, for example, Stephen Schwartz, *The Two Faces of Islam: The House of Sa'ud from Tradition to Terror* (New York: Doubleday, 2002) and Dore Gold, *Hatred's Kingdom: How Saudi Arabia Supports the New Global Terrorism* (Washington, DC: Regnery Publishing Inc., 2003).

16. Robert Baer, *Sleeping with the Devil: How Washington Sold Our Soul for Saudi Crude* (New York: Crown Publishers, 2003).

17. Dore Gold, *Hatred's Kingdom: How Saudi Arabia Supports the New Global Terrorism* (Washington, DC: Regnery Publishing, 2003).

18. Timothy L. O'Brien with Don Van Natta Jr., "Links of Saudis to Charities Come under Senate Review," *New York Times*, July 31, 2003.

19. Simon Henderson, "The Saudi Way," *Wall Street Journal*, August 12, 2002.

20. Daniel Pipes, "Make the Saudis Pay for Terror," *New York Post*, April 15, 2002. See also Daniel Pipes, "Sue the Saudis," *New York Post*, February 18, 2002.

21. Craig Unger, *House of Bush, House of Saud: The Secret Relationship between the World's Two Most Powerful Dynasties* (New York: Scribner, 2004).

22. David E. Sanger, "Bush Officials Praise Saudis for Aiding Terror Fight," *New York Times*, November 27, 2002.

23. Judith Miller and Jeff Garth, "Trade in Honey is Said to Provide Money and Cover for Bin Laden," *New York Times*, October 11, 2001.

24. Nick Kochan, *The Washing Machine: How Money Laundering and Terrorist Financing Soils Us* (Mason, OH: Thomson, 2005), p 77.

25. *Wall Street Journal*, September 24, 2001.

26. *Guardian*, September 18, 2001.

27. "Bin Laden 'share gains' probe," BBC News, September 18, 2001, http://news.bbc.co.uk/2/hi/business/1548118.stm.

28. Ibrahim Warde, "Vers des dommages boursiers collatéraux," *Le Monde diplomatique*, November 2001.

29. *Ibid.*

30. Long believed to have been the twentieth hijacker, French terrorist Zacarias Moussaoui, though a member of Al-Qaeda, was apparently not directly involved in the September 11 plot. See Scott Shane and Neil A. Lewis, "At September 11 Trial, Tale of Missteps and Management," *New York Times*, March 31, 2006.

31. *The 9/11 Commission Report*, p 172.

32. *Ibid.*, p 499.

33. Paul Thompson, *The Terror Timeline: A Comprehensive Chronicle of the Road to 9/11–and America's Response* (New York: Regan Books, 2004), pp 59–68.

34. See Chapters 2 and 3.

35. Halpern: *What You Need to Know About: Terror*, p 83.

36. William F. Wechsler, "Strangling the Hydra: Targeting Al Qaeda's Finances" in James Hoge, Jr., and Gideon Rose (eds), *How Did This Happen: Terrorism and the New War* (New York: Public Affairs, 2001), p 134.

37. War on Terrorism: CDI Primer: Terrorist Finances, http://www.cdi.org/friendlyversion/printversion.cfm?documentID=372.

38. Howard LaFranchi, "Lessons from Drug War: It Takes Time, Allies: Combatting terrorism, like narcotics, is expected to involve unlikely partners," *Christian Science Monitor*, October 1, 2001.

39. George Parker and Vicky Burnett, "Afghanistan described as 'narco-economy,'" *Financial Times*, November 18, 2004.

40. *Ibid.* See also Ashraf Ghani, "Where Democracy's Greatest Enemy Is a Flower," *New York Times*, December 11, 2004, and Eric Schmitt, "Drug Eradication: Afghans' Gains Face Big Threat in Drug Traffic," *New York Times*, December 11, 2004.

41. *The 9/11 Commission Report*, p 171.

42. *Ibid.*, p 140.

43. Barry R. McCaffrey and John A. Basso, "Narcotics, Terrorism, and International Crime: The Convergence Phenomenon" in Russell D. Howard and Reid L. Sawyer (eds), *Terrorism and Counterterrorism: Understanding the New Security Environment* (Guilford, CT: McGraw Hill, 2004), p 208.

44. See Chapters 1 and 4.

45. Bovard, *Terrorism and Tyranny*.

46. Somini Sengupta, "U.N. Report Says Al Qaeda May Be Diversifying Its Finances," *New York Times*, May 23, 2002.

47. According to Security Council Resolution 1373, all 189 United Nations members were to freeze financial assets and impose arms embargoes and travel bans on individuals and groups associated with Bin Laden, Al-Qaeda, and the Taliban.

48. Sengupta, "U.N. Report Says Al Qaeda May Be Diversifying Its Finances," *New York Times*, May 23, 2002.

49. *Ibid.*

50. See, for example, Lt. Col. Gordon Cucullu, "Terrorists: Swimming in Saudi Money – Drugs, money laundering, and illegal birds," *FrontPageMagazine.com*, November 8, 2005.

51. See Chapter 4.

52. *The 9/11 Commission Report*, p 23.

53. See Chapter 1.

54. Toby Harnden, "How cut-price diamonds are traded for weapons," *Daily Tele-*

graph, November 3, 2001.

55. Douglas Farah, *Blood for Stones: The Secret Financial Network of Terror* (New York: Broadway Books, 2004), pp 9–10.

56. Barton Gellman, "Struggles inside the Government Defined Campaign," *Washington Post*, December 20, 2001.

57. *Ibid.*

58. John K. Cooley, "Al-Qaida's elusive money men," *Le Monde diplomatique*, November 2002.

59. Douglas Frantz, "Ancient Secret System Moves Money Globally," *New York Times*, October 3, 2001.

60. Meenakshi Ganguly, "A Banking System Built for Terrorism: 'Hawala' can move millions of dollars around the globe with no paper trail and no questions asked," *Time*, October 5, 2001.

61. *Ibid.*

62. Diogo Teixeira and Shahjehan Cheema, "Bring Underground Payment Systems into the Mainstream," *The American Banker*, October 12, 2001.

63. The newspaper of record had initially described it as a Hindi word meaning "in trust." The October 5, 2001 correction stated that "the word, originally Arabic and now used in several languages in Southwest Asia, means a bill of exchange or promissory note, not trust or in trust."

64. Mathers, *Crime School, Money Laundering*, pp 183–4. See also Jack A. Blum, Michael Levi, R. Thomas Naylor, and Phil Williams, "Financial Havens, Banking Secrecy and Money Laundering." A study prepared on behalf of the United Nations under the auspices of the Global Programme against Money Laundering, Office for Drug Control and Crime Prevention, undated, p 42.

65. Colonel Thomas X. Hammes, *The Sling and the Stone: On War in the 21st Century* (Saint Paul, MN: Zenith Press, 2004), p 199.

66. John Daniszewski and Paul Watson, "Age-Old Way of Moving Cash Leaves Little Trail: U.S. effort to deny funds to terrorists may run into difficulty, as transactions in Muslim world often avoid banks," *Los Angeles Times*, September 26, 2001.

67. *The 9/11 Commission Report*, p 67.

68. "Terror Money," *Wall Street Journal*, October 26, 2001.

69. Jean-Philippe Rémy, "La Somalie tente de mettre sous surveillance les transferts de fonds des hawalas," *Le Monde*, December 18, 2003.

70. "Hawala: The Invisible Bank," *U.S. Customs Today*, April 2002.

71. *The 9/11 Commission Report*, pp 499, 140. Leftover funds were wired back to the United Arab Emirates in the days before September 11 through Western Union. The money was transferred to bank accounts and two exchange houses in the United Arab Emirates (p 141).

72. See Chapter 7.

73. Duncan Campbell, Alison Langley, David Pallister, and Khaled Daoud, "US targets Bin Laden's money men: Aim is to hit Islamist networks to starve al-Qaida of funds," *Guardian*, November 8, 2001.

THE PRICE OF FEAR

74. Khalid M. Medani, "Financing Terrorism or Survival? Informal Finance and State Collapse in Somalia, and the US War on Terrorism," *Middle East Report*, Summer 2002.

75. Richard Labévière, *Dollars for Terror: The United States and Islam* (New York: Algora Publishing, 2000), pp 86–7, 134–40; Jean-Charles Brisard and Guillaume Dasquié, *Forbidden Truth: U.S.–Taliban Secret Oil Diplomacy, Saudi Arabia and the Failed Search for bin Laden* (New York: Nation Books, 2002), p 81.

76. James M. Dorsey, "Saudis Monitor Key Bank Accounts for Terror Funding at U.S. Request," *Wall Street Journal*, February 6, 2002.

77. Gene J. Koprowski, "Islamic Banking Is Not the Enemy," *Wall Street Journal Europe*, October 1, 2001.

78. *Wall Street Journal*, March 12, 2002.

79. "Treasury Launches New Islamic Finance Scholar-in-Residence Program," Office of Public Affairs, Department of the Treasury, June 2, 2004.

80. Rachel Ehrenfeld and Alyssa A. Lappen, "Financial Jihad," *Human Events Online*, September 22, 2005.

81. Clement M. Henry and Rodney Wilson (eds), *The Politics of Islamic Finance* (Edinburgh: Edinburgh University Press, 2004).

82. *Gulf News*, November 12, 2001.

Chapter 6. Dynamics of the Financial War

1. Woodward, *Bush at War*, p 15.

2. David Cole, *Enemy Aliens: Double Standards and Constitutional Freedoms in the War on Terrorism* (New York: The New Press, 2003).

3. Andrew J. Bacevich, "Unsafe for Democracy," *Los Angeles Times*, November 8, 2004.

4. Warren Rudman and Gary Hart, "Restructuring for Security," *New York Times*, June 13, 2002.

5. See Chapter 11.

6. Donald H. Rumsfeld, "A New Kind of War," *New York Times*, September 27, 2001.

7. Dana Priest, *The Mission: Waging War and Keeping Peace with America's Military* (New York: W.W. Norton & Company, 2003). See also Robert Dreyfuss. "Humpty Dumpty in Baghdad: How the Pentagon plans to dominate post-war Iraq," *The American Prospect*, May 1, 2003.

8. See also Chapter 11.

9. Rob Garver, "Task Force Asked to Give Terrorists No 'Safe Harbor,'" *American Banker*, October 30, 2001.

10. Between 2001 and 2006, the wars in Iraq and Afghanistan have cost close to half a trillion dollars. "Detailing Proposed War Spending," *New York Times*, July 8, 2006.

11. Andrew J. Bacevich, *The New American Militarism: How Americans Are Seduced by War* (Oxford: Oxford University Press, 2005).

12. Chalmers Johnson, *The Sorrows of Empire: Militarism Secrecy, and the End of the Republic* (New York, 2004); Bacevich, *The New American Militarism*; P.W. Singer, *Corporate Warriors: The Rise of the Privatized Military Industry* (Cornell University Press); Ken Silverstein, *Private Warriors* (London: Verso, 2000); William D. Hartung, "Making Money on Terrorism," *The Nation*, February 23, 2004; Marie-Béatrice Baudet and Jean-Pierre Stroobants, "La lutte anti-terroriste, un business qui rapporte," *Le Monde*, October 11, 2005.

13. Peter Ford, "Tough trail of terror's money," *Christian Science Monitor*, October 19, 2001.

14. James Mann, *Rise of the Vulcans: The History of Bush's War Cabinet* (New York: Penguin Books, 2004).

15. Walter Isaacson and Evan Thomas, *The Wise Men: Six Friends and the World They Made* (New York: Simon and Schuster, 1986).

16. James Bamford, *A Pretext for War: 9/11, Iraq, and the Abuse of America's Intelligence Agencies* (New York: Doubleday, 2004), pp 261–99.

17. Suskind, *The One Percent Doctrine*, pp 148–52.

18. Chalmers Johnson, *Blowback*, pp 15–16.

19. David Von Drehle, "'Shock and awe' is obscure no more: Swift, stunning attack is meant to bring fast surrender, backers say," *Washington Post*, March 23, 2003.

20. "The needle in the haystack," *The Economist*, December 12, 2002.

21. Quoted in Michael A. Dawson, Deputy Assistant Secretary Critical Infrastructure Protection and Compliance Policy, "Remarks to the Bankers' Association for Finance and Trade, Washington, DC, July 15, 2003, Office of Public Affairs, Department of the Treasury.

22. Andrew F. Tully, "U.S.: Washington Struggles To Wage Effective Financial War On Terror," *Radio Free Europe/Radio Liberty*, October 24 2003.

23. Bob Woodward, *Plan of Attack*, pp 5, 26.

24. Karen DeYoung and Douglas Farah, "Al Qaeda Shifts Assets to Gold: U.S. Agency Turf Battles Hamper Hunt for Untraceable Commodities," *Washington Post*, June 18, 2002.

25. Suskind, *The One Percent Doctrine*, p 78.

26. See Linda Feldmann, "Bush moves to shore up war-on-terror credentials: His speeches on security this week signal that Republicans will use the terrorism issue for the third election in a row," *Christian Science Monitor*, September 8, 2006. See also Peter Wallsten, "GOP Leaders Are Hoping to Turn the War into a Winner," *Los Angeles Times*, August 8, 2006.

27. Much later it would be revealed that the intelligence community had caught a lot of "chatter" in the weeks preceding September 11, about a major Al-Qaeda attack in the United States involving airplanes. These threats had been communicated to the President.

28. Clarke, *Against All Enemies*, pp 30–3.

29. Woodward, *Bush at War*, p 25.

30. "Demand of Leadership," *New York Times*, September 13, 2001.

31. See Introduction.
32. Suskind, *The One Percent Doctrine*, p 141.
33. See Chapter 3.
34. Woodward, *Bush at War*, p 49.
35. *Ibid.*, p 111.
36. *Ibid.*, p 112.
37. *Ibid.*
38. Suskind, *The Price of Loyalty*, p 193.
39. *Ibid.*
40. Woodward, *Bush at War*, p 120.
41. Karen DeYoung, "Past Efforts to Stop Money Flow Ineffective," *Washington Post*, September 25, 2001. This was also noted by former Clinton administration officials who stressed the parallels between the Bush asset freeze and that ordered by Bill Clinton following the August 1998 African embassy bombings. See William F. Wechsler, "Strangling the Hydra: Targeting Al Qaeda's Finances" in James Hoge, Jr., and Gideon Rose (eds), *How Did This Happen: Terrorism and the New War* (New York: Public Affairs, 2001), p. 129, and Daniel Benjamin and Steven Simon, *The Age of Sacred Terror: Radical Islam's War against America* (New York: Random House, 2003), p 269.
42. See Chapter 3.
43. "Money Laundering And Financial Crimes," International Narcotics Control Strategy Report 1997, released by the Bureau for International Narcotics and Law Enforcement Affairs, US Department of State, Washington, DC, March 1998.
44. Suskind, *The Price of Loyalty*, p 181.
45. See Chapter 3.
46. *Wall Street Journal*, September 17, 2001.
47. Reuter and Truman, *Chasing Dirty Money*, p 7.
48. Central Intelligence Agency, Department of Homeland Security (Bureau of Customs and Border Protection, Bureau of Immigration and Customs Enforcement, US Secret Service), Justice Department (Bureau of Alcohol, Tobacco, Firearms, and Explosives (ATF), Civil Division, Criminal Division, Drug Enforcement Administration (DEA), Federal Bureau of Investigation (FBI), National Security Council, State Department (Bureau of Economic and Business Affairs, Bureau of International Narcotics and Law Enforcement Affairs, Office of the Coordinator for Counterterrorism), Treasury Department (Executive Office for Terrorist Financing and Financial Crime, Financial Crimes Enforcement Network (FinCEN), Internal Revenue Service (IRS) Criminal Investigation, IRS Tax Exempt and Government Entities, Office of Foreign Assets Control, Office of the General Counsel, Office of International Affairs). General Accounting Office, "Terrorist Financing: U.S. Agencies Should Systematically Assess Terrorists' Use of Alternative Financing Mechanisms," Report to Congressional Requesters, Washington, DC: General Accounting Office, November 2003, p 8.

49. T.D. Allman, "Blowback" in Mike Gray (ed), *Busted: Stone Cowboys, Narco-Lords and Washington's War on Drugs* (New York: Thunder 's Mouth Press/ Nation Books, 2002), p 16.

50. Elisabeth Rosenthal, "Threats and Responses: The FBI," *York Times*, October 25, 2002.

51. Tom Regan, "Iraq is becoming 'free fraud' zone: Corruption in Iraq under US-led CPA may dwarf UN oil-for-food scandal," *Christian Science Monitor*, April 7, 2005. http://www.csmonitor.com.

52. Testimony of Juan Carlos Zarate, Assistant Secretary Terrorist Financing and Financial Crimes US Department of the Treasury before the Senate Permanent Subcommittee on Investigations of the Committee on Governmental Affairs, Department of the Treasury, Office of Public Affairs, November 15, 2004.

53. See, for example, James Risen, *State of War: The Secret History of the CIA and the Bush Administration* (New York: Free Press, 2006), pp 65-84.

54. The Iran–Contra affair started with "off the book" sales of US anti-tank missiles, advanced military radars, and other military equipment to Iran in order to obtain that country's cooperation in securing the release of four US hostages in Lebanon. It was later revealed that the proceeds from Iranian arms sales were laundered to finance weapon sales to the Nicaraguan Contras. Iran–Contra was a disaster on many levels. First, the scheme itself was harebrained and its implementation inept. Second, the transactions were illegal and contravened official policy. Indeed, Congress had passed a law in 1984 prohibiting military support for the Contras. Ronald Reagan had also asserted that there would be no deals with Iran and no negotiations with hostage-takers. The United States had also been pressuring its allies to stop arm sales to Iran. Third and most significantly, the whole affair was a subversion of democracy. And most of the people involved pleaded guilty to perjury or to lying to Congress.

55. Michael Crowley, "Elliott Abrams: From Iran–Contra to Bush's democracy czar," *Slate*, February 17, 2005.

56. Other notable appointees include Otto J. Reich as President Bush's special envoy to Latin America, and John Negroponte as US Permanent Representative to the United Nations, and later ambassador to Iraq. In 2005 he became the first Director of National Intelligence (DNI).

57. Calvin Trillin, "New Federal Hires," *The Nation*, December 30, 2002.

58. Farhad Manjoo, "Total Information Awareness: Down, but not out," *Salon*, January 29, 2003.

59. Carl Hulse, "Pentagon Prepares a Futures Market on Terror Attacks," *New York Times*, July 29, 2003.

60. *Wall Street Journal*, July 29, 2003.

61. Christopher Marquis, "The Right and Wrong Stuff of Thinking outside a Box," *New York Times*, July 31, 2005.

62. Allan Gerson and Jerry Adler, *The Price of Terror: Lessons of Lockerbie for a*

World on the Brink (New York: HarperCollins, 2001). See Roger Parloff, "Sue Afghanistan!," *New York Times*, December 23, 2001.

63. "Families of 9/11 victims sue Saudi officials, institutions," *USA Today*, August 15, 2002.

64. Seth Stern, "Can a trillion-dollar lawsuit stop Saudi terror-cash flow?," *Christian Science Monitor*, August 20, 2002.

65. The first two as government officials were later dismissed from the suit (Burnett v. Al Baraka Inv. & Dev. Corp.)

66. David Usborne, "Families of twin towers victims sue 'al-Qa'ida backers,'" *Independent*, August 16, 2002.

67. *Ibid.*

68. Oliver Burkeman, "Legal action jeopardises 9/11 compensation," *Guardian*, September 20, 2002.

69. Willie Sutton is the legendary bank robber who in answer to the question "Why do you rob banks?," reportedly answered, "Because that's where the money is."

70. U.S. v. Bin Laden, 2001 U.S. Dist. LEXIS 15484 (S.D.N.Y. Oct. 2, 2001.

71. "New anti-terrorist legislation, passed in the wake of the attacks, makes it significantly more feasible for victims to sue terrorists in the US, by amending §2331 of Title 18 of the US Code to include a definition of domestic terrorism, a right of action, and jurisdiction for acts that occur primarily within the territorial jurisdiction of the United States. Fundamentally changing a criminal code provision for acts of terrorism 'transcending national boundaries,' the USA Patriot Act added 'domestic terrorism' to US law if the act is a violation of the criminal laws of the United States and occurs primarily within US territory, allowing a civil action in which the victim (only US nationals) or survivors 'may recover threefold the damage' as well as attorneys' fees, and which stops the terrorist defendant from denying the allegations of any prior criminal conviction, granting exclusive jurisdiction to US district courts. Victims of the September attacks may be thus able to make use of both the new legislation and earlier bills." Pamela S. Falk, "Families of Missing Have Three Options," *New York Law Journal*, October 29, 2004, http://www.law.com/jsp/nylj/index.jsp.

72. Jennifer Senior, "Intruders in the House of Saud," *New York Times Magazine*, March 14, 2004.

73. Tina Kelley, "Legal Action: Suit by Victims' Kin Says Iraq Knew of 9/11 Plans," *New York Times*, September 5, 2003.

74. *Ibid.*

75. Larry Neumeister, "Cantor Fitzgerald sues Saudis for losses," *Boston Globe*, September 3, 2004.

76. *Ibid.*

77. *Ibid.*

78. Seth Stern, "Can a trillion-dollar lawsuit stop Saudi terror-cash flow?," *Christian Science Monitor*, August 20, 2002.

79. Julian Borger, "Saudi royals face trillion-dollar lawsuit over September 11," *Guardian*, August 16, 2002.

80. Oliver Burkeman, "Legal action jeopardises 9/11 compensation," *Guardian*, September 20, 2002.

81. Unger, *House of Bush, House of Saud*; Kevin Phillips, *American Dynasty: Aristocracy, Fortune, and the Politics of Deceit in the House of Bush* (New York: Viking, 2004).

82. Senior, "Intruders in the House of Saud," *New York Times Magazine*, March 14, 2004.

83. See Chapter 9.

84. Seth Stern, "Can a trillion-dollar lawsuit stop Saudi terror-cash flow?," *Christian Science Monitor*, August 20, 2002.

85. Allan Gerson and Ron Motley, "Is Saudi Arabia Tough Enough on Terrorism?," *New York Times*, December 30, 2002.

86. Benjamin Wallace-Wells, "Private Jihad: How Rita Katz got into the spying business," *The New Yorker*, May 29, 2006.

87. Senior, "Intruders in the House of Saud," *New York Times Magazine*, March 14, 2004.

88. Jack Shafer,"The PowerPoint That Rocked the Pentagon: The LaRouchie defector who's advising the defense establishment on Saudi Arabia," *Slate*, August 7, 2002.

89. See Chapter 1.

90. Senior, "Intruders in the House of Saud," *New York Times Magazine*, March 14, 2004.

91. *Ibid.*

92. According to the lawsuit, a columnist writing under the byline Naeem Abd Muhalhal—who according to a former associate had been connected with Iraqi intelligence since the early 1980s—described Bin Laden thinking "seriously, with the seriousness of the Bedouin of the desert, about the way he will try to bomb the Pentagon after he destroys the White House." The columnist also stated that Bin Laden was "insisting very convincingly that he will strike America on the arm that is already hurting," which could be interpreted as a reference to the 1993 bombing of the World Trade Center. "11 September victims sue Iraq," BBC News, September 4, 2002. http://news.bbc.co.uk/2/low/americas/2237332.htm.

93. Mark Hamblett, "Sept. 11 Plaintiffs Win Case against Iraq," *New York Law Journal*, May 8, 2003.

Chapter 7. Targets and Collateral Damage

1. *The 9/11 Commission Report*, p 39.

2. Clarke, *Against All Enemies*, p 24.

3. *Ibid.*, p 31.

4. Woodward, *Bush at War*, p 83.

5. *The 9/11 Commission Report*, pp 559–60. See also Douglas J. Feith, "A War

Plan That Cast a Wide Net," *Washington Post*, August 7, 2004.

6. Ledeen, *The War against the Terror Masters*.

7. Marina Hyde, "Diary," *Guardian*, June 30, 2004.

8. Michael Savage, *The Savage Nation: Saving America from the Liberal Assault on Our Borders, Language and Culture* (Nashville, TN: Thomas Nelson Publishers, 2002), p 23.

9. Tamar Lewin and Gustav Niebuhr, "Attacks and Harassment Continue on Middle Eastern People and Mosques," *New York Times*, September 19, 2001.

10. Tamar Lewin, "Sikh Owner of Gas Station Is Fatally Shot in Rampage," *New York Times*, September 17, 2001, and Laurie Goodstein and Tamar Lewin, "Victims of Mistaken Identity: Sikhs Pay a Price for Turbans," *New York Times*, September 19, 2001.

11. Robert Kagan, "We Must Fight This War," *Washington Post*, September 12, 2001.

12. Quoted in Paul de Zardain, "The impact of energy sanctions on Iran's petroleum sector," *Daily Star*, February 16, 2004.

13. Thomas L. Friedman, "Because We Could," *New York Times*, June 4, 2003.

14. Another institution Al-Taqwa (a financial institution based in Switzerland and associated with the Muslim Brotherhood movement), mistakenly identified as a money-transmittal business, was also shut down the same day.

15. Duncan Campbell, Alison Langley, David Pallister, and Khaled Daoud, "US targets Bin Laden's money men: Aim is to hit Islamist networks to starve al-Qaida of funds," *Guardian*, November 8, 2001.

16. Edward Alden and Mark Huband, "Al-Qaeda: Terrorism after Afghanistan: Case still open on 'terror's quartermasters,'" *Financial Times*, February 21, 2002.

17. Kathleen Day, "Bin Laden may own an Islamic money exchange in U.S.: FBI, CIA investigating role of age-old Muslim banking system," *Washington Post*, November 7, 2001.

18. Paul Beckett, "Shutdown of Al Barakaat Severs Lifeline for Many Somalia Residents," *Wall Street Journal*, December 4, 2001.

19. *Ibid.*

20. Tim Golden, "5 Months after Sanctions against Somali Company, Scant Proof of Qaeda Tie," *New York Times*, April 13, 2002.

21. Michael M. Phillips, "U.S. Estimates $20 Million in Funds for Terrorists Have Been Cut Off," *Wall Street Journal*, January 29, 2002.

22. Glenn R. Simpson, "Bayh Claims Treasury Department Received Warning on Al Barakaat," *Wall Street Journal*, November 14, 2001.

23. Khalid M. Medani, "Financing Terrorism or Survival? Informal Finance and State Collapse in Somalia, and the US War on Terrorism," *Middle East Report*, Summer 2002.

24. Different accounts place the establishment of the company in 1985, 1987, and 1989.

25. *The 9/11 Commission Report*, p 67.

26. See for example Roger D. McGrath, "Coming to America: The Great Somali Welfare Hunt," *The American Conservative*, November 18, 2002; Somali Immigrants Rile Maine Mayor, CBS News, October 14, 2002, http://www.cbsnews.com.

27. *The 9/11 Commission Report*, p 69. In reality, the amounts mentioned in the 9/11 report on terrorist financing were not necessarily large, considering that a significant chunk of the Somalis' income was sent home.

28. See Chapter 3.

29. *The 9/11 Commission Report*, p 69.

30. *Ibid.*, p 10.

31. Davan Maharaj, "U.S. Is Urged Not to Attack Somalia, Africa: Nation may be target in terror war. U.N. official says strike would disrupt a fragile security and worsen the poverty," *Los Angeles Times*, January 10, 2002.

32. "Somalia and terrorism: Who is using whom?," *The Economist*, December 20, 2001.

33. *The 9/11 Commission Report*, p 76.

34. *Monograph on Terrorist Financing*, p 79.

35. The accusations rested on a theory which was itself based on questionable assertions about Al-Qaeda's presence in Somalia, about ties between Mohammed Farah Aideed, the Somali warlord who caused the withdrawal of American soldiers in 1993, and Al-Ittihad, and indeed about the very existence of Al-Ittihaad Al-Islamiya (AIAI) as a functioning organization.

36. Edward Alden and Mark Huband, "Al-Qaeda: Terrorism after Afghanistan: Case still open on 'terror's quartermasters,'" *Financial Times*, February 21, 2002.

37. Mike Crawley, "Somali banking under scrutiny: The US closure of suspected Al Qaeda fronts deals Somalia's battered economy another blow," *Christian Science Monitor*, November 28, 2001.

38. *Ibid.*

39. Edward Alden and Mark Huband, "Al-Qaeda: Terrorism after Afghanistan: Case still open on 'terror's quartermasters,'" *Financial Times*, February 21, 2002.

40. *Ibid.*

41. *Ibid.*

42. See Chapter 5.

43. *The 9/11 Commission Report*, p 10.

44. Christopher Cooper, "Crackdown on Terrorism Financing Ties Hands of Businessman in Sweden," *Wall Street Journal*, May 6, 2002.

45. Paul Beckett, "Shutdown of Al Barakaat Severs Lifeline for Many Somalia Residents," *Wall Street Journal*, December 4, 2001.

46. "Canada snubs U.S. extradition request," *The Globe and Mail*, June 3, 2002, and "Terror-funding suspect won't be extradited," *The Globe and Mail*, June 4, 2002.

47. Cooper, "Crackdown on Terrorism Financing Ties Hands of Businessman in

Sweden," *Wall Street Journal*, May 6, 2002.

48. "Canadian sentenced for illegal cash moves," *The Globe and Mail*, July 23, 2002.

49. Paul Beckett and Glenn R. Simpson, "Network Suspected of Funding Terrorists Used Major Banks for Money Transfers," *Wall Street Journal*, November 9, 2001.

50. Testimony of Kenneth Dam, "Terrorist Financing: A Progress Report on Implementation of the USA PATRIOT Act," Office of Public Affairs, US Department of the Treasury, September 19, 2002. PO-3439.

51. *The Financial War on Terror: A Guide* by the Financial Action Task Force (Paris: FATF, 2004), p 9.

52. *The 9/11 Commission Report*, p 10.

53. The Associated Press, August 27, 2002.

54. Tim Golden, "5 Months after Sanctions against Somali Company, Scant Proof of Qaeda Tie," *New York Times*, April 13, 2002.

55. Mike Crawley, "Somali banking under scrutiny: The US closure of suspected Al Qaeda fronts deals Somalia's battered economy another blow," *Christian Science Monitor*, November 28, 2001.

56. *Ibid.*

57. Christopher Cooper and Ian Johnson, "Though Its Corporate Face Is Gone, Barakaat Remains Active in Europe," *Wall Street Journal*, April 22, 2002.

58. Donald G. McNeil, "How Blocking Assets Erased a Wisp of Prosperity," *New York Times*, April 13, 2002.

59. "Les islamistes somaliens se dotent d'une direction 'dure'," *Le Monde*, June 27, 2006.

60. Cooper, "Crackdown on Terrorism Financing Ties Hands of Businessman in Sweden," *Wall Street Journal*, May 6, 2002.

61. Golden, "5 Months after Sanctions against Somali Company, Scant Proof of Qaeda Tie," *New York Times*, April 13, 2002.

62. "Did US Rush to Judge Somali Company?," The East African on the Web, September 9, 2002.

63. Golden, "5 Months after Sanctions against Somali Company, Scant Proof of Qaeda Tie," *New York Times*, April 13, 2002.

64. Suskind, *The Price of Loyalty*, pp 198-9.

65. *The 9/11 Commission Report*, p 62.

66. Heather Timmons and Mike McNamee, "Freeze Assets Now, Ask Questions Later," *Business Week Online*, October 15, 2001.

67. See Chapter 3.

68. Timmons and McNamee, "Freeze Assets Now, Ask Questions Later," *Business Week Online*, October 15, 2001.

69. Sageman, *Understanding Terror Networks*, p 67.

70. Michael Moss, "False Terrorism Tips to F.B.I. Uproot the Lives of Suspects," *Wall Street Journal*. February 12, 2002, and Bob Drogin, "Most Arrested by 'Mistake' - Coalition Intelligence Put Numbers at 70% to 90% of Iraqi pris-

oners, says a February Red Cross report, which details further abuses," *Los Angeles Times*, May 11, 2004.

71. "Terror Crackdown Nabs Headlines But Not Planners of Sept. 11 Attacks," *Wall Street Journal*, February 12, 2002.

72. Timmons and McNamee, "Freeze Assets Now, Ask Questions Later," *Business Week Online*, October 15, 2001.

73. James Risen, "To Bomb Sudan Plant, or Not: A Year Later, Debates Rankle," *New York Times*, October 27, 1999.

74. Bovard, *Terrorism and Tyranny*, pp 40–3.

75. Barton Gellman, "The Covert Hunt for bin Laden: Broad Effort Launched After '98 Attacks," *Washington Post*, December 19, 2001.

76. Michael Moss, "False Terrorism Tips to F.B.I. Uproot the Lives of Suspects," *New York Times*, June 19, 2003.

77. James M. Dorsey, "O'Neill Promises U.S. Caution in Citing Saudi Terror Links," *Wall Street Journal*, March 7, 2002.

78. Money claimed by poor countries or suffering victims can languish for years because of the number of claimants, and the near-impossibility of sorting out who should get the money. In Switzerland, the fate of some $300 million from accounts associated with late Philippine ruler Ferdinand Marcos and his cronies (which has more than doubled because of accruing interest) has yet to be decided. See Roger Thurow, "Freezer Burn: Switzerland Has Discovered Thawing Assets Is Tougher Than Freezing," *Wall Street Journal*, November 14, 2001.

79. Sageman, *Understanding Terror Networks*, p 67.

80. Farhad Manjoo, "'Please step to the side, sir': The airlines' 'no-fly' list is riddled with cases of mistaken identity. But the government's solution may be even more invasive." *Salon*, April 10, 2003.

81. Rachel L. Swarns, "Senator? Terrorist? A Watch List Stops Kennedy at Airport," *New York Times*, August 20, 2004.

82. Ibid.

83. See Chapter 2.

84. Tim Golden, "How Dubious Evidence Spurred Relentless Guantánamo Spy Hunt," *New York Times*, December 19, 2004.

85. Michael Moss, "False Terrorism Tips to F.B.I. Uproot the Lives of Suspects," *New York Times*, June 19, 2003.

86. James M. Dorsey, "O'Neill Promises U.S. Caution in Citing Saudi Terror Links," *Wall Street Journal*, March 7, 2002.

87. Dana Milbank and Claudia Deane, "Hussein Link to 9/11 Lingers in Many Minds," *Washington Post*, September 6, 2003.

88. Ron Suskind spoke of "the one percent doctrine," the post-September 11 belief by Vice-President Dick Cheney that "even if there's just a one per cent chance of the unimaginable coming true, act as if it is a certainty." See Suskind, *The One Percent Doctrine*, p 62.

89. Chris Matthews, *Hardball: How Politics Is Played Told By One Who Knows the*

Game (New York: Free Press, 1999).

Chapter 8. "Gated Finance" and Other Contradictions of the Financial War

1. See David Cole, *Enemy Aliens: Double Standards and Constitutional Freedoms in the War on Terrorism* (New York: The New Press, 2003); Boaz Ganor, *The Counter-Terrorism Puzzle: A Guide for Decision-Makers*, pp 147–81, 187, 282; Jessica Stern, *The Ultimate Terrorists* (Harvard University Press, 1999), p. 2; Laura D. Tyson, "Financing the Fight against Terrorism," *New York Times*, October 8, 2001; Andrew Balls, "World Bank chief warns on terror focus," *Financial Times*, September 23, 2004.
2. See, for example, Robert Kuttner, *Everything for Sale: The Virtues and Limits of Markets* (New York: Alfred A. Knopf, 1997), pp 39–67. See also Stiglitz, *Globalization and Its Discontents*, p 40.
3. For an early discussion of these themes see Walter B. Wriston, *The Twilight of Sovereignty: How the Information Revolution is Transforming Our World* (New York: Charles Scribner's Sons, 1992), p 17.
4. Bacevich, *American Empire: The Realities and Consequences of U.S. Diplomacy*, p 26.
5. Thomas L. Friedman, "A Manifesto for the Fast World," *New York Times Magazine*, March 28, 1999.
6. Ronald I. McKinnon, *Money and Capital in Economic Development* (Washington, DC: Brookings Institution, 1973).
7. Warde, *Islamic Finance in the Global Economy*, pp 96–103.
8. Richard W. Stevenson, "Greenspan Urges More Aid to Third-World Banks," *New York Times*, December 5, 1997.
9. Ibrahim Warde, "Le projet de taxe Tobin, bête noire des spéculateurs, cible des censeurs," *Le Monde diplomatique*, February 1997.
10. Steven C. Clemons, "Globalization and the End of the High-Trust Era," paper presented at the conference on American Policy in Asia after September 11, organized by Sun Yat-sen America Center, National Sun Yat-sen University, March 2002.
11. Moises Naim, *Illicit: How Smugglers, Traffickers, and Copycats Are Hijacking the Global Economy* (New York: Doubleday, 2005).
12. John Kerry, *The New War: The Web of Crime That Threatens America's Security* (New York: Simon and Schuster, 1997), p 120.
13. For Jean-Baptiste Say, "Fraudulent activities for an economist are simply a displacement of wealth; the moralist will condemn an injustice" (1840). And for Léon Walras, "That a substance can be used by a doctor to heal or by an assassin to poison his family is indifferent to us, though it is very important from other standpoints" (1874). *L'Economie Politique*, No. 15, Third Quarter 2002, p 4.
14. Thomas Frank, *One Market under God: Extreme Capitalism, Market Populism, and the End of Economic Democracy* (New York: Doubleday, 2000), p 54.
15. Wriston, *The Twilight of Sovereignty*, cover, see also pp 16–17, 158–9.

16. Bacevich, *American Empire: The Realities and Consequences of U.S. Diplomacy*, p 232.
17. Cass R. Sunstein, *Radicals in Robes: Right-Wing Courts Are Wrong for America* (New York: Basic Books, 2005), pp 161–73.
18. Irvine H. Sprague, *Bailout: An Insider's Account of Bank Failures and Rescues* (New York: Basic Books, 1986), p 4.
19. *Ibid.*, p 27.
20. Ibrahim Warde, *The Regulation of Foreign Banking in the United States* (San Francisco: IBPC, 1997).
21. The Group of Thirty, "Global Institutions, National Supervision and Systemic Risk," (Washington, DC, 1997).
22. For an in-depth discussion of the problems arising from profiling, see David Cole, *Enemy Aliens*, pp 47–56.
23. See also Chapter 7.
24. Ibrahim Warde, "Global Politics, Islamic Finance and Islamist Politics: Before and after September 11, 2001," in Clement M. Henry and Rodney Wilson (eds), *The Politics of Islamic Finance*.
25. "Follow the money," *The Economist*, May 30, 2002.
26. James M. Dorsey, "Saudis Monitor Key Bank Accounts for Terror Funding at U.S. Request," *Wall Street Journal*, February 6, 2002.
27. "Les mains sales," *The Economist*, October 11, 2001; "Rich countries must obey their own rules against terrorist financing," *The Economist*, May 30, 2002.
28. William Maclean, "Money Freezes Hit Muslim Faith in Western Banks," Reuters, November 13, 2001.
29. See Michael Young, "A Perfect Storm of Stupidity," *Wall Street Journal*, July 5, 2006.
30. Sam Ali, "Muslims Troubled by Bank's Decision: Civil Rights Groups See Sept. 11 Backlash," *New Jersey Star-Ledger*, February 27, 2005.
31. David Pallister and Owen Bowcott, "Banks to shut doors on Saudi royal cash: King Fahd is moving large sums through Liechtenstein," *Guardian*, July 17, 2002.
32. The affair started as an investigation of the bank's dealings with the Saudi embassy in Washington, but the biggest fish netted in that scandal was former Chilean leader Augusto Pinochet, who had been laundering millions of dollars through the bank. The bank was fined $25 million for its lax controls.
33. Glenn R. Simpson, "His Cash Is Green, But Flags Raised Were Red: Reports on Bob Dole's Preference for Carrying Wads of C-Notes Is Strange Fallout of Riggs Affair," *Wall Street Journal*, September 3, 2004.
34. Alex Nussbaum, "N.J. investigates company over alleged terror ties," December 30, 2004, North Jersey Media Group, NorthJersey.com.
35. Evan Perez and Christina Binkley, "Anti-Saudi Backlash Sinks Development Deal in Florida," *Wall Street Journal*, April 10, 2003.

230 THE PRICE OF FEAR

36. David E. Sanger and Eric Lipton, "Bush Would Veto Any Bill Halting Dubai Port Deal," *New York Times*, February 22, 2006.
37. David Ignatius, "Burning Allies—and Ourselves," *Washington Post*, March 10, 2006.
38. Pam Belluck with Eric Lichtblau, "Federal Agents Raid a Software Company outside Boston, Seeking Links to Al Qaeda," *New York Times*, December 7, 2002.
39. John Mintz, "Terrorism Investigators Search Company in Mass. Probe Focused on Possible Link between Software Firm and Accused Al Qaeda Financier," *Washington Post*, December 7, 2002.
40. Rachel Ehrenfeld, "Dollars of Terror," FrontPageMagazine.com, April 18, 2005.
41. Mansoor Ijaz, "A Secret Weapon in the War against Terror: Inclusion," *Los Angeles Times*, April 20, 2004.
42. See for example Tamara Cofman Wittes, "The New U.S. Proposal for a Greater Middle East Initiative: An Evaluation," Saban Center Middle East Memo No. 2, Washington, DC: Brookings Institution, May 10, 2004.
43. Glenn R. Simpson, "U.S. Crackdown on Arab Bank Tangles Policy," *Wall Street Journal*, February 28, 2005.
44. Joel Mowbray, "Bankrupting Terror," FrontPageMagazine.com, January 7, 2005.
45. Glenn R. Simpson, "Compound Interests: Arab Bank's Link to Terrorism Poses Dilemma for U.S. Policy Jordan-Based Lender, Accused of Moving Jihadist Money, Has Also Helped the West, Fine Could Top $20 Million," *Wall Street Journal*, April 20, 2005.
46. *Ibid.*
47. *Ibid.*
48. Elliot Blair Smith, "Arab Bank retreats from U.S. market," *USA Today*, February 8, 2005.
49. Elliott Blair Smith, "Arab Bank agrees to $24M fine," *USA Today*, August 18, 2005.
50. "Arab Bank Helped Saudi Charity Pay Bomber Families, Suit Says," Bloomberg, January 27, 2005.
51. Olivier Roy, "The Business of Terror: Al-Qaida brand name ready for franchise," *Le Monde diplomatique*, September 2004.
52. *The Banker*, April 1990, p 12.
53. *The 9/11 Commission Report*, p 140.
54. William F. Wechsler, Testimony before the House Committee on Government Reform, Subcommittee on Criminal Justice, Drug Policy and Human Resources, June 23, 2000.
55. Suskind, *The Price of Loyalty*, p 186.
56. See Chapter 11.
57. Duncan Campbell, "Pakistan says al-Qaida link to plot found," *Guardian*, August 17, 2006.

58. Craig Murray, "The timing is political: We should be sceptical about this alleged plot, and wary of politicians who seek to benefit," *Guardian*, August 18, 2006.
59. Richard A. Clarke and Roger W. Cressey, "A Secret the Terrorists Already Knew," *New York Times*, June 30, 2006.
60. Hernando de Soto: *The Other Path: The Economic Answer to Terrorism* (New York: Basic Books, 1989, with a 2002 preface), p xxxix.
61. Randal, *Osama: The Making of a Terrorist*, p 200.
62. Hernando de Soto, *The Mystery of Capital: Why Capitalism Triumphs in the West and Fails Everywhere Else* (New York: Basic Books, 2000), p 21.
63. Ganor, *The Counter-Terrorism Puzzle*, p 195.
64. Randal, *Osama: The Making of a Terrorist*, p 127.
65. *Ibid.*, p 42.
66. See Chapter 1.
67. Judith Miller, "Whose Assets Will Be Frozen Are Just the First of Many, a U.S. Official Says," *New York Times*, September 25, 2001.
68. Suskind, *The One Percent Doctrine*, p 142.
69. Rob Garver, "Treasury Orders More Suspect Cash Blocked," *The American Banker*, October 15, 2001.
70. "UN Gives Panel Monitoring Al-Qaida Sanctions New Powers," *Wall Street Journal*, January 30, 2004.
71. Randal, *Osama: The Making of a Terrorist*, p 20.
72. Christopher Cooper, "Crackdown on Terrorism Financing Ties Hands of Businessman in Sweden," *Wall Street Journal*, May 6, 2002.
73. "Text: White House Freezes Suspected Terror Assets," *Washington Post*, December 4, 2001.
74. See Chapter 10.
75. Philip Shenon, "F.B.I. Raids 2 of the Biggest Muslim Charities; Assets of One are Seized," *New York Times*, December 14, 2001.
76. See Chapter 11.
77. James Mann, *Rise of the Vulcans: The History of Bush's War Cabinet* (New York: Penguin Books, 2004), p 309.
78. See Chapter 1.
79. On June 20, 2005, the US Department of the Treasury froze the assets of two Syrian officials, Interior Minister Ghazi Kanaan and military intelligence chief Rustum Ghazali. The action, according to Treasury Secretary John W. Snow, was intended to financially isolate bad actors supporting Syria's efforts to destabilize its neighbors. "Treasury Designation Targets Individuals Leading Syria's Military Presence in Lebanon," Department of the Treasury Press Release, June 20, 2005. http://www.ustreas.gov/press/releases/js2617.htm.
80. *Monograph on Terrorist Financing*, p 47.
81. See also Chapter 4.
82. Roula Khalaf, "Why they hate," *Financial Times*, October 4, 2001.
83. Nye, *The Paradox of American Power*.

84. *Ibid.*, p 40.
85. See Chapters 1 and 2.
86. Charles Krauthammer, "The New Unilateralism," *Washington Post*, June 8, 2001.
87. See Chapters 3 and 11.
88. See Chapter 11.
89. Ian Johnson and David S. Cloud, "New Evidence Backs Belief That Germany May Have Been Financing Hub of Attack," *Wall Street Journal*, September 26, 2001.
90. R.P. Eddy, "In the end, all terrorism is local," *The Times*, July 8, 2005.
91. Jackson Diehl, "Our Cold War Hangover," *Washington Post*, March 18, 2002.
92. Guy Dinmore, "US shifts anti-terror policy," *Financial Times*, August 1, 2005.
93. See Chapter 11.
94. Judith Miller, *God Has Ninety-Nine Names: A Reporter's Journey through a Militant Middle East* (New York: Simon and Schuster, 1996), p 163.
95. Martin Kramer, *Ivory Towers on Sand: The Failure of Middle Eastern Studies in America* (Washington, DC: Washington Institute for Near Eastern Policy, 2001).
96. See Chapter 4.
97. Quoted in Paul de Zardain, "The impact of energy sanctions on Iran's petroleum sector," *Daily Star*, February 16, 2004.
98. *Financial Times*, November 19, 2001.
99. James Dao and Eric Lichtblau, "Case Adds to Outrage for Muslims in Northern Virginia," *New York Times*, February 27, 2005.
100. Michael Young, "A Perfect Form of Stupidity," *Wall Street Journal*, July 5, 2006.
101. "L'association de sayyed Fadlallah apporte son aide aux milieux défavorisés: Les 'mabarrats' ou la bienfaisance au service de la tolérance dans la société libanaise," *L'Orient-Le Jour*, October 10, 2005.
102. Adib F. Farha, "US Ban on Siniora: How to lose friends and win enemies," *Daily Star*, July 5, 2003.
103. John Diamond, "CIA plans riskier, more aggressive espionage," *USA Today*, November 18, 2004.
104. Matthew Clark, "Shifting roles of US spies and special forces: Pentagon takes over some CIA spy operations while US 'super-secret' commandos get duty on US soil," *Christian Science Monitor*, January 25, 2005.
105. Barton Gellman, "Secret Unit Expands Rumsfeld's Domain: New Espionage Branch Delving into CIA Territory," *Washington Post*, January 23, 2005.
106. The term "blowback," meaning "the unintended consequences of the US government's international activities that have been kept secret from the American people," was popularized by political scientist Chalmers Johnson. See Chalmers Johnson, *Blowback: The Costs and Consequences of American*

Empire (New York: Henry Holt & Co., 2000), p 6.

107. Steve Coll, *Ghost Wars: The Secret History of the CIA, Afghanistan and bin Laden, from the Soviet Invasion to 10 September 2001* (New York: Penguin, 2004), p 182.
108. Massoud, perhaps the best-known "hero" of the Afghan jihad, was killed two days before the September 11 attacks, in all likelihood by Al-Qaeda.
109. Anonymous, *Imperial Hubris*, pp 49–51.
110. Knut Royce, "Agency: Chalabi group was front for Iran," *Newsday*, May 21, 2004.
111. Jane Mayer, "The Manipulator: Ahmad Chalabi pushed a tainted case for war. Can he survive the occupation?," *The New Yorker*, June 7, 2004.
112. *Ibid.*
113. Jonathan S. Landay, "Funds Halted for Iraq Informer Group," *Boston Globe*, May 19, 2004.
114. See Chapter 11.

Chapter 9. The Question of Islamic Charities

1. Suskind, *The Price of Loyalty*, p 179.
2. *Ibid.*
3. *Ibid.*
4. Rachel Ehrenfeld, *Funding Evil: How Terrorism Is Financed—and How to Stop It* (Chicago: Bonus Books, 2003), p 21.
5. Jack Shafer, "The PowerPoint That Rocked the Pentagon: The LaRouchie defector who's advising the defense establishment on Saudi Arabia," *Slate*, August 7, 2002.
6. *Wall Street Journal*, August 24, 1998.
7. Bill Maher, "Terrorists can't be charities," *Boston Globe*, April 8, 2003.
8. Glenn R. Simpson, "Holy Land Foundation Allegedly Mixed Charity Money with Funds for Bombers," *Wall Street Journal*, February 27, 2002.
9. Many Islamist organizations gained considerable political support as a result of their social and philanthropic action. The phenomenon was observed in numerous places, among them Egypt, Algeria, Lebanon, and Israel's occupied territories: following natural calamities or political violence, the efficient relief provided by the philanthropic wings of Islamic organizations contrasted with the inaction of the government and was a powerful factor in generating popular support. See Abdel-Rahman Ghandour, *Jihad humanitaire: Enquête sur les ONG islamiques* (Paris: Flammarion, 2002), pp 67–79. See also Declan Walsh, "Extremist measures: An Islamic aid group is proving to be one of the most popular relief providers in quake-hit Kashmir," *Guardian*, October 18, 2005.
10. James Adams, *The Financing of Terror: Behind the PLO, IRA, Red Brigades and M19 Stand the Paymasters* (New York: Simon and Schuster, 1986), p 141.
11. Dan Balz and Bob Woodward, "America's Chaotic Road to War: Bush's Global Strategy Began to Take Shape in First Frantic Hours after Attack,"

Washington Post, January 27, 2002.

12. Glenn R. Simpson, "Holy Land Foundation Allegedly Mixed Charity Money with Funds for Bombers," *Wall Street Journal*, February 27, 2002.

13. For a comprehensive overview, see Abdel-Rahman Ghandour, *Jihad humanitaire*. For case studies, see Janine Clark, *Islam, Social Welfare, and the Middle Class: Networks, Activism, and Charity in Egypt, Yemen, and Jordan* (Indiana University Press, 2003); Denis J. Sullivan, *Private Voluntary Organizations in Egypt: Islamic Development, Private Initiative, and State Control* (University of Florida Press, 1994); Carrie Rosevsky Wickham, *Mobilizing Islam: Religion, Activism and Political Change in Egypt* (Columbia University Press, 2002); Quintan Wiktorowicz, *The Management of Islamic Activism: Salafis, the Muslim Brotherhood, and State Power in Jordan* (State University of New York Press, 2001).

14. Ian Fisher, "Airplane Terrorism Case Prompts Questions about the Work of Islamic Charities in Britain," *New York Times*, August 24, 2006.

15. The other pillars are: the *shahada*, or profession of faith; the *salat*, or praying five times a day; the *sawm*, fasting from dawn to sunset during the month of Ramadan; and, if a believer is able to do so, making at least one pilgrimage to Mecca.

16. Koran 9:60 "[*Zakat*] charity is only for the poor and the needy, and those employed to administer it, and those whose hearts are made to incline [to truth], and [to free] the captives, and those in debt, and in the way of Allah and for the wayfarer—an ordinance from Allah. And Allah is Knowing, Wise."

17. Abdelhamid Brahimi, *Justice sociale et développement en économie islamique* (Paris: La Pensée Universelle, 1993). The author is a former prime minister of Algeria.

18. Chibli Mallat, *The Renewal of Islamic Law: Muhammad Baqer as-Sadr, Najaf and the Shi'i International* (Cambridge: Cambridge University Press 1993), p 120.

19. Tariq Ramadan, *Western Muslims and the Future of Islam* (Oxford: Oxford University Press, 2003), pp 151–95.

20. Plural form of *waqf*. See Adam Sabra, *Poverty and Charity in Medieval Islam: Mamluk Egypt, 1250–1517* (Cambridge: Cambridge University Press, 2000), p 69.

21. Daniel Benjamin and Steven Simon, *The Age of Sacred Terror: Radical Islam's War against America* (New York: Random House, 2003), p 144.

22. Edward Mortimer, *Faith and Power: The Politics of Islam* (London: Random House, 1982), pp 177–80.

23. As'ad Abukhalil, *The Battle for Saudi Arabia: Royalty, Fundamentalism, and Global Power* (New York: Seven Stories Press, 2004), p 140.

24. http://www.oic-oci.org.

25. Daniel Yergin, *The Prize: The Epic Quest for Oil, Money and Power* (New York: Simon and Schuster, 1991), pp 563–87.

26. Timur Kuran, *Islam and Mammon: The Economic Predicaments of Islamism*

(Princeton University Press, 2004), p xiii.

27. Steve Coll, *Ghost Wars: The Secret History of the CIA, Afghanistan and bin Laden, from the Soviet Invasion to 10 September 2001* (New York: Penguin, 2004), p 79.

28. Prince Turki Al Faisal, Special Address, Georgetown University, Center for Contemporary Arab Studies, February 3, 2002. See also John Cooley, *Unholy Wars: Afghanistan, America and International Terrorism* (London: Pluto Press, 2002), pp 15–18.

29. George Crile, *Charlie Wilson's War: The Extraordinary Story of the Largest Covert Operation in History* (New York: Atlantic Monthly Press, 2003), p 236.

30. Quoted in Abukhalil, *The Battle for Saudi Arabia*, p 194.

31. Rachel Bronson, "Recall, Reagan had Riyadh to thank," *Daily Star*, June 19, 2004.

32. Ibrahim Warde, *Islamic Finance in the Global Economy* (Edinburgh: Edinburgh University Press, 2000), p 93.

33. Coll, *Ghost Wars*, p 28.

34. Mahmood Mamdani, *Good Muslim, Bad Muslim : America, the Cold War, and the Roots of Terror* (New York: Pantheon, 2004).

35. A further dimension of the conflict was that Saudi Arabia itself had a sizable Shia minority, mostly centered around the oil-rich eastern part of the country.

36. Abukhalil, *The Battle for Saudi Arabia*, p 138.

37. Crile, *Charlie Wilson's War*, p 165.

38. Coll, *Ghost Wars*, p 35.

39. Abukhalil, *The Battle for Saudi Arabia*, p 139.

40. Rachel Bronson, *Thicker Than Oil: America's Uneasy Partnership with Saudi Arabia* (Oxford: Oxford University Press, 2006), pp 168–77.

41. See Chapter 8.

42. A few scholars had developed the argument that Islamic unrest would result in the disintegration of the Soviet Union.

43. Kiren Aziz Chaudhry, *The Price of Wealth: Economies and Institutions in the Middle East* (Cornell University Press, 1997), p 7.

44. Crile, *Charlie Wilson's War*, p 238. Another version asserts that a formal agreement to that effect was arrived at by the two countries' intelligence agencies in July 1980. See also Coll, *Ghost Wars*, p 81.

45. Coll, *Ghost Wars*, p 83.

46. Robert Gates, *From the Shadows*, p 349.

47. Coll, *Ghost Wars*, p 6.

48. Rohan Gunaratna, *Inside Al Qaeda: Global Network of Terror* (New York: Berkley Books, 2002), pp 274–9.

49. Coll, *Ghost Wars*, pp 294–7.

50. *Ibid.*, p 299.

51. *Ibid.*

52. Jonathan Randal, *Osama: The Making of a Terrorist*, pp 121–9.

53. Coll, *Ghost Wars*, pp 296–9.
54. Ibrahim Warde, "Les dividendes de l'opération 'bouclier du desert'," *Le Monde diplomatique*, November 1990.
55. Anatol Lieven, *America Right or Wrong: An Anatomy of American Nationalism* (Oxford: Oxford University Press, 2004), pp 143–9.
56. In the years following the September 11 attacks, many other natural catastrophes hit Islamic countries. In the year 2005 alone a devastating tsunami and a catastrophic earthquake caused tens of thousands of victims in Indonesia and Pakistan respectively.
57. Anonymous, *Imperial Hubris*, pp 42–4.
58. See Chapter 8.
59. "Be Wary of Scam Artists after a Disaster Strikes," *Los Angeles Times*, September 4, 2005.
60. Tom Zeller Jr., "After the Storm, the Swindlers," *New York Times*, September 8, 2005.
61. The case of Saudi-based Al-Haramein is revealing. See *The 9/11 Commission Report*, pp 114–30.
62. *The 9/11 Commission Report*, pp 21–2.
63. See Introduction.
64. See Chapter 8.
65. Philip Shenon, "Senate Committee Requests Tax and Fund-Raising Records for 27 Muslim Charities," *New York Times*, January 15, 2004; Laurie P. Cohen, Glenn Simpson, Mark Maremont, and Peter Fritsch, "Bush's Financial War on Terrorism Includes Strikes at Islamic Charities," *Wall Street Journal*, September 25, 2001; and Lisa Getter, Chuck Neubauer, and Robert J. Lopez, "Islamic American Nonprofits Face Increased Scrutiny in U.S.: Charities' financial records are sought to see if any money is funneled to terrorist groups." *Los Angeles Times*, November 4, 2001.
66. Glenn R. Simpson, "U.S. Indicts Head of Charity for Helping Fund al Qaeda: Government Uses 'Al Capone' Tax Charges for This and Other Terror-Financing Cases," *Wall Street Journal*, October 10, 2002.
67. See Chapter 4.
68. See Matt Kelley, "Ex-NBA Star's Mosque Named in Probe," Associated Press, March 31, 2005, and Patrick E. Tyler, "British Singer Calls His Deportation a Mistake," *New York Times*, September 24, 2004.
69. Viola Gienger, "Guantanamo detainee was charity worker," *Chicago Tribune*, June 6, 2002.
70. For a detailed discussion of that case, see *The 9/11 Commssion Report*, pp 87–113.
71. Laurie Cohen, "Charity rips U.S. claims of terror ties: Lawyers contend photos, messages seized in FBI raid outdated, tenuous," *Chicago Tribune*, May 11, 2002.
72. *Ibid.*
73. Michael Higgins, "Islamic charities chafe at charges; Fairness at issue with

perjury ploy," *Chicago Tribune* May 13, 2002.

74. Donna Freedman, "Rally backs jailed head of Islamic foundation," *Chicago Tribune*, September 18, 2002.

75. Matt O'Connor, "Lawyers hit U.S. jail actions; they say head of Islamic charity 'locked up like dog'," *Chicago Tribune*, July 20, 2002.

76. John Mintz, "Head of Muslim Charity Sentenced: Ill Man Diverted Funds to Militants; No Proof of Terror Link, Judge Says," *Washington Post*, August 19, 2003.

77. *Ibid.*

78. "Federal Judge Refuses to Increase Charity Director's Prison Time," *Wall Street Journal*, July 17, 2003.

79. *Daily Star*, June 18, 2002.

80. Dan Eggen and Julie Tate, "U.S. Campaign Produces Few Convictions on Terrorism Charges," *Washington Post*, June 12, 2005.

81. *The 9/11 Commission Report*, p 24.

82. A highly publicized case involved Kuwaiti-born Sami al-Arian, a University of South Florida computer science professor. Since the mid-1990s, his political activities in favor of Palestinian causes had aroused controversy. A few weeks after the September 11 attacks, he was suspended by the University on the grounds of alleged ties to Islamic Jihad, another blacklisted Palestinian organization. In February 2003, a 50-count indictment accused him of concealing a terrorist cell within "the structure, facilities and academic environment" of his university, using it to raise, manage, and channel funds in a decade-long global conspiracy. The case had been reinvigorated when prosecutors gained access to evidence collected under counter-intelligence warrants, which judges can issue based on less evidence of wrongdoing than criminal warrants require. Jess Bravin and Glenn R. Simpson, "Florida Professor, Seven Others Are Accused of Terror Funding," *Wall Street Journal*, February 21, 2003.

83. *The 9/11 Commission Report*, p 43.

84. Halper and Clarke, *America Alone*, p 106; George Packer, *The Assassins' Gate: America in Iraq* (New York: Farrar, Straus and Giroux, 2005), p 30.

85. David Firestone, "F.B.I. Traces Hamas's Plan to Finance Attacks to 93," *New York Times*, December 6, 2001.

86. Glenn R. Simpson, "Holy Land Foundation Allegedly Mixed Charity Money with Funds for Bombers," *Wall Street Journal*, February 27, 2002.

87. *Ibid.*

88. David E. Sanger and Judith Miller, "Bush Freezes Assets of Biggest U.S. Muslim Charity, Calling It a Deadly Terror Group," *New York Times*, December 5, 2001.

89. "US targets Hamas finances," BBC News, December 4, 2001, http://news.bbc.co.uk/2/hi/americas/1691961.stm

90. Laurie Goodstein, "Groups Protest Bush's Freezing of Foundation's Assets," *New York Times*, December 5, 2001.

91. *Ibid.*

92. John Mintz, "Muslim Charity, Officials Indicted: Funding Groups with Hamas Ties at Issue," *Washington Post*, July 28, 2004.

93. Sean O'Neill, "Britain rejects Bush's charges against charity," *Daily Telegraph*, September 25, 2003.

94. *Ibid.*

95. Mark Oliver "Group cleared of Hamas link," *Guardian*, September 25, 2003.

96. O'Neill, "Britain rejects Bush's charges against charity," *Daily Telegraph*, September 25, 2003.

97. Matthew VI.1: "When thou doest alms, let not thy left hand know what thy right hand doeth."

98. Ghandour, *Jihad humanitaire: Enquête sur les ONG islamiques*, pp 101, 132.

99. *Ibid.*, p 332.

100. Some estimates suggest that over 80 percent of the world's refugees are Muslim. See Ghandour, *Jihad humanitaire: Enquête sur les ONG islamiques*, p 151.

101. Kuran, *Islam and Mammon*, p 20.

102. Graham Fuller, *The Future of Political Islam* (New York: Palgrave Macmillan, 2003), pp 126-7.

103. Ghandour, *Jihad humanitaire: Enquête sur les ONG islamiques*, p 22.

104. William P. Fuller and Barnett F. Baron, "How war on terror hits charity," *Christian Science Monitor*, July 29, 2003.

105. Alan Dershowitz, *The Case for Israel* (New York: John Wiley & Sons, 2003), pp 166-70.

106. Laurie Goodstein, "Groups Protest Bush's Freezing of Foundation's Assets," *New York Times*, December 5, 2001.

107. Glenn R. Simpson, Paul Beckett, and Jonathan Karp, "White House Will Freeze Assets of Charity Accused by Israel of Having Ties to Hamas," *Wall Street Journal*, December 4, 2001.

108. Glenn R. Simpson, "Holy Land Foundation Allegedly Mixed Charity Money with Funds for Bombers," *Wall Street Journal*, February 27, 2002.

109. See Chapter 7.

110. Christopher Cooper, "Crackdown on Terrorism Financing Ties Hands of Businessman in Sweden," *Wall Street Journal*, May 6, 2002.

111. Adnan El-Ghoul, "Fadlallah says U.S. 'war on terror' hurts Muslim charities," *Daily Star*, August 3, 2005.

112. See Chapter 9.

113. Raid Qusti and Ghazanfar Ali Khan, "What Directive on Charity Donations?," *Arab News*, July 28, 2003.

114. US Department of the Treasury, "Anti-Terrorist Financing Guidelines: Voluntary Best Practices For U.S.-Based Charities," November 2002.

115. Stephanie Strom, "Small Charities Abroad Feel Pinch of U.S. War on Terror," *New York Times*, August 5, 2003.

116. William P. Fuller and Barnett F. Baron, "How war on terror hits charity," *Christian Science Monitor*, July 29, 2003.

117. Ibrahim Warde, "Les riches entre philanthropie et repentance," *Le Monde diplomatique*, December 1997.

118. See Marvin Olasky, "A Brand New Game," *Washington Post*, December 17, 2000.

119. Marvin Olasky, *Renewing American Compassion: A Citizen's Guide* (New York: Free Press), p 108.

120. Ibrahim Warde, *Islamic Finance in the Global Economy*, p 98.

121. An equally significant factor in the strong Republican slant of the Muslim vote was the presence of Senator Joseph Lieberman, an Orthodox Jew and fervent Zionist, on the Democratic ticket.

122. See for example "Charity Begins at Home," a series of articles published in the *Boston Globe*: "Some Officers of Charities Steer Assets to Selves," October 9, 2003, "Charity Money Funding Perks," November 9, 2003, "Foundations Veer into Business," December 3, 2003, "Foundation Lawyers Enjoy Privileged Position," December 17, 2003, "Philanthropist's Millions Enrich Family Retainers," December 21, 2003, "Foundations' Tax Returns Left Unchecked," December 29, 2003.

123. Timothy L. O'Brien, "Charity Said to Have Paid Terrorists Is under Investigation by the Saudis," *New York Times*, September 26, 2003.

124. Laurie Goodstein, "Muslims Hesitating on Gifts as U.S. Scrutinizes Charities," *New York Times*, April 17, 2003.

125. *Ibid.*; see also David Bank, "Companies Face Quandaries over Matching-Gift Programs," *Wall Street Journal*, February 18, 2003; Raja Kamal, "Muslim charities could use a helping hand," *Daily Star*, March 11, 2004; and Adnan El-Ghoul, "Fadlallah says U.S. 'war on terror' hurts Muslim charities," *Daily Star*, August 3, 2005.

126. "Timing of Charity Shutdown Troubles Muslims," All Things Considered, National Public Radio, October 26, 2004.

127. Gregory L. Vistica, "Frozen Assets Going to Legal Bills: U.S. Has Linked Confiscated Funds to Financing Terror," *Washington Post*, November 1, 2003.

128. Roger Thurow, "Christian Reaching Out: As Crises Mount, Global Aid Groups Tap Islamic Money; Post 9/11, Western Charities Find a Better Reception in Oil-Rich Arab Nations; Passing the Hat in Dubai Mall," *Wall Street Journal*, December 3, 2004.

129. See Chapter 11.

Chapter 10. "Catastrophic Successes": Assessing the Financial War

1. http://www.whitehouse.gov/news/releases/2001/12/100dayreport.html.

2. "Fact Sheet: President Bush Addresses the United Nations High-Level Plenary Meeting," Office of the Press Secretary, the White House, September 14, 2005.

3. *The 9/11 Commission Report*, p 382. See also Chapter 8.
4. Dan Eggen, "U.S. Is Given Failing Grades by 9/11 Panel," *Washington Post*, December 6, 2005.
5. "Treasury Official Who Halted Funds to Terrorists Will Resign," *Wall Street Journal*, September 2, 2003.
6. Testimony of Steven Emerson before the United States Senate Committee of Banking, Housing, and Urban Affairs, "Money Laundering and Terror Financing Issues in the Middle East," July 13, 2005.
7. David Teather, "Al-Qaida 'has regrouped,'" *Guardian*, October 18, 2002.
8. Hudson Morgan, "Laundry Bag: Treasury's Kid Gloves," *The New Republic*, April 14, 2003, Spencer Ackerman, "What Else You Got?," *The New Republic Online*, May 9, 2003.
9. Ackerman, "What Else You Got?," *The New Republic Online*, May 9, 2003.
10. Quoted in Graham Allison, *Nuclear Terrorism: The Ultimate Preventable Catastrophe* (New York: Times Books, 2004), p 179.
11. *The 9/11 Commission Report*, p 382.
12. See Chapters 1 and 9.
13. *Monograph on Terrorist Financing*, p 22.
14. "Insurgents Strike Baghdad Again; Two-Day Death Toll Nears 200," *New York Times*, September 16, 2005.
15. Eric Lichtblau, "U.S. Lacks Strategy to Curb Terror Funds, Agency Says," *New York Times*, November 29, 2005.
16. William Saletan, "Catastrophic Success: The worse Iraq gets, the more we must be winning," *Slate*, September 28, 2004.
17. Mike McNamee and Lorraine Woellert, "The Cash Squeeze on Terror Inc.: Key arrests could help choke off al Qaeda financing," *Business Week*, March 17, 2003.
18. 'U.S. Says Freezing Funds Has Hit Terrorist Finances,' Reuters, March 2, 2005.
19. Testimony of Stuart Levey, Undersecretary, Office of Terrorism and Financial Intelligence, US Department of the Treasury before the House Financial Services Subcommittee on Oversight and Investigations and the House International Relations Subcommittee on International Terrorism and Nonproliferation, Department of the Treasury, the Office Of Public Affairs, May 4, 2005.
20. "Terrorist finance: Moving target," *The Economist*, September 12, 2002.
21. See Chapter 8.
22. Matthew Clark, "The Big Catch That Wasn't? Pakistan's arrest of Libyan Al Qaeda suspect not as big a breakthrough as first thought," *Christian Science Monitor*, May 10, 2005.
23. Jo Johnson and Farhan Bokhari, "Al-Qaeda's back has been broken, says Musharraf," *Financial Times*, May 15, 2005.
24. Christina Lamb and Mohammad Shehzad "Captured Al-Qaeda kingpin is case of 'mistaken identity,'" *Sunday Times*, May 8, 2005.

25. Another Libyan with a similar name is on the FBI most-wanted list—Anas al-Liby, who is wanted over the 1998 East African embassy bombings—and some believe the Americans may have initially confused the two. Christina Lamb and Mohammad Shehzad, "Captured Al-Qaeda kingpin is case of 'mistaken identity,'" *Sunday Times*, May 8, 2005.

26. *Ibid.*

27. Timothy Noah, "Al-Qaida's Rule of Threes—Why are all al-Qaida captives 'No. 3'?," *Slate*, December 5, 2005. See also Timothy Noah, "Lieutenants by the Bushel: Al-Zarqawi's top-heavy army," *Slate*, December 9, 2005.

28. International terrorism is defined as "premeditated, politically motivated violence perpetrated against noncombatant targets" involving citizens or property from multiple countries, "usually intended to influence an audience." An event "is judged significant if it results in loss of life or serious injury to persons" or "major property damage." Alan B. Krueger and David Laitin, "Faulty Terror Report Card," *Washington Post*, May 17, 2004.

29. Susan B. Glasser, "U.S. Figures Show Sharp Global Rise in Terrorism: State Dept. Will Not Put Data in Report," *Washington Post*, April 27, 2005, and Tom Regan, "Global Terror Attacks Tripled in 2004: National Counterterrorism Center releases stats after State Department decides not to," *Christian Science Monitor*, April 26, 2005.

30. Alan B. Krueger and David Laitin, "Faulty Terror Report Card," *Washington Post*, May 17, 2004.

31. Jim Fisher-Thompson, "US Counterterrorism Official Reports Progress to Africans," The Washington File, Bureau of International Information Programs, US Department of State, May 5, 2004.

32. Alan B. Krueger, "How to Measure Terrorism Data," *New York Times*, July 22, 2004.

33. "Terrorist Attacks Tripled in 2004, U.S. Reports," *Los Angeles Times*, April 27, 2005.

34. See Chapter 6.

35. See Chapter 1.

36. Ellen Knickmeyer, "U.S. Claims Success in Iraq Despite Onslaught: Body Counts Now Cited as Benchmarks," *Washington Post*, September 19, 2005.

37. Richard W. Stevenson and Jodi Wilgoren, "Bush Forcefully Defends War, Citing Safety of U.S. and World," *New York Times*, July 13, 2004.

38. For a different perspective, see Daniel Benjamin and Steven Simon, *The Next Attack: The Failure of the War on Terror and a Strategy for Getting It Right* (New York: Times Books, 2005).

39. To which a columnist H.D.S. Greenway responded: "In Iraq, the war is actually helping Al Qaeda to recruit terrorists to one day attack us at home." H.D.S. Greenway, "How Will the Iraq War End?," *Boston Globe*, December 27, 2005.

40. E.J. Dionne, "The War's Realists," *Washington Post*, July 12, 2005.

41. Edward Alden, "Complex finances defy global policing," *Financial Times*,

February 21, 2002.

42. Ibid.

43. Chris Suellentrop, "What Is the Financial Crimes Enforcement Network?,"
     Slate, November 8, 2001.

44. Juan C. Zarate, Deputy Assistant Secretary, "Securing the Financial System
     against Rogue Capital," November 10, 2003, Keynote Address before the
     Investment Company Institute, US Department of the Treasury, Office of
     Public Affairs. He was approvingly quoting a line by Saudi Arabia's Crown
     Prince Abdullah to the effect that "US Treasury and Finance Ministries are
     the greatest enemies of the terrorists."

45. David E. Sanger and Joseph Kahn, "Bush Freezes Assets Linked to Terror
     Net; Russians Offer Airspace and Arms Support," New York Times, Septem-
     ber 25, 2001.

46. John Willman, Michael Mann, and Richard Wolffe, "US Has Frozen $6m of
     Assets Linked to Al-Qaeda," Financial Times, October 1, 2001.

47. See for example, Jeff Gerth and Judith Miller, "U.S. Makes Inroads in Isolat-
     ing Funds Of Terror Groups," New York Times, November 5, 2001; Faye
     Bowers, "Headway on the Al Qaeda money trail: Top Treasury official claims
     vast reduction in terrorist cash flow—with long road ahead," Christian Science
     Monitor, October 10, 2003; "The Cash Squeeze on Terror Inc.: Key arrests
     could help choke off al Qaeda financing," Business Week, March 17, 2003.

48. Karen DeYoung, "Officials Defend Financial Searches; Critics Assert Secret
     Program Invades Privacy," Washington Post, June 24, 2006.

49. Ibid.

50. Glenn Simpson, "Since 9/11, U.S. Has Used Subpoenas to Access Records
     from Fund-Transfer System," Wall Street Journal, June 23, 2006.

51. Dan Eggen and Julie Tate, "Few Terror Convictions in Cases since 9/11,"
     Washington Post, June 12, 2005.

52. Ibid.

53. Eggen and Tate, "U.S. Campaign Produces Few Convictions on Terrorism
     Charges," Washington Post, June 12, 2005.

54. Eggen and Tate, "Few Terror Convictions in Cases since 9/11," Washington
     Post, June 12, 2005.

55. Mary Beth Sheridan, "Immigration Law as Anti-Terrorism Tool," Washington
     Post, June 13, 2005.

56. Bovard, Terrorism and Tyranny, p 3.

57. Suskind, The One Percent Doctrine, p 41.

58. "Database Tagged 120,000 as Possible Terrorist Suspects," New York Times,
     May 21, 2004.

59. Ann Davis, Maureen Tkacik, and Andrea Petersen, "Ashcroft's Call to
     Report Suspicious Activity Pits Neighbor vs. Neighbor in War on Terror,"
     Wall Street Journal, November 21, 2001.

60. Ibid.

61. Ibid.

62. Edith M. Lederer, "Countries Urged to Beef Up Terror List," *Guardian*, January 20, 2006.

63. Walter Pincus and Dan Eggen, "325,000 Names on Terrorism List; Rights Groups Say Database May Include Innocent People," *Washington Post*, February 15, 2006.

64. http://www.db-bis.net/operationamerica/KYCtalkpoints.html.

65. "Terror Money," *Wall Street Journal*, October 26, 2001.

66. Mathers, *Crime School, Money Laundering*, p 125.

67. Edward Alden, "Financial companies plead for fewer 'suspicious activity' alerts," *Financial Times*, May 11, 2005.

68. Glenn R. Simpson, "His Cash Is Green, But Flags Raised Were Red: Reports on Bob Dole's Preference for Carrying Wads of C-Notes Is Strange Fallout of Riggs Affair," *Wall Street Journal*, September 3, 2004.

69. *Ibid.*

70. Joe Cantlupe, "Fear of prosecution, fines cause big surge in filings," Copley News Service, June 15, 2005.

71. "£20m for terror measures and bomb victims," *Guardian*, July 19, 2005.

72. Joe Cantlupe, "Fear of prosecution, fines cause big surge in filings," Copley News Service, June 15, 2005.

73. Edward Alden, "Financial companies plead for fewer 'suspicious activity' alerts," *Financial Times*, May 11, 2005.

74. *A Month in Money Laundering*, May 2005, www.deloitte.com/dtt/cda/doc/content/ uk_fs_month_in_money_laundering_may05.pdf.

75. *Ibid.*

76. *Ibid.*

77. Glenn R. Simpson, "Since 9/11, U.S. Has Used Subpoenas to Access Records from Fund-Transfer System," *Wall Street Journal*, June 23, 2006.

78. Eric Lichtblau, "U.S. Seeks Access to Bank Records to Deter Terror," *New York Times*, April 10, 2005.

Chapter 11. Rethinking Money and Terror

1. Nicholas Watt, "MI5 team to track terror cash: Money trail 'Bletchley Park' experts target bank network," *Guardian*, October 16, 2001.

2. Andy McSmith "Anti-terror role urged for Bletchley," *Independent*, February 11, 2006.

3. To cite only a few, Richard A. Clarke, *Against All Enemies: Inside America's War on Terror* (New York: Free Press, 2004); Daniel Benjamin and Steven Simon, *The Next Attack: The Failure of the War on Terror and a Strategy for Getting It Right* (New York: Times Books, 2005); Stefan Halper and Jonathan Clarke, *America Alone: The Neo-Conservatives and the Global Order* (Cambridge: Cambridge University Press, 2004); George Packer, *The Assassins' Gate: America in Iraq* (New York: Farrar, Straus, and Giroux, 2005).

4. Office of the Undersecretary of Defense for Acquisition, Technology, and Logistics, Report of the Defense Science Board Task Force on Strategic

Communication, Washington, DC, September 2004, p 40.

5.   *Ibid.*

6.   Rupert Cornwell, "Iraq now a terrorist breeding ground, say US officials," *Independent*, January 15, 2005.

7.   *Ibid.*

8.   Dana Priest and Josh White, "War Helps Recruit Terrorists, Hill Told," *Washington Post*, February 17, 2005.

9.   *Ibid.*

10. Some preferred the word "strategy" instead, as in "global strategy against violent extremism."

11. Eric Schmitt and Thom Shanker, "U.S. Officials Retool Slogan for Terror War," *New York Times*, July 26, 2005.

12. *Ibid.*

13. *Ibid.*

14. *Ibid.*

15. Richard W. Stevenson, "President Makes It Clear Phrase Is 'War on Terror,'" *New York Times*, August 4, 2005.

16. Dan Eggen, "U.S. Is Given Failing Grades by 9/11 Panel," *Washington Post*, December 6, 2005.

17. Stuart Levey, "The war on terrorist financing must be stepped up," *Financial Times*, September 26, 2005.

18. Michael Freedman, "Financing Terror: Why the U.S. Can't Stop the Flow of Billions to Drug Lords, Smugglers and Al Qaida," *Forbes*, October 17, 2005.

19. And a whole genre of course claims that not enough is being done to crack down on terrorist financing, and especially in regard to the roles of Saudi Arabia and Islamic charities. See Chapters 5 and 10.

20. Anonymous, *Through Our Enemies' Eyes*, pp 28–44.

21. Bovard, *Terrorism and Tyranny*, pp 81–132.

22. Richard A. Clarke, et al, *Defeating the Jihadists: A Blueprint for Action* (New York: The Century Foundation Press, 2004).

23. Maurice R. Greenberg, Chair, Mallory Factor, Vice Chair, William F. Wechsler and Lee S. Wolosky, Project Co-Directors, "Update on the Global Campaign against Terrorist Financing," Second Report of an Independent Task Force on Terrorist Financing, Sponsored by the Council on Foreign Relations, June 15, 2004.

24. Clarke, et al, *Defeating the Jihadists*, p 1.

25. *Ibid.*

26. David E. Sanger and Warren Hoge, "Bush Thanks World Leaders and Takes Conciliatory Tone," *New York Times*, September 15, 2005.

27. Clarke, et al, *Defeating the Jihadists*, pp 91–106.

28. *Ibid.*, p 6.

29. See Chapter 1.

30. Clarke, et al, *Defeating the Jihadists*, p 111.

31. *Ibid.*, p 5.

32. Devin Leonard and Peter Elkind, "Hank's Big Fall, 'All I Want in Life Is an Unfair Advantage,'" *Fortune*, July 25, 2005.

33. Maurice R. Greenberg, Chair, Mallory Factor, Vice Chair, William F. Wechsler and Lee S. Wolosky, Project Co-Directors, "Update on the Global Campaign against Terrorist Financing," Second Report of an Independent Task Force on Terrorist Financing, Sponsored by the Council on Foreign Relations, June 15, 2004.

34. See Chapter 1.

35. Paul Beckett, "Sept. 11 Attacks Cost $303,672; Plot Papers Lacking, FBI Says," *Wall Street Journal*, May 15, 2002.

36. Ibid.

37. *Monograph on Terrorist Financing*, p 141.

38. Ibid., p 141.

39. Ibid., p 133.

40. See Chapter 5.

41. Rumors originating in India placed the head of Pakistan's intelligence services behind the transfers. See Michael Meacher, "The Pakistan connection," *Guardian*, July 22, 2004.

42. *The 9/11 Commission Report*, p 172.

43. David E. Sanger and Joseph Kahn, "Bush Freezes Assets Linked to Terror Net; Russians Offer Airspace and Arms Support," *New York Times*, September 25, 2001.

44. *Monograph on Terrorist Financing*, p 28.

45. Ibid., p 27.

46. Benn Steil and Robert E. Litan, *Financial Statecraft: The Role of Financial Markets in American Foreign Policy* (Yale University Press, 2006), p 41.

47. Ibid.

48. Douglas Frantz, Josh Meyer, Sebastian Rotella, and Megan K. Stack, "Al Qaeda Seen as Wider Threat: The network has evolved into a looser, ideological movement that may no longer report to Bin Laden. Critics say the White House focus is misdirected," *Los Angeles Times*, September 26, 2004.

49. Hannah K. Strange, "July 7 bombings 'cost just $1,000,'" United Press International, January 3, 2006.

50. Preface and Introduction, "Patterns of Global Terrorism - 2001," Department of State Publication, Office of the Secretary of State, released by the Office of the Coordinator for Counterterrorism, May 2002.

51. Financial Action Task Force, "The Financial War on Terror" (Paris: FATF, 2004), p 7.

52. National Criminal Intelligence Service (NCIS), Overview of Money Laundering, http://www.ncis.co.uk.

53. See Chapter 3.

54. See Chapter 10.

55. "£20m for terror measures and bomb victims," *Guardian*, July 19, 2005.

56. See Introduction.

57. Jenny Booth, "EU agrees crackdown on terrorist finances," *The Times*, July 12, 2005.
58. Conal Walsh, "Banks on alert for 'backpacker' terrorists," *Observer*, July 17, 2005.
59. Conal Walsh, "Terrorism on the cheap—and with no paper trail," *Observer*, July 17, 2005.
60. Hannah K. Strange, "July 7 bombings 'cost just $1,000,'" United Press International, January 3, 2006.
61. Of the four suicide bombers of the July 7 attacks, three were born in Britain of Pakistani parents, and one came as a young man from Jamaica. As for the attempted bombings of July 21, 2005, the four suspects arrested were of East African origin. David Cracknell, "Focus: How we can stop this from happening again," *Sunday Times*, July 31, 2005.
62. Though it was reported that the men "paid off some of their debts and at least one bomber is understood to have written a will." Hannah K. Strange, "July 7 bombings 'cost just $1,000,'" United Press International, January 3, 2006.
63. Bernard Lewis, *What Went Wrong? The Clash between Islam and Modernity in the Middle East* (New York: Perennial HarperCollins, 2003), p 160.
64. Robert A. Pape, "Blowing Up an Assumption," *New York Times*, May 18, 2005.
65. Peter Bergen and Swati Pandey, "The Madrassa Myth," *New York Times*, June 14, 2005.
66. *The 9/11 Commission Report*, pp 497-9.
67. *The 9/11 Commission Report*, p 22.
68. See Introduction and Chapters 9 and 10.
69. *The 9/11 Commission Report*, p 22; see also Chapter 10.
70. Shibley Telhami, *The Stakes: America and the Middle East: The Consequences of Power and the Choice for Peace* (Boulder, CO: Westview Press, 2002), p 13.
71. *Ibid.*, p 14.
72. See, for example, Marc Sageman, *Understanding Terror Networks* (University of Pennsylvania Press, 2004); Karen J. Greenberg (ed), *Al Qaeda Now: Understanding Today's Terrorists* (Cambridge: Cambridge University Press, 2005); Olivier Roy, *Globalized Islam: The Search for a New Ummah* (Columbia University Press, 2006).
73. Gerges, *The Far Enemy*, pp 273-6.
74. David Ignatius, "Think Strategy, Not Numbers," *Washington Post*, August 26, 2003.
75. Daniel Schorr, "Serious US image problem abroad," *Christian Science Monitor*, October 1, 2004.
76. Most accounts of the Iraqi insurgency bear this out. See, for example, Anthony Shadid, *Night Draws Near: Iraq's People in the Shadow of America's War* (New York: Henry Holt and Company, 2005); George Packer, *The Assassins' Gate: America in Iraq* (New York: Farrar, Straus, and Giroux, 2005); Michael

R. Gordon and General Bernard E. Trainor, *Cobra II: The Inside Story of the Invasion and Occupation of Iraq* (New York: Pantheon, 2006).

77. See Chapters 2 and 3.

78. Richard W. Stevenson, "President, Marking Anniversary of War, Urges World to Unite to Combat Terrorism," *New York Times*, March 20, 2004.

79. Elisabeth Bumiller and Jane Perlez, "Bush and Top Aides Proclaim Policy of 'Ending' States That Back Terror; Local Airports Shut after an Arrest," *New York Times*, September 14, 2001.

80. See Chapter 4.

81. Dershowitz, *The Case for Israel*, pp 166–70.

82. Robert McNamara, *In Retrospect: The Tragedy and Lessons of Vietnam* (New York: Vintage, 1996), pp 321–3. See also Errol Morris, *The Fog of War* (2004).

83. T.E. Lawrence, *Seven Pillars of Wisdom: A Triumph* (New York: Anchor Books, 1991), p 42.

84. *Ibid.*

85. Quoted in Chalmers Johnson, "Baseworld: America's Military Colonialism," *Mother Jones*, January 20, 2004.

86. Green is the color of the dollar, but also the color of Islam.

87. One exception may be the $30 million awarded to the informer who led the United States military to Saddam Hussein's sons, Uday and Qusay Hussein. The new millionaire was immediately evacuated from Iraq. See Kari Haskell, "Turning In Terrorists: Take the Money and Run," *New York Times*, March 28, 2004.

88. Kari Haskell, "Turning In Terrorists: Take the Money and Run," *New York Times*, March 28, 2004.

89. Anonymous, *Imperial Hubris*, p 51.

90. Philip Shenon, "9/11 Panel Criticizes Reform Effort at the F.B.I.," *New York Times*, October 21, 2005.

91. David Johnston, "F.B.I. Counterterror Officials Lack Experience, Lawyer Says," *New York Times*, June 20, 2005.

92. Zachary Lockman, *Contending Visions of the Middle East: The History and Politics of Orientalism* (Cambridge: Cambridge University Press, 2004), pp 246–67.

93. John Solomon, "FBI Says Counterterror Experts Not Crucial," *Washington Post*, June 20, 2005.

94. *Ibid.*

95. Solomon, "FBI Chief Won't Mandate Terror Expertise," *Boston Globe*, June 21, 2005.

96. Solomon, "FBI Says Counterterror Experts Not Crucial," *Washington Post*, June 20, 2005.

97. *Ibid.*

98. Rashid Khalidi, *Resurrecting Empire: Western Footprints and America's Perilous Path in the Middle East* (Boston: Beacon Press, 2004), p 14.

99. Larry Diamond, *Squandered Victory: The American Occupation and the Bungled*

Effort to Bring Democracy to Iraq (New York: Times Books, 2005), p 294.

100. Robinson, *The Laundrymen*, p 97.
101. See Randal, *Osama: The Making of a Terrorist*, pp 197–237.
102. Eric Lichtblau and Timothy L. O'Brien, "Efforts to Fight Terror Financing Reported to Lag," *New York Times*, December 12, 2003.
103. Hernando de Soto, *The Mystery of Capital: Why Capitalism Triumphs in the West and Fails Everywhere Else* (New York: Basic Books, 2000), p 159.
104. Randal, *Osama: The Making of a Terrorist*, pp 199–200.
105. *Ibid.*, p 317.
106. Noura Boustany, "Lebanon Offers Aid for Rebuilding," *Washington Post*, August 31, 2006.
107. As described in Chapters 3, 4, and 5.
108. See Chapters 3 and 6.
109. Clarke, et al, *Defeating the Jihadists*, p 6.
110. "Terror Money," *Wall Street Journal*, October 26, 2001.
111. Sara Daly, "Fight Terrorism with Intelligence, Not Might," *Christian Science Monitor*, December 26, 2003. See also Warde,
112. See Chapter 9.
113. See, for example, David C. Hendrikson, "In Our Own Image: The Sources of American Conduct in World Affairs," *The National Interest*, Winter 1997.
114. R.P. Eddy, "In the end, all terrorism is local," *The Times*, July 8, 2005.
115. See Fukuyama, *America at the Crossroads*, and Suskind, *The One Percent Doctrine*.
116. See especially Chapters 7, 8, 9, and 10.
117. "Rumsfeld's war-on-terror memo," *USA Today*, October 22, 2003.

Epilogue. The Last Happy Warriors

1. Frank Rich, *The Greatest Story Ever Sold: The Decline and Fall of Truth From 9/11 to Katrina* (New York: Penguin Press, 2006), pp 56–72, 132–52.
2. John Mueller, *Overblown: How Politicians and the Terrorism Industry Inflate National Security Threats, and Why We Believe Them* (New York: Free Press, 2006), p 33.
3. Peter Beinart, "Elevated Threat," *The New Republic*, February 6, 2006.
4. Michael Abramowitz, "Bush Says 'America Loses' Under Democrats: White House Talk Heats Up as Polls Show Tight Races," *Washington Post*, October 31, 2006.
5. Mark Mazzetti, "Spy Agencies Say Iraq War Worsens Terror Threat," *The New York Times*, September 24, 2006. See also "The Terrorism Index," *Foreign Policy*, July–August 2006.
6. Peter Baker and Jon Cohen, "Americans Say U.S. Is Losing War; Public, Politicians Split on Iraq Panel's Ideas," *Washington Post*, December 13, 2006.
7. Mueller, *Overblown*, p 35.
8. See p 78.
9. Mueller, *Overblown*, p 1.

10. *Ibid.*, p 29.
11. Ian S. Lustick, *Trapped in the War on Terror* (University of Pennsylvania Press, 2006), p ix.
12. *Ibid.*, p 2.
13. *Ibid.*, p 97.
14. Clare Dyer, "'There is no war on terror': Outspoken DPP takes on Blair and Reid over fear-driven legal response to threat," *Guardian*, January 24, 2007.
15. Jason Burke, "Britain stops talk of 'war on terror': Foreign Office has asked ministers to ditch the phrase invented by Bush to avoid stirring up tensions within the Islamic world," *Observer*, December 10, 2006.
16. Tim Grieve, "Rumsfeld's Iraq regret: Calling the war a 'war on terror,'" *Salon*, December 12, 2006.
17. Quoted by Niall Ferguson, "Cowboys and Indians," *New York Times*, May 24, 2005.
18. James Risen, "The War on Terror, Under New Scrutiny," *New York Times*, December 3, 2006.
19. Peter W. Galbraith, *The End of Iraq: How American Incompetence Created a War Without End* (New York: Simon and Schuster, 2006), p 83.
20. See pp xvii–xviii.
21. Jean-Charles Brisard and Guillaume Dasquié, authors of *Forbidden Truth: U.S.-Taliban Secret Oil Diplomacy and the Failed Hunt for Bin Laden* (New York: Nation Books, 2002) had to pay "substantial damages" and publish apologies retracting "very serious and highly defamatory allegations about Sheikh Khalid Bin Mahfouz and Sheikh Abdulrahman Bin Mahfouz, alleging support for terrorism through their businesses, families and charities." Brisard and Dasquié also stated: "we accept and acknowledge that all of those allegations about you and your families, businesses and charities are entirely and manifestly false," *The Economist*, November 4, 2006. Brisard was also the author of a frequently cited report on "terrorist financing," which he falsely claimed to have been commissioned by the United Nations Security Council. On other cases of prominent Saudis exonerated from accusations of terrorist financing, see Barbara Ferguson, "US Court Throws Out Case Against Saleh Kamel," *Arab News*, December 19, 2006. On the subject of Islamic charities, see Greg Krikorian, "Evidence against Muslim charity appears fabricated: An official summary of an FBI-wiretapped conversation contains anti-Semitic slurs that do not appear in the actual transcript," *Los Angeles Times*, February 25, 2007.
22. A notable exception is R.T. Naylor, *Satanic Purses: Money, Myth, and Misinformation in the War on Terror* (Montreal & Kingston: McGill-Queen's University Press, 2006).
23. Lustick, *Trapped in the War on Terror*, p 125.
24. John Diamond, "Flow of terror funds being choked, U.S. says," *USA Today*, June 18, 2006.
25. See, for example, pp xiii–xxv.

26. http://www.foreignpolicy.com, February 13, 2007.

27. *Ibid.*

28. See p xvi.

29. John Ward Anderson, "Belgium Rules Sifting of Bank Data Illegal: Prime Minister Says SWIFT Group Wrongly Cooperated With U.S. Anti-Terrorism Effort," *Washington Post*, September 29, 2006.

30. Jeannine Aversa, "CIA has tracked bank transactions in terror hunt," *Independent*, June 24, 2006.

31. Ron Suskind, "Without a Doubt," *New York Times Magazine*, October 17, 2004.

32. See Chapter 3.

33. "Laundering clamp hailed," *Gulf Daily News*, December 6, 2006.

34. See Richard B. Schmitt, "U.S. May Want More Bank Data: The administration debates whether to force American institutions to turn over information on all international wire," *Los Angeles Times*, July 12, 2006; Mary Beth Sheridan and Spencer S. Hsu, "Localities Operate Intelligence Centers To Pool Terror Data: 'Fusion' Facilities Raise Privacy Worries As Wide Range of Information Is Collected," *Washington Post*, December 31, 2006.

35. Matthew Swibel, "Missouri Treasurer: Show Me You're Anti-Terror," July 12, 2006, www.forbes.com.

36. Gary Parkinson, "RBS used to channel funds to terrorist group, claims lawsuit," *Independent*, January 7, 2006. On the Interpal case, see pp 144–5.

37. John B. Taylor, *Global Financial Warriors: The Untold Story of International Finance in the Post-9/11 World* (New York: W.W. Norton & Company, 2007), p 10.

38. *Ibid.*, pp 28, 242.

39. Karen DeYoung, "Terrorist Attacks Rose Sharply in 2005, State Dept. Says," *Washington Post*, April 29, 2006. See also pp 156–7.

40. *Ibid.*

41. Ruth Gledhill, "Anti-American feelings soar among Muslims, study finds," *The Times*, February 21, 2007.

42. The Newshour with Jim Lehrer, PBS, September 19, 2001. See also pp 42–3, 82.

43. See, for example, John B. Taylor, *Global Financial Warriors*, p 22.

44. See also Chapter 8.

45. Anna Fifield, "Macao bank 'handled millions' for North Korea," *Financial Times*, December 17, 2006.

46. David E. Sanger, "Outside Pressures Broke Korean Deadlock," *New York Times*, February 14, 2007.

47. "Glaser to Meet With North Korean Officials," *Washington Post*, January 28, 2007.

48. Selig S. Harrison, "North Korea: A Nuclear Threat," *Newsweek*, October 16, 2006.

49. David Ignatius, "U.S. Sanctions With Teeth," *Washington Post*, February 28,

2007.

50. Ibrahim Warde, "L'ordre américain coûte que coûte," *Le Monde diplomatique*, April 2003.

51. Glenn Kessler, "U.S. Moves to Isolate Iranian Banks: Treasury Cuts Off Bank Saderat as Part of Plan to Stymie Terrorist Financing," *Washington Post*, September 9, 2006.

52. Peter S. Goodman, "Treasury Warns G-7 About Iran: Paulson Describes Financial Network to Help Nuclear Drive," *Washington Post*, September 17, 2006.

53. "Sanctions US contre des firmes ayant vendu des armes à l'Iran et la Syrie", Le Monde.fr, January 6, 2007.

54. Kevin G. Hall and Warren P. Strobel, "U.S. sanctions one of Iran's largest banks," *San Jose Mercury News*, January 9, 2007.

55. Tara Perkins, "Royal Bank clarifies rule on sanctions: Some exceptions on U.S. accounts," *Toronto Star*, January 18, 2007.

56. Ali Ansari, "Only the US hawks can save the Iranian president now," *Guardian*, January 30, 2007.

57. Vali Nasr and Ray Takeyh , "The Iran Option That Isn't on the Table," *Washington Post*, February 8, 2007.

58. Anthony Shadid, "With Iran Ascendant, U.S. Is Seen at Fault: Arab Allies in Region Feeling Pressure," *Washington Post*, January 30, 2007.

59. *Ibid.*

60. Andrew Higgins, "Fund-Raising Target: Branded Terrorist by U.S., Israel, Microcredit Czar Keeps Lending, Hezbollah Financier Endures Bomb Runs on Branch, Pursues His Mixed Mission; Money for Bullets, $865 Loans," *Wall Street Journal*, December 28, 2006.

61. See p 123.

62. Higgins, "Fund-Raising Target".

63. *Ibid.*

64. "Brazil rejects U.S. action against alleged terrorist links in tri-border area," *International Herald Tribune*, December 8, 2006.

65. On that subject, see Katherine Hughes, "Criminalizing Compassion in the War on Terror: Muslim Charities and the Case of Dr. Rafil A. Dhafir," http://www.zmag.org/content/showarticle.cfm?ItemID=11449.

66. Matthew Gutman, "Hamas' big win leads to a huge loss in financial support for Palestinians," *USA Today*, April 24, 2006.

67. Greg Myre, "Israel Bars Hamas Official Carrying Millions," *New York Times*, December 16, 2006.

68. Rajiv Chadrasekaran, *Imperial Life in the Emerald City: Inside Iraq's Green Zone* (New York: Alfred A. Knopf, 2006), pp 90–9.

69. John F. Burns and Kirk Semple, "U.S. Finds Iraq Insurgency Has Funds to Sustain Itself," *New York Times*, November 26, 2006.

70. *Ibid.*

71. *Ibid.*

72. See p xiii.
73. Burns and Semple, "U.S. Finds Iraq Insurgency Has Funds to Sustain Itself."
74. Jason Burke, "Family clues to Iraq's missing oil billions," *Observer*, December 31, 2006.
75. David Pallister, "How the US sent $12bn in cash to Iraq. And watched it vanish," *Guardian*, February 8, 2007.
76. See also Chapter 6.
77. See John B. Taylor, *Global Financial Warriors*, pp 17–19.
78. Mueller, *Overblown*, p. 6.
79. See pp 11–14.
80. See p xviii.
81. See pp 14–16.

Index

9/11
  attacks, xiii, xix, xxii, xxiv, 4, 10, 32, 36, 47,
    60, 69, 70, 87, 103, 112, 168, 169
  Commission, 6, 38, 71, 73, 77, 84, 97, 99,
    119, 142, 166, 169, 173
  Commission Report, 5, 6, 9, 60, 64, 69, 70,
    94, 99, 170, 187
  terrorist financing monograph, 5, 49, 58, 60,
    64, 97, 119, 154
9/11 Families United to Bankrupt Terrorism, 86

Abacha, Sani, 111
Abrams, Elliott, 84, 165
Abu-Baker, Shukri, 144
Aden, Abdirisak, 99
Aetna, 113
Afghan jihad, xxii, 6, 7, 133, 136, 139, 142
Afghanistan, ix, xii, 5, 7, 8, 64, 69, 70, 78–80,
    86, 94, 119, 121, 132, 134–8, 142, 146, 154,
    155, 158
African bombings of US embassies (1998), 7,
    103, 129
Ahmad, Mustafa Muhammad, 103
Ahmed, Mohammad, 103
AIAI see Al-Ittihaad Al-Islamiya
Air Force, 113
Al Aqsa Islamic Bank, 143
Al Baluchi, Ammar, 170
Al Baraka, 75
Al-Barakaat, ix, xxv, 14, 74, 93, 95–103, 118,
    128, 147
Al-Barakaat North America, 96
Al-Faisal, Haifa, 60
Al Hawsawi, Mustafa, 84, 170
Al-Hazmi, Nawaf, 60
Al-Ittihaad Al-Islamiya (AIAI), 98, 99
Al-Jazeera, 57
Al-Libbi, Abu Farraj, 156
Al-Midhar, Khalid, 60

Al-Qadi, Yassin, 113
Al-Qaeda, 8, 11, 17–19, 45, 46, 59, 64, 69, 80,
    86, 87, 89, 96, 98, 99, 140–2, 154–6, 158, 188
  budget, 8
  treasure, 13, 69
Al-Saud, King Fahd bin Abdul Aziz, 135
Al-Saud, King Faisal bin Abdul Aziz, 86
Al-Saud, Prince Bandar bin Sultan, 60, 133
Al-Saud, Prince Mohammed bin Faisal, 86
Al-Saud, Prince Sultan bin Abdul Aziz, 86
Al-Saud, Prince Turki bin Faisal, 85, 135
Al-Shami, Hussein, 191
Al-Zarqawi, Abu Musab, xvii
Al Zawahiri, 156
Ali, Ali Abdul Aziz, 84, 170
Allman, T.D., 83
American Airlines, 68
American Banking Association, 114
American Enterprise Institute, 94, 184
AML/CFT, 48, 83
Amman, 46
Anati, Muhammed, 147
Annunzio–Wylie Anti-Money Laundering Act,
    39
Anti-Drug Abuse Act, 39
anti-money laundering
  arsenal, viii, 13–15, 35, 36, 44, 49, 82
  controls, 35, 37, 40–2, 48, 80
  laws, xv, 40, 41, 47, 48, 82
  paradigm, 36, 46, 98, 171
Antiterrorism and Effective Death Penalty Act,
    45
Arab Bank, 88, 113, 114
Arabs, 3, 4, 18, 95, 113, 114, 139, 148, 179
  money, 3, 5
  rich, 4, 19, 65
Arafat, Yasser, 85, 121, 143
Armitage, Richard, 157
Arnaout, Enaam, 139–42

Ashcroft, John, 95
assets
  confiscation, 8, 28, 30, 37, 48, 66, 111, 123,
  128, 179
  forfeiture, 26-30, 43
  freezing, x, xi, xx, 48, 61, 75, 81, 83, 103, 117,
  144, 145
  unfreezing, 101
AT&T, 102
Atta, Mohamed, 72, 103
Aufhauser, David, 66, 79, 81, 96, 127, 155
Awqaf, 131

Baath Party, xvii
Baer, Harold, 89
Baer, Robert, 18
Baghdad, xviii
Bahrain, 74, 112
Baker, James, 184
Bali, 46, 154, 168
Balzac, Honoré de, 37
Banco Delta Asia, 190
Bank of Credit and Commerce International
  (BCCI), 28, 59, 109
Bank Saderat, 191
Bank Secrecy Act, 23, 39, 40
Bank Sepah, 191
banks and banking, viii, x, xii, xviii, xx, xxii, 13,
  23, 28, 31, 39, 40, 47, 72-4, 79, 88, 89, 97,
  99, 100, 102, 103, 109-15, 160, 161, 178, 179
  accounts, 27, 63, 65, 72, 103, 168, 169
  international, 38, 39
  officials, 28
Barakaat North America, 100
Barfod, Mikael, 33
Barr Arnold, Roseanne, 53
Barsky, Yehudit, xviii
Bartlett, Dan, 11
Basle Committee on Banking Supervision, 110
BCCI see Bank of Credit and Commerce
  International
Beit el Mal Holdings, 143
Benevolence International, 141
Benevolence International Foundation (BIF),
  119, 139, 140
Benjamin, Daniel, xiii, 16
Bergen, Peter, 9, 172
Berger, Sandy, 74
Berlin Wall, 32
Biden, Joseph, 10
BIF see Benevolence International Foundation
Bin Laden, Usama, ix, xiv, xxi, 4, 6-9, 16, 17, 19,
  45, 59, 64, 65, 67, 70, 71, 74, 86, 124, 139,
  140, 166, 177
  $300 million fortune, 4, 6, 17

Black, Cofer, 157
Blair, Tony, 158
Bletchley Park, 73, 163
Blitzer, Robert, 143
Blowback, 54, 124
Bosnia, 138-41, 146
Boston, 24
Bovard, James, 159, 166
Bowen, Stuart, 194
Brandeis, Louis D., 178
Bremer, Paul, 194
Brilliant, Ashleigh, 93
British Telecom, 102
Brown, Gordon, xv, xx, 163
Bruguière, Jean-Louis, xxii
bureaucracies, 37, 38, 47, 82-4, 93, 118, 139,
  160, 180, 181
Burma, xxiii, 34
Burnett v. Al Baraka Investment and
  Development Corporation, 13
Bush, George H.W., 9, 36, 55
Bush, George W., xviii-x, xiii, xv, xvi, 9, 10, 35,
  36, 46, 54, 56, 58-61, 67, 77, 80, 81, 84, 88,
  93-5, 121, 148, 149, 156-8
  administration, 5, 9-11, 14, 40, 53, 54, 67, 80,
  82, 113, 119, 125, 143, 154, 155, 164, 165
  appointees, 9
  doctrine(s), xxiv, 58, 61, 124, 175, 183-4
  executive order, x, xi
Byrne, John, 161

Cali drug cartel, 16
Camdessus, Michel, 13
Campus Watch, 56, 122
Canada, ix, 95
Cantor Fitzgerald Securities, 87
Capone, Al, 25, 26
Carlucci, Frank, 161
Carlyle, 60
Carter, Jimmy, 133
  administration, 42
Casablanca, 46, 63, 170
cash, 5, 19, 27, 28, 39, 48, 61, 71, 103, 115, 136,
  156, 169, 173, 179
CCCA see Comprehensive Crime and Control
  Act
Center for Defense Information (CDI), 69
Center for Economic and Policy Research, xiv
Central Asia, 121
Central Intelligence Agency (CIA), ix, 5, 45, 81,
  104, 124, 136, 166
  virtual Bin Laden station, 5, 124
Chalabi, Ahmed, 124, 125
charities, 13, 60, 63-6, 113, 114, 123, 127-31,
  136, 138-42, 144-50, 169

Christian, 149
controllable, 147
corrupt or fraudulent, 64, 87, 128, 129, 138, 139, 142
government-controlled, 138
informal, 138, 139, 147
non-Islamic, 148
politicized, 129
private, 148
religious, 148
underground, 132, 150
Charity Commission, 144, 145
Chechnya, 121, 138
Cheney, Dick, 4, 59, 93, 122, 158, 184–5
Chicago, 17, 172
China, 83, 121
Christian fundamentalists, 19
CIA see Central Intelligence Agency
CISPES see Committee in Solidarity with the People of El Salvador
Citibank, 103, 114, 115
Citicorp, xii
Civil Asset Forfeiture Reform Act, 29
Clancy, Tom, 18
Clarke, Richard, xviii, 5, 16, 18, 53, 79, 94, 166, 167, 180, 181
Clarke report, 166, 167
clash of civilizations, 57
clean money, 36, 46–8, 127, 128, 180
Clemons, Steven, 108
Clinton, Bill, 32, 44, 45, 55
administration, 17, 35, 40, 42, 46, 142
Colbert, Stephen, 19
Cold War, 24, 30, 31, 55, 124, 132, 133, 139
Coll, Steve, 124, 134, 136
collateral damage, 64, 91, 93, 95–7, 99, 101, 103, 105, 109, 115, 117, 147, 149, 182
Commission on National Security/21st Century, 77
Committee in Solidarity with the People of El Salvador (CISPES), 130
compassionate conservatism, 148
Comprehensive Crime and Control Act (CCCA), 26, 27
Concert Communications, 102
Confucius, 153
Conlon, Suzanne, 141
Cooksey, John, 94
Cooley, John, 72
Council on American Islamic Relations, 146
Council on Foreign Relations, 64, 66, 140, 164, 166, 167
counterterrorism, xviii, 5, 45, 71, 79, 104, 112, 156, 157, 177, 178
Counter-Terrorist and Narco-Terrorist Reward

Program Act, 177
credit cards, 161, 169
Credit Lyonnais, 188
crime and criminals, xxii, xxv, 13–15, 19, 23, 24, 26–9, 35–7, 39, 41, 44, 46–8, 65, 69, 70, 104, 105, 108, 171, 178
financial, 14, 26, 40, 44, 47–9, 82, 83
organized, 15, 17, 18, 23–5, 43, 44, 46, 171, 175
terrorist-related, 45
Cuba, 32

Daawa, 135
Dam, Kenneth, 96
Daniel, Norman, 15
DARPA, 84, 85
DARPA, FutureMAP, 85
DARPA, Information Awareness Office, 84
DARPA Information Collection Program, 125
De Soto, Hernando, 116
"Deep Throat", 25
Defense Advance Research Projects Agency see DARPA
Defense Intelligence Agency, 124
Defense Policy Board, xiv, 60, 88, 128
Delhi, 72
Democratic Party, 5, 80
Department of Defense, xi, 31
see also Pentagon
Department of Energy, 113
Department of Homeland Security, 83, 104
Department of Justice, 29
Asset Forfeiture Office, 29
Diamond, Larry, 178
diamonds, 4, 19, 64, 65, 70, 71, 155
Didion, Joan, 4, 53
Diehl, Jackson, 120
dirty money, xxi, xxii, 24, 26
Dole, Robert, 161
drugs, 4, 13, 15, 24, 28, 29, 36–9, 44, 46, 48, 65, 69, 70, 83, 171, 180
dealers, 26, 27, 29, 37, 39, 45
lords, 15
trafficking, 14, 15, 18, 32, 35–7, 39, 44, 48, 64, 69, 70, 72, 80, 137, 159, 176
Dubai, ix, 95, 97, 112
Dubai Ports World, 112
Duffy, Joseph, 141
Dyer, Gwynne, 185
Dylan, Bob, 153

EBI see Emirates Bank International
ECHO see European Commission Humanitarian Organization
economic sanctions, 24, 32

economic warfare, 31
economics, 31, 79, 85
The Economist, xiv
Egypt, 19, 85, 132, 133
Einstein, Albert, 107
El Shifa, 103
Ellis, Dina, 41
embedded liberalism, 30
Emerson, Steven, 57, 63
Emirates Bank International (EBI), 97, 99
European Commission Humanitarian
   Organization (ECHO), 33
European Union xv, xx, xxi, 15
evidence, empirical, 10, 19, 47, 64, 115, 154, 168
evil, 11

factoids, 6, 8, 9, 64
Fadlallah, Mohammad Hussein, 123, 147
false positives, 93, 102, 103, 105
Farah, Douglas, 71
Farha, Adib, 123
FATF, viii, xxi, 36, 40, 47, 48, 76, 82, 83, 101, 118
FATF Report on Money Laundering Typologies,
   47
FATF-Style Regional Bodies, 48
Fatfat, Ahmed, 192
FBI, viii, ix, xi, 26, 69, 113, 130
Federal Deposit Insurance Corporation
   Improvement Act (FDICIA), 109
Federal Reserve Bank of New York, 112
Feith, Douglas, 56, 94
finance
   deregulation, 37, 39
   faith-based, 9
   framing the guilty, 25, 27, 29, 31, 33
   martial, 78-80
Financial Action Task Force see FATF
Financial Anti-Terrorism Act, 43
financial blowback, 107, 124
financial crimes, 14, 26, 40, 44, 47-9, 82, 83
Financial Crimes Enforcement Network see
   FinCEN
financial front, vii, ix, xi, xii, xiv-xvi, 38, 47, 80,
   93, 119, 120, 153, 154, 157, 174
financial system, 15, 36, 38, 46, 48, 110, 112
financial terrain, xi, xvi, xxii, xxiv, 23, 30, 81,
   105, 120, 168
Financial Times, xxi, 70, 99
financial war, 4-6, 14, 15, 36, 46, 60, 61, 77-1,
   83, 87-9, 95-7, 101, 102, 118, 153-5, 166-8,
   173, 181, 182
   100-day report, 5
   commentators and "experts", 16, 47, 48, 53,
      56, 61, 64, 72, 74, 75, 88, 122, 166, 177, 180
   contradictions, 35, 89, 107, 109, 113, 122,

   135, 147, 156
   different paradigm, 163, 165, 167, 169, 171,
      173, 175, 177, 179, 181
   dynamics, 51, 79, 81, 83, 85, 87, 89
   dysfunctions, 15
   global, 120
   lawsuits, 13, 85-9, 101, 111, 114, 177
   paradigm, 118, 173
   role of lawyers, 13, 45, 85-7, 89, 100, 140, 144
financial warriors, xii, xxi-xxiii, xxv, 14, 48, 64,
   78, 84, 96, 116, 155, 158, 159, 163, 166, 168,
   170, 171, 179
   blinders, 14, 175, 176
   groupthink, 14
   knowledgeable ignorance, 14-16
   trained incapacity, 14, 15, 46
   tropes and blinders, 14
FinCEN, 40, 72, 161
First Data Corporation, viii
First Gulf War, 9, 32, 137
fishing expeditions, xxiii, 26, 111, 131, 139, 149,
   162
Fisk, Robert, 179
Fitzgerald, Patrick, 141
Fleischer, Ari, 67
Florida, 28
Follett, Ken, 18
"following the money", 23, 107, 115
Forbes, 14
Ford administration, 42
Foreign Terrorist Asset Tracking Center (FTAT),
   82
Fox News, xx
"framing the guilty", 23, 24, 70
France, 133
Friedman, Thomas, 95, 108
front companies, 63-5, 169
Frum, David, 18
FSRBs, 48
FTAT see Foreign Terrorist Asset Tracking Center
Funding Evil: How Terrorism is Financed–and How
   to Stop It, 12, 128

Galbraith, John Kenneth, 23
Galbraith, Peter, 187
Gannon, Donald, 53
Ganor, Boaz, xviii, 117
gated finance, xxv, 107, 109, 111, 113, 115, 117,
   119, 121, 123, 125, 156
Gates, Robert, 137, 184
GCIBFI see General Council for Islamic Banks
   and Financial Institutions
Geithner, Timothy, 112
General Council for Islamic Banks and Financial
   Institutions (GCIBFI), 75

Georgetown University, 133
Georgia, 95
Gerson, Allan, 85, 87
global economy, 74, 109–11, 113, 123
Global Relief Foundation, 119, 139, 140
global struggle against violent extremism, 122, 165
global war on terror, 122, 165
globalization, xxiii, 31, 35, 39, 108, 109
GMEI *see* Greater Middle East Initiative
God Has Ninety-Nine Names, 122
Goldwater, Barry, 105
Google, 6
Government Accountability Office, 155
Gramm, Phil, 41, 42
Greater Middle East Initiative (GMEI), 113
Greed, 19
Greenberg, Maurice, 167, 180
    reports, 180, 181
Greenspan, Alan, 108
Gross Criminal Product, 14
Group of Thirty, 110
GSAVE *see* global struggle against violent extremism
Guantanamo Bay, 105, 186
Gurule, Jimmy, 96
GWOT *see* global war on terror

Haddad, Amin, 114
hadith, 131
Hadley, Steven, 165
Halberstam, David, 55
Hall, Peter, 55
Hallen, Jay, 193
Hamas, ix, 44, 188, 191, 192
Hamilton, Lee, 184
Haniya, Ismail, 192–3
Hariri, Rafik, 114
Harrison, Selig, 190
Hart, Gary, 77
Hartz, Louis, 35
Hashi, Ahmed Abdi, 101
Hassan, Abdiquassim Salad, 98
Hatred's Kingdom, 67
Hauptmann, Bruno Richard, 26
hawalas ix, 4, 19, 48, 65, 71–4, 98, 99, 116, 169
Hekmatyar, Gulbuddin, 142
Helms–Burton Act, 32
Hersh, Seymour, 59, 60
Hewitt, Ibrahim, 145
Hezbollah, ix, 44, 119, 143, 172, 179, 188, 190, 191–2
Higgins, Andrew, 192
high politics, 31
Hill, Christopher, 190

Hoffman, Bruce, 159
Hollywood, 4
Holy Land Foundation, 118, 119, 129, 139, 142–4, 147
Honduras, 84
Hooper, Ibrahim, 146
Hoover, J. Edgar, 25, 26
House Committee on Appropriations, x
House Judiciary Committee, 29
Hughes, Karen, 81, 164
Hunt, David, xx
Hurricane Katrina, 138
Hussein, Liban, 96, 100
Hussein, Mohamed, 96, 100
Hyde, Henry, 29

IBM, 113
Idris, Salah, 104
IEDs *see* improvised explosive devices
IEEPA *see* International Emergency Economic Powers Act
IIRO *see* International Islamic Relief Organization
Iklé, Fred, 58
IMF *see* International Monetary Fund
improvised explosive devices (IEDs), xix
India, 121
insurgency, xi, xvii, 83, 173–6, 181
intelligence
    community, xi, 16, 61, 133, 164
    failure of, 53, 164, 177
Internal Revenue Service (IRS), ix, 42, 98
international cooperation, 42, 81, 97, 102, 119, 120, 167, 168
International Emergency Economic Powers Act (IEEPA), xiii, 16
International Islamic Relief Organization (IIRO), 134
International Monetary Fund (IMF), viii, xxi, 13, 31, 40
International Money Laundering Abatement, 43
International Narcotics Control Strategy Report, 27
International Symposium on Economic Crime, 49
Interpal, 144, 145
Investcorp, 112
Iran, 32, 133, 190–1
Iran–Contra scandal, 18, 59, 84
Iran–Libya Sanctions Act, 32
Iraq, 11, 19, 46, 54, 56, 57, 59, 61, 83–7, 89, 94, 112, 155, 158, 164, 176–9, 193
    assets, 83, 87, 89
    frozen funds, 89
    insurgency, 193–4

National Congress, 125
    war, 10, 55, 56, 61, 80, 95, 122, 164, 183–4
Iraq Study Group, 184, 189
IRS see Internal Revenue Service
Islam
    global, 132
    mainstream, 129, 139
    war on, 18, 119, 156
Islam, Yusuf (Cat Stevens), 139
Islamic Americans, 149
Islamic banks, xxv, 64, 65, 74–5, 103, 143, 169
Islamic charities, 4, 19, 65, 66, 88, 116, 119,
    127–35, 137–41, 143, 145–9, 156
Islamic countries, 111, 115, 132, 172
Islamic foundations, 13, 109, 136, 143, 144, 147
Islamic moderates, xxv, 57, 107, 121–3
Islamic NGOs, 128–30, 133–6, 146
    see also Islamic charities
Islamic Resistance Movement, 143
Ismail, Abdullahi Sheikh, 98
Israel, 30, 85, 88, 114, 115, 118, 143, 144, 146,
    164, 179, 192
Israel Discount Bank, 114
Issawi, Charles, 127
Istanbul, 168
Italy, 95

Jacoby, Lowell, 165
Jamaica, xxi, 172
James Bond, 18
Jeddah, 46, 136
Jewish Institute for National Security Affairs, 56
jihad, 7, 18, 89, 122, 124, 135, 137, 164, 166, 167
Johnson administration, 42
Johnson, Chalmers, 54
Johnson, Hiram, vii
Johnson, Larry, 156
Jordan, 19, 85, 114, 144, 165
Jost, Patrick, 72
Jumale, Ahmed Nur Ali, 99
Justice Department, 143, 144, 160
    Assets Forfeiture Fund, 27

Kabul, 137
Kagan, Robert, 94
Kamel, Sheikh Saleh, 75
Karimov, Islam, 120, 121
Kashmir, 121, 137
Kayyem, Juliette, 158
Kelley, Jack, 17, 65, 67
Kennedy, Edward, 42, 104
Kennedy, John F., 3
    assassination, 59
Kerry, John, xi, 108, 154, 184
Keynes, John Maynard, 30

Khan, Mujeeb, 141
Khartoum, 103
Khashoggi, Adnan, 59
Khashoggi, Jamal Ahmad, 142
Khomeini, Ayatollah Ruhollah, 134
Kinsley, Michael, 12
Koran, 57, 131, 134, 172
Kosovo, 32
Kramer, Martin, 122
Krauthammer, Charles, 120
Kreindler, James, 86, 87
Kromberg, Gordon, 29
Kuwait, 154
Kwiatkowski, Karen, 56

LaFalce, John xv
Lander, Stephen, xxi
Lane, Charles, 17
Lang, W. Patrick, 194
language skills, 55, 56, 67, 80, 82, 122, 176–80,
    181
Lansky, Meyer, 38
LaRouche, Lyndon, 66
Latin America, 15, 48, 82
law enforcement, viii, x, xvi, xxii, 5, 13, 15, 24,
    27, 28, 30, 43, 64, 71, 96, 107, 130, 156, 169
    agencies, 15, 26, 28, 29, 45, 69, 98, 99, 103,
    111
    logic, 131, 145, 146
    officials, 99, 103, 105
Lawrence, T.E., 163, 176
Ledeen, Michael, 94
Left Behind, 18
Levey, Stuart, xxi, 155, 158
Levin, Carl, 158
Levin, Jonathan, 57
Lewis, Bernard, 58, 122, 172
Lewis, Michael, 3, 4
Liar's Poker, 3
Libby, L. "Scooter", 18
liberalization, financial, 35, 37, 43, 107, 108
Liberia, 71
Libya, 32, 85, 86
Lindbergh, Charles, 26
Lindsey, Lawrence, 10, 40
Lippmann, Walter, 3
Lo, Claire, 78
Lockheed Martin, 103
Lomasney, Martin, 24
London, 46, 168
    bombings (July 2005), xix–xxi, 158, 171
    plot (August 2006), 80, 116
Los Angeles Times, xii
low politics, 30, 31
Luce, Clare Boothe, 127

Lustick, Ian, 185, 187

McCaffrey, Barry, 70
Macdonald, Sir Ken, 186
McGill University, 13
McVeigh, Timothy, 45
madrassas, xxiii, 57, 172, 173
Madrid, 46, 168
Marcos, Ferdinand, 31, 59, 111
market fundamentalism, 109
Martino, Antonio, 68
Marx, Groucho, 35
Massachusetts, 95, 104
Massachusetts Division of Banks, 100
Massoud, Ahmed Shah, 124
Matrix, 160
Matthews, Chris, 105
Mearsheimer, John, 59
Mencken, H.L., 35
MEPI *see* Middle East Partnership Initiative
MI5, xxi
Middle East Media Research Institute, 56
Middle East Partnership Initiative (MEPI), 113
Middle Eastern Studies Association, 122
military-industrial-security complex, 78
Miller, Judith, 122
Miller, Zell, 95
Minneapolis, 97, 98
Minnesota, 95
Mintzberg, Henry, 16
Mitchell, John, 25
MLTF, 48
Mobutu, Joseph, 111
Mogadishu, 101
money
   clean, 36, 46–8, 127, 128, 180
   dirty, xxi, xxii, 24, 26
   as oxygen of terror, 61, 103, 118, 155, 170
   trail, 23, 25, 26, 39, 40, 46, 47, 60, 72, 115–17, 120, 171
   transfers, 17, 64, 65, 71, 83, 99, 98, 100, 171
money laundering, viii, xi, xxi, xxiv, 13, 25, 35, 36, 38–44, 46–9, 72, 82, 110, 111, 114, 118, 121, 127, 161, 171, 180
   criminalization of, 24, 28, 35, 40, 44
   internationalization, 14, 180
   template, 35–7, 39, 41, 43, 45, 47, 49
   see also anti-money laundering
Money Laundering Alert, 161
Money Laundering and Financial Crimes Strategy Act, 39
Money Laundering Control Act, 35
Money Laundering Suppression Act, 39
MoneyGram, 97
Moore, Michael, 60

Morgenthau, Robert, xxi, 61
Morocco, 133, 165
Motley, Ron, 77, 85, 88
Motorola, 113
Mubarak, Husni, 117
Mueller, John, 185
Mueller, Robert, 177, 178
Mujahideen, 136–8
Multi-State Anti-Terrorism Information Exchange
   see Matrix
Munich Re, 68
Murawiec, Laurent, 66, 88, 128
Murray, Craig, 116
Musharraf, Pervez, 156
Muslim Brotherhood, 118
Muslim World League, 132, 134
Myers, Richard, 165

narco-terrorism, 13, 44, 48
Nasser, Gamal Abdul, 132
National Counterterrorism Center, 142, 160
National Economic Council, 40
National Money Laundering Strategy, 47
National Review, 122
National Security Council, xiii, 8, 16, 66, 71, 81, 84, 167
national security fundamentalism, 109
National Security Strategy, 61
NatWest, 188
Nauru, xxi
Naylor, R.T., 13
Negroponte, John, 84, 191
neo-conservatives, 54, 56-8, 66, 67, 94, 97, 122, 165, 181
New International Economic Order, 133
New Jersey, 112
New Republic, 17
New York, 102
New York Post, 122
New York Sun, 122
New York Times, xvii, xviii, 72, 95, 102
Newcomb, Richard, 16
Nicaragua, 33
Nichols, Rob, 101
Nietzsche, Friedrich, 154
Nigeria, xxi, 111
Nixon, Richard, 25
   administration, 25, 42
Noah, Timothy, 59
Norquist, Grover, 149
Norris, Kathleen, 12
North, Oliver, 18
North Korea, 189–90
Northern Ireland Aid Committee (Noraid), 129
Nye, Joseph, xxiii, 120

O'Brien, Pat, 191
Odierno, Raymond, xvii
OECD *see* Organization for Economic
    Cooperation and Development
Office of Foreign Assets Control (OFAC), ix, 16,
    101, 103, 155
Ohio, 95
OIC *see* Organization of the Islamic Conference
oil, x, 4, 65–7, 132–8, 145
Oil & Gas Journal, 95
Oklahoma City, 45
Olajuwon, Hakeem, 139
Olasky, Marvin, 148
O'Neill, Paul, vii, xii, 3, 5, 10, 41–3, 61, 74, 81,
    82, 95, 96, 104, 115, 118, 128, 189
Operation Green Quest, 82, 96
Operation Infinite Reach, 103
Organization for Economic Cooperation and
    Development (OECD), 40, 42
Organization of the Islamic Conference (OIC),
    132
organized crime, 15, 17, 18, 23–5, 43, 44, 46,
    171, 175
Orwell, George, vii
Osler, William, 107
Oslo peace process, 114, 142, 143

P&O, 112
Palestinian Authority, 115, 143, 192
Pandey, Swati, 172
The Paradox of American Power, xxiii, 120
Parenti, Christian, 28
Patterns of Global Terrorism, 156, 157
peacetime wars, 31
Pearl Harbor, 109
Pentagon, xvii, xxiv, 36, 56, 60, 75, 78, 94, 109,
    121, 124, 144, 164, 167
    Near East South Asia Directorate, 56
    Office of Special Plans, 56
    see also Department of Defense
Perle, Richard, xiv, 18, 59, 60, 66, 77, 78, 165
Philippines, 31, 111
Phillips, Kevin, 33
Pillar, Paul, 104
Pipes, Daniel, 56, 67
Pittsburgh Press Gazette, 28
Plamegate scandal, 18
PLO, 30
Poindexter, John, 84, 85
political grievances, 57, 58
post-Cold War, 32
post-September 11, 8, 11, 15, 47, 60, 65, 71, 79,
    86, 98, 115, 119, 147, 163, 166–8
Powell, Colin, ix, 69, 95, 112
power, structural, 32

Praeger, Dennis, 127
The Price of Loyalty, 81
public diplomacy, 164, 181
Pulitzer Prize, 17
Pyrrhus, 153

Qatar, 57

Rabin, Itzhak, 143
Racketeer Influenced and Corrupt Organizations
    Act (RICO), 23, 25, 26
Rand Corporation, 159
Randal, Jonathan, 117
Reagan, Ronald, 11, 27, 133
remittance systems, 72–4, 97, 98, 101, 102
Renewing American Compassion, 148
Republican Party, 5, 9, 80
Reuter, Peter, 49
Rice, Condoleezza, 157
RICO *see* Racketeer Influenced and Corrupt
    Organizations Act
Ridge, Tom, 104
Riggs Bank, 111
Risen, James, 186
Riyadh, 88
Robinson, Jeffrey, 13
Rose Garden Strategy, vii, 118
Roy, Sara, 56
Rudman, Warren, 77
Rumsfeld, Donald, xxiii, xxiv, 59, 78, 93, 104,
    157, 165, 172, 182, 184, 186
    "long, hard slog" memo, xxiii, xxiv, 182
Ryan, Chris, 19

Saddam Hussein, x, xvii, 11, 83, 105, 122, 194
Safari Club, 133
Safire, William, 59
sanctions, 32–4, 42, 48, 95, 102, 121, 147, 179
Santo Domingo, 33
SARs *see* suspicious activity reports
Saudi Arabia, xii, xx, 7, 8, 18–19, 47, 57, 59,
    64–7, 74, 85–6, 88, 104, 114, 124, 128, 132–8,
    142, 165, 167
    charities, 128, 134
    establishment, 7, 8
    government, 7, 8, 87, 114, 133, 135, 136, 138
    Mecca uprising, 132
Saudi Arabian Monetary Authority, 74
Saudi Binladin Group (SBG), 7, 86
Saudi Committee for the Relief of the Palestinian
    People, 114
Savage, Michael, 94
SBG *see* Saudi Binladin Group
Scheuer, Michael, 5, 124, 166
Schlesinger, James, 33

Schons, Gary, 29
Schwartz, Stephen, 60
Scotland, xxi
Securities and Exchange Commission (SEC), 68, 69
Senate Banking Committee, xviii, 41
September 11
   attacks, xiii, xix, xxii, xxiv, 4, 10, 32, 36, 47, 60, 69, 70, 87, 103, 112, 168, 169
   Commission, 6, 7, 49, 58–60, 71, 73, 99, 119, 142, 153, 155, 166, 169, 173
   Commission Report, 5, 6, 9, 60, 64, 69, 70, 94, 99, 170
   terrorist financing monograph, 5, 49, 58, 60, 64, 97, 119, 154
Serious and Organized Crime Agency, xx
Shaheen, Jack, 4
Shanghai, 109
Sharon, Ariel, 121
Sierra Leone, 71
Simon, Steven, xiii, 16
Siniora, Fouad, 123, 191–2
six degrees of separation, 58, 88, 114, 139, 149, 175
skills, cultural and linguistic, 15, 82, 172, 177, 178, 181
Sleeping with the Devil, 67
Snow, John, xi, 112, 158, 162, 188
Society for Worldwide Interbank Financial Telecommunications, 36, 47, 158, 188
soft power, 79, 107, 120, 174, 181
Somali Swedes, 100
Somalia, ix, xxi, 97–9, 101, 102, 146, 147, 178
The Sopranos, 19
South America, 94
Southeast Asia, 94, 134
Soviet Union, 11, 136
Specially Designated Terrorists, 104
Sprint, 113
Sri Lanka, 146, 172
State Department, 27, 114, 121
   Bureau of Narcotics and Law Enforcement, 82
Stevens, Cat *see* Islam, Yusuf
Stiglitz, Joseph, 33
Strange, Susan, 32
Sturgeon, Theodore, 107
subsidiarity, 181
Sudan, 7, 16, 86
suicide bombers, 17, 89, 116, 118, 119, 143, 144, 146, 147, 172
Summers, Lawrence, 26
SunTrust Banks, 169
Suskind, Ron, 9, 10, 81, 127, 160
suspicious activity reports (SARs), 98, 160, 161, 169, 171, 179

Sutton's Law, 86
Sweden, ix, 100
SWIFT *see* Society for Worldwide Interbank Financial Telecommunications
Switzerland, 31, 95
   banks and bank accounts, 30, 31
Syria, xvii, 85
   banks, xvii

Taliban, xi, 7, 69, 70
Tamil Tigers, 146
Tarrow, Sidney, 55
Taylor, John B., 189
Telhami, Shibley, 173, 174
Tenet, George, 81, 154
terror
   economy, 13, 14
   market, xviii, 85
terrorism, vii–ix, xi, xii, xiv–xv, 12, 16, 17, 36, 43–9, 57, 58, 69, 71, 72, 100, 101, 115–17, 121–3, 141, 153–6, 158–60, 170, 171, 176, 177
   fighting, vii–ix, xiv–xxi, xxv, 86, 142, 147, 159, 178
   financing, xii, xiv, xv, xvii, 48, 49, 75, 86, 149
   fronts, 74, 99, 130, 138
   international, 43, 85, 121, 158
   material support, 45, 87, 89, 144
   paymasters, 47, 64, 170, 171, 173
   support networks, 5, 7, 141, 174, 175, 181
terrorist attacks, xv, xvi, xviii–xx, xxii–xxv, 16, 33, 64, 65, 71, 85, 95, 103, 104, 110, 115, 116, 130, 139, 144, 168, 170–3, 178
   cost, xx, 10, 32, 38, 41, 42, 49, 72, 84, 102, 116, 136, 160, 166, 168–71
Terrorist Finance Tracking Program, 82, 162
Terrorist Financing Task Force, 82
terrorists xv, xvi, xviii–xx, xxii–xxv, 9, 12, 46, 58–61, 63–5, 83, 85, 96, 103, 104, 112, 113, 115–17, 128, 129, 149, 150, 160, 170–5
   assumptions, 6, 14, 166–8, 173, 176
   axioms, xv, 6, 14, 46, 61, 166–8, 173, 176
   discourse, 4, 13, 19
   fantasy, 5, 7, 9, 11, 13, 15, 17, 19
   fiction, 3, 5, 7, 9, 11, 13, 15, 17–19
   fighting, 36, 69, 83, 115, 167
   financiers, xvi, 4, 15, 60, 86, 118, 150, 180
   financing, 3–5, 7–9, 11–17, 19, 43–9, 57, 58, 66, 67, 69–71, 81–4, 86, 87, 115–18, 153, 154, 163, 166–8, 180, 181
   financing, usual suspects, 4, 16, 19, 63–7, 69, 71, 73, 75, 81, 128
   funding, disruption of, 80–2, 95, 155, 167
   lifeblood or oxygen metaphors, 37, 46, 65, 103, 154, 155, 166, 170
   narrative, 12, 55, 57, 59, 61, 128, 131, 138,

172, 180
networks, 8, 9, 15, 99, 149, 174
organizations, 44, 45, 48, 68, 87, 96, 98, 117, 123, 129, 142, 144, 146, 148, 172
paradigm, xx, 47
parallel universe, xiv, xv, xvii, 4, 11
potential, xxii, 116
puzzle, 45, 73
Texas, 40, 67, 143, 144
Tikrit, xix
Thornburgh, Richard, 27
Through Our Enemies' Eye, 166
Thucydides, 93
Time, 72
Treasury Department, ix–xii, xv, 5, 10, 16, 27, 40–2, 47, 74, 79, 81–3, 95, 96, 99–104, 110, 115, 118, 161
Truman, Edwin, 49
"truthiness", 19
Turabi, Hassan, 117, 122
Turkey, 85
The Twilight of Sovereignty, 109

Uighur, 121
Ullman, Harlan, 79
underground economy, 73, 116, 147
Unger, Craig, 60
United Airlines, 68
United Arab Emirates, 95, 98, 170
United Kingdom, xx, xxi, 30, 33, 104, 131, 144, 145, 161, 171
United Nations, xi, 9, 70, 153
  Monitoring Committee, 118
  Security Council, viii, 8, 16, 66, 71, 81, 84, 102, 167
Uniting and Strengthening America by Providing Appropriate Tools Required to Intercept and Obstruct Terrorism *see* USA PATRIOT Act
US Congress, 4, 25, 29, 33, 43, 54, 55, 66, 67, 84, 95, 112, 133, 155, 167
US Constitution
  First Amendment, 130
  Fourth Amendment, 41
US District Court, 85
US Navy, 113
US News and World Report, xviii
US Office of the Comptroller of the Currency, 114
USA PATRIOT Act, 30, 43, 79, 86, 110
USA Today, xxiii
Uzbekistan, 121

Veblen, Thorstein, 15
Victim Compensation Fund, 88
Vienna, 40

Vienna Convention on Diplomatic Relations, 112
Vietnam War, 133
Virginia, 29, 40

Wade, James, 79
Wahhabism, 57, 67, 134
Wall Street, 3, 30
Wall Street Journal, 63, 102
war on crime, 24
war on drugs, xvi, xxiv, xxv, 23, 24, 27
war on terror, xiv, 78, 112
  first strike, 43, 80, 82, 103, 128, 158
  global, 165
  rhetoric, 165
Washington, 4, 95, 136
Washington Institute for Near East Policy, 56, 143
Washington Post, 95, 159
Watergate scandal, 36, 59, 133
Waxman, Henry, 157
weapons of mass destruction, 11, 12, 19, 34, 59, 122, 173
Wechsler, William, 16, 42, 46, 71
Wedtech, 59
Weekly Standard, 60, 122
Weisbrot, Mark, xiv
Werner, Robert, 155
West Bank, 114, 142, 143
Western Union, 97
Wilson, Joseph, 122
Wolcott, James, 54
Wolfowitz, Paul, x, 11, 94, 165
Woolsey, James, 78
World Bank, 31, 33
World Trade Organization, 31
World War I, 32
World War II, 30
Wriston, Walter, 109

Xinjiang, 121
XL Capital, 68

Yeats, W.B., 77
Yee, James, 105
Yemen, 67, 154
  honey business, 67

Zaire, 111
zakat, 128
Zarate, Juan, xi, 83, 193
Zeldin, Michael, 29